Effective Java

Third Edition

Effective Java

Third Edition

Joshua Bloch

♦ Addison-Wesley

Boston • Columbus • Indianapolis • New York • San Francisco • Amsterdam • Cape Town
Dubai • London • Madrid • Milan • Munich • Paris • Montreal • Toronto • Delhi • Mexico City
São Paulo • Sydney • Hong Kong • Seoul • Singapore • Taipei • Tokyo

Library of Congress Control Number: 2017956176

ISBN-13: 978-0-13-468599-1
ISBN-10: 0-13-468599-7

1   17

To my family: Cindy, Tim, and Matt

Contents

Foreword

IF a colleague were to say to you, "Spouse of me this night today manufactures the unusual meal in a home. You will join?" three things would likely cross your mind: third, that you had been invited to dinner; second, that English was not your colleague's first language; and first, a good deal of puzzlement.

If you have ever studied a second language yourself and then tried to use it outside the classroom, you know that there are three things you must master: how the language is structured (grammar), how to name things you want to talk about (vocabulary), and the customary and effective ways to say everyday things (usage). Too often only the first two are covered in the classroom, and you find native speakers constantly suppressing their laughter as you try to make yourself understood.

It is much the same with a programming language. You need to understand the core language: is it algorithmic, functional, object-oriented? You need to know the vocabulary: what data structures, operations, and facilities are provided by the standard libraries? And you need to be familiar with the customary and effective ways to structure your code. Books about programming languages often cover only the first two, or discuss usage only spottily. Maybe that's because the first two are in some ways easier to write about. Grammar and vocabulary are properties of the language alone, but usage is characteristic of a community that uses it.

The Java programming language, for example, is object-oriented with single inheritance and supports an imperative (statement-oriented) coding style within each method. The libraries address graphic display support, networking, distributed computing, and security. But how is the language best put to use in practice?

There is another point. Programs, unlike spoken sentences and unlike most books and magazines, are likely to be changed over time. It's typically not enough to produce code that operates effectively and is readily understood by other persons; one must also organize the code so that it is easy to modify. There may be ten ways to write code for some task T. Of those ten ways, seven will be awkward, inefficient, or puzzling. Of the other three, which is most likely to be similar to the code needed for the task T' in next year's software release?

There are numerous books from which you can learn the grammar of the Java programming language, including *The Java™ Programming Language* by Arnold, Gosling, and Holmes, or *The Java™ Language Specification* by Gosling, Joy, yours truly, and Bracha. Likewise, there are dozens of books on the libraries and APIs associated with the Java programming language.

This book addresses your third need: customary and effective usage. Joshua Bloch has spent years extending, implementing, and using the Java programming language at Sun Microsystems; he has also read a lot of other people's code, including mine. Here he offers good advice, systematically organized, on how to structure your code so that it works well, so that other people can understand it, so that future modifications and improvements are less likely to cause headaches—perhaps, even, so that your programs will be pleasant, elegant, and graceful.

Guy L. Steele Jr.
Burlington, Massachusetts
April 2001

Preface

Preface to the Third Edition

IN 1997, when Java was new, James Gosling (the father of Java), described it as a "blue collar language" that was "pretty simple" [Gosling97]. At about the same time, Bjarne Stroustrup (the father of C++) described C++ as a "multi-paradigm language" that "deliberately differs from languages designed to support a single way of writing programs" [Stroustrup95]. Stroustrup warned:

> Much of the relative simplicity of Java is—like for most new languages—partly an illusion and partly a function of its incompleteness. As time passes, Java will grow significantly in size and complexity. It will double or triple in size and grow implementation-dependent extensions or libraries. [Stroustrup]

Now, twenty years later, it's fair to say that Gosling and Stroustrup were both right. Java is now large and complex, with multiple abstractions for many things, from parallel execution, to iteration, to the representation of dates and times.

I still like Java, though my ardor has cooled a bit as the platform has grown. Given its increased size and complexity, the need for an up-to-date best-practices guide is all the more critical. With this third edition of *Effective Java*, I did my best to provide you with one. I hope this edition continues to satisfy the need, while staying true to the spirit of the first two editions.

Small is beautiful, but simple ain't easy.

San Jose, California
November 2017

P.S. I would be remiss if I failed to mention an industry-wide best practice that has occupied a fair amount of my time lately. Since the birth of our field in the 1950's, we have freely reimplemented each others' APIs. This practice was critical to the meteoric success of computer technology. I am active in the effort to preserve this freedom [CompSci17], and I encourage you to join me. It is crucial to the continued health of our profession that we retain the right to reimplement each others' APIs.

Preface to the Second Edition

A lot has happened to the Java platform since I wrote the first edition of this book in 2001, and it's high time for a second edition. The most significant set of changes was the addition of generics, enum types, annotations, autoboxing, and the for-each loop in Java 5. A close second was the addition of the new concurrency library, `java.util.concurrent`, also released in Java 5. With Gilad Bracha, I had the good fortune to lead the teams that designed the new language features. I also had the good fortune to serve on the team that designed and developed the concurrency library, which was led by Doug Lea.

The other big change in the platform is the widespread adoption of modern Integrated Development Environments (IDEs), such as Eclipse, IntelliJ IDEA, and NetBeans, and of static analysis tools, such as FindBugs. While I have not been involved in these efforts, I've benefited from them immensely and learned how they affect the Java development experience.

In 2004, I moved from Sun to Google, but I've continued my involvement in the development of the Java platform over the past four years, contributing to the concurrency and collections APIs through the good offices of Google and the Java Community Process. I've also had the pleasure of using the Java platform to develop libraries for use within Google. Now I know what it feels like to be a user.

As was the case in 2001 when I wrote the first edition, my primary goal is to share my experience with you so that you can imitate my successes while avoiding my failures. The new material continues to make liberal use of real-world examples from the Java platform libraries.

The first edition succeeded beyond my wildest expectations, and I've done my best to stay true to its spirit while covering all of the new material that was required to bring the book up to date. It was inevitable that the book would grow, and grow it did, from fifty-seven items to seventy-eight. Not only did I add twenty-three items, but I thoroughly revised all the original material and retired a few items whose better days had passed. In the Appendix, you can see how the material in this edition relates to the material in the first edition.

In the Preface to the First Edition, I wrote that the Java programming language and its libraries were immensely conducive to quality and productivity, and a joy to work with. The changes in releases 5 and 6 have taken a good thing and made it better. The platform is much bigger now than it was in 2001 and more complex, but once you learn the patterns and idioms for using the new features, they make your programs better and your life easier. I hope this edition captures my continued enthusiasm for the platform and helps make your use of the platform and its new features more effective and enjoyable.

San Jose, California
April 2008

Preface to the First Edition

In 1996 I pulled up stakes and headed west to work for JavaSoft, as it was then known, because it was clear that that was where the action was. In the intervening five years I've served as Java platform libraries architect. I've designed, implemented, and maintained many of the libraries and served as a consultant for many others. Presiding over these libraries as the Java platform matured was a once-in-a-lifetime opportunity. It is no exaggeration to say that I had the privilege to work with some of the great software engineers of our generation. In the process, I learned a lot about the Java programming language—what works, what doesn't, and how to use the language and its libraries to best effect.

This book is my attempt to share my experience with you so that you can imitate my successes while avoiding my failures. I borrowed the format from Scott Meyers's *Effective C++*, which consists of fifty items, each conveying one specific rule for improving your programs and designs. I found the format to be singularly effective, and I hope you do too.

In many cases, I took the liberty of illustrating the items with real-world examples from the Java platform libraries. When describing something that could have been done better, I tried to pick on code that I wrote myself, but occasionally I pick on something written by a colleague. I sincerely apologize if, despite my best efforts, I've offended anyone. Negative examples are cited not to cast blame but in the spirit of cooperation, so that all of us can benefit from the experience of those who've gone before.

While this book is not targeted solely at developers of reusable components, it is inevitably colored by my experience writing such components over the past two decades. I naturally think in terms of exported APIs (Application Programming Interfaces), and I encourage you to do likewise. Even if you aren't developing reusable components, thinking in these terms tends to improve the quality of the software you write. Furthermore, it's not uncommon to write a reusable component without knowing it: You write something useful, share it with your buddy across the hall, and before long you have half a dozen users. At this point, you no longer have the flexibility to change the API at will and are thankful for all the effort that you put into designing the API when you first wrote the software.

My focus on API design may seem a bit unnatural to devotees of the new lightweight software development methodologies, such as *Extreme Programming*. These methodologies emphasize writing the simplest program that could possibly work. If you're using one of these methodologies, you'll find that a focus on API design serves you well in the *refactoring* process. The fundamental goals of refactoring are the improvement of system structure and the avoidance of code duplication. These goals are impossible to achieve in the absence of well-designed APIs for the components of the system.

No language is perfect, but some are excellent. I have found the Java programming language and its libraries to be immensely conducive to quality and productivity, and a joy to work with. I hope this book captures my enthusiasm and helps make your use of the language more effective and enjoyable.

Cupertino, California
April 2001

Acknowledgments

Acknowledgments for the Third Edition

I thank the readers of the first two editions of this book for giving it such a kind and enthusiastic reception, for taking its ideas to heart, and for letting me know what a positive influence it had on them and their work. I thank the many professors who used the book in their courses, and the many engineering teams that adopted it.

I thank the whole team at Addison-Wesley and Pearson for their kindness, professionalism, patience, and grace under extreme pressure. Through it all, my editor Greg Doench remained unflappable: a fine editor and a perfect gentleman. I'm afraid his hair may have turned a bit gray as a result of this project, and I humbly apologize. My project manager, Julie Nahil, and my project editor, Dana Wilson, were all I could hope for: diligent, prompt, organized, and friendly. My copy editor, Kim Wimpsett, was meticulous and tasteful.

I have yet again been blessed with the best team of reviewers imaginable, and I give my sincerest thanks to each of them. The core team, who reviewed most every chapter, consisted of Cindy Bloch, Brian Kernighan, Kevin Bourrillion, Joe Bowbeer, William Chargin, Joe Darcy, Brian Goetz, Tim Halloran, Stuart Marks, Tim Peierls, and Yoshiki Shibata, Other reviewers included Marcus Biel, Dan Bloch, Beth Bottos, Martin Buchholz, Michael Diamond, Charlie Garrod, Tom Hawtin, Doug Lea, Aleksey Shipilëv, Lou Wasserman, and Peter Weinberger. These reviewers made numerous suggestions that led to great improvements in this book and saved me from many embarrassments.

I give special thanks to William Chargin, Doug Lea, and Tim Peierls, who served as sounding boards for many of the ideas in this book. William, Doug, and Tim were unfailingly generous with their time and knowledge.

Finally, I thank my wife, Cindy Bloch, for encouraging me to write, for reading each item in raw form, for writing the index, for helping me with all of the things that invariably come up when you take on a big project, and for putting up with me while I wrote.

Acknowledgments for the Second Edition

I thank the readers of the first edition of this book for giving it such a kind and enthusiastic reception, for taking its ideas to heart, and for letting me know what a positive influence it had on them and their work. I thank the many professors who used the book in their courses, and the many engineering teams that adopted it.

I thank the whole team at Addison-Wesley for their kindness, professionalism, patience, and grace under pressure. Through it all, my editor Greg Doench remained unflappable: a fine editor and a perfect gentleman. My production manager, Julie Nahil, was everything that a production manager should be: diligent, prompt, organized, and friendly. My copy editor, Barbara Wood, was meticulous and tasteful.

I have once again been blessed with the best team of reviewers imaginable, and I give my sincerest thanks to each of them. The core team, who reviewed every chapter, consisted of Lexi Baugher, Cindy Bloch, Beth Bottos, Joe Bowbeer, Brian Goetz, Tim Halloran, Brian Kernighan, Rob Konigsberg, Tim Peierls, Bill Pugh, Yoshiki Shibata, Peter Stout, Peter Weinberger, and Frank Yellin. Other reviewers included Pablo Bellver, Dan Bloch, Dan Bornstein, Kevin Bourrillion, Martin Buchholz, Joe Darcy, Neal Gafter, Laurence Gonsalves, Aaron Greenhouse, Barry Hayes, Peter Jones, Angelika Langer, Doug Lea, Bob Lee, Jeremy Manson, Tom May, Mike McCloskey, Andriy Tereshchenko, and Paul Tyma. Again, these reviewers made numerous suggestions that led to great improvements in this book and saved me from many embarrassments. And again, any remaining embarrassments are my responsibility.

I give special thanks to Doug Lea and Tim Peierls, who served as sounding boards for many of the ideas in this book. Doug and Tim were unfailingly generous with their time and knowledge.

I thank my manager at Google, Prabha Krishna, for her continued support and encouragement.

Finally, I thank my wife, Cindy Bloch, for encouraging me to write, for reading each item in raw form, for helping me with Framemaker, for writing the index, and for putting up with me while I wrote.

Acknowledgments for the First Edition

I thank Patrick Chan for suggesting that I write this book and for pitching the idea to Lisa Friendly, the series managing editor; Tim Lindholm, the series technical editor; and Mike Hendrickson, executive editor of Addison-Wesley. I thank Lisa, Tim, and Mike for encouraging me to pursue the project and for their superhuman patience and unyielding faith that I would someday write this book.

I thank James Gosling and his original team for giving me something great to write about, and I thank the many Java platform engineers who followed in James's footsteps. In particular, I thank my colleagues in Sun's Java Platform Tools and Libraries Group for their insights, their encouragement, and their support. The team consists of Andrew Bennett, Joe Darcy, Neal Gafter, Iris Garcia, Konstantin Kladko, Ian Little, Mike McCloskey, and Mark Reinhold. Former members include Zhenghua Li, Bill Maddox, and Naveen Sanjeeva.

I thank my manager, Andrew Bennett, and my director, Larry Abrahams, for lending their full and enthusiastic support to this project. I thank Rich Green, the VP of Engineering at Java Software, for providing an environment where engineers are free to think creatively and to publish their work.

I have been blessed with the best team of reviewers imaginable, and I give my sincerest thanks to each of them: Andrew Bennett, Cindy Bloch, Dan Bloch, Beth Bottos, Joe Bowbeer, Gilad Bracha, Mary Campione, Joe Darcy, David Eckhardt, Joe Fialli, Lisa Friendly, James Gosling, Peter Haggar, David Holmes, Brian Kernighan, Konstantin Kladko, Doug Lea, Zhenghua Li, Tim Lindholm, Mike McCloskey, Tim Peierls, Mark Reinhold, Ken Russell, Bill Shannon, Peter Stout, Phil Wadler, and two anonymous reviewers. They made numerous suggestions that led to great improvements in this book and saved me from many embarrassments. Any remaining embarrassments are my responsibility.

Numerous colleagues, inside and outside Sun, participated in technical discussions that improved the quality of this book. Among others, Ben Gomes, Steffen Grarup, Peter Kessler, Richard Roda, John Rose, and David Stoutamire contributed useful insights. A special thanks is due Doug Lea, who served as a sounding board for many of the ideas in this book. Doug has been unfailingly generous with his time and his knowledge.

I thank Julie Dinicola, Jacqui Doucette, Mike Hendrickson, Heather Olszyk, Tracy Russ, and the whole team at Addison-Wesley for their support and professionalism. Even under an impossibly tight schedule, they were always friendly and accommodating.

I thank Guy Steele for writing the Foreword. I am honored that he chose to participate in this project.

Finally, I thank my wife, Cindy Bloch, for encouraging and occasionally threatening me to write this book, for reading each item in its raw form, for helping me with Framemaker, for writing the index, and for putting up with me while I wrote.

CHAPTER 1

Introduction

THIS book is designed to help you make effective use of the Java programming language and its fundamental libraries: `java.lang`, `java.util`, and `java.io`, and subpackages such as `java.util.concurrent` and `java.util.function`. Other libraries are discussed from time to time.

This book consists of ninety items, each of which conveys one rule. The rules capture practices generally held to be beneficial by the best and most experienced programmers. The items are loosely grouped into eleven chapters, each covering one broad aspect of software design. The book is not intended to be read from cover to cover: each item stands on its own, more or less. The items are heavily cross-referenced so you can easily plot your own course through the book.

Many new features were added to the platform since the last edition of this book was published. Most of the items in this book use these features in some way. This table shows you where to go for primary coverage of key features:

Feature	Items	Release
Lambdas	Items 42–44	Java 8
Streams	Items 45–48	Java 8
Optionals	Item 55	Java 8
Default methods in interfaces	Item 21	Java 8
try-with-resources	Item 9	Java 7
@SafeVarargs	Item 32	Java 7
Modules	Item 15	Java 9

Most items are illustrated with program examples. A key feature of this book is that it contains code examples illustrating many design patterns and idioms. Where appropriate, they are cross-referenced to the standard reference work in this area [Gamma95].

Many items contain one or more program examples illustrating some practice to be avoided. Such examples, sometimes known as *antipatterns,* are clearly labeled with a comment such as **// Never do this!**. In each case, the item explains why the example is bad and suggests an alternative approach.

This book is not for beginners: it assumes that you are already comfortable with Java. If you are not, consider one of the many fine introductory texts, such as Peter Sestoft's *Java Precisely* [Sestoft16]. While *Effective Java* is designed to be accessible to anyone with a working knowledge of the language, it should provide food for thought even for advanced programmers.

Most of the rules in this book derive from a few fundamental principles. Clarity and simplicity are of paramount importance. The user of a component should never be surprised by its behavior. Components should be as small as possible but no smaller. (As used in this book, the term *component* refers to any reusable software element, from an individual method to a complex framework consisting of multiple packages.) Code should be reused rather than copied. The dependencies between components should be kept to a minimum. Errors should be detected as soon as possible after they are made, ideally at compile time.

While the rules in this book do not apply 100 percent of the time, they do characterize best programming practices in the great majority of cases. You should not slavishly follow these rules, but violate them only occasionally and with good reason. Learning the art of programming, like most other disciplines, consists of first learning the rules and then learning when to break them.

For the most part, this book is not about performance. It is about writing programs that are clear, correct, usable, robust, flexible, and maintainable. If you can do that, it's usually a relatively simple matter to get the performance you need (Item 67). Some items do discuss performance concerns, and a few of these items provide performance numbers. These numbers, which are introduced with the phrase "On my machine," should be regarded as approximate at best.

For what it's worth, my machine is an aging homebuilt 3.5GHz quad-core Intel Core i7-4770K with 16 gigabytes of DDR3-1866 CL9 RAM, running Azul's Zulu 9.0.0.15 release of OpenJDK, atop Microsoft Windows 7 Professional SP1 (64-bit).

When discussing features of the Java programming language and its libraries, it is sometimes necessary to refer to specific releases. For convenience, this book uses nicknames in preference to official release names. This table shows the mapping between release names and nicknames:

Official Release Name	Nickname
JDK 1.0.x	Java 1.0
JDK 1.1.x	Java 1.1
Java 2 Platform, Standard Edition, v1.2	Java 2
Java 2 Platform, Standard Edition, v1.3	Java 3
Java 2 Platform, Standard Edition, v1.4	Java 4
Java 2 Platform, Standard Edition, v5.0	Java 5
Java Platform, Standard Edition 6	Java 6
Java Platform, Standard Edition 7	Java 7
Java Platform, Standard Edition 8	Java 8
Java Platform, Standard Edition 9	Java 9

The examples are reasonably complete, but favor readability over completeness. They freely use classes from packages `java.util` and `java.io`. In order to compile examples, you may have to add one or more import declarations, or other such boilerplate. The book's website, `http://joshbloch.com/effectivejava`, contains an expanded version of each example, which you can compile and run.

For the most part, this book uses technical terms as they are defined in *The Java Language Specification, Java SE 8 Edition* [JLS]. A few terms deserve special mention. The language supports four kinds of types: *interfaces* (including *annotations*), *classes* (including *enums*), *arrays*, and *primitives*. The first three are known as *reference types*. Class instances and arrays are *objects*; primitive values are not. A class's *members* consist of its *fields*, *methods*, *member classes*, and *member interfaces*. A method's *signature* consists of its name and the types of its formal parameters; the signature does *not* include the method's return type.

This book uses a few terms differently from *The Java Language Specification*. Unlike *The Java Language Specification*, this book uses *inheritance* as a synonym for *subclassing*. Instead of using the term inheritance for interfaces, this book simply states that a class *implements* an interface or that one interface *extends* another. To describe the access level that applies when none is specified, this book uses the traditional *package-private* instead of the technically correct *package access* [JLS, 6.6.1].

This book uses a few technical terms that are not defined in *The Java Language Specification*. The term *exported API*, or simply *API*, refers to the classes, interfaces, constructors, members, and serialized forms by which a programmer accesses a class, interface, or package. (The term *API*, which is short for *application programming interface*, is used in preference to the otherwise preferable term *interface* to avoid confusion with the language construct of that name.) A programmer who writes a program that uses an API is referred to as a *user* of the API. A class whose implementation uses an API is a *client* of the API.

Classes, interfaces, constructors, members, and serialized forms are collectively known as *API elements*. An exported API consists of the API elements that are accessible outside of the package that defines the API. These are the API elements that any client can use and the author of the API commits to support. Not coincidentally, they are also the elements for which the Javadoc utility generates documentation in its default mode of operation. Loosely speaking, the exported API of a package consists of the public and protected members and constructors of every public class or interface in the package.

In Java 9, a *module system* was added to the platform. If a library makes use of the module system, its exported API is the union of the exported APIs of all the packages exported by the library's module declaration.

CHAPTER 2

Creating and Destroying Objects

THIS chapter concerns creating and destroying objects: when and how to create them, when and how to avoid creating them, how to ensure they are destroyed in a timely manner, and how to manage any cleanup actions that must precede their destruction.

Item 1: Consider static factory methods instead of constructors

The traditional way for a class to allow a client to obtain an instance is to provide a public constructor. There is another technique that should be a part of every programmer's toolkit. A class can provide a public *static factory method*, which is simply a static method that returns an instance of the class. Here's a simple example from Boolean (the *boxed primitive* class for boolean). This method translates a boolean primitive value into a Boolean object reference:

```
public static Boolean valueOf(boolean b) {
    return b ? Boolean.TRUE : Boolean.FALSE;
}
```

Note that a static factory method is not the same as the *Factory Method* pattern from *Design Patterns* [Gamma95]. The static factory method described in this item has no direct equivalent in *Design Patterns*.

A class can provide its clients with static factory methods instead of, or in addition to, public constructors. Providing a static factory method instead of a public constructor has both advantages and disadvantages.

One advantage of static factory methods is that, unlike constructors, they have names. If the parameters to a constructor do not, in and of themselves, describe the object being returned, a static factory with a well-chosen name is easier to use and the resulting client code easier to read. For example, the

5

constructor `BigInteger(int, int, Random)`, which returns a `BigInteger` that is probably prime, would have been better expressed as a static factory method named `BigInteger.probablePrime`. (This method was added in Java 4.)

A class can have only a single constructor with a given signature. Programmers have been known to get around this restriction by providing two constructors whose parameter lists differ only in the order of their parameter types. This is a really bad idea. The user of such an API will never be able to remember which constructor is which and will end up calling the wrong one by mistake. People reading code that uses these constructors will not know what the code does without referring to the class documentation.

Because they have names, static factory methods don't share the restriction discussed in the previous paragraph. In cases where a class seems to require multiple constructors with the same signature, replace the constructors with static factory methods and carefully chosen names to highlight their differences.

A second advantage of static factory methods is that, unlike constructors, they are not required to create a new object each time they're invoked. This allows immutable classes (Item 17) to use preconstructed instances, or to cache instances as they're constructed, and dispense them repeatedly to avoid creating unnecessary duplicate objects. The `Boolean.valueOf(boolean)` method illustrates this technique: it *never* creates an object. This technique is similar to the *Flyweight* pattern [Gamma95]. It can greatly improve performance if equivalent objects are requested often, especially if they are expensive to create.

The ability of static factory methods to return the same object from repeated invocations allows classes to maintain strict control over what instances exist at any time. Classes that do this are said to be *instance-controlled*. There are several reasons to write instance-controlled classes. Instance control allows a class to guarantee that it is a singleton (Item 3) or noninstantiable (Item 4). Also, it allows an immutable value class (Item 17) to make the guarantee that no two equal instances exist: `a.equals(b)` if and only if a == b. This is the basis of the *Flyweight* pattern [Gamma95]. Enum types (Item 34) provide this guarantee.

A third advantage of static factory methods is that, unlike constructors, they can return an object of any subtype of their return type. This gives you great flexibility in choosing the class of the returned object.

One application of this flexibility is that an API can return objects without making their classes public. Hiding implementation classes in this fashion leads to a very compact API. This technique lends itself to *interface-based frameworks* (Item 20), where interfaces provide natural return types for static factory methods.

Prior to Java 8, interfaces couldn't have static methods. By convention, static factory methods for an interface named *Type* were put in a *noninstantiable companion class* (Item 4) named *Types*. For example, the Java Collections Framework has forty-five utility implementations of its interfaces, providing unmodifiable collections, synchronized collections, and the like. Nearly all of these implementations are exported via static factory methods in one noninstantiable class (`java.util.Collections`). The classes of the returned objects are all nonpublic.

The Collections Framework API is much smaller than it would have been had it exported forty-five separate public classes, one for each convenience implementation. It is not just the *bulk* of the API that is reduced but the *conceptual weight:* the number and difficulty of the concepts that programmers must master in order to use the API. The programmer knows that the returned object has precisely the API specified by its interface, so there is no need to read additional class documentation for the implementation class. Furthermore, using such a static factory method requires the client to refer to the returned object by interface rather than implementation class, which is generally good practice (Item 64).

As of Java 8, the restriction that interfaces cannot contain static methods was eliminated, so there is typically little reason to provide a noninstantiable companion class for an interface. Many public static members that would have been at home in such a class should instead be put in the interface itself. Note, however, that it may still be necessary to put the bulk of the implementation code behind these static methods in a separate package-private class. This is because Java 8 requires all static members of an interface to be public. Java 9 allows private static methods, but static fields and static member classes are still required to be public.

A fourth advantage of static factories is that the class of the returned object can vary from call to call as a function of the input parameters. Any subtype of the declared return type is permissible. The class of the returned object can also vary from release to release.

The `EnumSet` class (Item 36) has no public constructors, only static factories. In the OpenJDK implementation, they return an instance of one of two subclasses, depending on the size of the underlying enum type: if it has sixty-four or fewer elements, as most enum types do, the static factories return a `RegularEnumSet` instance, which is backed by a single `long`; if the enum type has sixty-five or more elements, the factories return a `JumboEnumSet` instance, backed by a `long` array.

The existence of these two implementation classes is invisible to clients. If `RegularEnumSet` ceased to offer performance advantages for small enum types, it could be eliminated from a future release with no ill effects. Similarly, a future release could add a third or fourth implementation of `EnumSet` if it proved beneficial for performance. Clients neither know nor care about the class of the object they get back from the factory; they care only that it is some subclass of EnumSet.

A fifth advantage of static factories is that the class of the returned object need not exist when the class containing the method is written. Such flexible static factory methods form the basis of *service provider frameworks*, like the Java Database Connectivity API (JDBC). A service provider framework is a system in which providers implement a service, and the system makes the implementations available to clients, decoupling the clients from the implementations.

There are three essential components in a service provider framework: a *service interface*, which represents an implementation; a *provider registration API*, which providers use to register implementations; and a *service access API*, which clients use to obtain instances of the service. The service access API may allow clients to specify criteria for choosing an implementation. In the absence of such criteria, the API returns an instance of a default implementation, or allows the client to cycle through all available implementations. The service access API is the flexible static factory that forms the basis of the service provider framework.

An optional fourth component of a service provider framework is a *service provider interface*, which describes a factory object that produce instances of the service interface. In the absence of a service provider interface, implementations must be instantiated reflectively (Item 65). In the case of JDBC, Connection plays the part of the service interface, DriverManager.registerDriver is the provider registration API, DriverManager.getConnection is the service access API, and Driver is the service provider interface.

There are many variants of the service provider framework pattern. For example, the service access API can return a richer service interface to clients than the one furnished by providers. This is the *Bridge* pattern [Gamma95]. Dependency injection frameworks (Item 5) can be viewed as powerful service providers. Since Java 6, the platform includes a general-purpose service provider framework, java.util.ServiceLoader, so you needn't, and generally shouldn't, write your own (Item 59). JDBC doesn't use ServiceLoader, as the former predates the latter.

The main limitation of providing only static factory methods is that classes without public or protected constructors cannot be subclassed. For example, it is impossible to subclass any of the convenience implementation classes in the Collections Framework. Arguably this can be a blessing in disguise because it encourages programmers to use composition instead of inheritance (Item 18), and is required for immutable types (Item 17).

A second shortcoming of static factory methods is that they are hard for programmers to find. They do not stand out in API documentation in the way that constructors do, so it can be difficult to figure out how to instantiate a class that provides static factory methods instead of constructors. The Javadoc tool may someday draw attention to static factory methods. In the meantime, you can reduce this problem by drawing attention to static factories in class or interface documentation and by adhering to common naming conventions. Here are some common names for static factory methods. This list is far from exhaustive:

- **from**—A *type-conversion method* that takes a single parameter and returns a corresponding instance of this type, for example:

  ```
  Date d = Date.from(instant);
  ```

- **of**—An *aggregation method* that takes multiple parameters and returns an instance of this type that incorporates them, for example:

  ```
  Set<Rank> faceCards = EnumSet.of(JACK, QUEEN, KING);
  ```

- **valueOf**—A more verbose alternative to from and of, for example:

  ```
  BigInteger prime = BigInteger.valueOf(Integer.MAX_VALUE);
  ```

- **instance** or **getInstance**—Returns an instance that is described by its parameters (if any) but cannot be said to have the same value, for example:

  ```
  StackWalker luke = StackWalker.getInstance(options);
  ```

- **create** or **newInstance**—Like instance or getInstance, except that the method guarantees that each call returns a new instance, for example:

  ```
  Object newArray = Array.newInstance(classObject, arrayLen);
  ```

- **get*Type***—Like getInstance, but used if the factory method is in a different class. *Type* is the type of object returned by the factory method, for example:

  ```
  FileStore fs = Files.getFileStore(path);
  ```

- **new*Type***—Like newInstance, but used if the factory method is in a different class. *Type* is the type of object returned by the factory method, for example:

  ```
  BufferedReader br = Files.newBufferedReader(path);
  ```

- ***type***—A concise alternative to get*Type* and new*Type*, for example:

  ```
  List<Complaint> litany = Collections.list(legacyLitany);
  ```

In summary, static factory methods and public constructors both have their uses, and it pays to understand their relative merits. Often static factories are preferable, so avoid the reflex to provide public constructors without first considering static factories.

Item 2: Consider a builder when faced with many constructor parameters

Static factories and constructors share a limitation: they do not scale well to large numbers of optional parameters. Consider the case of a class representing the Nutrition Facts label that appears on packaged foods. These labels have a few required fields—serving size, servings per container, and calories per serving—and more than twenty optional fields—total fat, saturated fat, trans fat, cholesterol, sodium, and so on. Most products have nonzero values for only a few of these optional fields.

What sort of constructors or static factories should you write for such a class? Traditionally, programmers have used the *telescoping constructor* pattern, in which you provide a constructor with only the required parameters, another with a single optional parameter, a third with two optional parameters, and so on, culminating in a constructor with all the optional parameters. Here's how it looks in practice. For brevity's sake, only four optional fields are shown:

```java
// Telescoping constructor pattern - does not scale well!
public class NutritionFacts {
    private final int servingSize;  // (mL)            required
    private final int servings;     // (per container) required
    private final int calories;     // (per serving)   optional
    private final int fat;          // (g/serving)     optional
    private final int sodium;       // (mg/serving)    optional
    private final int carbohydrate; // (g/serving)     optional

    public NutritionFacts(int servingSize, int servings) {
        this(servingSize, servings, 0);
    }

    public NutritionFacts(int servingSize, int servings,
            int calories) {
        this(servingSize, servings, calories, 0);
    }

    public NutritionFacts(int servingSize, int servings,
            int calories, int fat) {
        this(servingSize, servings, calories, fat, 0);
    }

    public NutritionFacts(int servingSize, int servings,
            int calories, int fat, int sodium) {
        this(servingSize, servings, calories, fat, sodium, 0);
    }
```

```java
    public NutritionFacts(int servingSize, int servings,
            int calories, int fat, int sodium, int carbohydrate) {
        this.servingSize  = servingSize;
        this.servings     = servings;
        this.calories     = calories;
        this.fat          = fat;
        this.sodium       = sodium;
        this.carbohydrate = carbohydrate;
    }
}
```

When you want to create an instance, you use the constructor with the shortest parameter list containing all the parameters you want to set:

```java
NutritionFacts cocaCola =
    new NutritionFacts(240, 8, 100, 0, 35, 27);
```

Typically this constructor invocation will require many parameters that you don't want to set, but you're forced to pass a value for them anyway. In this case, we passed a value of 0 for fat. With "only" six parameters this may not seem so bad, but it quickly gets out of hand as the number of parameters increases.

In short, **the telescoping constructor pattern works, but it is hard to write client code when there are many parameters, and harder still to read it.** The reader is left wondering what all those values mean and must carefully count parameters to find out. Long sequences of identically typed parameters can cause subtle bugs. If the client accidentally reverses two such parameters, the compiler won't complain, but the program will misbehave at runtime (Item 51).

A second alternative when you're faced with many optional parameters in a constructor is the *JavaBeans* pattern, in which you call a parameterless constructor to create the object and then call setter methods to set each required parameter and each optional parameter of interest:

```java
// JavaBeans Pattern - allows inconsistency, mandates mutability
public class NutritionFacts {
    // Parameters initialized to default values (if any)
    private int servingSize  = -1; // Required; no default value
    private int servings     = -1; // Required; no default value
    private int calories     = 0;
    private int fat          = 0;
    private int sodium       = 0;
    private int carbohydrate = 0;

    public NutritionFacts() { }
```

```
    // Setters
    public void setServingSize(int val)  { servingSize = val; }
    public void setServings(int val)     { servings = val; }
    public void setCalories(int val)     { calories = val; }
    public void setFat(int val)          { fat = val; }
    public void setSodium(int val)       { sodium = val; }
    public void setCarbohydrate(int val) { carbohydrate = val; }
}
```

This pattern has none of the disadvantages of the telescoping constructor pattern. It is easy, if a bit wordy, to create instances, and easy to read the resulting code:

```
NutritionFacts cocaCola = new NutritionFacts();
cocaCola.setServingSize(240);
cocaCola.setServings(8);
cocaCola.setCalories(100);
cocaCola.setSodium(35);
cocaCola.setCarbohydrate(27);
```

Unfortunately, the JavaBeans pattern has serious disadvantages of its own. Because construction is split across multiple calls, **a JavaBean may be in an inconsistent state partway through its construction.** The class does not have the option of enforcing consistency merely by checking the validity of the constructor parameters. Attempting to use an object when it's in an inconsistent state may cause failures that are far removed from the code containing the bug and hence difficult to debug. A related disadvantage is that **the JavaBeans pattern precludes the possibility of making a class immutable** (Item 17) and requires added effort on the part of the programmer to ensure thread safety.

It is possible to reduce these disadvantages by manually "freezing" the object when its construction is complete and not allowing it to be used until frozen, but this variant is unwieldy and rarely used in practice. Moreover, it can cause errors at runtime because the compiler cannot ensure that the programmer calls the freeze method on an object before using it.

Luckily, there is a third alternative that combines the safety of the telescoping constructor pattern with the readability of the JavaBeans pattern. It is a form of the *Builder* pattern [Gamma95]. Instead of making the desired object directly, the client calls a constructor (or static factory) with all of the required parameters and gets a *builder object*. Then the client calls setter-like methods on the builder object to set each optional parameter of interest. Finally, the client calls a parameterless build method to generate the object, which is typically immutable. The builder is typically a static member class (Item 24) of the class it builds. Here's how it looks in practice:

```java
// Builder Pattern
public class NutritionFacts {
    private final int servingSize;
    private final int servings;
    private final int calories;
    private final int fat;
    private final int sodium;
    private final int carbohydrate;

    public static class Builder {
        // Required parameters
        private final int servingSize;
        private final int servings;

        // Optional parameters - initialized to default values
        private int calories      = 0;
        private int fat           = 0;
        private int sodium        = 0;
        private int carbohydrate  = 0;

        public Builder(int servingSize, int servings) {
            this.servingSize = servingSize;
            this.servings    = servings;
        }

        public Builder calories(int val)
            { calories = val;      return this; }
        public Builder fat(int val)
            { fat = val;           return this; }
        public Builder sodium(int val)
            { sodium = val;        return this; }
        public Builder carbohydrate(int val)
            { carbohydrate = val;  return this; }

        public NutritionFacts build() {
            return new NutritionFacts(this);
        }
    }

    private NutritionFacts(Builder builder) {
        servingSize  = builder.servingSize;
        servings     = builder.servings;
        calories     = builder.calories;
        fat          = builder.fat;
        sodium       = builder.sodium;
        carbohydrate = builder.carbohydrate;
    }
}
```

The NutritionFacts class is immutable, and all parameter default values are in one place. The builder's setter methods return the builder itself so that invocations can be chained, resulting in a *fluent API*. Here's how the client code looks:

```
NutritionFacts cocaCola = new NutritionFacts.Builder(240, 8)
        .calories(100).sodium(35).carbohydrate(27).build();
```

This client code is easy to write and, more importantly, easy to read. **The Builder pattern simulates named optional parameters** as found in Python and Scala.

Validity checks were omitted for brevity. To detect invalid parameters as soon as possible, check parameter validity in the builder's constructor and methods. Check invariants involving multiple parameters in the constructor invoked by the build method. To ensure these invariants against attack, do the checks on object fields after copying parameters from the builder (Item 50). If a check fails, throw an IllegalArgumentException (Item 72) whose detail message indicates which parameters are invalid (Item 75).

The Builder pattern is well suited to class hierarchies. Use a parallel hierarchy of builders, each nested in the corresponding class. Abstract classes have abstract builders; concrete classes have concrete builders. For example, consider an abstract class at the root of a hierarchy representing various kinds of pizza:

```
// Builder pattern for class hierarchies
public abstract class Pizza {
    public enum Topping { HAM, MUSHROOM, ONION, PEPPER, SAUSAGE }
    final Set<Topping> toppings;

    abstract static class Builder<T extends Builder<T>> {
        EnumSet<Topping> toppings = EnumSet.noneOf(Topping.class);
        public T addTopping(Topping topping) {
            toppings.add(Objects.requireNonNull(topping));
            return self();
        }

        abstract Pizza build();

        // Subclasses must override this method to return "this"
        protected abstract T self();
    }
    Pizza(Builder<?> builder) {
        toppings = builder.toppings.clone(); // See Item 50
    }
}
```

Note that Pizza.Builder is a *generic type* with a *recursive type parameter* (Item 30). This, along with the abstract self method, allows method chaining to work properly in subclasses, without the need for casts. This workaround for the fact that Java lacks a self type is known as the *simulated self-type* idiom.

Here are two concrete subclasses of Pizza, one of which represents a standard New-York-style pizza, the other a calzone. The former has a required size parameter, while the latter lets you specify whether sauce should be inside or out:

```java
public class NyPizza extends Pizza {
    public enum Size { SMALL, MEDIUM, LARGE }
    private final Size size;

    public static class Builder extends Pizza.Builder<Builder> {
        private final Size size;

        public Builder(Size size) {
            this.size = Objects.requireNonNull(size);
        }

        @Override public NyPizza build() {
            return new NyPizza(this);
        }

        @Override protected Builder self() { return this; }
    }

    private NyPizza(Builder builder) {
        super(builder);
        size = builder.size;
    }
}

public class Calzone extends Pizza {
    private final boolean sauceInside;

    public static class Builder extends Pizza.Builder<Builder> {
        private boolean sauceInside = false; // Default

        public Builder sauceInside() {
            sauceInside = true;
            return this;
        }

        @Override public Calzone build() {
            return new Calzone(this);
        }

        @Override protected Builder self() { return this; }
    }

    private Calzone(Builder builder) {
        super(builder);
        sauceInside = builder.sauceInside;
    }
}
```

Note that the build method in each subclass's builder is declared to return the correct subclass: the build method of NyPizza.Builder returns NyPizza, while the one in Calzone.Builder returns Calzone. This technique, wherein a subclass method is declared to return a subtype of the return type declared in the superclass, is known as *covariant return typing*. It allows clients to use these builders without the need for casting.

The client code for these "hierarchical builders" is essentially identical to the code for the simple NutritionFacts builder. The example client code shown next assumes static imports on enum constants for brevity:

```
NyPizza pizza = new NyPizza.Builder(SMALL)
        .addTopping(SAUSAGE).addTopping(ONION).build();
Calzone calzone = new Calzone.Builder()
        .addTopping(HAM).sauceInside().build();
```

A minor advantage of builders over constructors is that builders can have multiple varargs parameters because each parameter is specified in its own method. Alternatively, builders can aggregate the parameters passed into multiple calls to a method into a single field, as demonstrated in the addTopping method earlier.

The Builder pattern is quite flexible. A single builder can be used repeatedly to build multiple objects. The parameters of the builder can be tweaked between invocations of the build method to vary the objects that are created. A builder can fill in some fields automatically upon object creation, such as a serial number that increases each time an object is created.

The Builder pattern has disadvantages as well. In order to create an object, you must first create its builder. While the cost of creating this builder is unlikely to be noticeable in practice, it could be a problem in performance-critical situations. Also, the Builder pattern is more verbose than the telescoping constructor pattern, so it should be used only if there are enough parameters to make it worthwhile, say four or more. But keep in mind that you may want to add more parameters in the future. But if you start out with constructors or static factories and switch to a builder when the class evolves to the point where the number of parameters gets out of hand, the obsolete constructors or static factories will stick out like a sore thumb. Therefore, it's often better to start with a builder in the first place.

In summary, **the Builder pattern is a good choice when designing classes whose constructors or static factories would have more than a handful of parameters**, especially if many of the parameters are optional or of identical type. Client code is much easier to read and write with builders than with telescoping constructors, and builders are much safer than JavaBeans.

Item 3:   Enforce the singleton property with a private constructor or an enum type

A *singleton* is simply a class that is instantiated exactly once [Gamma95]. Singletons typically represent either a stateless object such as a function (Item 24) or a system component that is intrinsically unique. **Making a class a singleton can make it difficult to test its clients** because it's impossible to substitute a mock implementation for a singleton unless it implements an interface that serves as its type.

There are two common ways to implement singletons. Both are based on keeping the constructor private and exporting a public static member to provide access to the sole instance. In one approach, the member is a final field:

```
// Singleton with public final field
public class Elvis {
    public static final Elvis INSTANCE = new Elvis();
    private Elvis() { ... }

    public void leaveTheBuilding() { ... }
}
```

The private constructor is called only once, to initialize the public static final field Elvis.INSTANCE. The lack of a public or protected constructor *guarantees* a "monoelvistic" universe: exactly one Elvis instance will exist once the Elvis class is initialized—no more, no less. Nothing that a client does can change this, with one caveat: a privileged client can invoke the private constructor reflectively (Item 65) with the aid of the AccessibleObject.setAccessible method. If you need to defend against this attack, modify the constructor to make it throw an exception if it's asked to create a second instance.

In the second approach to implementing singletons, the public member is a static factory method:

```
// Singleton with static factory
public class Elvis {
    private static final Elvis INSTANCE = new Elvis();
    private Elvis() { ... }
    public static Elvis getInstance() { return INSTANCE; }

    public void leaveTheBuilding() { ... }
}
```

All calls to Elvis.getInstance return the same object reference, and no other Elvis instance will ever be created (with the same caveat mentioned earlier).

The main advantage of the public field approach is that the API makes it clear that the class is a singleton: the public static field is final, so it will always contain the same object reference. The second advantage is that it's simpler.

One advantage of the static factory approach is that it gives you the flexibility to change your mind about whether the class is a singleton without changing its API. The factory method returns the sole instance, but it could be modified to return, say, a separate instance for each thread that invokes it. A second advantage is that you can write a *generic singleton factory* if your application requires it (Item 30). A final advantage of using a static factory is that a *method reference* can be used as a supplier, for example `Elvis::instance` is a `Supplier<Elvis>`. Unless one of these advantages is relevant, the public field approach is preferable.

To make a singleton class that uses either of these approaches *serializable* (Chapter 12), it is not sufficient merely to add `implements Serializable` to its declaration. To maintain the singleton guarantee, declare all instance fields `transient` and provide a `readResolve` method (Item 89). Otherwise, each time a serialized instance is deserialized, a new instance will be created, leading, in the case of our example, to spurious `Elvis` sightings. To prevent this from happening, add this `readResolve` method to the `Elvis` class:

```
// readResolve method to preserve singleton property
private Object readResolve() {
    // Return the one true Elvis and let the garbage collector
    // take care of the Elvis impersonator.
    return INSTANCE;
}
```

A third way to implement a singleton is to declare a single-element enum:

```
// Enum singleton - the preferred approach
public enum Elvis {
    INSTANCE;

    public void leaveTheBuilding() { ... }
}
```

This approach is similar to the public field approach, but it is more concise, provides the serialization machinery for free, and provides an ironclad guarantee against multiple instantiation, even in the face of sophisticated serialization or reflection attacks. This approach may feel a bit unnatural, but **a single-element enum type is often the best way to implement a singleton**. Note that you can't use this approach if your singleton must extend a superclass other than `Enum` (though you *can* declare an enum to implement interfaces).

Item 4:   Enforce noninstantiability with a private constructor

Occasionally you'll want to write a class that is just a grouping of static methods and static fields. Such classes have acquired a bad reputation because some people abuse them to avoid thinking in terms of objects, but they do have valid uses. They can be used to group related methods on primitive values or arrays, in the manner of java.lang.Math or java.util.Arrays. They can also be used to group static methods, including factories (Item 1), for objects that implement some interface, in the manner of java.util.Collections. (As of Java 8, you can also put such methods *in* the interface, assuming it's yours to modify.) Lastly, such classes can be used to group methods on a final class, since you can't put them in a subclass.

Such *utility classes* were not designed to be instantiated: an instance would be nonsensical. In the absence of explicit constructors, however, the compiler provides a public, parameterless *default constructor*. To a user, this constructor is indistinguishable from any other. It is not uncommon to see unintentionally instantiable classes in published APIs.

Attempting to enforce noninstantiability by making a class abstract does not work. The class can be subclassed and the subclass instantiated. Furthermore, it misleads the user into thinking the class was designed for inheritance (Item 19). There is, however, a simple idiom to ensure noninstantiability. A default constructor is generated only if a class contains no explicit constructors, so **a class can be made noninstantiable by including a private constructor**:

```
// Noninstantiable utility class
public class UtilityClass {
    // Suppress default constructor for noninstantiability
    private UtilityClass() {
        throw new AssertionError();
    }
    ...  // Remainder omitted
}
```

Because the explicit constructor is private, it is inaccessible outside the class. The AssertionError isn't strictly required, but it provides insurance in case the constructor is accidentally invoked from within the class. It guarantees the class will never be instantiated under any circumstances. This idiom is mildly counterintuitive because the constructor is provided expressly so that it cannot be invoked. It is therefore wise to include a comment, as shown earlier.

As a side effect, this idiom also prevents the class from being subclassed. All constructors must invoke a superclass constructor, explicitly or implicitly, and a subclass would have no accessible superclass constructor to invoke.

Item 5:   Prefer dependency injection to hardwiring resources

Many classes depend on one or more underlying resources. For example, a spell checker depends on a dictionary. It is not uncommon to see such classes implemented as static utility classes (Item 4):

```
// Inappropriate use of static utility - inflexible & untestable!
public class SpellChecker {
    private static final Lexicon dictionary = ...;

    private SpellChecker() {} // Noninstantiable

    public static boolean isValid(String word) { ... }
    public static List<String> suggestions(String typo) { ... }
}
```

Similarly, it's not uncommon to see them implemented as singletons (Item 3):

```
// Inappropriate use of singleton - inflexible & untestable!
public class SpellChecker {
    private final Lexicon dictionary = ...;

    private SpellChecker(...) {}
    public static INSTANCE = new SpellChecker(...);

    public boolean isValid(String word) { ... }
    public List<String> suggestions(String typo) { ... }
}
```

Neither of these approaches is satisfactory, because they assume that there is only one dictionary worth using. In practice, each language has its own dictionary, and special dictionaries are used for special vocabularies. Also, it may be desirable to use a special dictionary for testing. It is wishful thinking to assume that a single dictionary will suffice for all time.

You could try to have SpellChecker support multiple dictionaries by making the dictionary field nonfinal and adding a method to change the dictionary in an existing spell checker, but this would be awkward, error-prone, and unworkable in a concurrent setting. **Static utility classes and singletons are inappropriate for classes whose behavior is parameterized by an underlying resource.**

What is required is the ability to support multiple instances of the class (in our example, SpellChecker), each of which uses the resource desired by the client (in our example, the dictionary). A simple pattern that satisfies this requirement is to **pass the resource into the constructor when creating a new instance**. This is one form of *dependency injection*: the dictionary is a *dependency* of the spell checker and is *injected* into the spell checker when it is created.

```
// Dependency injection provides flexibility and testability
public class SpellChecker {
    private final Lexicon dictionary;

    public SpellChecker(Lexicon dictionary) {
        this.dictionary = Objects.requireNonNull(dictionary);
    }

    public boolean isValid(String word) { ... }
    public List<String> suggestions(String typo) { ... }
}
```

The dependency injection pattern is so simple that many programmers use it for years without knowing it has a name. While our spell checker example had only a single resource (the dictionary), dependency injection works with an arbitrary number of resources and arbitrary dependency graphs. It preserves immutability (Item 17), so multiple clients can share dependent objects (assuming the clients desire the same underlying resources). Dependency injection is equally applicable to constructors, static factories (Item 1), and builders (Item 2).

A useful variant of the pattern is to pass a resource *factory* to the constructor. A factory is an object that can be called repeatedly to create instances of a type. Such factories embody the *Factory Method* pattern [Gamma95]. The Supplier<T> interface, introduced in Java 8, is perfect for representing factories. Methods that take a Supplier<T> on input should typically constrain the factory's type parameter using a *bounded wildcard type* (Item 31) to allow the client to pass in a factory that creates any subtype of a specified type. For example, here is a method that makes a mosaic using a client-provided factory to produce each tile:

```
Mosaic create(Supplier<? extends Tile> tileFactory) { ... }
```

Although dependency injection greatly improves flexibility and testability, it can clutter up large projects, which typically contain thousands of dependencies. This clutter can be all but eliminated by using a *dependency injection framework*, such as Dagger [Dagger], Guice [Guice], or Spring [Spring]. The use of these frameworks is beyond the scope of this book, but note that APIs designed for manual dependency injection are trivially adapted for use by these frameworks.

In summary, do not use a singleton or static utility class to implement a class that depends on one or more underlying resources whose behavior affects that of the class, and do not have the class create these resources directly. Instead, pass the resources, or factories to create them, into the constructor (or static factory or builder). This practice, known as dependency injection, will greatly enhance the flexibility, reusability, and testability of a class.

Item 6:   Avoid creating unnecessary objects

It is often appropriate to reuse a single object instead of creating a new functionally equivalent object each time it is needed. Reuse can be both faster and more stylish. An object can always be reused if it is immutable (Item 17).

As an extreme example of what not to do, consider this statement:

```
String s = new String("bikini");  // DON'T DO THIS!
```

The statement creates a new String instance each time it is executed, and none of those object creations is necessary. The argument to the String constructor ("bikini") is itself a String instance, functionally identical to all of the objects created by the constructor. If this usage occurs in a loop or in a frequently invoked method, millions of String instances can be created needlessly.

The improved version is simply the following:

```
String s = "bikini";
```

This version uses a single String instance, rather than creating a new one each time it is executed. Furthermore, it is guaranteed that the object will be reused by any other code running in the same virtual machine that happens to contain the same string literal [JLS, 3.10.5].

You can often avoid creating unnecessary objects by using *static factory methods* (Item 1) in preference to constructors on immutable classes that provide both. For example, the factory method Boolean.valueOf(String) is preferable to the constructor Boolean(String), which was deprecated in Java 9. The constructor *must* create a new object each time it's called, while the factory method is never required to do so and won't in practice. In addition to reusing immutable objects, you can also reuse mutable objects if you know they won't be modified.

Some object creations are much more expensive than others. If you're going to need such an "expensive object" repeatedly, it may be advisable to cache it for reuse. Unfortunately, it's not always obvious when you're creating such an object. Suppose you want to write a method to determine whether a string is a valid Roman numeral. Here's the easiest way to do this using a regular expression:

```
// Performance can be greatly improved!
static boolean isRomanNumeral(String s) {
    return s.matches("^(?=.)M*(C[MD]|D?C{0,3})"
            + "(X[CL]|L?X{0,3})(I[XV]|V?I{0,3})$");
}
```

The problem with this implementation is that it relies on the String.matches method. **While String.matches is the easiest way to check if a string matches a regular expression, it's not suitable for repeated use in performance-critical situations.** The problem is that it internally creates a Pattern instance for the regular expression and uses it only once, after which it becomes eligible for garbage collection. Creating a Pattern instance is expensive because it requires compiling the regular expression into a finite state machine.

To improve the performance, explicitly compile the regular expression into a Pattern instance (which is immutable) as part of class initialization, cache it, and reuse the same instance for every invocation of the isRomanNumeral method:

```
// Reusing expensive object for improved performance
public class RomanNumerals {
    private static final Pattern ROMAN = Pattern.compile(
            "^(?=.)M*(C[MD]|D?C{0,3})"
            + "(X[CL]|L?X{0,3})(I[XV]|V?I{0,3})$");

    static boolean isRomanNumeral(String s) {
        return ROMAN.matcher(s).matches();
    }
}
```

The improved version of isRomanNumeral provides significant performance gains if invoked frequently. On my machine, the original version takes 1.1 µs on an 8-character input string, while the improved version takes 0.17 µs, which is 6.5 times faster. Not only is the performance improved, but arguably, so is clarity. Making a static final field for the otherwise invisible Pattern instance allows us to give it a name, which is far more readable than the regular expression itself.

If the class containing the improved version of the isRomanNumeral method is initialized but the method is never invoked, the field ROMAN will be initialized needlessly. It would be possible to eliminate the initialization by *lazily initializing* the field (Item 83) the first time the isRomanNumeral method is invoked, but this is *not* recommended. As is often the case with lazy initialization, it would complicate the implementation with no measurable performance improvement (Item 67).

When an object is immutable, it is obvious it can be reused safely, but there are other situations where it is far less obvious, even counterintuitive. Consider the case of *adapters* [Gamma95], also known as *views*. An adapter is an object that delegates to a backing object, providing an alternative interface. Because an adapter has no state beyond that of its backing object, there's no need to create more than one instance of a given adapter to a given object.

For example, the keySet method of the Map interface returns a Set view of the Map object, consisting of all the keys in the map. Naively, it would seem that every call to keySet would have to create a new Set instance, but every call to keySet on a given Map object may return the same Set instance. Although the returned Set instance is typically mutable, all of the returned objects are functionally identical: when one of the returned objects changes, so do all the others, because they're all backed by the same Map instance. While it is largely harmless to create multiple instances of the keySet view object, it is unnecessary and has no benefits.

Another way to create unnecessary objects is *autoboxing*, which allows the programmer to mix primitive and boxed primitive types, boxing and unboxing automatically as needed. **Autoboxing blurs but does not erase the distinction between primitive and boxed primitive types.** There are subtle semantic distinctions and not-so-subtle performance differences (Item 61). Consider the following method, which calculates the sum of all the positive int values. To do this, the program has to use long arithmetic because an int is not big enough to hold the sum of all the positive int values:

```
// Hideously slow! Can you spot the object creation?
private static long sum() {
    Long sum = 0L;
    for (long i = 0; i <= Integer.MAX_VALUE; i++)
        sum += i;

    return sum;
}
```

This program gets the right answer, but it is *much* slower than it should be, due to a one-character typographical error. The variable sum is declared as a Long instead of a long, which means that the program constructs about 2^{31} unnecessary Long instances (roughly one for each time the long i is added to the Long sum). Changing the declaration of sum from Long to long reduces the runtime from 6.3 seconds to 0.59 seconds on my machine. The lesson is clear: **prefer primitives to boxed primitives, and watch out for unintentional autoboxing.**

This item should not be misconstrued to imply that object creation is expensive and should be avoided. On the contrary, the creation and reclamation of small objects whose constructors do little explicit work is cheap, especially on modern JVM implementations. Creating additional objects to enhance the clarity, simplicity, or power of a program is generally a good thing.

Conversely, avoiding object creation by maintaining your own *object pool* is a bad idea unless the objects in the pool are extremely heavyweight. The classic example of an object that *does* justify an object pool is a database connection. The cost of establishing the connection is sufficiently high that it makes sense to reuse these objects. Generally speaking, however, maintaining your own object pools clutters your code, increases memory footprint, and harms performance. Modern JVM implementations have highly optimized garbage collectors that easily outperform such object pools on lightweight objects.

The counterpoint to this item is Item 50 on *defensive copying*. The present item says, "Don't create a new object when you should reuse an existing one," while Item 50 says, "Don't reuse an existing object when you should create a new one." Note that the penalty for reusing an object when defensive copying is called for is far greater than the penalty for needlessly creating a duplicate object. Failing to make defensive copies where required can lead to insidious bugs and security holes; creating objects unnecessarily merely affects style and performance.

Item 7:   Eliminate obsolete object references

If you switched from a language with manual memory management, such as C or C++, to a garbage-collected language such as Java, your job as a programmer was made much easier by the fact that your objects are automatically reclaimed when you're through with them. It seems almost like magic when you first experience it. It can easily lead to the impression that you don't have to think about memory management, but this isn't quite true.

Consider the following simple stack implementation:

```java
// Can you spot the "memory leak"?
public class Stack {
    private Object[] elements;
    private int size = 0;
    private static final int DEFAULT_INITIAL_CAPACITY = 16;

    public Stack() {
        elements = new Object[DEFAULT_INITIAL_CAPACITY];
    }

    public void push(Object e) {
        ensureCapacity();
        elements[size++] = e;
    }

    public Object pop() {
        if (size == 0)
            throw new EmptyStackException();
        return elements[--size];
    }

    /**
     * Ensure space for at least one more element, roughly
     * doubling the capacity each time the array needs to grow.
     */
    private void ensureCapacity() {
        if (elements.length == size)
            elements = Arrays.copyOf(elements, 2 * size + 1);
    }
}
```

There's nothing obviously wrong with this program (but see Item 29 for a generic version). You could test it exhaustively, and it would pass every test with flying colors, but there's a problem lurking. Loosely speaking, the program has a "memory leak," which can silently manifest itself as reduced performance due to increased garbage collector activity or increased memory footprint. In extreme cases, such memory leaks can cause disk paging and even program failure with an OutOfMemoryError, but such failures are relatively rare.

So where is the memory leak? If a stack grows and then shrinks, the objects that were popped off the stack will not be garbage collected, even if the program using the stack has no more references to them. This is because the stack maintains *obsolete references* to these objects. An obsolete reference is simply a reference that will never be dereferenced again. In this case, any references outside of the "active portion" of the element array are obsolete. The active portion consists of the elements whose index is less than size.

Memory leaks in garbage-collected languages (more properly known as *unintentional object retentions*) are insidious. If an object reference is unintentionally retained, not only is that object excluded from garbage collection, but so too are any objects referenced by that object, and so on. Even if only a few object references are unintentionally retained, many, many objects may be prevented from being garbage collected, with potentially large effects on performance.

The fix for this sort of problem is simple: null out references once they become obsolete. In the case of our Stack class, the reference to an item becomes obsolete as soon as it's popped off the stack. The corrected version of the pop method looks like this:

```
public Object pop() {
    if (size == 0)
        throw new EmptyStackException();
    Object result = elements[--size];
    elements[size] = null; // Eliminate obsolete reference
    return result;
}
```

An added benefit of nulling out obsolete references is that if they are subsequently dereferenced by mistake, the program will immediately fail with a NullPointerException, rather than quietly doing the wrong thing. It is always beneficial to detect programming errors as quickly as possible.

When programmers are first stung by this problem, they may overcompensate by nulling out every object reference as soon as the program is finished using it. This is neither necessary nor desirable; it clutters up the program unnecessarily. **Nulling out object references should be the exception rather than the norm.** The best way to eliminate an obsolete reference is to let the variable that contained the reference fall out of scope. This occurs naturally if you define each variable in the narrowest possible scope (Item 57).

So when should you null out a reference? What aspect of the Stack class makes it susceptible to memory leaks? Simply put, it *manages its own memory*. The *storage pool* consists of the elements of the elements array (the object reference cells, not the objects themselves). The elements in the active portion of the array (as defined earlier) are *allocated*, and those in the remainder of the array are *free*. The garbage collector has no way of knowing this; to the garbage collector, all of the object references in the elements array are equally valid. Only the programmer knows that the inactive portion of the array is unimportant. The programmer effectively communicates this fact to the garbage collector by manually nulling out array elements as soon as they become part of the inactive portion.

Generally speaking, **whenever a class manages its own memory, the programmer should be alert for memory leaks**. Whenever an element is freed, any object references contained in the element should be nulled out.

Another common source of memory leaks is caches. Once you put an object reference into a cache, it's easy to forget that it's there and leave it in the cache long after it becomes irrelevant. There are several solutions to this problem. If you're lucky enough to implement a cache for which an entry is relevant exactly so long as there are references to its key outside of the cache, represent the cache as a WeakHashMap; entries will be removed automatically after they become obsolete. Remember that WeakHashMap is useful only if the desired lifetime of cache entries is determined by external references to the key, not the value.

More commonly, the useful lifetime of a cache entry is less well defined, with entries becoming less valuable over time. Under these circumstances, the cache should occasionally be cleansed of entries that have fallen into disuse. This can be done by a background thread (perhaps a ScheduledThreadPoolExecutor) or as a side effect of adding new entries to the cache. The LinkedHashMap class facilitates the latter approach with its removeEldestEntry method. For more sophisticated caches, you may need to use java.lang.ref directly.

A third common source of memory leaks is listeners and other callbacks. If you implement an API where clients register callbacks but don't deregister them explicitly, they will accumulate unless you take some action. One way to ensure that callbacks are garbage collected promptly is to store only *weak references* to them, for instance, by storing them only as keys in a WeakHashMap.

Because memory leaks typically do not manifest themselves as obvious failures, they may remain present in a system for years. They are typically discovered only as a result of careful code inspection or with the aid of a debugging tool known as a *heap profiler*. Therefore, it is very desirable to learn to anticipate problems like this before they occur and prevent them from happening.

Item 8:   Avoid finalizers and cleaners

Finalizers are unpredictable, often dangerous, and generally unnecessary. Their use can cause erratic behavior, poor performance, and portability problems. Finalizers have a few valid uses, which we'll cover later in this item, but as a rule, you should avoid them. As of Java 9, finalizers have been deprecated, but they are still being used by the Java libraries. The Java 9 replacement for finalizers is *cleaners.* **Cleaners are less dangerous than finalizers, but still unpredictable, slow, and generally unnecessary.**

C++ programmers are cautioned not to think of finalizers or cleaners as Java's analogue of C++ destructors. In C++, destructors are the normal way to reclaim the resources associated with an object, a necessary counterpart to constructors. In Java, the garbage collector reclaims the storage associated with an object when it becomes unreachable, requiring no special effort on the part of the programmer. C++ destructors are also used to reclaim other nonmemory resources. In Java, a try-with-resources or `try-finally` block is used for this purpose (Item 9).

One shortcoming of finalizers and cleaners is that there is no guarantee they'll be executed promptly [JLS, 12.6]. It can take arbitrarily long between the time that an object becomes unreachable and the time its finalizer or cleaner runs. This means that you should **never do anything time-critical in a finalizer or cleaner.** For example, it is a grave error to depend on a finalizer or cleaner to close files because open file descriptors are a limited resource. If many files are left open as a result of the system's tardiness in running finalizers or cleaners, a program may fail because it can no longer open files.

The promptness with which finalizers and cleaners are executed is primarily a function of the garbage collection algorithm, which varies widely across implementations. The behavior of a program that depends on the promptness of finalizer or cleaner execution may likewise vary. It is entirely possible that such a program will run perfectly on the JVM on which you test it and then fail miserably on the one favored by your most important customer.

Tardy finalization is not just a theoretical problem. Providing a finalizer for a class can arbitrarily delay reclamation of its instances. A colleague debugged a long-running GUI application that was mysteriously dying with an `OutOfMemoryError`. Analysis revealed that at the time of its death, the application had thousands of graphics objects on its finalizer queue just waiting to be finalized and reclaimed. Unfortunately, the finalizer thread was running at a lower priority than another application thread, so objects weren't getting finalized at the rate they became eligible for finalization. The language specification makes no guarantees as to which thread will execute finalizers, so there is no portable way to prevent this sort of problem other than to refrain from using finalizers. Cleaners are a bit better than finalizers in this regard because class authors have control over their own cleaner threads, but cleaners still run in the background, under the control of the garbage collector, so there can be no guarantee of prompt cleaning.

Not only does the specification provide no guarantee that finalizers or cleaners will run promptly; it provides no guarantee that they'll run at all. It is entirely possible, even likely, that a program terminates without running them on some objects that are no longer reachable. As a consequence, you should **never depend on a finalizer or cleaner to update persistent state.** For example, depending on a finalizer or cleaner to release a persistent lock on a shared resource such as a database is a good way to bring your entire distributed system to a grinding halt.

Don't be seduced by the methods System.gc and System.runFinalization. They may increase the odds of finalizers or cleaners getting executed, but they don't guarantee it. Two methods once claimed to make this guarantee: System.runFinalizersOnExit and its evil twin, Runtime.runFinalizersOnExit. These methods are fatally flawed and have been deprecated for decades [ThreadStop].

Another problem with finalizers is that an uncaught exception thrown during finalization is ignored, and finalization of that object terminates [JLS, 12.6]. Uncaught exceptions can leave other objects in a corrupt state. If another thread attempts to use such a corrupted object, arbitrary nondeterministic behavior may result. Normally, an uncaught exception will terminate the thread and print a stack trace, but not if it occurs in a finalizer—it won't even print a warning. Cleaners do not have this problem because a library using a cleaner has control over its thread.

There is a *severe* performance penalty for using finalizers and cleaners. On my machine, the time to create a simple AutoCloseable object, to close it using try-with-resources, and to have the garbage collector reclaim it is about 12 ns. Using a finalizer instead increases the time to 550 ns. In other words, it is about 50 times slower to create and destroy objects with finalizers. This is primarily because finalizers inhibit efficient garbage collection. Cleaners are comparable in speed to finalizers if you use them to clean all instances of the class (about 500 ns per instance on my machine), but cleaners are much faster if you use them only as a safety net, as discussed below. Under these circumstances, creating, cleaning, and destroying an object takes about 66 ns on my machine, which means you pay a factor of five (not fifty) for the insurance of a safety net *if* you don't use it.

Finalizers have a serious security problem: they open your class up to *finalizer attacks*. The idea behind a finalizer attack is simple: If an exception is thrown from a constructor or its serialization equivalents—the readObject and readResolve methods (Chapter 12)—the finalizer of a malicious subclass can run on the partially constructed object that should have "died on the vine." This finalizer can record a reference to the object in a static field, preventing it from being garbage collected. Once the malformed object has been recorded, it is a simple matter to invoke arbitrary methods on this object that should never have been allowed to exist in the first place. **Throwing an exception from a constructor should be sufficient to prevent an object from coming into existence; in the presence of finalizers, it is not.** Such attacks can have dire consequences. Final classes are immune to finalizer attacks because no one can write a malicious subclass of a final class. **To protect nonfinal classes from finalizer attacks, write a final finalize method that does nothing.**

So what should you do instead of writing a finalizer or cleaner for a class whose objects encapsulate resources that require termination, such as files or threads? Just **have your class implement AutoCloseable,** and require its clients to invoke the close method on each instance when it is no longer needed, typically using try-with-resources to ensure termination even in the face of exceptions (Item 9). One detail worth mentioning is that the instance must keep track of whether it has been closed: the close method must record in a field that the object is no longer valid, and other methods must check this field and throw an IllegalStateException if they are called after the object has been closed.

So what, if anything, are cleaners and finalizers good for? They have perhaps two legitimate uses. One is to act as a safety net in case the owner of a resource neglects to call its close method. While there's no guarantee that the cleaner or finalizer will run promptly (or at all), it is better to free the resource late than never if the client fails to do so. If you're considering writing such a safety-net finalizer, think long and hard about whether the protection is worth the cost. Some Java library classes, such as FileInputStream, FileOutputStream, ThreadPoolExecutor, and java.sql.Connection, have finalizers that serve as safety nets.

A second legitimate use of cleaners concerns objects with *native peers*. A native peer is a native (non-Java) object to which a normal object delegates via native methods. Because a native peer is not a normal object, the garbage collector doesn't know about it and can't reclaim it when its Java peer is reclaimed. A cleaner or finalizer may be an appropriate vehicle for this task, assuming the performance is acceptable and the native peer holds no critical resources. If the performance is unacceptable or the native peer holds resources that must be reclaimed promptly, the class should have a close method, as described earlier.

Cleaners are a bit tricky to use. Below is a simple Room class demonstrating the facility. Let's assume that rooms must be cleaned before they are reclaimed. The Room class implements AutoCloseable; the fact that its automatic cleaning safety net uses a cleaner is merely an implementation detail. Unlike finalizers, cleaners do not pollute a class's public API:

```
// An autocloseable class using a cleaner as a safety net
public class Room implements AutoCloseable {
    private static final Cleaner cleaner = Cleaner.create();

    // Resource that requires cleaning. Must not refer to Room!
    private static class State implements Runnable {
        int numJunkPiles; // Number of junk piles in this room

        State(int numJunkPiles) {
            this.numJunkPiles = numJunkPiles;
        }

        // Invoked by close method or cleaner
        @Override public void run() {
            System.out.println("Cleaning room");
            numJunkPiles = 0;
        }
    }

    // The state of this room, shared with our cleanable
    private final State state;

    // Our cleanable. Cleans the room when it's eligible for gc
    private final Cleaner.Cleanable cleanable;

    public Room(int numJunkPiles) {
        state = new State(numJunkPiles);
        cleanable = cleaner.register(this, state);
    }

    @Override public void close() {
        cleanable.clean();
    }
}
```

The static nested State class holds the resources that are required by the cleaner to clean the room. In this case, it is simply the numJunkPiles field, which represents the amount of mess in the room. More realistically, it might be a final long that contains a pointer to a native peer. State implements Runnable, and its run method is called at most once, by the Cleanable that we get when we register our State instance with our cleaner in the Room constructor. The call to the run method will be triggered by one of two things: Usually it is triggered by a call to

Room's close method calling Cleanable's clean method. If the client fails to call the close method by the time a Room instance is eligible for garbage collection, the cleaner will (hopefully) call State's run method.

It is critical that a State instance does not refer to its Room instance. If it did, it would create a circularity that would prevent the Room instance from becoming eligible for garbage collection (and from being automatically cleaned). Therefore, State must be a *static* nested class because nonstatic nested classes contain references to their enclosing instances (Item 24). It is similarly inadvisable to use a lambda because they can easily capture references to enclosing objects.

As we said earlier, Room's cleaner is used only as a safety net. If clients surround all Room instantiations in try-with-resource blocks, automatic cleaning will never be required. This well-behaved client demonstrates that behavior:

```
public class Adult {
    public static void main(String[] args) {
        try (Room myRoom = new Room(7)) {
            System.out.println("Goodbye");
        }
    }
}
```

As you'd expect, running the Adult program prints Goodbye, followed by Cleaning room. But what about this ill-behaved program, which never cleans its room?

```
public class Teenager {
    public static void main(String[] args) {
        new Room(99);
        System.out.println("Peace out");
    }
}
```

You might expect it to print Peace out, followed by Cleaning room, but on my machine, it never prints Cleaning room; it just exits. This is the unpredictability we spoke of earlier. The Cleaner spec says, "The behavior of cleaners during System.exit is implementation specific. No guarantees are made relating to whether cleaning actions are invoked or not." While the spec does not say it, the same holds true for normal program exit. On my machine, adding the line System.gc() to Teenager's main method is enough to make it print Cleaning room prior to exit, but there's no guarantee that you'll see the same behavior on your machine.

In summary, don't use cleaners, or in releases prior to Java 9, finalizers, except as a safety net or to terminate noncritical native resources. Even then, beware the indeterminacy and performance consequences.

Item 9:   Prefer try-with-resources to try-finally

The Java libraries include many resources that must be closed manually by invoking a close method. Examples include InputStream, OutputStream, and java.sql.Connection. Closing resources is often overlooked by clients, with predictably dire performance consequences. While many of these resources use finalizers as a safety net, finalizers don't work very well (Item 8).

Historically, a try-finally statement was the best way to guarantee that a resource would be closed properly, even in the face of an exception or return:

```
// try-finally - No longer the best way to close resources!
static String firstLineOfFile(String path) throws IOException {
    BufferedReader br = new BufferedReader(new FileReader(path));
    try {
        return br.readLine();
    } finally {
        br.close();
    }
}
```

This may not look bad, but it gets worse when you add a second resource:

```
// try-finally is ugly when used with more than one resource!
static void copy(String src, String dst) throws IOException {
    InputStream in = new FileInputStream(src);
    try {
        OutputStream out = new FileOutputStream(dst);
        try {
            byte[] buf = new byte[BUFFER_SIZE];
            int n;
            while ((n = in.read(buf)) >= 0)
                out.write(buf, 0, n);
        } finally {
            out.close();
        }
    } finally {
        in.close();
    }
}
```

It may be hard to believe, but even good programmers got this wrong most of the time. For starters, I got it wrong on page 88 of *Java Puzzlers* [Bloch05], and no one noticed for years. In fact, two-thirds of the uses of the close method in the Java libraries were wrong in 2007.

Even the correct code for closing resources with try-finally statements, as illustrated in the previous two code examples, has a subtle deficiency. The code in both the try block and the finally block is capable of throwing exceptions. For example, in the firstLineOfFile method, the call to readLine could throw an exception due to a failure in the underlying physical device, and the call to close could then fail for the same reason. Under these circumstances, the second exception completely obliterates the first one. There is no record of the first exception in the exception stack trace, which can greatly complicate debugging in real systems—usually it's the first exception that you want to see in order to diagnose the problem. While it is possible to write code to suppress the second exception in favor of the first, virtually no one did because it's just too verbose.

All of these problems were solved in one fell swoop when Java 7 introduced the try-with-resources statement [JLS, 14.20.3]. To be usable with this construct, a resource must implement the AutoCloseable interface, which consists of a single void-returning close method. Many classes and interfaces in the Java libraries and in third-party libraries now implement or extend AutoCloseable. If you write a class that represents a resource that must be closed, your class should implement AutoCloseable too.

Here's how our first example looks using try-with-resources:

```java
// try-with-resources - the the best way to close resources!
static String firstLineOfFile(String path) throws IOException {
    try (BufferedReader br = new BufferedReader(
            new FileReader(path))) {
        return br.readLine();
    }
}
```

And here's how our second example looks using try-with-resources:

```java
// try-with-resources on multiple resources - short and sweet
static void copy(String src, String dst) throws IOException {
    try (InputStream   in = new FileInputStream(src);
         OutputStream out = new FileOutputStream(dst)) {
        byte[] buf = new byte[BUFFER_SIZE];
        int n;
        while ((n = in.read(buf)) >= 0)
            out.write(buf, 0, n);
    }
}
```

Not only are the try-with-resources versions shorter and more readable than the originals, but they provide far better diagnostics. Consider the firstLineOfFile method. If exceptions are thrown by both the readLine call and the (invisible) close, the latter exception is *suppressed* in favor of the former. In fact, multiple exceptions may be suppressed in order to preserve the exception that you actually want to see. These suppressed exceptions are not merely discarded; they are printed in the stack trace with a notation saying that they were suppressed. You can also access them programmatically with the getSuppressed method, which was added to Throwable in Java 7.

You can put catch clauses on try-with-resources statements, just as you can on regular try-finally statements. This allows you to handle exceptions without sullying your code with another layer of nesting. As a slightly contrived example, here's a version our firstLineOfFile method that does not throw exceptions, but takes a default value to return if it can't open the file or read from it:

```java
// try-with-resources with a catch clause
static String firstLineOfFile(String path, String defaultVal) {
    try (BufferedReader br = new BufferedReader(
            new FileReader(path))) {
        return br.readLine();
    } catch (IOException e) {
        return defaultVal;
    }
}
```

The lesson is clear: Always use try-with-resources in preference to try-finally when working with resources that must be closed. The resulting code is shorter and clearer, and the exceptions that it generates are more useful. The try-with-resources statement makes it easy to write correct code using resources that must be closed, which was practically impossible using try-finally.

CHAPTER 3

Methods Common to All Objects

ALTHOUGH Object is a concrete class, it is designed primarily for extension. All of its nonfinal methods (equals, hashCode, toString, clone, and finalize) have explicit *general contracts* because they are designed to be overridden. It is the responsibility of any class overriding these methods to obey their general contracts; failure to do so will prevent other classes that depend on the contracts (such as HashMap and HashSet) from functioning properly in conjunction with the class.

This chapter tells you when and how to override the nonfinal Object methods. The finalize method is omitted from this chapter because it was discussed in Item 8. While not an Object method, Comparable.compareTo is discussed in this chapter because it has a similar character.

Item 10: Obey the general contract when overriding equals

Overriding the equals method seems simple, but there are many ways to get it wrong, and consequences can be dire. The easiest way to avoid problems is not to override the equals method, in which case each instance of the class is equal only to itself. This is the right thing to do if any of the following conditions apply:

- **Each instance of the class is inherently unique.** This is true for classes such as Thread that represent active entities rather than values. The equals implementation provided by Object has exactly the right behavior for these classes.

- **There is no need for the class to provide a "logical equality" test.** For example, java.util.regex.Pattern could have overridden equals to check whether two Pattern instances represented exactly the same regular expression, but the designers didn't think that clients would need or want this functionality. Under these circumstances, the equals implementation inherited from Object is ideal.

- **A superclass has already overridden equals, and the superclass behavior is appropriate for this class.** For example, most Set implementations inherit their equals implementation from AbstractSet, List implementations from AbstractList, and Map implementations from AbstractMap.

- **The class is private or package-private, and you are certain that its equals method will never be invoked.** If you are extremely risk-averse, you can override the equals method to ensure that it isn't invoked accidentally:

```
@Override public boolean equals(Object o) {
    throw new AssertionError(); // Method is never called
}
```

So when is it appropriate to override equals? It is when a class has a notion of *logical equality* that differs from mere object identity and a superclass has not already overridden equals. This is generally the case for *value classes*. A value class is simply a class that represents a value, such as Integer or String. A programmer who compares references to value objects using the equals method expects to find out whether they are logically equivalent, not whether they refer to the same object. Not only is overriding the equals method necessary to satisfy programmer expectations, it enables instances to serve as map keys or set elements with predictable, desirable behavior.

One kind of value class that does *not* require the equals method to be overridden is a class that uses instance control (Item 1) to ensure that at most one object exists with each value. Enum types (Item 34) fall into this category. For these classes, logical equality is the same as object identity, so Object's equals method functions as a logical equals method.

When you override the equals method, you must adhere to its general contract. Here is the contract, from the specification for Object :

The equals method implements an *equivalence relation*. It has these properties:

- *Reflexive*: For any non-null reference value x, x.equals(x) must return true.

- *Symmetric*: For any non-null reference values x and y, x.equals(y) must return true if and only if y.equals(x) returns true.

- *Transitive*: For any non-null reference values x, y, z, if x.equals(y) returns true and y.equals(z) returns true, then x.equals(z) must return true.

- *Consistent*: For any non-null reference values x and y, multiple invocations of x.equals(y) must consistently return true or consistently return false, provided no information used in equals comparisons is modified.

- For any non-null reference value x, x.equals(null) must return false.

Unless you are mathematically inclined, this might look a bit scary, but do not ignore it! If you violate it, you may well find that your program behaves erratically or crashes, and it can be very difficult to pin down the source of the failure. To paraphrase John Donne, no class is an island. Instances of one class are frequently passed to another. Many classes, including all collections classes, depend on the objects passed to them obeying the equals contract.

Now that you are aware of the dangers of violating the equals contract, let's go over the contract in detail. The good news is that, appearances notwithstanding, it really isn't very complicated. Once you understand it, it's not hard to adhere to it.

So what is an equivalence relation? Loosely speaking, it's an operator that partitions a set of elements into subsets whose elements are deemed equal to one another. These subsets are known as *equivalence classes*. For an equals method to be useful, all of the elements in each equivalence class must be interchangeable from the perspective of the user. Now let's examine the five requirements in turn:

Reflexivity—The first requirement says merely that an object must be equal to itself. It's hard to imagine violating this one unintentionally. If you were to violate it and then add an instance of your class to a collection, the contains method might well say that the collection didn't contain the instance that you just added.

Symmetry—The second requirement says that any two objects must agree on whether they are equal. Unlike the first requirement, it's not hard to imagine violating this one unintentionally. For example, consider the following class, which implements a case-insensitive string. The case of the string is preserved by toString but ignored in equals comparisons:

```java
// Broken - violates symmetry!
public final class CaseInsensitiveString {
    private final String s;

    public CaseInsensitiveString(String s) {
        this.s = Objects.requireNonNull(s);
    }

    // Broken - violates symmetry!
    @Override public boolean equals(Object o) {
        if (o instanceof CaseInsensitiveString)
            return s.equalsIgnoreCase(
                ((CaseInsensitiveString) o).s);
        if (o instanceof String)  // One-way interoperability!
            return s.equalsIgnoreCase((String) o);
        return false;
    }
    ...  // Remainder omitted
}
```

The well-intentioned `equals` method in this class naively attempts to interoperate with ordinary strings. Let's suppose that we have one case-insensitive string and one ordinary one:

```
CaseInsensitiveString cis = new CaseInsensitiveString("Polish");
String s = "polish";
```

As expected, `cis.equals(s)` returns `true`. The problem is that while the `equals` method in `CaseInsensitiveString` knows about ordinary strings, the `equals` method in `String` is oblivious to case-insensitive strings. Therefore, `s.equals(cis)` returns `false`, a clear violation of symmetry. Suppose you put a case-insensitive string into a collection:

```
List<CaseInsensitiveString> list = new ArrayList<>();
list.add(cis);
```

What does `list.contains(s)` return at this point? Who knows? In the current OpenJDK implementation, it happens to return `false`, but that's just an implementation artifact. In another implementation, it could just as easily return `true` or throw a runtime exception. **Once you've violated the `equals` contract, you simply don't know how other objects will behave when confronted with your object.**

To eliminate the problem, merely remove the ill-conceived attempt to interoperate with `String` from the `equals` method. Once you do this, you can refactor the method into a single return statement:

```
@Override public boolean equals(Object o) {
    return o instanceof CaseInsensitiveString &&
        ((CaseInsensitiveString) o).s.equalsIgnoreCase(s);
}
```

Transitivity—The third requirement of the `equals` contract says that if one object is equal to a second and the second object is equal to a third, then the first object must be equal to the third. Again, it's not hard to imagine violating this requirement unintentionally. Consider the case of a subclass that adds a new *value component* to its superclass. In other words, the subclass adds a piece of information that affects equals comparisons. Let's start with a simple immutable two-dimensional integer point class:

```
public class Point {
    private final int x;
    private final int y;

    public Point(int x, int y) {
        this.x = x;
        this.y = y;
    }

    @Override public boolean equals(Object o) {
        if (!(o instanceof Point))
            return false;
        Point p = (Point)o;
        return p.x == x && p.y == y;
    }

    ... // Remainder omitted
}
```

Suppose you want to extend this class, adding the notion of color to a point:

```
public class ColorPoint extends Point {
    private final Color color;

    public ColorPoint(int x, int y, Color color) {
        super(x, y);
        this.color = color;
    }

    ... // Remainder omitted
}
```

How should the equals method look? If you leave it out entirely, the implementation is inherited from Point and color information is ignored in equals comparisons. While this does not violate the equals contract, it is clearly unacceptable. Suppose you write an equals method that returns true only if its argument is another color point with the same position and color:

```
// Broken - violates symmetry!
@Override public boolean equals(Object o) {
    if (!(o instanceof ColorPoint))
        return false;
    return super.equals(o) && ((ColorPoint) o).color == color;
}
```

The problem with this method is that you might get different results when comparing a point to a color point and vice versa. The former comparison ignores color, while the latter comparison always returns `false` because the type of the argument is incorrect. To make this concrete, let's create one point and one color point:

```
Point p = new Point(1, 2);
ColorPoint cp = new ColorPoint(1, 2, Color.RED);
```

Then `p.equals(cp)` returns `true`, while `cp.equals(p)` returns `false`. You might try to fix the problem by having `ColorPoint.equals` ignore color when doing "mixed comparisons":

```
// Broken - violates transitivity!
@Override public boolean equals(Object o) {
    if (!(o instanceof Point))
        return false;

    // If o is a normal Point, do a color-blind comparison
    if (!(o instanceof ColorPoint))
        return o.equals(this);

    // o is a ColorPoint; do a full comparison
    return super.equals(o) && ((ColorPoint) o).color == color;
}
```

This approach does provide symmetry, but at the expense of transitivity:

```
ColorPoint p1 = new ColorPoint(1, 2, Color.RED);
Point p2 = new Point(1, 2);
ColorPoint p3 = new ColorPoint(1, 2, Color.BLUE);
```

Now `p1.equals(p2)` and `p2.equals(p3)` return `true`, while `p1.equals(p3)` returns `false`, a clear violation of transitivity. The first two comparisons are "color-blind," while the third takes color into account.

Also, this approach can cause infinite recursion: Suppose there are two subclasses of `Point`, say `ColorPoint` and `SmellPoint`, each with this sort of equals method. Then a call to `myColorPoint.equals(mySmellPoint)` will throw a `StackOverflowError`.

So what's the solution? It turns out that this is a fundamental problem of equivalence relations in object-oriented languages. **There is no way to extend an instantiable class and add a value component while preserving the equals contract**, unless you're willing to forgo the benefits of object-oriented abstraction.

You may hear it said that you can extend an instantiable class and add a value component while preserving the equals contract by using a getClass test in place of the instanceof test in the equals method:

```
// Broken - violates Liskov substitution principle (page 43)
@Override public boolean equals(Object o) {
    if (o == null || o.getClass() != getClass())
        return false;
    Point p = (Point) o;
    return p.x == x && p.y == y;
}
```

This has the effect of equating objects only if they have the same implementation class. This may not seem so bad, but the consequences are unacceptable: An instance of a subclass of Point is still a Point, and it still needs to function as one, but it fails to do so if you take this approach! Let's suppose we want to write a method to tell whether a point is on the unit circle. Here is one way we could do it:

```
// Initialize unitCircle to contain all Points on the unit circle
private static final Set<Point> unitCircle = Set.of(
        new Point( 1,  0), new Point( 0,  1),
        new Point(-1,  0), new Point( 0, -1));

public static boolean onUnitCircle(Point p) {
    return unitCircle.contains(p);
}
```

While this may not be the fastest way to implement the functionality, it works fine. Suppose you extend Point in some trivial way that doesn't add a value component, say, by having its constructor keep track of how many instances have been created:

```
public class CounterPoint extends Point {
    private static final AtomicInteger counter =
        new AtomicInteger();

    public CounterPoint(int x, int y) {
        super(x, y);
        counter.incrementAndGet();
    }
    public static int numberCreated() { return counter.get(); }
}
```

The *Liskov substitution principle* says that any important property of a type should also hold for all its subtypes so that any method written for the type should work equally well on its subtypes [Liskov87]. This is the formal statement of our earlier claim that a subclass of Point (such as CounterPoint) is still a Point and must act as one. But suppose we pass a CounterPoint to the onUnitCircle method. If the Point class uses a getClass-based equals method, the onUnitCircle method will return false regardless of the CounterPoint instance's x and y coordinates. This is so because most collections, including the HashSet used by the onUnitCircle method, use the equals method to test for containment, and no CounterPoint instance is equal to any Point. If, however, you use a proper instanceof-based equals method on Point, the same onUnitCircle method works fine when presented with a CounterPoint instance.

While there is no satisfactory way to extend an instantiable class and add a value component, there is a fine workaround: Follow the advice of Item 18, "Favor composition over inheritance." Instead of having ColorPoint extend Point, give ColorPoint a private Point field and a public *view* method (Item 6) that returns the point at the same position as this color point:

```java
// Adds a value component without violating the equals contract
public class ColorPoint {
    private final Point point;
    private final Color color;

    public ColorPoint(int x, int y, Color color) {
        point = new Point(x, y);
        this.color = Objects.requireNonNull(color);
    }

    /**
     * Returns the point-view of this color point.
     */
    public Point asPoint() {
        return point;
    }

    @Override public boolean equals(Object o) {
        if (!(o instanceof ColorPoint))
            return false;
        ColorPoint cp = (ColorPoint) o;
        return cp.point.equals(point) && cp.color.equals(color);
    }

    ... // Remainder omitted
}
```

There are some classes in the Java platform libraries that do extend an instantiable class and add a value component. For example, java.sql.Timestamp extends `java.util.Date` and adds a nanoseconds field. The `equals` implementation for `Timestamp` does violate symmetry and can cause erratic behavior if `Timestamp` and `Date` objects are used in the same collection or are otherwise intermixed. The `Timestamp` class has a disclaimer cautioning programmers against mixing dates and timestamps. While you won't get into trouble as long as you keep them separate, there's nothing to prevent you from mixing them, and the resulting errors can be hard to debug. This behavior of the `Timestamp` class was a mistake and should not be emulated.

Note that you *can* add a value component to a subclass of an *abstract* class without violating the `equals` contract. This is important for the sort of class hierarchies that you get by following the advice in Item 23, "Prefer class hierarchies to tagged classes." For example, you could have an abstract class `Shape` with no value components, a subclass `Circle` that adds a `radius` field, and a subclass `Rectangle` that adds `length` and `width` fields. Problems of the sort shown earlier won't occur so long as it is impossible to create a superclass instance directly.

Consistency—The fourth requirement of the `equals` contract says that if two objects are equal, they must remain equal for all time unless one (or both) of them is modified. In other words, mutable objects can be equal to different objects at different times while immutable objects can't. When you write a class, think hard about whether it should be immutable (Item 17). If you conclude that it should, make sure that your `equals` method enforces the restriction that equal objects remain equal and unequal objects remain unequal for all time.

Whether or not a class is immutable, **do not write an `equals` method that depends on unreliable resources.** It's extremely difficult to satisfy the consistency requirement if you violate this prohibition. For example, `java.net.URL`'s `equals` method relies on comparison of the IP addresses of the hosts associated with the URLs. Translating a host name to an IP address can require network access, and it isn't guaranteed to yield the same results over time. This can cause the URL `equals` method to violate the `equals` contract and has caused problems in practice. The behavior of URL's `equals` method was a big mistake and should not be emulated. Unfortunately, it cannot be changed due to compatibility requirements. To avoid this sort of problem, `equals` methods should perform only deterministic computations on memory-resident objects.

Non-nullity—The final requirement lacks an official name, so I have taken the liberty of calling it "non-nullity." It says that all objects must be unequal to `null`. While it is hard to imagine accidentally returning `true` in response to the invocation `o.equals(null)`, it isn't hard to imagine accidentally throwing a

NullPointerException. The general contract prohibits this. Many classes have equals methods that guard against it with an explicit test for null:

```
@Override public boolean equals(Object o) {
    if (o == null)
        return false;
    ...
}
```

This test is unnecessary. To test its argument for equality, the equals method must first cast its argument to an appropriate type so its accessors can be invoked or its fields accessed. Before doing the cast, the method must use the instanceof operator to check that its argument is of the correct type:

```
@Override public boolean equals(Object o) {
    if (!(o instanceof MyType))
        return false;
    MyType mt = (MyType) o;
    ...
}
```

If this type check were missing and the equals method were passed an argument of the wrong type, the equals method would throw a ClassCastException, which violates the equals contract. But the instanceof operator is specified to return false if its first operand is null, regardless of what type appears in the second operand [JLS, 15.20.2]. Therefore, the type check will return false if null is passed in, so you don't need an explicit null check.

Putting it all together, here's a recipe for a high-quality equals method:

1. **Use the == operator to check if the argument is a reference to this object.** If so, return true. This is just a performance optimization but one that is worth doing if the comparison is potentially expensive.

2. **Use the instanceof operator to check if the argument has the correct type.** If not, return false. Typically, the correct type is the class in which the method occurs. Occasionally, it is some interface implemented by this class. Use an interface if the class implements an interface that refines the equals contract to permit comparisons across classes that implement the interface. Collection interfaces such as Set, List, Map, and Map.Entry have this property.

3. **Cast the argument to the correct type.** Because this cast was preceded by an instanceof test, it is guaranteed to succeed.

4. **For each "significant" field in the class, check if that field of the argument matches the corresponding field of this object.** If all these tests succeed, return `true`; otherwise, return `false`. If the type in Step 2 is an interface, you must access the argument's fields via interface methods; if the type is a class, you may be able to access the fields directly, depending on their accessibility.

For primitive fields whose type is not `float` or `double`, use the `==` operator for comparisons; for object reference fields, call the `equals` method recursively; for `float` fields, use the static `Float.compare(float, float)` method; and for `double` fields, use `Double.compare(double, double)`. The special treatment of `float` and `double` fields is made necessary by the existence of `Float.NaN`, `-0.0f` and the analogous `double` values; see JLS 15.21.1 or the documentation of `Float.equals` for details. While you could compare `float` and `double` fields with the static methods `Float.equals` and `Double.equals`, this would entail autoboxing on every comparison, which would have poor performance. For array fields, apply these guidelines to each element. If every element in an array field is significant, use one of the `Arrays.equals` methods.

Some object reference fields may legitimately contain `null`. To avoid the possibility of a `NullPointerException`, check such fields for equality using the static method `Objects.equals(Object, Object)`.

For some classes, such as `CaseInsensitiveString` above, field comparisons are more complex than simple equality tests. If this is the case, you may want to store a *canonical form* of the field so the `equals` method can do a cheap exact comparison on canonical forms rather than a more costly nonstandard comparison. This technique is most appropriate for immutable classes (Item 17); if the object can change, you must keep the canonical form up to date.

The performance of the `equals` method may be affected by the order in which fields are compared. For best performance, you should first compare fields that are more likely to differ, less expensive to compare, or, ideally, both. You must not compare fields that are not part of an object's logical state, such as lock fields used to synchronize operations. You need not compare *derived fields*, which can be calculated from "significant fields," but doing so may improve the performance of the `equals` method. If a derived field amounts to a summary description of the entire object, comparing this field will save you the expense of comparing the actual data if the comparison fails. For example, suppose you have a `Polygon` class, and you cache the area. If two polygons have unequal areas, you needn't bother comparing their edges and vertices.

When you are finished writing your equals method, ask yourself three questions: Is it symmetric? Is it transitive? Is it consistent? And don't just ask yourself; write unit tests to check, unless you used AutoValue (page 49) to generate your equals method, in which case you can safely omit the tests. If the properties fail to hold, figure out why, and modify the equals method accordingly. Of course your equals method must also satisfy the other two properties (reflexivity and non-nullity), but these two usually take care of themselves.

An equals method constructed according to the previous recipe is shown in this simplistic PhoneNumber class:

```java
// Class with a typical equals method
public final class PhoneNumber {
    private final short areaCode, prefix, lineNum;

    public PhoneNumber(int areaCode, int prefix, int lineNum) {
        this.areaCode = rangeCheck(areaCode, 999, "area code");
        this.prefix   = rangeCheck(prefix,    999, "prefix");
        this.lineNum  = rangeCheck(lineNum, 9999, "line num");
    }

    private static short rangeCheck(int val, int max, String arg) {
        if (val < 0 || val > max)
            throw new IllegalArgumentException(arg + ": " + val);
        return (short) val;
    }

    @Override public boolean equals(Object o) {
        if (o == this)
            return true;
        if (!(o instanceof PhoneNumber))
            return false;
        PhoneNumber pn = (PhoneNumber)o;
        return pn.lineNum == lineNum && pn.prefix == prefix
                && pn.areaCode == areaCode;
    }
    ... // Remainder omitted
}
```

Here are a few final caveats:

- **Always override hashCode when you override equals** (Item 11).

- **Don't try to be too clever.** If you simply test fields for equality, it's not hard to adhere to the equals contract. If you are overly aggressive in searching for equivalence, it's easy to get into trouble. It is generally a bad idea to take any form of aliasing into account. For example, the File class shouldn't attempt to equate symbolic links referring to the same file. Thankfully, it doesn't.

- **Don't substitute another type for Object in the equals declaration.** It is not uncommon for a programmer to write an equals method that looks like this and then spend hours puzzling over why it doesn't work properly:

```
// Broken - parameter type must be Object!
public boolean equals(MyClass o) {
    ...
}
```

The problem is that this method does not *override* Object.equals, whose argument is of type Object, but *overloads* it instead (Item 52). It is unacceptable to provide such a "strongly typed" equals method even in addition to the normal one, because it can cause Override annotations in subclasses to generate false positives and provide a false sense of security.

Consistent use of the Override annotation, as illustrated throughout this item, will prevent you from making this mistake (Item 40). This equals method won't compile, and the error message will tell you exactly what is wrong:

```
// Still broken, but won't compile
@Override public boolean equals(MyClass o) {
    ...
}
```

Writing and testing equals (and hashCode) methods is tedious, and the resulting code is mundane. An excellent alternative to writing and testing these methods manually is to use Google's open source AutoValue framework, which automatically generates these methods for you, triggered by a single annotation on the class . In most cases, the methods generated by AutoValue are essentially identical to those you'd write yourself.

IDEs, too, have facilities to generate equals and hashCode methods, but the resulting source code is more verbose and less readable than code that uses AutoValue, does not track changes in the class automatically, and therefore requires testing. That said, having IDEs generate equals (and hashCode) methods is generally preferable to implementing them manually because IDEs do not make careless mistakes, and humans do.

In summary, don't override the equals method unless you have to: in many cases, the implementation inherited from Object does exactly what you want. If you do override equals, make sure to compare all of the class's significant fields and to compare them in a manner that preserves all five provisions of the equals contract.

Item 11: Always override `hashCode` when you override `equals`

You must override `hashCode` in every class that overrides `equals`. If you fail to do so, your class will violate the general contract for `hashCode`, which will prevent it from functioning properly in collections such as `HashMap` and `HashSet`. Here is the contract, adapted from the `Object` specification :

- When the `hashCode` method is invoked on an object repeatedly during an execution of an application, it must consistently return the same value, provided no information used in `equals` comparisons is modified. This value need not remain consistent from one execution of an application to another.

- If two objects are equal according to the `equals(Object)` method, then calling `hashCode` on the two objects must produce the same integer result.

- If two objects are unequal according to the `equals(Object)` method, it is *not* required that calling `hashCode` on each of the objects must produce distinct results. However, the programmer should be aware that producing distinct results for unequal objects may improve the performance of hash tables.

The key provision that is violated when you fail to override `hashCode` is the second one: equal objects must have equal hash codes. Two distinct instances may be logically equal according to a class's `equals` method, but to `Object`'s `hashCode` method, they're just two objects with nothing much in common. Therefore, `Object`'s `hashCode` method returns two seemingly random numbers instead of two equal numbers as required by the contract.

For example, suppose you attempt to use instances of the `PhoneNumber` class from Item 10 as keys in a `HashMap`:

```
Map<PhoneNumber, String> m = new HashMap<>();
m.put(new PhoneNumber(707, 867, 5309), "Jenny");
```

At this point, you might expect `m.get(new PhoneNumber(707, 867, 5309))` to return `"Jenny"`, but instead, it returns `null`. Notice that two `PhoneNumber` instances are involved: one is used for insertion into the `HashMap`, and a second, equal instance is used for (attempted) retrieval. The `PhoneNumber` class's failure to override `hashCode` causes the two equal instances to have unequal hash codes, in violation of the `hashCode` contract. Therefore, the `get` method is likely to look for the phone number in a different hash bucket from the one in which it was stored by the `put` method. Even if the two instances happen to hash to the same bucket, the `get` method will almost certainly return `null`, because `HashMap` has an optimization that caches the hash code associated with each entry and doesn't bother checking for object equality if the hash codes don't match.

Fixing this problem is as simple as writing a proper hashCode method for PhoneNumber. So what should a hashCode method look like? It's trivial to write a bad one. This one, for example, is always legal but should never be used:

```
// The worst possible legal hashCode implementation - never use!
@Override public int hashCode() { return 42; }
```

It's legal because it ensures that equal objects have the same hash code. It's atrocious because it ensures that *every* object has the same hash code. Therefore, every object hashes to the same bucket, and hash tables degenerate to linked lists. Programs that should run in linear time instead run in quadratic time. For large hash tables, this is the difference between working and not working.

A good hash function tends to produce unequal hash codes for unequal instances. This is exactly what is meant by the third part of the hashCode contract. Ideally, a hash function should distribute any reasonable collection of unequal instances uniformly across all int values. Achieving this ideal can be difficult. Luckily it's not too hard to achieve a fair approximation. Here is a simple recipe:

1. Declare an int variable named result, and initialize it to the hash code c for the first significant field in your object, as computed in step 2.a. (Recall from Item 10 that a significant field is a field that affects equals comparisons.)

2. For every remaining significant field f in your object, do the following:

   a. Compute an int hash code c for the field:

      i. If the field is of a primitive type, compute *Type*.hashCode(f), where *Type* is the boxed primitive class corresponding to f's type.

      ii. If the field is an object reference and this class's equals method compares the field by recursively invoking equals, recursively invoke hashCode on the field. If a more complex comparison is required, compute a "canonical representation" for this field and invoke hashCode on the canonical representation. If the value of the field is null, use 0 (or some other constant, but 0 is traditional).

      iii. If the field is an array, treat it as if each significant element were a separate field. That is, compute a hash code for each significant element by applying these rules recursively, and combine the values per step 2.b. If the array has no significant elements, use a constant, preferably not 0. If all elements are significant, use Arrays.hashCode.

   b. Combine the hash code c computed in step 2.a into result as follows:
      ```
      result = 31 * result + c;
      ```

3. Return result.

When you are finished writing the hashCode method, ask yourself whether equal instances have equal hash codes. Write unit tests to verify your intuition (unless you used AutoValue to generate your equals and hashCode methods, in which case you can safely omit these tests). If equal instances have unequal hash codes, figure out why and fix the problem.

You may exclude *derived fields* from the hash code computation. In other words, you may ignore any field whose value can be computed from fields included in the computation. You *must* exclude any fields that are not used in equals comparisons, or you risk violating the second provision of the hashCode contract.

The multiplication in step 2.b makes the result depend on the order of the fields, yielding a much better hash function if the class has multiple similar fields. For example, if the multiplication were omitted from a String hash function, all anagrams would have identical hash codes. The value 31 was chosen because it is an odd prime. If it were even and the multiplication overflowed, information would be lost, because multiplication by 2 is equivalent to shifting. The advantage of using a prime is less clear, but it is traditional. A nice property of 31 is that the multiplication can be replaced by a shift and a subtraction for better performance on some architectures: 31 * i == (i << 5) - i. Modern VMs do this sort of optimization automatically.

Let's apply the previous recipe to the PhoneNumber class:

```java
// Typical hashCode method
@Override public int hashCode() {
    int result = Short.hashCode(areaCode);
    result = 31 * result + Short.hashCode(prefix);
    result = 31 * result + Short.hashCode(lineNum);
    return result;
}
```

Because this method returns the result of a simple deterministic computation whose only inputs are the three significant fields in a PhoneNumber instance, it is clear that equal PhoneNumber instances have equal hash codes. This method is, in fact, a perfectly good hashCode implementation for PhoneNumber, on par with those in the Java platform libraries. It is simple, is reasonably fast, and does a reasonable job of dispersing unequal phone numbers into different hash buckets.

While the recipe in this item yields reasonably good hash functions, they are not state-of-the-art. They are comparable in quality to the hash functions found in the Java platform libraries' value types and are adequate for most uses. If you have a bona fide need for hash functions less likely to produce collisions, see Guava's com.google.common.hash.Hashing [Guava].

The Objects class has a static method that takes an arbitrary number of objects and returns a hash code for them. This method, named hash, lets you write one-line hashCode methods whose quality is comparable to those written according to the recipe in this item. Unfortunately, they run more slowly because they entail array creation to pass a variable number of arguments, as well as boxing and unboxing if any of the arguments are of primitive type. This style of hash function is recommended for use only in situations where performance is not critical. Here is a hash function for PhoneNumber written using this technique:

```
// One-line hashCode method - mediocre performance
@Override public int hashCode() {
    return Objects.hash(lineNum, prefix, areaCode);
}
```

If a class is immutable and the cost of computing the hash code is significant, you might consider caching the hash code in the object rather than recalculating it each time it is requested. If you believe that most objects of this type will be used as hash keys, then you should calculate the hash code when the instance is created. Otherwise, you might choose to *lazily initialize* the hash code the first time hash-Code is invoked. Some care is required to ensure that the class remains thread-safe in the presence of a lazily initialized field (Item 83). Our PhoneNumber class does not merit this treatment, but just to show you how it's done, here it is. Note that the initial value for the hashCode field (in this case, 0) should not be the hash code of a commonly created instance:

```
// hashCode method with lazily initialized cached hash code
private int hashCode; // Automatically initialized to 0

@Override public int hashCode() {
    int result = hashCode;
    if (result == 0) {
        result = Short.hashCode(areaCode);
        result = 31 * result + Short.hashCode(prefix);
        result = 31 * result + Short.hashCode(lineNum);
        hashCode = result;
    }
    return result;
}
```

Do not be tempted to exclude significant fields from the hash code computation to improve performance. While the resulting hash function may run faster, its poor quality may degrade hash tables' performance to the point where they become unusable. In particular, the hash function may be confronted with a large collection of instances that differ mainly in regions you've chosen to ignore. If this happens, the hash function will map all these instances to a few hash codes, and programs that should run in linear time will instead run in quadratic time.

This is not just a theoretical problem. Prior to Java 2, the String hash function used at most sixteen characters evenly spaced throughout the string, starting with the first character. For large collections of hierarchical names, such as URLs, this function displayed exactly the pathological behavior described earlier.

Don't provide a detailed specification for the value returned by hashCode, so clients can't reasonably depend on it; this gives you the flexibility to change it. Many classes in the Java libraries, such as String and Integer, specify the exact value returned by their hashCode method as a function of the instance value. This is *not* a good idea but a mistake that we're forced to live with: It impedes the ability to improve the hash function in future releases. If you leave the details unspecified and a flaw is found in the hash function or a better hash function is discovered, you can change it in a subsequent release.

In summary, you *must* override hashCode every time you override equals, or your program will not run correctly. Your hashCode method must obey the general contract specified in Object and must do a reasonable job assigning unequal hash codes to unequal instances. This is easy to achieve, if slightly tedious, using the recipe on page 51. As mentioned in Item 10, the AutoValue framework provides a fine alternative to writing equals and hashCode methods manually, and IDEs also provide some of this functionality.

Item 12: Always override `toString`

While `Object` provides an implementation of the `toString` method, the string that it returns is generally not what the user of your class wants to see. It consists of the class name followed by an "at" sign (@) and the unsigned hexadecimal representation of the hash code, for example, `PhoneNumber@163b91`. The general contract for `toString` says that the returned string should be "a concise but informative representation that is easy for a person to read." While it could be argued that `PhoneNumber@163b91` is concise and easy to read, it isn't very informative when compared to `707-867-5309`. The `toString` contract goes on to say, "It is recommended that all subclasses override this method." Good advice, indeed!

While it isn't as critical as obeying the `equals` and `hashCode` contracts (Items 10 and 11), **providing a good `toString` implementation makes your class much more pleasant to use and makes systems using the class easier to debug**. The `toString` method is automatically invoked when an object is passed to `println`, `printf`, the string concatenation operator, or `assert`, or is printed by a debugger. Even if you never call `toString` on an object, others may. For example, a component that has a reference to your object may include the string representation of the object in a logged error message. If you fail to override `toString`, the message may be all but useless.

If you've provided a good `toString` method for `PhoneNumber`, generating a useful diagnostic message is as easy as this:

```
System.out.println("Failed to connect to " + phoneNumber);
```

Programmers will generate diagnostic messages in this fashion whether or not you override `toString`, but the messages won't be useful unless you do. The benefits of providing a good `toString` method extend beyond instances of the class to objects containing references to these instances, especially collections. Which would you rather see when printing a map, `{Jenny=PhoneNumber@163b91}` or `{Jenny=707-867-5309}`?

When practical, the `toString` method should return *all* of the interesting information contained in the object, as shown in the phone number example. It is impractical if the object is large or if it contains state that is not conducive to string representation. Under these circumstances, `toString` should return a summary such as `Manhattan residential phone directory (1487536 listings)` or `Thread[main,5,main]`. Ideally, the string should be self-explanatory. (The `Thread` example flunks this test.) A particularly annoying penalty for failing to include all of an object's interesting information in its string representation is test failure reports that look like this:

```
Assertion failure: expected {abc, 123}, but was {abc, 123}.
```

One important decision you'll have to make when implementing a toString method is whether to specify the format of the return value in the documentation. It is recommended that you do this for *value classes*, such as phone number or matrix. The advantage of specifying the format is that it serves as a standard, unambiguous, human-readable representation of the object. This representation can be used for input and output and in persistent human-readable data objects, such as CSV files. If you specify the format, it's usually a good idea to provide a matching static factory or constructor so programmers can easily translate back and forth between the object and its string representation. This approach is taken by many value classes in the Java platform libraries, including BigInteger, BigDecimal, and most of the boxed primitive classes.

The disadvantage of specifying the format of the toString return value is that once you've specified it, you're stuck with it for life, assuming your class is widely used. Programmers will write code to parse the representation, to generate it, and to embed it into persistent data. If you change the representation in a future release, you'll break their code and data, and they will yowl. By choosing not to specify a format, you preserve the flexibility to add information or improve the format in a subsequent release.

Whether or not you decide to specify the format, you should clearly document your intentions. If you specify the format, you should do so precisely. For example, here's a toString method to go with the PhoneNumber class in Item 11:

```java
/**
 * Returns the string representation of this phone number.
 * The string consists of twelve characters whose format is
 * "XXX-YYY-ZZZZ", where XXX is the area code, YYY is the
 * prefix, and ZZZZ is the line number. Each of the capital
 * letters represents a single decimal digit.
 *
 * If any of the three parts of this phone number is too small
 * to fill up its field, the field is padded with leading zeros.
 * For example, if the value of the line number is 123, the last
 * four characters of the string representation will be "0123".
 */
@Override public String toString() {
    return String.format("%03d-%03d-%04d",
            areaCode, prefix, lineNum);
}
```

If you decide not to specify a format, the documentation comment should read something like this:

```
/**
 * Returns a brief description of this potion. The exact details
 * of the representation are unspecified and subject to change,
 * but the following may be regarded as typical:
 *
 * "[Potion #9: type=love, smell=turpentine, look=india ink]"
 */
@Override public String toString() { ... }
```

After reading this comment, programmers who produce code or persistent data that depends on the details of the format will have no one but themselves to blame when the format is changed.

Whether or not you specify the format, **provide programmatic access to the information contained in the value returned by toString.** For example, the PhoneNumber class should contain accessors for the area code, prefix, and line number. If you fail to do this, you *force* programmers who need this information to parse the string. Besides reducing performance and making unnecessary work for programmers, this process is error-prone and results in fragile systems that break if you change the format. By failing to provide accessors, you turn the string format into a de facto API, even if you've specified that it's subject to change.

It makes no sense to write a toString method in a static utility class (Item 4). Nor should you write a toString method in most enum types (Item 34) because Java provides a perfectly good one for you. You should, however, write a toString method in any abstract class whose subclasses share a common string representation. For example, the toString methods on most collection implementations are inherited from the abstract collection classes.

Google's open source AutoValue facility, discussed in Item 10, will generate a toString method for you, as will most IDEs. These methods are great for telling you the contents of each field but aren't specialized to the *meaning* of the class. So, for example, it would be inappropriate to use an automatically generated toString method for our PhoneNumber class (as phone numbers have a standard string representation), but it would be perfectly acceptable for our Potion class. That said, an automatically generated toString method is far preferable to the one inherited from Object, which tells you *nothing* about an object's value.

To recap, override Object's toString implementation in every instantiable class you write, unless a superclass has already done so. It makes classes much more pleasant to use and aids in debugging. The toString method should return a concise, useful description of the object, in an aesthetically pleasing format.

Item 13: Override `clone` judiciously

The `Cloneable` interface was intended as a *mixin interface* (Item 20) for classes to advertise that they permit cloning. Unfortunately, it fails to serve this purpose. Its primary flaw is that it lacks a `clone` method, and `Object`'s `clone` method is protected. You cannot, without resorting to *reflection* (Item 65), invoke `clone` on an object merely because it implements `Cloneable`. Even a reflective invocation may fail, because there is no guarantee that the object has an accessible `clone` method. Despite this flaw and many others, the facility is in reasonably wide use, so it pays to understand it. This item tells you how to implement a well-behaved `clone` method, discusses when it is appropriate to do so, and presents alternatives.

So what *does* `Cloneable` do, given that it contains no methods? It determines the behavior of `Object`'s protected `clone` implementation: if a class implements `Cloneable`, `Object`'s `clone` method returns a field-by-field copy of the object; otherwise it throws `CloneNotSupportedException`. This is a highly atypical use of interfaces and not one to be emulated. Normally, implementing an interface says something about what a class can do for its clients. In this case, it modifies the behavior of a protected method on a superclass.

Though the specification doesn't say it, **in practice, a class implementing `Cloneable` is expected to provide a properly functioning public `clone` method.** In order to achieve this, the class and all of its superclasses must obey a complex, unenforceable, thinly documented protocol. The resulting mechanism is fragile, dangerous, and *extralinguistic*: it creates objects without calling a constructor.

The general contract for the `clone` method is weak. Here it is, copied from the `Object` specification :

Creates and returns a copy of this object. The precise meaning of "copy" may depend on the class of the object. The general intent is that, for any object x, the expression

```
x.clone() != x
```

will be `true`, and the expression

```
x.clone().getClass() == x.getClass()
```

will be `true`, but these are not absolute requirements. While it is typically the case that

```
x.clone().equals(x)
```

will be `true`, this is not an absolute requirement.

By convention, the object returned by this method should be obtained by calling `super.clone`. If a class and all of its superclasses (except `Object`) obey this convention, it will be the case that

`x.clone().getClass() == x.getClass()`.

By convention, the returned object should be independent of the object being cloned. To achieve this independence, it may be necessary to modify one or more fields of the object returned by `super.clone` before returning it.

This mechanism is vaguely similar to constructor chaining, except that it isn't enforced: if a class's `clone` method returns an instance that is *not* obtained by calling `super.clone` but by calling a constructor, the compiler won't complain, but if a subclass of that class calls `super.clone`, the resulting object will have the wrong class, preventing the subclass from `clone` method from working properly. If a class that overrides `clone` is final, this convention may be safely ignored, as there are no subclasses to worry about. But if a final class has a `clone` method that does not invoke `super.clone`, there is no reason for the class to implement `Cloneable`, as it doesn't rely on the behavior of `Object`'s clone implementation.

Suppose you want to implement `Cloneable` in a class whose superclass provides a well-behaved `clone` method. First call `super.clone`. The object you get back will be a fully functional replica of the original. Any fields declared in your class will have values identical to those of the original. If every field contains a primitive value or a reference to an immutable object, the returned object may be exactly what you need, in which case no further processing is necessary. This is the case, for example, for the `PhoneNumber` class in Item 11, but note that **immutable classes should never provide a clone method** because it would merely encourage wasteful copying. With that caveat, here's how a `clone` method for PhoneNumber would look:

```
// Clone method for class with no references to mutable state
@Override public PhoneNumber clone() {
    try {
        return (PhoneNumber) super.clone();
    } catch (CloneNotSupportedException e) {
        throw new AssertionError();  // Can't happen
    }
}
```

In order for this method to work, the class declaration for PhoneNumber would have to be modified to indicate that it implements `Cloneable`. Though `Object`'s clone method returns `Object`, this `clone` method returns `PhoneNumber`. It is legal and desirable to do this because Java supports *covariant return types*. In other words, an overriding method's return type can be a subclass of the overridden method's return type. This eliminates the need for casting in the client. We must cast the result of super.clone from Object to PhoneNumber before returning it, but the cast is guaranteed to succeed.

The call to super.clone is contained in a try-catch block. This is because Object declares its clone method to throw CloneNotSupportedException, which is a *checked exception*. Because PhoneNumber implements Cloneable, we know the call to super.clone will succeed. The need for this boilerplate indicates that CloneNotSupportedException should have been unchecked (Item 71).

If an object contains fields that refer to mutable objects, the simple clone implementation shown earlier can be disastrous. For example, consider the Stack class in Item 7:

```java
public class Stack {
    private Object[] elements;
    private int size = 0;
    private static final int DEFAULT_INITIAL_CAPACITY = 16;

    public Stack() {
        this.elements = new Object[DEFAULT_INITIAL_CAPACITY];
    }

    public void push(Object e) {
        ensureCapacity();
        elements[size++] = e;
    }

    public Object pop() {
        if (size == 0)
            throw new EmptyStackException();
        Object result = elements[--size];
        elements[size] = null; // Eliminate obsolete reference
        return result;
    }

    // Ensure space for at least one more element.
    private void ensureCapacity() {
        if (elements.length == size)
            elements = Arrays.copyOf(elements, 2 * size + 1);
    }
}
```

Suppose you want to make this class cloneable. If the clone method merely returns super.clone(), the resulting Stack instance will have the correct value in its `size` field, but its `elements` field will refer to the same array as the original `Stack` instance. Modifying the original will destroy the invariants in the clone and vice versa. You will quickly find that your program produces nonsensical results or throws a `NullPointerException`.

This situation could never occur as a result of calling the sole constructor in the `Stack` class. **In effect, the `clone` method functions as a constructor; you must ensure that it does no harm to the original object and that it properly establishes invariants on the clone.** In order for the `clone` method on `Stack` to work properly, it must copy the internals of the stack. The easiest way to do this is to call `clone` recursively on the `elements` array:

```java
// Clone method for class with references to mutable state
@Override public Stack clone() {
    try {
        Stack result = (Stack) super.clone();
        result.elements = elements.clone();
        return result;
    } catch (CloneNotSupportedException e) {
        throw new AssertionError();
    }
}
```

Note that we do not have to cast the result of `elements.clone` to `Object[]`. Calling `clone` on an array returns an array whose runtime and compile-time types are identical to those of the array being cloned. This is the preferred idiom to duplicate an array. In fact, arrays are the sole compelling use of the `clone` facility.

Note also that the earlier solution would not work if the `elements` field were final because `clone` would be prohibited from assigning a new value to the field. This is a fundamental problem: like serialization, **the `Cloneable` architecture is incompatible with normal use of final fields referring to mutable objects**, except in cases where the mutable objects may be safely shared between an object and its clone. In order to make a class cloneable, it may be necessary to remove `final` modifiers from some fields.

It is not always sufficient merely to call `clone` recursively. For example, suppose you are writing a `clone` method for a hash table whose internals consist of an array of buckets, each of which references the first entry in a linked list of key-value pairs. For performance, the class implements its own lightweight singly linked list instead of using `java.util.LinkedList` internally:

```java
public class HashTable implements Cloneable {
    private Entry[] buckets = ...;
```

```java
    private static class Entry {
        final Object key;
        Object value;
        Entry  next;

        Entry(Object key, Object value, Entry next) {
            this.key   = key;
            this.value = value;
            this.next  = next;
        }
    }
}
    ... // Remainder omitted
}
```

Suppose you merely clone the bucket array recursively, as we did for Stack:

```java
// Broken clone method - results in shared mutable state!
@Override public HashTable clone() {
    try {
        HashTable result = (HashTable) super.clone();
        result.buckets = buckets.clone();
        return result;
    } catch (CloneNotSupportedException e) {
        throw new AssertionError();
    }
}
```

Though the clone has its own bucket array, this array references the same linked lists as the original, which can easily cause nondeterministic behavior in both the clone and the original. To fix this problem, you'll have to copy the linked list that comprises each bucket. Here is one common approach:

```java
// Recursive clone method for class with complex mutable state
public class HashTable implements Cloneable {
    private Entry[] buckets = ...;

    private static class Entry {
        final Object key;
        Object value;
        Entry  next;

        Entry(Object key, Object value, Entry next) {
            this.key   = key;
            this.value = value;
            this.next  = next;
        }
```

```java
    // Recursively copy the linked list headed by this Entry
    Entry deepCopy() {
        return new Entry(key, value,
            next == null ? null : next.deepCopy());
    }
}

@Override public HashTable clone() {
    try {
        HashTable result = (HashTable) super.clone();
        result.buckets = new Entry[buckets.length];
        for (int i = 0; i < buckets.length; i++)
            if (buckets[i] != null)
                result.buckets[i] = buckets[i].deepCopy();
        return result;
    } catch (CloneNotSupportedException e) {
        throw new AssertionError();
    }
}
... // Remainder omitted
}
```

The private class `HashTable.Entry` has been augmented to support a "deep copy" method. The `clone` method on `HashTable` allocates a new `buckets` array of the proper size and iterates over the original `buckets` array, deep-copying each nonempty bucket. The `deepCopy` method on `Entry` invokes itself recursively to copy the entire linked list headed by the entry. While this technique is cute and works fine if the buckets aren't too long, it is not a good way to clone a linked list because it consumes one stack frame for each element in the list. If the list is long, this could easily cause a stack overflow. To prevent this from happening, you can replace the recursion in deepCopy with iteration:

```java
// Iteratively copy the linked list headed by this Entry
Entry deepCopy() {
    Entry result = new Entry(key, value, next);
    for (Entry p = result; p.next != null; p = p.next)
        p.next = new Entry(p.next.key, p.next.value, p.next.next);
    return result;
}
```

A final approach to cloning complex mutable objects is to call `super.clone`, set all of the fields in the resulting object to their initial state, and then call higher-level methods to regenerate the state of the original object. In the case of our `HashTable` example, the `buckets` field would be initialized to a new bucket array, and the `put(key, value)` method (not shown) would be invoked for each key-value mapping in the hash table being cloned. This approach typically yields a simple, reasonably elegant `clone` method that does not run as quickly as one that directly manipulates the innards of the clone. While this approach is clean, it is antithetical to the whole `Cloneable` architecture because it blindly overwrites the field-by-field object copy that forms the basis of the architecture.

Like a constructor, a `clone` method must never invoke an overridable method on the clone under construction (Item 19). If `clone` invokes a method that is overridden in a subclass, this method will execute before the subclass has had a chance to fix its state in the clone, quite possibly leading to corruption in the clone and the original. Therefore, the `put(key, value)` method discussed in the previous paragraph should be either final or private. (If it is private, it is presumably the "helper method" for a nonfinal public method.)

`Object`'s `clone` method is declared to throw `CloneNotSupportedException`, but overriding methods need not. **Public `clone` methods should omit the throws clause**, as methods that don't throw checked exceptions are easier to use (Item 71).

You have two choices when designing a class for inheritance (Item 19), but whichever one you choose, the class should *not* implement `Cloneable`. You may choose to mimic the behavior of `Object` by implementing a properly functioning protected `clone` method that is declared to throw `CloneNotSupportedException`. This gives subclasses the freedom to implement `Cloneable` or not, just as if they extended `Object` directly. Alternatively, you may choose *not* to implement a working `clone` method, and to prevent subclasses from implementing one, by providing the following degenerate `clone` implementation:

```
// clone method for extendable class not supporting Cloneable
@Override
protected final Object clone() throws CloneNotSupportedException {
    throw new CloneNotSupportedException();
}
```

There is one more detail that bears noting. If you write a thread-safe class that implements `Cloneable`, remember that its `clone` method must be properly synchronized, just like any other method (Item 78). `Object`'s `clone` method is not synchronized, so even if its implementation is otherwise satisfactory, you may have to write a synchronized `clone` method that returns `super.clone()`.

To recap, all classes that implement `Cloneable` should override `clone` with a public method whose return type is the class itself. This method should first call `super.clone`, then fix any fields that need fixing. Typically, this means copying any mutable objects that comprise the internal "deep structure" of the object and replacing the clone's references to these objects with references to their copies.

While these internal copies can usually be made by calling `clone` recursively, this is not always the best approach. If the class contains only primitive fields or references to immutable objects, then it is likely the case that no fields need to be fixed. There are exceptions to this rule. For example, a field representing a serial number or other unique ID will need to be fixed even if it is primitive or immutable.

Is all this complexity really necessary? Rarely. If you extend a class that already implements `Cloneable`, you have little choice but to implement a well-behaved `clone` method. Otherwise, you are usually better off providing an alternative means of object copying. **A better approach to object copying is to provide a** *copy constructor* **or** *copy factory.* A copy constructor is simply a constructor that takes a single argument whose type is the class containing the constructor, for example,

```
// Copy constructor
public Yum(Yum yum) { ... };
```

A copy factory is the static factory (Item 1) analogue of a copy constructor:

```
// Copy factory
public static Yum newInstance(Yum yum) { ... };
```

The copy constructor approach and its static factory variant have many advantages over `Cloneable/clone`: they don't rely on a risk-prone extralinguistic object creation mechanism; they don't demand unenforceable adherence to thinly documented conventions; they don't conflict with the proper use of final fields; they don't throw unnecessary checked exceptions; and they don't require casts.

Furthermore, a copy constructor or factory can take an argument whose type is an interface implemented by the class. For example, by convention all general-purpose collection implementations provide a constructor whose argument is of type `Collection` or `Map`. Interface-based copy constructors and factories, more properly known as *conversion constructors* and *conversion factories*, allow the client to choose the implementation type of the copy rather than forcing the client to accept the implementation type of the original. For example, suppose you have a `HashSet`, `s`, and you want to copy it as a `TreeSet`. The `clone` method can't offer this functionality, but it's easy with a conversion constructor: `new TreeSet<>(s)`.

Given all the problems associated with `Cloneable`, new interfaces should not extend it, and new extendable classes should not implement it. While it's less harmful for final classes to implement `Cloneable`, this should be viewed as a performance optimization, reserved for the rare cases where it is justified (Item 67). As a rule, copy functionality is best provided by constructors or factories. A notable exception to this rule is arrays, which are best copied with the clone method.

Item 14: Consider implementing `Comparable`

Unlike the other methods discussed in this chapter, the `compareTo` method is not declared in `Object`. Rather, it is the sole method in the `Comparable` interface. It is similar in character to `Object`'s `equals` method, except that it permits order comparisons in addition to simple equality comparisons, and it is generic. By implementing `Comparable`, a class indicates that its instances have a *natural ordering*. Sorting an array of objects that implement `Comparable` is as simple as this:

```
Arrays.sort(a);
```

It is similarly easy to search, compute extreme values, and maintain automatically sorted collections of `Comparable` objects. For example, the following program, which relies on the fact that `String` implements `Comparable`, prints an alphabetized list of its command-line arguments with duplicates eliminated:

```
public class WordList {
    public static void main(String[] args) {
        Set<String> s = new TreeSet<>();
        Collections.addAll(s, args);
        System.out.println(s);
    }
}
```

By implementing `Comparable`, you allow your class to interoperate with all of the many generic algorithms and collection implementations that depend on this interface. You gain a tremendous amount of power for a small amount of effort. Virtually all of the value classes in the Java platform libraries, as well as all enum types (Item 34), implement `Comparable`. If you are writing a value class with an obvious natural ordering, such as alphabetical order, numerical order, or chronological order, you should implement the `Comparable` interface:

```
public interface Comparable<T> {
    int compareTo(T t);
}
```

The general contract of the `compareTo` method is similar to that of `equals`:

Compares this object with the specified object for order. Returns a negative integer, zero, or a positive integer as this object is less than, equal to, or greater than the specified object. Throws `ClassCastException` if the specified object's type prevents it from being compared to this object.

In the following description, the notation sgn(*expression*) designates the mathematical *signum* function, which is defined to return -1, 0, or 1, according to whether the value of *expression* is negative, zero, or positive.

- The implementor must ensure that sgn(x.compareTo(y)) == -sgn(y.compareTo(x)) for all x and y. (This implies that x.compareTo(y) must throw an exception if and only if y.compareTo(x) throws an exception.)

- The implementor must also ensure that the relation is transitive: (x.compareTo(y) > 0 && y.compareTo(z) > 0) implies x.compareTo(z) > 0.

- Finally, the implementor must ensure that x.compareTo(y) == 0 implies that sgn(x.compareTo(z)) == sgn(y.compareTo(z)), for all z.

- It is strongly recommended, but not required, that (x.compareTo(y) == 0) == (x.equals(y)). Generally speaking, any class that implements the Comparable interface and violates this condition should clearly indicate this fact. The recommended language is "Note: This class has a natural ordering that is inconsistent with equals."

Don't be put off by the mathematical nature of this contract. Like the equals contract (Item 10), this contract isn't as complicated as it looks. Unlike the equals method, which imposes a global equivalence relation on all objects, compareTo doesn't have to work across objects of different types: when confronted with objects of different types, compareTo is permitted to throw ClassCastException. Usually, that is exactly what it does. The contract does *permit* intertype comparisons, which are typically defined in an interface implemented by the objects being compared.

Just as a class that violates the hashCode contract can break other classes that depend on hashing, a class that violates the compareTo contract can break other classes that depend on comparison. Classes that depend on comparison include the sorted collections TreeSet and TreeMap and the utility classes Collections and Arrays, which contain searching and sorting algorithms.

Let's go over the provisions of the compareTo contract. The first provision says that if you reverse the direction of a comparison between two object references, the expected thing happens: if the first object is less than the second, then the second must be greater than the first; if the first object is equal to the second, then the second must be equal to the first; and if the first object is greater than the second, then the second must be less than the first. The second provision says that if one object is greater than a second and the second is greater than a third, then the first must be greater than the third. The final provision says that all objects that compare as equal must yield the same results when compared to any other object.

One consequence of these three provisions is that the equality test imposed by a compareTo method must obey the same restrictions imposed by the equals contract: reflexivity, symmetry, and transitivity. Therefore, the same caveat applies: there is no way to extend an instantiable class with a new value component while preserving the compareTo contract, unless you are willing to forgo the benefits of object-oriented abstraction (Item 10). The same workaround applies, too. If you want to add a value component to a class that implements Comparable, don't extend it; write an unrelated class containing an instance of the first class. Then provide a "view" method that returns the contained instance. This frees you to implement whatever compareTo method you like on the containing class, while allowing its client to view an instance of the containing class as an instance of the contained class when needed.

The final paragraph of the compareTo contract, which is a strong suggestion rather than a true requirement, simply states that the equality test imposed by the compareTo method should generally return the same results as the equals method. If this provision is obeyed, the ordering imposed by the compareTo method is said to be *consistent with equals*. If it's violated, the ordering is said to be *inconsistent with equals*. A class whose compareTo method imposes an order that is inconsistent with equals will still work, but sorted collections containing elements of the class may not obey the general contract of the appropriate collection interfaces (Collection, Set, or Map). This is because the general contracts for these interfaces are defined in terms of the equals method, but sorted collections use the equality test imposed by compareTo in place of equals. It is not a catastrophe if this happens, but it's something to be aware of.

For example, consider the BigDecimal class, whose compareTo method is inconsistent with equals. If you create an empty HashSet instance and then add new BigDecimal("1.0") and new BigDecimal("1.00"), the set will contain two elements because the two BigDecimal instances added to the set are unequal when compared using the equals method. If, however, you perform the same procedure using a TreeSet instead of a HashSet, the set will contain only one element because the two BigDecimal instances are equal when compared using the compareTo method. (See the BigDecimal documentation for details.)

Writing a compareTo method is similar to writing an equals method, but there are a few key differences. Because the Comparable interface is parameterized, the compareTo method is statically typed, so you don't need to type check or cast its argument. If the argument is of the wrong type, the invocation won't even compile. If the argument is null, the invocation should throw a NullPointer-Exception, and it will, as soon as the method attempts to access its members.

In a compareTo method, fields are compared for order rather than equality. To compare object reference fields, invoke the compareTo method recursively. If a field does not implement Comparable or you need a nonstandard ordering, use a Comparator instead. You can write your own comparator or use an existing one, as in this compareTo method for CaseInsensitiveString in Item 10:

```java
// Single-field Comparable with object reference field
public final class CaseInsensitiveString
        implements Comparable<CaseInsensitiveString> {
    public int compareTo(CaseInsensitiveString cis) {
        return String.CASE_INSENSITIVE_ORDER.compare(s, cis.s);
    }
    ... // Remainder omitted
}
```

Note that CaseInsensitiveString implements Comparable<CaseInsensitiveString>. This means that a CaseInsensitiveString reference can be compared only to another CaseInsensitiveString reference. This is the normal pattern to follow when declaring a class to implement Comparable.

Prior editions of this book recommended that compareTo methods compare integral primitive fields using the relational operators < and >, and floating point primitive fields using the static methods Double.compare and Float.compare. In Java 7, static compare methods were added to all of Java's boxed primitive classes. **Use of the relational operators < and > in compareTo methods is verbose and error-prone and no longer recommended.**

If a class has multiple significant fields, the order in which you compare them is critical. Start with the most significant field and work your way down. If a comparison results in anything other than zero (which represents equality), you're done; just return the result. If the most significant field is equal, compare the next-most-significant field, and so on, until you find an unequal field or compare the least significant field. Here is a compareTo method for the PhoneNumber class in Item 11 demonstrating this technique:

```java
// Multiple-field Comparable with primitive fields
public int compareTo(PhoneNumber pn) {
    int result = Short.compare(areaCode, pn.areaCode);
    if (result == 0)  {
        result = Short.compare(prefix, pn.prefix);
        if (result == 0)
            result = Short.compare(lineNum, pn.lineNum);
    }
    return result;
}
```

In Java 8, the Comparator interface was outfitted with a set of *comparator construction methods*, which enable fluent construction of comparators. These comparators can then be used to implement a compareTo method, as required by the Comparable interface. Many programmers prefer the conciseness of this approach, though it does come at a modest performance cost: sorting arrays of PhoneNumber instances is about 10% slower on my machine. When using this approach, consider using Java's *static import* facility so you can refer to static comparator construction methods by their simple names for clarity and brevity. Here's how the compareTo method for PhoneNumber looks using this approach:

```
// Comparable with comparator construction methods
private static final Comparator<PhoneNumber> COMPARATOR =
        comparingInt((PhoneNumber pn) -> pn.areaCode)
          .thenComparingInt(pn -> pn.prefix)
          .thenComparingInt(pn -> pn.lineNum);

public int compareTo(PhoneNumber pn) {
    return COMPARATOR.compare(this, pn);
}
```

This implementation builds a comparator at class initialization time, using two comparator construction methods. The first is comparingInt. It is a static method that takes a *key extractor function* that maps an object reference to a key of type int and returns a comparator that orders instances according to that key. In the previous example, comparingInt takes a *lambda* () that extracts the area code from a PhoneNumber and returns a Comparator<PhoneNumber> that orders phone numbers according to their area codes. Note that the lambda explicitly specifies the type of its input parameter (PhoneNumber pn). It turns out that in this situation, Java's type inference isn't powerful enough to figure the type out for itself, so we're forced to help it in order to make the program compile.

If two phone numbers have the same area code, we need to further refine the comparison, and that's exactly what the second comparator construction method, thenComparingInt, does. It is an instance method on Comparator that takes an int key extractor function, and returns a comparator that first applies the original comparator and then uses the extracted key to break ties. You can stack up as many calls to thenComparingInt as you like, resulting in a *lexicographic ordering*. In the example above, we stack up two calls to thenComparingInt, resulting in an ordering whose secondary key is the prefix and whose tertiary key is the line number. Note that we did *not* have to specify the parameter type of the key extractor function passed to either of the calls to thenComparingInt: Java's type inference was smart enough to figure this one out for itself.

The Comparator class has a full complement of construction methods. There are analogues to comparingInt and thenComparingInt for the primitive types long and double. The int versions can also be used for narrower integral types, such as short, as in our PhoneNumber example. The double versions can also be used for float. This provides coverage of all of Java's numerical primitive types.

There are also comparator construction methods for object reference types. The static method, named comparing, has two overloadings. One takes a key extractor and uses the keys' natural order. The second takes both a key extractor and a comparator to be used on the extracted keys. There are three overloadings of the instance method, which is named thenComparing. One overloading takes only a comparator and uses it to provide a secondary order. A second overloading takes only a key extractor and uses the key's natural order as a secondary order. The final overloading takes both a key extractor and a comparator to be used on the extracted keys.

Occasionally you may see compareTo or compare methods that rely on the fact that the difference between two values is negative if the first value is less than the second, zero if the two values are equal, and positive if the first value is greater. Here is an example:

```
// BROKEN difference-based comparator - violates transitivity!
static Comparator<Object> hashCodeOrder = new Comparator<>() {
    public int compare(Object o1, Object o2) {
        return o1.hashCode() - o2.hashCode();
    }
};
```

Do not use this technique. It is fraught with danger from integer overflow and IEEE 754 floating point arithmetic artifacts [JLS 15.20.1, 15.21.1]. Furthermore, the resulting methods are unlikely to be significantly faster than those written using the techniques described in this item. Use either a static compare method:

```
// Comparator based on static compare method
static Comparator<Object> hashCodeOrder = new Comparator<>() {
    public int compare(Object o1, Object o2) {
        return Integer.compare(o1.hashCode(), o2.hashCode());
    }
};
```

or a comparator construction method:

```
// Comparator based on Comparator construction method
static Comparator<Object> hashCodeOrder =
        Comparator.comparingInt(o -> o.hashCode());
```

In summary, whenever you implement a value class that has a sensible ordering, you should have the class implement the `Comparable` interface so that its instances can be easily sorted, searched, and used in comparison-based collections. When comparing field values in the implementations of the `compareTo` methods, avoid the use of the < and > operators. Instead, use the static `compare` methods in the boxed primitive classes or the comparator construction methods in the `Comparator` interface.

CHAPTER 4

Classes and Interfaces

CLASSES and interfaces lie at the heart of the Java programming language. They are its basic units of abstraction. The language provides many powerful elements that you can use to design classes and interfaces. This chapter contains guidelines to help you make the best use of these elements so that your classes and interfaces are usable, robust, and flexible.

Item 15: Minimize the accessibility of classes and members

The single most important factor that distinguishes a well-designed component from a poorly designed one is the degree to which the component hides its internal data and other implementation details from other components. A well-designed component hides all its implementation details, cleanly separating its API from its implementation. Components then communicate only through their APIs and are oblivious to each others' inner workings. This concept, known as *information hiding* or *encapsulation*, is a fundamental tenet of software design [Parnas72].

Information hiding is important for many reasons, most of which stem from the fact that it *decouples* the components that comprise a system, allowing them to be developed, tested, optimized, used, understood, and modified in isolation. This speeds up system development because components can be developed in parallel. It eases the burden of maintenance because components can be understood more quickly and debugged or replaced with little fear of harming other components. While information hiding does not, in and of itself, cause good performance, it enables effective performance tuning: once a system is complete and profiling has determined which components are causing performance problems (Item 67), those components can be optimized without affecting the correctness of others. Information hiding increases software reuse because components that aren't tightly coupled often prove useful in other contexts besides the ones for which they were developed. Finally, information hiding decreases the risk in building large systems because individual components may prove successful even if the system does not.

Java has many facilities to aid in information hiding. The *access control* mechanism [JLS, 6.6] specifies the *accessibility* of classes, interfaces, and members. The accessibility of an entity is determined by the location of its declaration and by which, if any, of the access modifiers (`private`, `protected`, and `public`) is present on the declaration. Proper use of these modifiers is essential to information hiding.

The rule of thumb is simple: **make each class or member as inaccessible as possible.** In other words, use the lowest possible access level consistent with the proper functioning of the software that you are writing.

For top-level (non-nested) classes and interfaces, there are only two possible access levels: *package-private* and *public*. If you declare a top-level class or interface with the `public` modifier, it will be public; otherwise, it will be package-private. If a top-level class or interface can be made package-private, it should be. By making it package-private, you make it part of the implementation rather than the exported API, and you can modify it, replace it, or eliminate it in a subsequent release without fear of harming existing clients. If you make it public, you are obligated to support it forever to maintain compatibility.

If a package-private top-level class or interface is used by only one class, consider making the top-level class a private static nested class of the sole class that uses it (Item 24). This reduces its accessibility from all the classes in its package to the one class that uses it. But it is far more important to reduce the accessibility of a gratuitously public class than of a package-private top-level class: the public class is part of the package's API, while the package-private top-level class is already part of its implementation.

For members (fields, methods, nested classes, and nested interfaces), there are four possible access levels, listed here in order of increasing accessibility:

- **private**—The member is accessible only from the top-level class where it is declared.

- **package-private**—The member is accessible from any class in the package where it is declared. Technically known as *default* access, this is the access level you get if no access modifier is specified (except for interface members, which are public by default).

- **protected**—The member is accessible from subclasses of the class where it is declared (subject to a few restrictions [JLS, 6.6.2]) and from any class in the package where it is declared.

- **public**—The member is accessible from anywhere.

After carefully designing your class's public API, your reflex should be to make all other members private. Only if another class in the same package really needs to access a member should you remove the `private` modifier, making the member package-private. If you find yourself doing this often, you should reexamine the design of your system to see if another decomposition might yield classes that are better decoupled from one another. That said, both private and package-private members are part of a class's implementation and do not normally impact its exported API. These fields can, however, "leak" into the exported API if the class implements `Serializable` (Items 86 and 87).

For members of public classes, a huge increase in accessibility occurs when the access level goes from package-private to protected. A protected member is part of the class's exported API and must be supported forever. Also, a protected member of an exported class represents a public commitment to an implementation detail (Item 19). The need for protected members should be relatively rare.

There is a key rule that restricts your ability to reduce the accessibility of methods. If a method overrides a superclass method, it cannot have a more restrictive access level in the subclass than in the superclass [JLS, 8.4.8.3]. This is necessary to ensure that an instance of the subclass is usable anywhere that an instance of the superclass is usable (the *Liskov substitution principle*, see Item 15). If you violate this rule, the compiler will generate an error message when you try to compile the subclass. A special case of this rule is that if a class implements an interface, all of the class methods that are in the interface must be declared public in the class.

To facilitate testing your code, you may be tempted to make a class, interface, or member more accessible than otherwise necessary. This is fine up to a point. It is acceptable to make a private member of a public class package-private in order to test it, but it is not acceptable to raise the accessibility any higher. In other words, it is not acceptable to make a class, interface, or member a part of a package's exported API to facilitate testing. Luckily, it isn't necessary either because tests can be made to run as part of the package being tested, thus gaining access to its package-private elements.

Instance fields of public classes should rarely be public (Item 16). If an instance field is nonfinal or is a reference to a mutable object, then by making it public, you give up the ability to limit the values that can be stored in the field. This means you give up the ability to enforce invariants involving the field. Also, you give up the ability to take any action when the field is modified, so **classes with public mutable fields are not generally thread-safe.** Even if a field is final and refers to an immutable object, by making it public you give up the flexibility to switch to a new internal data representation in which the field does not exist.

The same advice applies to static fields, with one exception. You can expose constants via public static final fields, assuming the constants form an integral part of the abstraction provided by the class. By convention, such fields have names consisting of capital letters, with words separated by underscores (Item 68). It is critical that these fields contain either primitive values or references to immutable objects (Item 17). a field containing a reference to a mutable object has all the disadvantages of a nonfinal field. While the reference cannot be modified, the referenced object can be modified—with disastrous results.

Note that a nonzero-length array is always mutable, so **it is wrong for a class to have a public static final array field, or an accessor that returns such a field.** If a class has such a field or accessor, clients will be able to modify the contents of the array. This is a frequent source of security holes:

```
// Potential security hole!
public static final Thing[] VALUES =  { ... };
```

Beware of the fact that some IDEs generate accessors that return references to private array fields, resulting in exactly this problem. There are two ways to fix the problem. You can make the public array private and add a public immutable list:

```
private static final Thing[] PRIVATE_VALUES = { ... };
public static final List<Thing> VALUES =
    Collections.unmodifiableList(Arrays.asList(PRIVATE_VALUES));
```

Alternatively, you can make the array private and add a public method that returns a copy of a private array:

```
private static final Thing[] PRIVATE_VALUES = { ... };
public static final Thing[] values() {
    return PRIVATE_VALUES.clone();
}
```

To choose between these alternatives, think about what the client is likely to do with the result. Which return type will be more convenient? Which will give better performance?

As of Java 9, there are two additional, implicit access levels introduced as part of the *module system.* A module is a grouping of packages, like a package is a grouping of classes. A module may explicitly export some of its packages via *export declarations* in its *module declaration* (which is by convention contained in a source file named module-info.java). Public and protected members of unexported packages in a module are inaccessible outside the module; within the module, accessibility is unaffected by export declarations. Using the module system allows you to share classes among packages within a module without making them visible to the entire world. Public and protected members of public classes in unexported packages give rise to the two implicit access levels, which are intramodular analogues of the normal public and protected levels. The need for this kind of sharing is relatively rare and can often be eliminated by rearranging the classes within your packages.

Unlike the four main access levels, the two module-based levels are largely advisory. If you place a module's JAR file on your application's class path instead of its module path, the packages in the module revert to their non-modular behavior: all of the public and protected members of the packages' public classes have their normal accessibility, regardless of whether the packages are exported by the module [Reinhold, 1.2]. The one place where the newly introduced access levels are strictly enforced is the JDK itself: the unexported packages in the Java libraries are truly inaccessible outside of their modules.

Not only is the access protection afforded by modules of limited utility to the typical Java programmer, and largely advisory in nature; in order to take advantage of it, you must group your packages into modules, make all of their dependencies explicit in module declarations, rearrange your source tree, and take special actions to accommodate any access to non-modularized packages from within your modules [Reinhold, 3]. It is too early to say whether modules will achieve widespread use outside of the JDK itself. In the meantime, it seems best to avoid them unless you have a compelling need.

To summarize, you should reduce accessibility of program elements as much as possible (within reason). After carefully designing a minimal public API, you should prevent any stray classes, interfaces, or members from becoming part of the API. With the exception of public static final fields, which serve as constants, public classes should have no public fields. Ensure that objects referenced by public static final fields are immutable.

Item 16: In public classes, use accessor methods, not public fields

Occasionally, you may be tempted to write degenerate classes that serve no purpose other than to group instance fields:

```
// Degenerate classes like this should not be public!
class Point {
    public double x;
    public double y;
}
```

Because the data fields of such classes are accessed directly, these classes do not offer the benefits of *encapsulation* (Item 15). You can't change the representation without changing the API, you can't enforce invariants, and you can't take auxiliary action when a field is accessed. Hard-line object-oriented programmers feel that such classes are anathema and should always be replaced by classes with private fields and public *accessor methods* (getters) and, for mutable classes, *mutators* (setters):

```
// Encapsulation of data by accessor methods and mutators
class Point {
    private double x;
    private double y;

    public Point(double x, double y) {
        this.x = x;
        this.y = y;
    }

    public double getX() { return x; }
    public double getY() { return y; }

    public void setX(double x) { this.x = x; }
    public void setY(double y) { this.y = y; }
}
```

Certainly, the hard-liners are correct when it comes to public classes: **if a class is accessible outside its package, provide accessor methods** to preserve the flexibility to change the class's internal representation. If a public class exposes its data fields, all hope of changing its representation is lost because client code can be distributed far and wide.

However, **if a class is package-private or is a private nested class, there is nothing inherently wrong with exposing its data fields**—assuming they do an adequate job of describing the abstraction provided by the class. This approach generates less visual clutter than the accessor-method approach, both in the class definition and in the client code that uses it. While the client code is tied to the class's internal representation, this code is confined to the package containing the class. If a change in representation becomes desirable, you can make the change without touching any code outside the package. In the case of a private nested class, the scope of the change is further restricted to the enclosing class.

Several classes in the Java platform libraries violate the advice that public classes should not expose fields directly. Prominent examples include the Point and Dimension classes in the java.awt package. Rather than examples to be emulated, these classes should be regarded as cautionary tales. As described in Item 67, the decision to expose the internals of the Dimension class resulted in a serious performance problem that is still with us today.

While it's never a good idea for a public class to expose fields directly, it is less harmful if the fields are immutable. You can't change the representation of such a class without changing its API, and you can't take auxiliary actions when a field is read, but you can enforce invariants. For example, this class guarantees that each instance represents a valid time:

```java
// Public class with exposed immutable fields - questionable
public final class Time {
    private static final int HOURS_PER_DAY    = 24;
    private static final int MINUTES_PER_HOUR = 60;

    public final int hour;
    public final int minute;

    public Time(int hour, int minute) {
        if (hour < 0 || hour >= HOURS_PER_DAY)
            throw new IllegalArgumentException("Hour: " + hour);
        if (minute < 0 || minute >= MINUTES_PER_HOUR)
            throw new IllegalArgumentException("Min: " + minute);
        this.hour = hour;
        this.minute = minute;
    }
    ... // Remainder omitted
}
```

In summary, public classes should never expose mutable fields. It is less harmful, though still questionable, for public classes to expose immutable fields. It is, however, sometimes desirable for package-private or private nested classes to expose fields, whether mutable or immutable.

Item 17: Minimize mutability

An immutable class is simply a class whose instances cannot be modified. All of the information contained in each instance is fixed for the lifetime of the object, so no changes can ever be observed. The Java platform libraries contain many immutable classes, including String, the boxed primitive classes, and BigInteger and BigDecimal. There are many good reasons for this: Immutable classes are easier to design, implement, and use than mutable classes. They are less prone to error and are more secure.

To make a class immutable, follow these five rules:

1. **Don't provide methods that modify the object's state** (known as *mutators*).

2. **Ensure that the class can't be extended.** This prevents careless or malicious subclasses from compromising the immutable behavior of the class by behaving as if the object's state has changed. Preventing subclassing is generally accomplished by making the class final, but there is an alternative that we'll discuss later.

3. **Make all fields final.** This clearly expresses your intent in a manner that is enforced by the system. Also, it is necessary to ensure correct behavior if a reference to a newly created instance is passed from one thread to another without synchronization, as spelled out in the *memory model* [JLS, 17.5; Goetz06, 16].

4. **Make all fields private.** This prevents clients from obtaining access to mutable objects referred to by fields and modifying these objects directly. While it is technically permissible for immutable classes to have public final fields containing primitive values or references to immutable objects, it is not recommended because it precludes changing the internal representation in a later release (Items 15 and 16).

5. **Ensure exclusive access to any mutable components.** If your class has any fields that refer to mutable objects, ensure that clients of the class cannot obtain references to these objects. Never initialize such a field to a client-provided object reference or return the field from an accessor. Make *defensive copies* (Item 50) in constructors, accessors, and readObject methods (Item 88).

Many of the example classes in previous items are immutable. One such class is PhoneNumber in Item 11, which has accessors for each attribute but no corresponding mutators. Here is a slightly more complex example:

```java
// Immutable complex number class
public final class Complex {
    private final double re;
    private final double im;

    public Complex(double re, double im) {
        this.re = re;
        this.im = im;
    }

    public double realPart()      { return re; }
    public double imaginaryPart() { return im; }

    public Complex plus(Complex c) {
        return new Complex(re + c.re, im + c.im);
    }

    public Complex minus(Complex c) {
        return new Complex(re - c.re, im - c.im);
    }

    public Complex times(Complex c) {
        return new Complex(re * c.re - im * c.im,
                           re * c.im + im * c.re);
    }

    public Complex dividedBy(Complex c) {
        double tmp = c.re * c.re + c.im * c.im;
        return new Complex((re * c.re + im * c.im) / tmp,
                           (im * c.re - re * c.im) / tmp);
    }

    @Override public boolean equals(Object o) {
        if (o == this)
            return true;
        if (!(o instanceof Complex))
            return false;
        Complex c = (Complex) o;

        // See page 47 to find out why we use compare instead of ==
        return Double.compare(c.re, re) == 0
            && Double.compare(c.im, im) == 0;
    }
    @Override public int hashCode() {
        return 31 * Double.hashCode(re) + Double.hashCode(im);
    }

    @Override public String toString() {
        return "(" + re + " + " + im + "i)";
    }
}
```

This class represents a *complex number* (a number with both real and imaginary parts). In addition to the standard Object methods, it provides accessors for the real and imaginary parts and provides the four basic arithmetic operations: addition, subtraction, multiplication, and division. Notice how the arithmetic operations create and return a new Complex instance rather than modifying this instance. This pattern is known as the *functional* approach because methods return the result of applying a function to their operand, without modifying it. Contrast it to the *procedural* or *imperative* approach in which methods apply a procedure to their operand, causing its state to change. Note that the method names are prepositions (such as plus) rather than verbs (such as add). This emphasizes the fact that methods don't change the values of the objects. The BigInteger and BigDecimal classes did *not* obey this naming convention, and it led to many usage errors.

The functional approach may appear unnatural if you're not familiar with it, but it enables immutability, which has many advantages. **Immutable objects are simple.** An immutable object can be in exactly one state, the state in which it was created. If you make sure that all constructors establish class invariants, then it is guaranteed that these invariants will remain true for all time, with no further effort on your part or on the part of the programmer who uses the class. Mutable objects, on the other hand, can have arbitrarily complex state spaces. If the documentation does not provide a precise description of the state transitions performed by mutator methods, it can be difficult or impossible to use a mutable class reliably.

Immutable objects are inherently thread-safe; they require no synchronization. They cannot be corrupted by multiple threads accessing them concurrently. This is far and away the easiest approach to achieve thread safety. Since no thread can ever observe any effect of another thread on an immutable object, **immutable objects can be shared freely.** Immutable classes should therefore encourage clients to reuse existing instances wherever possible. One easy way to do this is to provide public static final constants for commonly used values. For example, the Complex class might provide these constants:

```
public static final Complex ZERO = new Complex(0, 0);
public static final Complex ONE  = new Complex(1, 0);
public static final Complex I    = new Complex(0, 1);
```

This approach can be taken one step further. An immutable class can provide static factories (Item 1) that cache frequently requested instances to avoid creating new instances when existing ones would do. All the boxed primitive classes and BigInteger do this. Using such static factories causes clients to share instances instead of creating new ones, reducing memory footprint and garbage collection costs. Opting for static factories in place of public constructors when designing a new class gives you the flexibility to add caching later, without modifying clients.

A consequence of the fact that immutable objects can be shared freely is that you never have to make *defensive copies* of them (Item 50). In fact, you never have to make any copies at all because the copies would be forever equivalent to the originals. Therefore, you need not and should not provide a clone method or *copy constructor* (Item 13) on an immutable class. This was not well understood in the early days of the Java platform, so the String class does have a copy constructor, but it should rarely, if ever, be used (Item 6).

Not only can you share immutable objects, but they can share their internals. For example, the BigInteger class uses a sign-magnitude representation internally. The sign is represented by an int, and the magnitude is represented by an int array. The negate method produces a new BigInteger of like magnitude and opposite sign. It does not need to copy the array even though it is mutable; the newly created BigInteger points to the same internal array as the original.

Immutable objects make great building blocks for other objects, whether mutable or immutable. It's much easier to maintain the invariants of a complex object if you know that its component objects will not change underneath it. A special case of this principle is that immutable objects make great map keys and set elements: you don't have to worry about their values changing once they're in the map or set, which would destroy the map or set's invariants.

Immutable objects provide failure atomicity for free (Item 76). Their state never changes, so there is no possibility of a temporary inconsistency.

The major disadvantage of immutable classes is that they require a separate object for each distinct value. Creating these objects can be costly, especially if they are large. For example, suppose that you have a million-bit BigInteger and you want to change its low-order bit:

```
BigInteger moby = ...;
moby = moby.flipBit(0);
```

The flipBit method creates a new BigInteger instance, also a million bits long, that differs from the original in only one bit. The operation requires time and space proportional to the size of the BigInteger. Contrast this to java.util.BitSet. Like BigInteger, BitSet represents an arbitrarily long sequence of bits, but unlike BigInteger, BitSet is mutable. The BitSet class provides a method that allows you to change the state of a single bit of a million-bit instance in constant time:

```
BitSet moby = ...;
moby.flip(0);
```

The performance problem is magnified if you perform a multistep operation that generates a new object at every step, eventually discarding all objects except the final result. There are two approaches to coping with this problem. The first is to guess which multistep operations will be commonly required and to provide them as primitives. If a multistep operation is provided as a primitive, the immutable class does not have to create a separate object at each step. Internally, the immutable class can be arbitrarily clever. For example, BigInteger has a package-private mutable "companion class" that it uses to speed up multistep operations such as modular exponentiation. It is much harder to use the mutable companion class than to use BigInteger, for all of the reasons outlined earlier. Luckily, you don't have to use it: the implementors of BigInteger did the hard work for you.

The package-private mutable companion class approach works fine if you can accurately predict which complex operations clients will want to perform on your immutable class. If not, then your best bet is to provide a *public* mutable companion class. The main example of this approach in the Java platform libraries is the String class, whose mutable companion is StringBuilder (and its obsolete predecessor, StringBuffer).

Now that you know how to make an immutable class and you understand the pros and cons of immutability, let's discuss a few design alternatives. Recall that to guarantee immutability, a class must not permit itself to be subclassed. This can be done by making the class final, but there is another, more flexible alternative. Instead of making an immutable class final, you can make all of its constructors private or package-private and add public static factories in place of the public constructors (Item 1). To make this concrete, here's how Complex would look if you took this approach:

```java
// Immutable class with static factories instead of constructors
public class Complex {
    private final double re;
    private final double im;

    private Complex(double re, double im) {
        this.re = re;
        this.im = im;
    }

    public static Complex valueOf(double re, double im) {
        return new Complex(re, im);
    }

    ... // Remainder unchanged
}
```

This approach is often the best alternative. It is the most flexible because it allows the use of multiple package-private implementation classes. To its clients that reside outside its package, the immutable class is effectively final because it is impossible to extend a class that comes from another package and that lacks a public or protected constructor. Besides allowing the flexibility of multiple implementation classes, this approach makes it possible to tune the performance of the class in subsequent releases by improving the object-caching capabilities of the static factories.

It was not widely understood that immutable classes had to be effectively final when BigInteger and BigDecimal were written, so all of their methods may be overridden. Unfortunately, this could not be corrected after the fact while preserving backward compatibility. If you write a class whose security depends on the immutability of a BigInteger or BigDecimal argument from an untrusted client, you must check to see that the argument is a "real" BigInteger or BigDecimal, rather than an instance of an untrusted subclass. If it is the latter, you must defensively copy it under the assumption that it might be mutable (Item 50):

```
public static BigInteger safeInstance(BigInteger val) {
    return val.getClass() == BigInteger.class ?
            val : new BigInteger(val.toByteArray());
}
```

The list of rules for immutable classes at the beginning of this item says that no methods may modify the object and that all its fields must be final. In fact these rules are a bit stronger than necessary and can be relaxed to improve performance. In truth, no method may produce an *externally visible* change in the object's state. However, some immutable classes have one or more nonfinal fields in which they cache the results of expensive computations the first time they are needed. If the same value is requested again, the cached value is returned, saving the cost of recalculation. This trick works precisely because the object is immutable, which guarantees that the computation would yield the same result if it were repeated.

For example, PhoneNumber's hashCode method (Item 11, page 53) computes the hash code the first time it's invoked and caches it in case it's invoked again. This technique, an example of *lazy initialization* (Item 83), is also used by String.

One caveat should be added concerning serializability. If you choose to have your immutable class implement Serializable and it contains one or more fields that refer to mutable objects, you must provide an explicit readObject or readResolve method, or use the ObjectOutputStream.writeUnshared and

ObjectInputStream.readUnshared methods, even if the default serialized form is acceptable. Otherwise an attacker could create a mutable instance of your class. This topic is covered in detail in Item 88.

To summarize, resist the urge to write a setter for every getter. **Classes should be immutable unless there's a very good reason to make them mutable.** Immutable classes provide many advantages, and their only disadvantage is the potential for performance problems under certain circumstances. You should always make small value objects, such as PhoneNumber and Complex, immutable. (There are several classes in the Java platform libraries, such as java.util.Date and java.awt.Point, that should have been immutable but aren't.) You should seriously consider making larger value objects, such as String and BigInteger, immutable as well. You should provide a public mutable companion class for your immutable class *only* once you've confirmed that it's necessary to achieve satisfactory performance (Item 67).

There are some classes for which immutability is impractical. **If a class cannot be made immutable, limit its mutability as much as possible.** Reducing the number of states in which an object can exist makes it easier to reason about the object and reduces the likelihood of errors. Therefore, make every field final unless there is a compelling reason to make it nonfinal. Combining the advice of this item with that of Item 15, your natural inclination should be to **declare every field private final unless there's a good reason to do otherwise.**

Constructors should create fully initialized objects with all of their invariants established. Don't provide a public initialization method separate from the constructor or static factory unless there is a *compelling* reason to do so. Similarly, don't provide a "reinitialize" method that enables an object to be reused as if it had been constructed with a different initial state. Such methods generally provide little if any performance benefit at the expense of increased complexity.

The CountDownLatch class exemplifies these principles. It is mutable, but its state space is kept intentionally small. You create an instance, use it once, and it's done: once the countdown latch's count has reached zero, you may not reuse it.

A final note should be added concerning the Complex class in this item. This example was meant only to illustrate immutability. It is not an industrial-strength complex number implementation. It uses the standard formulas for complex multiplication and division, which are not correctly rounded and provide poor semantics for complex NaNs and infinities [Kahan91, Smith62, Thomas94].

Item 18: Favor composition over inheritance

Inheritance is a powerful way to achieve code reuse, but it is not always the best tool for the job. Used inappropriately, it leads to fragile software. It is safe to use inheritance within a package, where the subclass and the superclass implementations are under the control of the same programmers. It is also safe to use inheritance when extending classes specifically designed and documented for extension (Item 19). Inheriting from ordinary concrete classes across package boundaries, however, is dangerous. As a reminder, this book uses the word "inheritance" to mean *implementation inheritance* (when one class extends another). The problems discussed in this item do not apply to *interface inheritance* (when a class implements an interface or when one interface extends another).

Unlike method invocation, inheritance violates encapsulation [Snyder86]. In other words, a subclass depends on the implementation details of its superclass for its proper function. The superclass's implementation may change from release to release, and if it does, the subclass may break, even though its code has not been touched. As a consequence, a subclass must evolve in tandem with its superclass, unless the superclass's authors have designed and documented it specifically for the purpose of being extended.

To make this concrete, let's suppose we have a program that uses a HashSet. To tune the performance of our program, we need to query the HashSet as to how many elements have been added since it was created (not to be confused with its current size, which goes down when an element is removed). To provide this functionality, we write a HashSet variant that keeps count of the number of attempted element insertions and exports an accessor for this count. The HashSet class contains two methods capable of adding elements, add and addAll, so we override both of these methods:

```
// Broken - Inappropriate use of inheritance!
public class InstrumentedHashSet<E> extends HashSet<E> {
    // The number of attempted element insertions
    private int addCount = 0;

    public InstrumentedHashSet() {
    }

    public InstrumentedHashSet(int initCap, float loadFactor) {
        super(initCap, loadFactor);
    }
```

```java
    @Override public boolean add(E e) {
        addCount++;
        return super.add(e);
    }
    @Override public boolean addAll(Collection<? extends E> c) {
        addCount += c.size();
        return super.addAll(c);
    }
    public int getAddCount() {
        return addCount;
    }
}
```

This class looks reasonable, but it doesn't work. Suppose we create an instance and add three elements using the addAll method. Incidentally, note that we create a list using the static factory method List.of, which was added in Java 9; if you're using an earlier release, use Arrays.asList instead:

```java
InstrumentedHashSet<String> s = new InstrumentedHashSet<>();
s.addAll(List.of("Snap", "Crackle", "Pop"));
```

We would expect the getAddCount method to return three at this point, but it returns six. What went wrong? Internally, HashSet's addAll method is implemented on top of its add method, although HashSet, quite reasonably, does not document this implementation detail. The addAll method in Instrumented-HashSet added three to addCount and then invoked HashSet's addAll implementation using super.addAll. This in turn invoked the add method, as overridden in InstrumentedHashSet, once for each element. Each of these three invocations added one more to addCount, for a total increase of six: each element added with the addAll method is double-counted.

We could "fix" the subclass by eliminating its override of the addAll method. While the resulting class would work, it would depend for its proper function on the fact that HashSet's addAll method is implemented on top of its add method. This "self-use" is an implementation detail, not guaranteed to hold in all implementations of the Java platform and subject to change from release to release. Therefore, the resulting InstrumentedHashSet class would be fragile.

It would be slightly better to override the addAll method to iterate over the specified collection, calling the add method once for each element. This would guarantee the correct result whether or not HashSet's addAll method were implemented atop its add method because HashSet's addAll implementation would no longer be invoked. This technique, however, does not solve all our problems. It amounts to reimplementing superclass methods that may or may not result in self-use, which is difficult, time-consuming, error-prone, and may reduce performance. Additionally, it isn't always possible because some methods cannot be implemented without access to private fields inaccessible to the subclass.

A related cause of fragility in subclasses is that their superclass can acquire new methods in subsequent releases. Suppose a program depends for its security on the fact that all elements inserted into some collection satisfy some predicate. This can be guaranteed by subclassing the collection and overriding each method capable of adding an element to ensure that the predicate is satisfied before adding the element. This works fine until a new method capable of inserting an element is added to the superclass in a subsequent release. Once this happens, it becomes possible to add an "illegal" element merely by invoking the new method, which is not overridden in the subclass. This is not a purely theoretical problem. Several security holes of this nature had to be fixed when Hashtable and Vector were retrofitted to participate in the Collections Framework.

Both of these problems stem from overriding methods. You might think that it is safe to extend a class if you merely add new methods and refrain from overriding existing methods. While this sort of extension is much safer, it is not without risk. If the superclass acquires a new method in a subsequent release and you have the bad luck to have given the subclass a method with the same signature and a different return type, your subclass will no longer compile [JLS, 8.4.8.3]. If you've given the subclass a method with the same signature and return type as the new superclass method, then you're now overriding it, so you're subject to the problems described earlier. Furthermore, it is doubtful that your method will fulfill the contract of the new superclass method, because that contract had not yet been written when you wrote the subclass method.

Luckily, there is a way to avoid all of the problems described above. Instead of extending an existing class, give your new class a private field that references an instance of the existing class. This design is called *composition* because the existing class becomes a component of the new one. Each instance method in the new class invokes the corresponding method on the contained instance of the existing class and returns the results. This is known as *forwarding*, and the methods in the new class are known as *forwarding methods*. The resulting class will be rock solid, with no dependencies on the implementation details of the existing class. Even adding new methods to the existing class will have no impact on the new class. To make this concrete, here's a replacement for InstrumentedHashSet that uses the composition-and-forwarding approach. Note that the implementation is broken into two pieces, the class itself and a reusable *forwarding class,* which contains all of the forwarding methods and nothing else:

```java
// Wrapper class - uses composition in place of inheritance
public class InstrumentedSet<E> extends ForwardingSet<E> {
    private int addCount = 0;

    public InstrumentedSet(Set<E> s) {
        super(s);
    }

    @Override public boolean add(E e) {
        addCount++;
        return super.add(e);
    }
    @Override public boolean addAll(Collection<? extends E> c) {
        addCount += c.size();
        return super.addAll(c);
    }
    public int getAddCount() {
        return addCount;
    }
}

// Reusable forwarding class
public class ForwardingSet<E> implements Set<E> {
    private final Set<E> s;
    public ForwardingSet(Set<E> s) { this.s = s; }

    public void clear()               { s.clear();            }
    public boolean contains(Object o) { return s.contains(o); }
    public boolean isEmpty()          { return s.isEmpty();   }
    public int size()                 { return s.size();      }
    public Iterator<E> iterator()     { return s.iterator();  }
    public boolean add(E e)           { return s.add(e);      }
    public boolean remove(Object o)   { return s.remove(o);   }
    public boolean containsAll(Collection<?> c)
                                      { return s.containsAll(c); }
    public boolean addAll(Collection<? extends E> c)
                                      { return s.addAll(c);     }
    public boolean removeAll(Collection<?> c)
                                      { return s.removeAll(c);  }
    public boolean retainAll(Collection<?> c)
                                      { return s.retainAll(c);  }
    public Object[] toArray()         { return s.toArray();  }
    public <T> T[] toArray(T[] a)     { return s.toArray(a); }
    @Override public boolean equals(Object o)
                                      { return s.equals(o);  }
    @Override public int hashCode()   { return s.hashCode(); }
    @Override public String toString() { return s.toString(); }
}
```

The design of the InstrumentedSet class is enabled by the existence of the Set interface, which captures the functionality of the HashSet class. Besides being robust, this design is extremely flexible. The InstrumentedSet class implements the Set interface and has a single constructor whose argument is also of type Set. In essence, the class transforms one Set into another, adding the instrumentation functionality. Unlike the inheritance-based approach, which works only for a single concrete class and requires a separate constructor for each supported constructor in the superclass, the wrapper class can be used to instrument any Set implementation and will work in conjunction with any preexisting constructor:

```
Set<Instant> times = new InstrumentedSet<>(new TreeSet<>(cmp));
Set<E> s = new InstrumentedSet<>(new HashSet<>(INIT_CAPACITY));
```

The InstrumentedSet class can even be used to temporarily instrument a set instance that has already been used without instrumentation:

```
static void walk(Set<Dog> dogs) {
    InstrumentedSet<Dog> iDogs = new InstrumentedSet<>(dogs);
    ... // Within this method use iDogs instead of dogs
}
```

The InstrumentedSet class is known as a *wrapper* class because each InstrumentedSet instance contains ("wraps") another Set instance. This is also known as the *Decorator* pattern [Gamma95] because the InstrumentedSet class "decorates" a set by adding instrumentation. Sometimes the combination of composition and forwarding is loosely referred to as *delegation.* Technically it's not delegation unless the wrapper object passes itself to the wrapped object [Lieberman86; Gamma95].

The disadvantages of wrapper classes are few. One caveat is that wrapper classes are not suited for use in *callback frameworks*, wherein objects pass self-references to other objects for subsequent invocations ("callbacks"). Because a wrapped object doesn't know of its wrapper, it passes a reference to itself (this) and callbacks elude the wrapper. This is known as the *SELF problem* [Lieberman86]. Some people worry about the performance impact of forwarding method invocations or the memory footprint impact of wrapper objects. Neither turn out to have much impact in practice. It's tedious to write forwarding methods, but you have to write the reusable forwarding class for each interface only once, and forwarding classes may be provided for you. For example, Guava provides forwarding classes for all of the collection interfaces [Guava].

Inheritance is appropriate only in circumstances where the subclass really is a *subtype* of the superclass. In other words, a class B should extend a class A only if an "is-a" relationship exists between the two classes. If you are tempted to have a class B extend a class A, ask yourself the question: Is every B really an A? If you cannot truthfully answer yes to this question, B should not extend A. If the answer is no, it is often the case that B should contain a private instance of A and expose a different API: A is not an essential part of B, merely a detail of its implementation.

There are a number of obvious violations of this principle in the Java platform libraries. For example, a stack is not a vector, so `Stack` should not extend `Vector`. Similarly, a property list is not a hash table, so `Properties` should not extend `Hashtable`. In both cases, composition would have been preferable.

If you use inheritance where composition is appropriate, you needlessly expose implementation details. The resulting API ties you to the original implementation, forever limiting the performance of your class. More seriously, by exposing the internals you let clients access them directly. At the very least, it can lead to confusing semantics. For example, if p refers to a `Properties` instance, then `p.getProperty(key)` may yield different results from `p.get(key)`: the former method takes defaults into account, while the latter method, which is inherited from `Hashtable`, does not. Most seriously, the client may be able to corrupt invariants of the subclass by modifying the superclass directly. In the case of `Properties`, the designers intended that only strings be allowed as keys and values, but direct access to the underlying `Hashtable` allows this invariant to be violated. Once violated, it is no longer possible to use other parts of the `Properties` API (`load` and `store`). By the time this problem was discovered, it was too late to correct it because clients depended on the use of non-string keys and values.

There is one last set of questions you should ask yourself before deciding to use inheritance in place of composition. Does the class that you contemplate extending have any flaws in its API? If so, are you comfortable propagating those flaws into your class's API? Inheritance propagates any flaws in the superclass's API, while composition lets you design a new API that hides these flaws.

To summarize, inheritance is powerful, but it is problematic because it violates encapsulation. It is appropriate only when a genuine subtype relationship exists between the subclass and the superclass. Even then, inheritance may lead to fragility if the subclass is in a different package from the superclass and the superclass is not designed for inheritance. To avoid this fragility, use composition and forwarding instead of inheritance, especially if an appropriate interface to implement a wrapper class exists. Not only are wrapper classes more robust than subclasses, they are also more powerful.

Item 19: Design and document for inheritance or else prohibit it

Item 18 alerted you to the dangers of subclassing a "foreign" class that was not designed and documented for inheritance. So what does it mean for a class to be designed and documented for inheritance?

First, the class must document precisely the effects of overriding any method. In other words, **the class must document its *self-use* of overridable methods.** For each public or protected method, the documentation must indicate which overridable methods the method invokes, in what sequence, and how the results of each invocation affect subsequent processing. (By *overridable*, we mean nonfinal and either public or protected.) More generally, a class must document any circumstances under which it might invoke an overridable method. For example, invocations might come from background threads or static initializers.

A method that invokes overridable methods contains a description of these invocations at the end of its documentation comment. The description is in a special section of the specification, labeled "Implementation Requirements," which is generated by the Javadoc tag @implSpec. This section describes the inner workings of the method. Here's an example, copied from the specification for `java.util.AbstractCollection`:

> `public boolean remove(Object o)`
>
> Removes a single instance of the specified element from this collection, if it is present (optional operation). More formally, removes an element e such that `Objects.equals(o, e)`, if this collection contains one or more such elements. Returns `true` if this collection contained the specified element (or equivalently, if this collection changed as a result of the call).
>
> **Implementation Requirements:** This implementation iterates over the collection looking for the specified element. If it finds the element, it removes the element from the collection using the iterator's `remove` method. Note that this implementation throws an `UnsupportedOperationException` if the iterator returned by this collection's `iterator` method does not implement the `remove` method and this collection contains the specified object.

This documentation leaves no doubt that overriding the `iterator` method will affect the behavior of the `remove` method. It also describes exactly how the behavior of the `Iterator` returned by the `iterator` method will affect the behavior of the `remove` method. Contrast this to the situation in Item 18, where the programmer subclassing `HashSet` simply could not say whether overriding the `add` method would affect the behavior of the `addAll` method.

But doesn't this violate the dictum that good API documentation should describe *what* a given method does and not *how* it does it? Yes, it does! This is an unfortunate consequence of the fact that inheritance violates encapsulation. To document a class so that it can be safely subclassed, you must describe implementation details that should otherwise be left unspecified.

The @implSpec tag was added in Java 8 and used heavily in Java 9. This tag should be enabled by default, but as of Java 9, the Javadoc utility still ignores it unless you pass the command line switch -tag "apiNote:a:API Note:".

Designing for inheritance involves more than just documenting patterns of self-use. To allow programmers to write efficient subclasses without undue pain, **a class may have to provide hooks into its internal workings in the form of judiciously chosen protected methods** or, in rare instances, protected fields. For example, consider the removeRange method from java.util.AbstractList:

protected void removeRange(int fromIndex, int toIndex)

> Removes from this list all of the elements whose index is between fromIndex, inclusive, and toIndex, exclusive. Shifts any succeeding elements to the left (reduces their index). This call shortens the list by (toIndex - fromIndex) elements. (If toIndex == fromIndex, this operation has no effect.)
>
> This method is called by the clear operation on this list and its sublists. Overriding this method to take advantage of the internals of the list implementation can substantially improve the performance of the clear operation on this list and its sublists.
>
> **Implementation Requirements:** This implementation gets a list iterator positioned before fromIndex and repeatedly calls ListIterator.next followed by ListIterator.remove, until the entire range has been removed. **Note: If ListIterator.remove requires linear time, this implementation requires quadratic time.**
>
> Parameters:
>> fromIndex   index of first element to be removed.
>>
>> toIndex   index after last element to be removed.

This method is of no interest to end users of a List implementation. It is provided solely to make it easy for subclasses to provide a fast clear method on sublists. In the absence of the removeRange method, subclasses would have to make do with quadratic performance when the clear method was invoked on sublists or rewrite the entire subList mechanism from scratch—not an easy task!

So how do you decide what protected members to expose when you design a class for inheritance? Unfortunately, there is no magic bullet. The best you can do is to think hard, take your best guess, and then test it by writing subclasses. You should expose as few protected members as possible because each one represents a commitment to an implementation detail. On the other hand, you must not expose too few because a missing protected member can render a class practically unusable for inheritance.

The *only* way to test a class designed for inheritance is to write subclasses. If you omit a crucial protected member, trying to write a subclass will make the omission painfully obvious. Conversely, if several subclasses are written and none uses a protected member, you should probably make it private. Experience shows that three subclasses are usually sufficient to test an extendable class. One or more of these subclasses should be written by someone other than the superclass author.

When you design for inheritance a class that is likely to achieve wide use, realize that you are committing *forever* to the self-use patterns that you document and to the implementation decisions implicit in its protected methods and fields. These commitments can make it difficult or impossible to improve the performance or functionality of the class in a subsequent release. Therefore, **you must test your class by writing subclasses *before* you release it.**

Also, note that the special documentation required for inheritance clutters up normal documentation, which is designed for programmers who create instances of your class and invoke methods on them. As of this writing, there is little in the way of tools to separate ordinary API documentation from information of interest only to programmers implementing subclasses.

There are a few more restrictions that a class must obey to allow inheritance. **Constructors must not invoke overridable methods,** directly or indirectly. If you violate this rule, program failure will result. The superclass constructor runs before the subclass constructor, so the overriding method in the subclass will get invoked before the subclass constructor has run. If the overriding method depends on any initialization performed by the subclass constructor, the method will not behave as expected. To make this concrete, here's a class that violates this rule:

```
public class Super {
    // Broken - constructor invokes an overridable method
    public Super() {
        overrideMe();
    }
    public void overrideMe() {
    }
}
```

Here's a subclass that overrides the overrideMe method, which is erroneously invoked by Super's sole constructor:

```
public final class Sub extends Super {
    // Blank final, set by constructor
    private final Instant instant;

    Sub() {
        instant = Instant.now();
    }

    // Overriding method invoked by superclass constructor
    @Override public void overrideMe() {
        System.out.println(instant);
    }

    public static void main(String[] args) {
        Sub sub = new Sub();
        sub.overrideMe();
    }
}
```

You might expect this program to print out the instant twice, but it prints out null the first time because overrideMe is invoked by the Super constructor before the Sub constructor has a chance to initialize the instant field. Note that this program observes a final field in two different states! Note also that if overrideMe had invoked any method on instant, it would have thrown a NullPointerException when the Super constructor invoked overrideMe. The only reason this program doesn't throw a NullPointerException as it stands is that the println method tolerates null parameters.

Note that it *is* safe to invoke private methods, final methods, and static methods, none of which are overridable, from a constructor.

The Cloneable and Serializable interfaces present special difficulties when designing for inheritance. It is generally not a good idea for a class designed for inheritance to implement either of these interfaces because they place a substantial burden on programmers who extend the class. There are, however, special actions that you can take to allow subclasses to implement these interfaces without mandating that they do so. These actions are described in Item 13 and Item 86.

If you do decide to implement either Cloneable or Serializable in a class that is designed for inheritance, you should be aware that because the clone and readObject methods behave a lot like constructors, a similar restriction applies: **neither clone nor readObject may invoke an overridable method, directly or indirectly.** In the case of readObject, the overriding method will run before the subclass's state has been deserialized. In the case of `clone`, the overriding method will run before the subclass's `clone` method has a chance to fix the clone's state. In either case, a program failure is likely to follow. In the case of `clone`, the failure can damage the original object as well as the clone. This can happen, for example, if the overriding method assumes it is modifying the clone's copy of the object's deep structure, but the copy hasn't been made yet.

Finally, if you decide to implement `Serializable` in a class designed for inheritance and the class has a `readResolve` or `writeReplace` method, you must make the `readResolve` or `writeReplace` method protected rather than private. If these methods are private, they will be silently ignored by subclasses. This is one more case where an implementation detail becomes part of a class's API to permit inheritance.

By now it should be apparent that **designing a class for inheritance requires great effort and places substantial limitations on the class.** This is not a decision to be undertaken lightly. There are some situations where it is clearly the right thing to do, such as abstract classes, including *skeletal implementations* of interfaces (Item 20). There are other situations where it is clearly the wrong thing to do, such as immutable classes (Item 17).

But what about ordinary concrete classes? Traditionally, they are neither final nor designed and documented for subclassing, but this state of affairs is dangerous. Each time a change is made in such a class, there is a chance that subclasses extending the class will break. This is not just a theoretical problem. It is not uncommon to receive subclassing-related bug reports after modifying the internals of a nonfinal concrete class that was not designed and documented for inheritance.

The best solution to this problem is to prohibit subclassing in classes that are not designed and documented to be safely subclassed. There are two ways to prohibit subclassing. The easier of the two is to declare the class final. The alternative is to make all the constructors private or package-private and to add public static factories in place of the constructors. This alternative, which provides the flexibility to use subclasses internally, is discussed in Item 17. Either approach is acceptable.

This advice may be somewhat controversial because many programmers have grown accustomed to subclassing ordinary concrete classes to add facilities such as instrumentation, notification, and synchronization or to limit functionality. If a class implements some interface that captures its essence, such as `Set`, `List`, or `Map`, then you should feel no compunction about prohibiting subclassing. The *wrapper class* pattern, described in Item 18, provides a superior alternative to inheritance for augmenting the functionality.

If a concrete class does not implement a standard interface, then you may inconvenience some programmers by prohibiting inheritance. If you feel that you must allow inheritance from such a class, one reasonable approach is to ensure that the class never invokes any of its overridable methods and to document this fact. In other words, eliminate the class's self-use of overridable methods entirely. In doing so, you'll create a class that is reasonably safe to subclass. Overriding a method will never affect the behavior of any other method.

You can eliminate a class's self-use of overridable methods mechanically, without changing its behavior. Move the body of each overridable method to a private "helper method" and have each overridable method invoke its private helper method. Then replace each self-use of an overridable method with a direct invocation of the overridable method's private helper method.

In summary, designing a class for inheritance is hard work. You must document all of its self-use patterns, and once you've documented them, you must commit to them for the life of the class. If you fail to do this, subclasses may become dependent on implementation details of the superclass and may break if the implementation of the superclass changes. To allow others to write *efficient* subclasses, you may also have to export one or more protected methods. Unless you know there is a real need for subclasses, you are probably better off prohibiting inheritance by declaring your class final or ensuring that there are no accessible constructors.

Item 20: Prefer interfaces to abstract classes

Java has two mechanisms to define a type that permits multiple implementations: interfaces and abstract classes. Since the introduction of *default methods* for interfaces in Java 8 [JLS 9.4.3], both mechanisms allow you to provide implementations for some instance methods. A major difference is that to implement the type defined by an abstract class, a class must be a subclass of the abstract class. Because Java permits only single inheritance, this restriction on abstract classes severely constrains their use as type definitions. Any class that defines all the required methods and obeys the general contract is permitted to implement an interface, regardless of where the class resides in the class hierarchy.

Existing classes can easily be retrofitted to implement a new interface. All you have to do is to add the required methods, if they don't yet exist, and to add an `implements` clause to the class declaration. For example, many existing classes were retrofitted to implement the `Comparable`, `Iterable`, and `Autocloseable` interfaces when they were added to the platform. Existing classes cannot, in general, be retrofitted to extend a new abstract class. If you want to have two classes extend the same abstract class, you have to place it high up in the type hierarchy where it is an ancestor of both classes. Unfortunately, this can cause great collateral damage to the type hierarchy, forcing all descendants of the new abstract class to subclass it, whether or not it is appropriate.

Interfaces are ideal for defining mixins. Loosely speaking, a *mixin* is a type that a class can implement in addition to its "primary type," to declare that it provides some optional behavior. For example, `Comparable` is a mixin interface that allows a class to declare that its instances are ordered with respect to other mutually comparable objects. Such an interface is called a mixin because it allows the optional functionality to be "mixed in" to the type's primary functionality. Abstract classes can't be used to define mixins for the same reason that they can't be retrofitted onto existing classes: a class cannot have more than one parent, and there is no reasonable place in the class hierarchy to insert a mixin.

Interfaces allow for the construction of nonhierarchical type frameworks. Type hierarchies are great for organizing some things, but other things don't fall neatly into a rigid hierarchy. For example, suppose we have an interface representing a singer and another representing a songwriter:

```java
public interface Singer {
    AudioClip sing(Song s);
}
```

```
public interface Songwriter {
    Song compose(int chartPosition);
}
```

In real life, some singers are also songwriters. Because we used interfaces rather than abstract classes to define these types, it is perfectly permissible for a single class to implement both Singer and Songwriter. In fact, we can define a third interface that extends both Singer and Songwriter and adds new methods that are appropriate to the combination:

```
public interface SingerSongwriter extends Singer, Songwriter {
    AudioClip strum();
    void actSensitive();
}
```

You don't always need this level of flexibility, but when you do, interfaces are a lifesaver. The alternative is a bloated class hierarchy containing a separate class for every supported combination of attributes. If there are n attributes in the type system, there are 2^n possible combinations that you might have to support. This is what's known as a *combinatorial explosion*. Bloated class hierarchies can lead to bloated classes with many methods that differ only in the type of their arguments because there are no types in the class hierarchy to capture common behaviors.

Interfaces enable safe, powerful functionality enhancements via the *wrapper class* idiom (Item 18). If you use abstract classes to define types, you leave the programmer who wants to add functionality with no alternative but inheritance. The resulting classes are less powerful and more fragile than wrapper classes.

When there is an obvious implementation of an interface method in terms of other interface methods, consider providing implementation assistance to programmers in the form of a default method. For an example of this technique, see the removeIf method on page 104. If you provide default methods, be sure to document them for inheritance using the @implSpec Javadoc tag (Item 19).

There are limits on how much implementation assistance you can provide with default methods. Although many interfaces specify the behavior of Object methods such as equals and hashCode, you are not permitted to provide default methods for them. Also, interfaces are not permitted to contain instance fields or nonpublic static members (with the exception of private static methods). Finally, you can't add default methods to an interface that you don't control.

You can, however, combine the advantages of interfaces and abstract classes by providing an abstract *skeletal implementation class* to go with an interface. The interface defines the type, perhaps providing some default methods, while the skeletal implementation class implements the remaining non-primitive interface methods atop the primitive interface methods. Extending a skeletal implementation takes most of the work out of implementing an interface. This is the *Template Method* pattern [Gamma95].

By convention, skeletal implementation classes are called Abstract*Interface*, where *Interface* is the name of the interface they implement. For example, the Collections Framework provides a skeletal implementation to go along with each main collection interface: AbstractCollection, AbstractSet, AbstractList, and AbstractMap. Arguably it would have made sense to call them SkeletalCollection, SkeletalSet, SkeletalList, and SkeletalMap, but the Abstract convention is now firmly established. When properly designed, skeletal implementations (whether a separate abstract class, or consisting solely of default methods on an interface) can make it *very* easy for programmers to provide their own implementations of an interface. For example, here's a static factory method containing a complete, fully functional List implementation atop AbstractList:

```java
// Concrete implementation built atop skeletal implementation
static List<Integer> intArrayAsList(int[] a) {
    Objects.requireNonNull(a);

    // The diamond operator is only legal here in Java 9 and later
    // If you're using an earlier release, specify <Integer>
    return new AbstractList<>() {
        @Override public Integer get(int i) {
            return a[i];  // Autoboxing (Item 6)
        }

        @Override public Integer set(int i, Integer val) {
            int oldVal = a[i];
            a[i] = val;       // Auto-unboxing
            return oldVal;    // Autoboxing
        }

        @Override public int size() {
            return a.length;
        }
    };
}
```

When you consider all that a List implementation does for you, this example is an impressive demonstration of the power of skeletal implementations. Incidentally, this example is an *Adapter* [Gamma95] that allows an int array to be viewed as a list of Integer instances. Because of all the translation back and forth between int values and Integer instances (boxing and unboxing), its performance is not terribly good. Note that the implementation takes the form of an *anonymous class* (Item 24).

The beauty of skeletal implementation classes is that they provide all of the implementation assistance of abstract classes without imposing the severe constraints that abstract classes impose when they serve as type definitions. For most implementors of an interface with a skeletal implementation class, extending this class is the obvious choice, but it is strictly optional. If a class cannot be made to extend the skeletal implementation, the class can always implement the interface directly. The class still benefits from any default methods present on the interface itself. Furthermore, the skeletal implementation can still aid the implementor's task. The class implementing the interface can forward invocations of interface methods to a contained instance of a private inner class that extends the skeletal implementation. This technique, known as *simulated multiple inheritance*, is closely related to the wrapper class idiom discussed in Item 18. It provides many of the benefits of multiple inheritance, while avoiding the pitfalls.

Writing a skeletal implementation is a relatively simple, if somewhat tedious, process. First, study the interface and decide which methods are the primitives in terms of which the others can be implemented. These primitives will be the abstract methods in your skeletal implementation. Next, provide default methods in the interface for all of the methods that can be implemented directly atop the primitives, but recall that you may not provide default methods for Object methods such as equals and hashCode. If the primitives and default methods cover the interface, you're done, and have no need for a skeletal implementation class. Otherwise, write a class declared to implement the interface, with implementations of all of the remaining interface methods. The class may contain any nonpublic fields ands methods appropriate to the task.

As a simple example, consider the Map.Entry interface. The obvious primitives are getKey, getValue, and (optionally) setValue. The interface specifies the behavior of equals and hashCode, and there is an obvious implementation of toString in terms of the primitives. Since you are not allowed to provide default implementations for the Object methods, all implementations are placed in the skeletal implementation class:

```
// Skeletal implementation class
public abstract class AbstractMapEntry<K,V>
        implements Map.Entry<K,V> {
    // Entries in a modifiable map must override this method
    @Override public V setValue(V value) {
        throw new UnsupportedOperationException();
    }
```

```java
    // Implements the general contract of Map.Entry.equals
    @Override public boolean equals(Object o) {
        if (o == this)
            return true;
        if (!(o instanceof Map.Entry))
            return false;
        Map.Entry<?,?> e = (Map.Entry) o;
        return Objects.equals(e.getKey(),   getKey())
            && Objects.equals(e.getValue(), getValue());
    }

    // Implements the general contract of Map.Entry.hashCode
    @Override public int hashCode() {
        return Objects.hashCode(getKey())
             ^ Objects.hashCode(getValue());
    }

    @Override public String toString() {
        return getKey() + "=" + getValue();
    }
}
```

Note that this skeletal implementation could not be implemented in the Map.Entry interface or as a subinterface because default methods are not permitted to override Object methods such as equals, hashCode, and toString.

Because skeletal implementations are designed for inheritance, you should follow all of the design and documentation guidelines in Item 19. For brevity's sake, the documentation comments were omitted from the previous example, but **good documentation is absolutely essential in a skeletal implementation,** whether it consists of default methods on an interface or a separate abstract class.

A minor variant on the skeletal implementation is the *simple implementation,* exemplified by AbstractMap.SimpleEntry. A simple implementation is like a skeletal implementation in that it implements an interface and is designed for inheritance, but it differs in that it isn't abstract: it is the simplest possible working implementation. You can use it as it stands or subclass it as circumstances warrant.

To summarize, an interface is generally the best way to define a type that permits multiple implementations. If you export a nontrivial interface, you should strongly consider providing a skeletal implementation to go with it. To the extent possible, you should provide the skeletal implementation via default methods on the interface so that all implementors of the interface can make use of it. That said, restrictions on interfaces typically mandate that a skeletal implementation take the form of an abstract class.

Item 21: Design interfaces for posterity

Prior to Java 8, it was impossible to add methods to interfaces without breaking existing implementations. If you added a new method to an interface, existing implementations would, in general, lack the method, resulting in a compile-time error. In Java 8, the *default method* construct was added [JLS 9.4], with the intent of allowing the addition of methods to existing interfaces. But adding new methods to existing interfaces is fraught with risk.

The declaration for a default method includes a *default implementation* that is used by all classes that implement the interface but do not implement the default method. While the addition of default methods to Java makes it possible to add methods to an existing interface, there is no guarantee that these methods will work in all preexisting implementations. Default methods are "injected" into existing implementations without the knowledge or consent of their implementors. Before Java 8, these implementations were written with the tacit understanding that their interfaces would *never* acquire any new methods.

Many new default methods were added to the core collection interfaces in Java 8, primarily to facilitate the use of lambdas (Chapter 6). The Java libraries' default methods are high-quality general-purpose implementations, and in most cases, they work fine. But **it is not always possible to write a default method that maintains all invariants of every conceivable implementation.**

For example, consider the `removeIf` method, which was added to the `Collection` interface in Java 8. This method removes all elements for which a given boolean function (or *predicate*) returns `true`. The default implementation is specified to traverse the collection using its iterator, invoking the predicate on each element, and using the iterator's `remove` method to remove the elements for which the predicate returns `true`. Presumably the declaration looks something like this:

```
// Default method added to the Collection interface in Java 8
default boolean removeIf(Predicate<? super E> filter) {
    Objects.requireNonNull(filter);
    boolean result = false;
    for (Iterator<E> it = iterator(); it.hasNext(); ) {
        if (filter.test(it.next())) {
            it.remove();
            result = true;
        }
    }
    return result;
}
```

This is the best general-purpose implementation one could possibly write for the `removeIf` method, but sadly, it fails on some real-world `Collection` implementations. For example, consider `org.apache.commons.collections4.-collection.SynchronizedCollection`. This class, from the Apache Commons library, is similar to the one returned by the static factory `Collections.-synchronizedCollection` in `java.util`. The Apache version additionally provides the ability to use a client-supplied object for locking, in place of the collection. In other words, it is a wrapper class (Item 18), all of whose methods synchronize on a locking object before delegating to the wrapped collection.

The Apache `SynchronizedCollection` class is still being actively maintained, but as of this writing, it does not override the `removeIf` method. If this class is used in conjunction with Java 8, it will therefore inherit the default implementation of `removeIf`, which does not, indeed *cannot*, maintain the class's fundamental promise: to automatically synchronize around each method invocation. The default implementation knows nothing about synchronization and has no access to the field that contains the locking object. If a client calls the `removeIf` method on a `SynchronizedCollection` instance in the presence of concurrent modification of the collection by another thread, a `ConcurrentModificationException` or other unspecified behavior may result.

In order to prevent this from happening in similar Java platform libraries implementations, such as the package-private class returned by `Collections.synchronizedCollection`, the JDK maintainers had to override the default `removeIf` implementation and other methods like it to perform the necessary synchronization before invoking the default implementation. Preexisting collection implementations that were not part of the Java platform did not have the opportunity to make analogous changes in lockstep with the interface change, and some have yet to do so.

In the presence of default methods, existing implementations of an interface may compile without error or warning but fail at runtime. While not terribly common, this problem is not an isolated incident either. A handful of the methods added to the collections interfaces in Java 8 are known to be susceptible, and a handful of existing implementations are known to be affected.

Using default methods to add new methods to existing interfaces should be avoided unless the need is critical, in which case you should think long and hard about whether an existing interface implementation might be broken by your default method implementation. Default methods are, however, extremely useful for providing standard method implementations when an interface is created, to ease the task of implementing the interface (Item 20).

It is also worth noting that default methods were not designed to support removing methods from interfaces or changing the signatures of existing methods. Neither of these interface changes is possible without breaking existing clients.

The moral is clear. Even though default methods are now a part of the Java platform, **it is still of the utmost importance to design interfaces with great care.** While default methods make it *possible* to add methods to existing interfaces, there is great risk in doing so. If an interface contains a minor flaw, it may irritate its users forever; if an interface is severely deficient, it may doom the API that contains it.

Therefore, it is critically important to test each new interface before you release it. Multiple programmers should implement each interface in different ways. At a minimum, you should aim for three diverse implementations. Equally important is to write multiple client programs that use instances of each new interface to perform various tasks. This will go a long way toward ensuring that each interface satisfies all of its intended uses. These steps will allow you to discover flaws in interfaces before they are released, when you can still correct them easily. **While it may be possible to correct some interface flaws after an interface is released, you cannot count on it.**

Item 22: Use interfaces only to define types

When a class implements an interface, the interface serves as a *type* that can be used to refer to instances of the class. That a class implements an interface should therefore say something about what a client can do with instances of the class. It is inappropriate to define an interface for any other purpose.

One kind of interface that fails this test is the so-called *constant interface*. Such an interface contains no methods; it consists solely of static final fields, each exporting a constant. Classes using these constants implement the interface to avoid the need to qualify constant names with a class name. Here is an example:

```
// Constant interface antipattern - do not use!
public interface PhysicalConstants {
    // Avogadro's number (1/mol)
    static final double AVOGADROS_NUMBER   = 6.022_140_857e23;

    // Boltzmann constant (J/K)
    static final double BOLTZMANN_CONSTANT = 1.380_648_52e-23;

    // Mass of the electron (kg)
    static final double ELECTRON_MASS      = 9.109_383_56e-31;
}
```

The constant interface pattern is a poor use of interfaces. That a class uses some constants internally is an implementation detail. Implementing a constant interface causes this implementation detail to leak into the class's exported API. It is of no consequence to the users of a class that the class implements a constant interface. In fact, it may even confuse them. Worse, it represents a commitment: if in a future release the class is modified so that it no longer needs to use the constants, it still must implement the interface to ensure binary compatibility. If a nonfinal class implements a constant interface, all of its subclasses will have their namespaces polluted by the constants in the interface.

There are several constant interfaces in the Java platform libraries, such as `java.io.ObjectStreamConstants`. These interfaces should be regarded as anomalies and should not be emulated.

If you want to export constants, there are several reasonable choices. If the constants are strongly tied to an existing class or interface, you should add them to the class or interface. For example, all of the boxed numerical primitive classes, such as `Integer` and `Double`, export `MIN_VALUE` and `MAX_VALUE` constants. If the constants are best viewed as members of an enumerated type, you should export them with an *enum type* (Item 34). Otherwise, you should export the constants with a noninstantiable *utility class* (Item 4). Here is a utility class version of the PhysicalConstants example shown earlier:

```
// Constant utility class
package com.effectivejava.science;

public class PhysicalConstants {
  private PhysicalConstants() { }  // Prevents instantiation

    public static final double AVOGADROS_NUMBER = 6.022_140_857e23;
    public static final double BOLTZMANN_CONST  = 1.380_648_52e-23;
    public static final double ELECTRON_MASS    = 9.109_383_56e-31;
}
```

Incidentally, note the use of the underscore character (_) in the numeric literals. Underscores, which have been legal since Java 7, have no effect on the values of numeric literals, but can make them much easier to read if used with discretion. Consider adding underscores to numeric literals, whether fixed of floating point, if they contain five or more consecutive digits. For base ten literals, whether integral or floating point, you should use underscores to separate literals into groups of three digits indicating positive and negative powers of one thousand.

Normally a utility class requires clients to qualify constant names with a class name, for example, PhysicalConstants.AVOGADROS_NUMBER. If you make heavy use of the constants exported by a utility class, you can avoid the need for qualifying the constants with the class name by making use of the *static import* facility:

```
// Use of static import to avoid qualifying constants
import static com.effectivejava.science.PhysicalConstants.*;

public class Test {
    double atoms(double mols) {
        return AVOGADROS_NUMBER * mols;
    }
    ...
    // Many more uses of PhysicalConstants justify static import
}
```

In summary, interfaces should be used only to define types. They should not be used merely to export constants.

Item 23: Prefer class hierarchies to tagged classes

Occasionally you may run across a class whose instances come in two or more flavors and contain a *tag* field indicating the flavor of the instance. For example, consider this class, which is capable of representing a circle or a rectangle:

```
// Tagged class - vastly inferior to a class hierarchy!
class Figure {
    enum Shape { RECTANGLE, CIRCLE };

    // Tag field - the shape of this figure
    final Shape shape;

    // These fields are used only if shape is RECTANGLE
    double length;
    double width;

    // This field is used only if shape is CIRCLE
    double radius;

    // Constructor for circle
    Figure(double radius) {
        shape = Shape.CIRCLE;
        this.radius = radius;
    }

    // Constructor for rectangle
    Figure(double length, double width) {
        shape = Shape.RECTANGLE;
        this.length = length;
        this.width = width;
    }

    double area() {
        switch(shape) {
          case RECTANGLE:
            return length * width;
          case CIRCLE:
            return Math.PI * (radius * radius);
          default:
            throw new AssertionError(shape);
        }
    }
}
```

Such *tagged classes* have numerous shortcomings. They are cluttered with boilerplate, including enum declarations, tag fields, and switch statements. Readability is further harmed because multiple implementations are jumbled together in a single class. Memory footprint is increased because instances are burdened with irrelevant fields belonging to other flavors. Fields can't be made final unless constructors initialize irrelevant fields, resulting in more boilerplate. Constructors must set the tag field and initialize the right data fields with no help from the compiler: if you initialize the wrong fields, the program will fail at runtime. You can't add a flavor to a tagged class unless you can modify its source file. If you do add a flavor, you must remember to add a case to every switch statement, or the class will fail at runtime. Finally, the data type of an instance gives no clue as to its flavor. In short, **tagged classes are verbose, error-prone, and inefficient.**

Luckily, object-oriented languages such as Java offer a far better alternative for defining a single data type capable of representing objects of multiple flavors: subtyping. **A tagged class is just a pallid imitation of a class hierarchy.**

To transform a tagged class into a class hierarchy, first define an abstract class containing an abstract method for each method in the tagged class whose behavior depends on the tag value. In the Figure class, there is only one such method, which is area. This abstract class is the root of the class hierarchy. If there are any methods whose behavior does not depend on the value of the tag, put them in this class. Similarly, if there are any data fields used by all the flavors, put them in this class. There are no such flavor-independent methods or fields in the Figure class.

Next, define a concrete subclass of the root class for each flavor of the original tagged class. In our example, there are two: circle and rectangle. Include in each subclass the data fields particular to its flavor. In our example, radius is particular to circle, and length and width are particular to rectangle. Also include in each subclass the appropriate implementation of each abstract method in the root class. Here is the class hierarchy corresponding to the original Figure class:

```
// Class hierarchy replacement for a tagged class
abstract class Figure {
    abstract double area();
}

class Circle extends Figure {
    final double radius;

    Circle(double radius) { this.radius = radius; }

    @Override double area() { return Math.PI * (radius * radius); }
}
```

```
class Rectangle extends Figure {
    final double length;
    final double width;

    Rectangle(double length, double width) {
        this.length = length;
        this.width  = width;
    }
    @Override double area() { return length * width; }
}
```

This class hierarchy corrects every shortcoming of tagged classes noted previously. The code is simple and clear, containing none of the boilerplate found in the original. The implementation of each flavor is allotted its own class, and none of these classes is encumbered by irrelevant data fields. All fields are final. The compiler ensures that each class's constructor initializes its data fields and that each class has an implementation for every abstract method declared in the root class. This eliminates the possibility of a runtime failure due to a missing switch case. Multiple programmers can extend the hierarchy independently and interoperably without access to the source for the root class. There is a separate data type associated with each flavor, allowing programmers to indicate the flavor of a variable and to restrict variables and input parameters to a particular flavor.

Another advantage of class hierarchies is that they can be made to reflect natural hierarchical relationships among types, allowing for increased flexibility and better compile-time type checking. Suppose the tagged class in the original example also allowed for squares. The class hierarchy could be made to reflect the fact that a square is a special kind of rectangle (assuming both are immutable):

```
class Square extends Rectangle {
    Square(double side) {
        super(side, side);
    }
}
```

Note that the fields in the above hierarchy are accessed directly rather than by accessor methods. This was done for brevity and would be a poor design if the hierarchy were public (Item 16).

In summary, tagged classes are seldom appropriate. If you're tempted to write a class with an explicit tag field, think about whether the tag could be eliminated and the class replaced by a hierarchy. When you encounter an existing class with a tag field, consider refactoring it into a hierarchy.

Item 24: Favor static member classes over nonstatic

A *nested class* is a class defined within another class. A nested class should exist only to serve its enclosing class. If a nested class would be useful in some other context, then it should be a top-level class. There are four kinds of nested classes: *static member classes, nonstatic member classes, anonymous classes,* and *local classes.* All but the first kind are known as *inner classes.* This item tells you when to use which kind of nested class and why.

A static member class is the simplest kind of nested class. It is best thought of as an ordinary class that happens to' be declared inside another class and has access to all of the enclosing class's members, even those declared private. A static member class is a static member of its enclosing class and obeys the same accessibility rules as other static members. If it is declared private, it is accessible only within the enclosing class, and so forth.

One common use of a static member class is as a public helper class, useful only in conjunction with its outer class. For example, consider an enum describing the operations supported by a calculator (Item 34). The Operation enum should be a public static member class of the Calculator class. Clients of Calculator could then refer to operations using names like Calculator.Operation.PLUS and Calculator.Operation.MINUS.

Syntactically, the only difference between static and nonstatic member classes is that static member classes have the modifier static in their declarations. Despite the syntactic similarity, these two kinds of nested classes are very different. Each instance of a nonstatic member class is implicitly associated with an *enclosing instance* of its containing class. Within instance methods of a nonstatic member class, you can invoke methods on the enclosing instance or obtain a reference to the enclosing instance using the *qualified this* construct [JLS, 15.8.4]. If an instance of a nested class can exist in isolation from an instance of its enclosing class, then the nested class *must* be a static member class: it is impossible to create an instance of a nonstatic member class without an enclosing instance.

The association between a nonstatic member class instance and its enclosing instance is established when the member class instance is created and cannot be modified thereafter. Normally, the association is established automatically by invoking a nonstatic member class constructor from within an instance method of the enclosing class. It is possible, though rare, to establish the association manually using the expression enclosingInstance.new MemberClass(args). As you would expect, the association takes up space in the nonstatic member class instance and adds time to its construction.

One common use of a nonstatic member class is to define an *Adapter* [Gamma95] that allows an instance of the outer class to be viewed as an instance of some unrelated class. For example, implementations of the Map interface typically use nonstatic member classes to implement their *collection views*, which are returned by Map's keySet, entrySet, and values methods. Similarly, implementations of the collection interfaces, such as Set and List, typically use nonstatic member classes to implement their iterators:

```java
// Typical use of a nonstatic member class
public class MySet<E> extends AbstractSet<E> {
    ... // Bulk of the class omitted

    @Override public Iterator<E> iterator() {
        return new MyIterator();
    }

    private class MyIterator implements Iterator<E> {
        ...
    }
}
```

If you declare a member class that does not require access to an enclosing instance, *always* **put the static modifier in its declaration,** making it a static rather than a nonstatic member class. If you omit this modifier, each instance will have a hidden extraneous reference to its enclosing instance. As previously mentioned, storing this reference takes time and space. More seriously, it can result in the enclosing instance being retained when it would otherwise be eligible for garbage collection (Item 7). The resulting memory leak can be catastrophic. It is often difficult to detect because the reference is invisible.

A common use of private static member classes is to represent components of the object represented by their enclosing class. For example, consider a Map instance, which associates keys with values. Many Map implementations have an internal Entry object for each key-value pair in the map. While each entry is associated with a map, the methods on an entry (getKey, getValue, and setValue) do not need access to the map. Therefore, it would be wasteful to use a nonstatic member class to represent entries: a private static member class is best. If you accidentally omit the static modifier in the entry declaration, the map will still work, but each entry will contain a superfluous reference to the map, which wastes space and time.

It is doubly important to choose correctly between a static and a nonstatic member class if the class in question is a public or protected member of an exported class. In this case, the member class is an exported API element and cannot be changed from a nonstatic to a static member class in a subsequent release without violating backward compatibility.

As you would expect, an anonymous class has no name. It is not a member of its enclosing class. Rather than being declared along with other members, it is simultaneously declared and instantiated at the point of use. Anonymous classes are permitted at any point in the code where an expression is legal. Anonymous classes have enclosing instances if and only if they occur in a nonstatic context. But even if they occur in a static context, they cannot have any static members other than *constant variables*, which are final primitive or string fields initialized to constant expressions [JLS, 4.12.4].

There are many limitations on the applicability of anonymous classes. You can't instantiate them except at the point they're declared. You can't perform instanceof tests or do anything else that requires you to name the class. You can't declare an anonymous class to implement multiple interfaces or to extend a class and implement an interface at the same time. Clients of an anonymous class can't invoke any members except those it inherits from its supertype. Because anonymous classes occur in the midst of expressions, they must be kept short—about ten lines or fewer—or readability will suffer.

Before lambdas were added to Java (Chapter 6), anonymous classes were the preferred means of creating small *function objects* and *process objects* on the fly, but lambdas are now preferred (Item 42). Another common use of anonymous classes is in the implementation of static factory methods (see intArrayAsList in Item 20).

Local classes are the least frequently used of the four kinds of nested classes. A local class can be declared practically anywhere a local variable can be declared and obeys the same scoping rules. Local classes have attributes in common with each of the other kinds of nested classes. Like member classes, they have names and can be used repeatedly. Like anonymous classes, they have enclosing instances only if they are defined in a nonstatic context, and they cannot contain static members. And like anonymous classes, they should be kept short so as not to harm readability.

To recap, there are four different kinds of nested classes, and each has its place. If a nested class needs to be visible outside of a single method or is too long to fit comfortably inside a method, use a member class. If each instance of a member class needs a reference to its enclosing instance, make it nonstatic; otherwise, make it static. Assuming the class belongs inside a method, if you need to create instances from only one location and there is a preexisting type that characterizes the class, make it an anonymous class; otherwise, make it a local class.

Item 25: Limit source files to a single top-level class

While the Java compiler lets you define multiple top-level classes in a single source file, there are no benefits associated with doing so, and there are significant risks. The risks stem from the fact that defining multiple top-level classes in a source file makes it possible to provide multiple definitions for a class. Which definition gets used is affected by the order in which the source files are passed to the compiler.

To make this concrete, consider this source file, which contains only a Main class that refers to members of two other top-level classes (Utensil and Dessert):

```java
public class Main {
    public static void main(String[] args) {
        System.out.println(Utensil.NAME + Dessert.NAME);
    }
}
```

Now suppose you define both Utensil and Dessert in a single source file named Utensil.java:

```java
// Two classes defined in one file. Don't ever do this!
class Utensil {
    static final String NAME = "pan";
}

class Dessert {
    static final String NAME = "cake";
}
```

Of course the main program prints pancake.

Now suppose you accidentally make *another* source file named Dessert.java that defines the same two classes:

```java
// Two classes defined in one file. Don't ever do this!
class Utensil {
    static final String NAME = "pot";
}

class Dessert {
    static final String NAME = "pie";
}
```

If you're lucky enough to compile the program with the command javac Main.java Dessert.java, the compilation will fail, and the compiler will tell you that you've multiply defined the classes Utensil and Dessert. This is so because the compiler will first compile Main.java, and when it sees the reference to Utensil (which precedes the reference to Dessert), it will look in Utensil.java for this class and find both Utensil and Dessert. When the compiler encounters Dessert.java on the command line, it will pull in that file too, causing it to encounter both definitions of Utensil and Dessert.

If you compile the program with the command javac Main.java or javac Main.java Utensil.java, it will behave as it did before you wrote the Dessert.java file, printing pancake. But if you compile the program with the command javac Dessert.java Main.java, it will print potpie. The behavior of the program is thus affected by the order in which the source files are passed to the compiler, which is clearly unacceptable.

Fixing the problem is as simple as splitting the top-level classes (Utensil and Dessert, in the case of our example) into separate source files. If you are tempted to put multiple top-level classes into a single source file, consider using static member classes (Item 24) as an alternative to splitting the classes into separate source files. If the classes are subservient to another class, making them into static member classes is generally the better alternative because it enhances readability and makes it possible to reduce the accessibility of the classes by declaring them private (Item 15). Here is how our example looks with static member classes:

```java
// Static member classes instead of multiple top-level classes
public class Test {
    public static void main(String[] args) {
        System.out.println(Utensil.NAME + Dessert.NAME);
    }

    private static class Utensil {
        static final String NAME = "pan";
    }

    private static class Dessert {
        static final String NAME = "cake";
    }
}
```

The lesson is clear: **Never put multiple top-level classes or interfaces in a single source file.** Following this rule guarantees that you can't have multiple definitions for a single class at compile time. This in turn guarantees that the class files generated by compilation, and the behavior of the resulting program, are independent of the order in which the source files are passed to the compiler.

CHAPTER 5

Generics

SINCE Java 5, generics have been a part of the language. Before generics, you had to cast every object you read from a collection. If someone accidentally inserted an object of the wrong type, casts could fail at runtime. With generics, you tell the compiler what types of objects are permitted in each collection. The compiler inserts casts for you automatically and tells you *at compile time* if you try to insert an object of the wrong type. This results in programs that are both safer and clearer, but these benefits, which are not limited to collections, come at a price. This chapter tells you how to maximize the benefits and minimize the complications.

Item 26: Don't use raw types

First, a few terms. A class or interface whose declaration has one or more *type parameters* is a *generic* class or interface [JLS, 8.1.2, 9.1.2]. For example, the List interface has a single type parameter, E, representing its element type. The full name of the interface is List<E> (read "list of E"), but people often call it List for short. Generic classes and interfaces are collectively known as *generic types*.

Each generic type defines a set of *parameterized types*, which consist of the class or interface name followed by an angle-bracketed list of *actual type parameters* corresponding to the generic type's formal type parameters [JLS, 4.4, 4.5]. For example, List<String> (read "list of string") is a parameterized type representing a list whose elements are of type String. (String is the actual type parameter corresponding to the formal type parameter E.)

Finally, each generic type defines a *raw type*, which is the name of the generic type used without any accompanying type parameters [JLS, 4.8]. For example, the raw type corresponding to List<E> is List. Raw types behave as if all of the generic type information were erased from the type declaration. They exist primarily for compatibility with pre-generics code.

Before generics were added to Java, this would have been an exemplary collection declaration. As of Java 9, it is still legal, but far from exemplary:

```
// Raw collection type - don't do this!

// My stamp collection. Contains only Stamp instances.
private final Collection stamps = ... ;
```

If you use this declaration today and then accidentally put a coin into your stamp collection, the erroneous insertion compiles and runs without error (though the compiler does emit a vague warning):

```
// Erroneous insertion of coin into stamp collection
stamps.add(new Coin( ... )); // Emits "unchecked call" warning
```

You don't get an error until you try to retrieve the coin from the stamp collection:

```
// Raw iterator type - don't do this!
for (Iterator i = stamps.iterator(); i.hasNext(); )
    Stamp stamp = (Stamp) i.next(); // Throws ClassCastException
        stamp.cancel();
```

As mentioned throughout this book, it pays to discover errors as soon as possible after they are made, ideally at compile time. In this case, you don't discover the error until runtime, long after it has happened, and in code that may be distant from the code containing the error. Once you see the ClassCastException, you have to search through the codebase looking for the method invocation that put the coin into the stamp collection. The compiler can't help you, because it can't understand the comment that says, "Contains only Stamp instances."

With generics, the type declaration contains the information, not the comment:

```
// Parameterized collection type - typesafe
private final Collection<Stamp> stamps = ... ;
```

From this declaration, the compiler knows that stamps should contain only Stamp instances and *guarantees* it to be true, assuming your entire codebase compiles without emitting (or suppressing; see Item 27) any warnings. When stamps is declared with a parameterized type declaration, the erroneous insertion generates a compile-time error message that tells you *exactly* what is wrong:

```
Test.java:9: error: incompatible types: Coin cannot be converted
to Stamp
    c.add(new Coin());
       ^
```

The compiler inserts invisible casts for you when retrieving elements from collections and guarantees that they won't fail (assuming, again, that all of your code did not generate or suppress any compiler warnings). While the prospect of accidentally inserting a coin into a stamp collection may appear far-fetched, the problem is real. For example, it is easy to imagine putting a BigInteger into a collection that is supposed to contain only BigDecimal instances.

As noted earlier, it is legal to use raw types (generic types without their type parameters), but you should never do it. **If you use raw types, you lose all the safety and expressiveness benefits of generics.** Given that you shouldn't use them, why did the language designers permit raw types in the first place? For compatibility. Java was about to enter its second decade when generics were added, and there was an enormous amount of code in existence that did not use generics. It was deemed critical that all of this code remain legal and interoperate with newer code that does use generics. It had to be legal to pass instances of parameterized types to methods that were designed for use with raw types, and vice versa. This requirement, known as *migration compatibility*, drove the decisions to support raw types and to implement generics using *erasure* (Item 28).

While you shouldn't use raw types such as List, it is fine to use types that are parameterized to allow insertion of arbitrary objects, such as List<Object>. Just what is the difference between the raw type List and the parameterized type List<Object>? Loosely speaking, the former has opted out of the generic type system, while the latter has explicitly told the compiler that it is capable of holding objects of any type. While you can pass a List<String> to a parameter of type List, you can't pass it to a parameter of type List<Object>. There are subtyping rules for generics, and List<String> is a subtype of the raw type List, but not of the parameterized type List<Object> (Item 28). As a consequence, **you lose type safety if you use a raw type such as List, but not if you use a parameterized type such as List<Object>.**

To make this concrete, consider the following program:

```
// Fails at runtime - unsafeAdd method uses a raw type (List)!
public static void main(String[] args) {
    List<String> strings = new ArrayList<>();
    unsafeAdd(strings, Integer.valueOf(42));
    String s = strings.get(0); // Has compiler-generated cast
}

private static void unsafeAdd(List list, Object o) {
    list.add(o);
}
```

This program compiles, but because it uses the raw type List, you get a warning:

```
Test.java:10: warning: [unchecked] unchecked call to add(E) as a
member of the raw type List
    list.add(o);
        ^
```

And indeed, if you run the program, you get a ClassCastException when the program tries to cast the result of the invocation strings.get(0), which is an Integer, to a String. This is a compiler-generated cast, so it's normally guaranteed to succeed, but in this case we ignored a compiler warning and paid the price.

If you replace the raw type List with the parameterized type List<Object> in the unsafeAdd declaration and try to recompile the program, you'll find that it no longer compiles but emits the error message:

```
Test.java:5: error: incompatible types: List<String> cannot be
converted to List<Object>
    unsafeAdd(strings, Integer.valueOf(42));
        ^
```

You might be tempted to use a raw type for a collection whose element type is unknown and doesn't matter. For example, suppose you want to write a method that takes two sets and returns the number of elements they have in common. Here's how you might write such a method if you were new to generics:

```
// Use of raw type for unknown element type - don't do this!
static int numElementsInCommon(Set s1, Set s2) {
    int result = 0;
    for (Object o1 : s1)
        if (s2.contains(o1))
            result++;
    return result;
}
```

This method works but it uses raw types, which are dangerous. The safe alternative is to use *unbounded wildcard types*. If you want to use a generic type but you don't know or care what the actual type parameter is, you can use a question mark instead. For example, the unbounded wildcard type for the generic type Set<E> is Set<?> (read "set of some type"). It is the most general parameterized Set type, capable of holding *any* set. Here is how the numElementsInCommon declaration looks with unbounded wildcard types:

```
// Uses unbounded wildcard type - typesafe and flexible
static int numElementsInCommon(Set<?> s1, Set<?> s2) { ... }
```

What is the difference between the unbounded wildcard type Set<?> and the raw type Set? Does the question mark really buy you anything? Not to belabor the point, but the wildcard type is safe and the raw type isn't. You can put *any* element into a collection with a raw type, easily corrupting the collection's type invariant (as demonstrated by the unsafeAdd method on page 119); **you can't put any element (other than null) into a Collection<?>.** Attempting to do so will generate a compile-time error message like this:

```
WildCard.java:13: error: incompatible types: String cannot be
converted to CAP#1
    c.add("verboten");
        ^
  where CAP#1 is a fresh type-variable:
    CAP#1 extends Object from capture of ?
```

Admittedly this error message leaves something to be desired, but the compiler has done its job, preventing you from corrupting the collection's type invariant, whatever its element type may be. Not only can't you put any element (other than null) into a Collection<?>, but you can't assume anything about the type of the objects that you get out. If these restrictions are unacceptable, you can use *generic methods* (Item 30) or *bounded wildcard types* (Item 31).

There are a few minor exceptions to the rule that you should not use raw types. **You must use raw types in class literals.** The specification does not permit the use of parameterized types (though it does permit array types and primitive types) [JLS, 15.8.2]. In other words, List.class, String[].class, and int.class are all legal, but List<String>.class and List<?>.class are not.

A second exception to the rule concerns the instanceof operator. Because generic type information is erased at runtime, it is illegal to use the instanceof operator on parameterized types other than unbounded wildcard types. The use of unbounded wildcard types in place of raw types does not affect the behavior of the instanceof operator in any way. In this case, the angle brackets and question marks are just noise. **This is the preferred way to use the instanceof operator with generic types:**

```
// Legitimate use of raw type - instanceof operator
if (o instanceof Set) {       // Raw type
    Set<?> s = (Set<?>) o;    // Wildcard type
    ...
}
```

Note that once you've determined that o is a Set, you must cast it to the wildcard type Set<?>, not the raw type Set. This is a checked cast, so it will not cause a compiler warning.

In summary, using raw types can lead to exceptions at runtime, so don't use them. They are provided only for compatibility and interoperability with legacy code that predates the introduction of generics. As a quick review, Set<Object> is a parameterized type representing a set that can contain objects of any type, Set<?> is a wildcard type representing a set that can contain only objects of some unknown type, and Set is a raw type, which opts out of the generic type system. The first two are safe, and the last is not.

For quick reference, the terms introduced in this item (and a few introduced later in this chapter) are summarized in the following table:

Term	Example	Item
Parameterized type	List<String>	Item 26
Actual type parameter	String	Item 26
Generic type	List<E>	Items 26, 29
Formal type parameter	E	Item 26
Unbounded wildcard type	List<?>	Item 26
Raw type	List	Item 26
Bounded type parameter	<E extends Number>	Item 29
Recursive type bound	<T extends Comparable<T>>	Item 30
Bounded wildcard type	List<? extends Number>	Item 31
Generic method	static <E> List<E> asList(E[] a)	Item 30
Type token	String.class	Item 33

Item 27: Eliminate unchecked warnings

When you program with generics, you will see many compiler warnings: unchecked cast warnings, unchecked method invocation warnings, unchecked parameterized vararg type warnings, and unchecked conversion warnings. The more experience you acquire with generics, the fewer warnings you'll get, but don't expect newly written code to compile cleanly.

Many unchecked warnings are easy to eliminate. For example, suppose you accidentally write this declaration:

```
Set<Lark> exaltation = new HashSet();
```

The compiler will gently remind you what you did wrong:

```
Venery.java:4: warning: [unchecked] unchecked conversion
        Set<Lark> exaltation = new HashSet();
                               ^
    required: Set<Lark>
    found:    HashSet
```

You can then make the indicated correction, causing the warning to disappear. Note that you don't actually have to specify the type parameter, merely to indicate that it's present with the *diamond operator* (<>), introduced in Java 7. The compiler will then *infer* the correct actual type parameter (in this case, Lark):

```
Set<Lark> exaltation = new HashSet<>();
```

Some warnings will be *much* more difficult to eliminate. This chapter is filled with examples of such warnings. When you get warnings that require some thought, persevere! **Eliminate every unchecked warning that you can.** If you eliminate all warnings, you are assured that your code is typesafe, which is a very good thing. It means that you won't get a ClassCastException at runtime, and it increases your confidence that your program will behave as you intended.

If you can't eliminate a warning, but you can prove that the code that provoked the warning is typesafe, then (and only then) suppress the warning with an @SuppressWarnings("unchecked") annotation. If you suppress warnings without first proving that the code is typesafe, you are giving yourself a false sense of security. The code may compile without emitting any warnings, but it can still throw a ClassCastException at runtime. If, however, you ignore unchecked warnings that you know to be safe (instead of suppressing them), you won't notice when a new warning crops up that represents a real problem. The new warning will get lost amidst all the false alarms that you didn't silence.

The SuppressWarnings annotation can be used on any declaration, from an individual local variable declaration to an entire class. **Always use the SuppressWarnings annotation on the smallest scope possible.** Typically this will be a variable declaration or a very short method or constructor. Never use SuppressWarnings on an entire class. Doing so could mask critical warnings.

If you find yourself using the SuppressWarnings annotation on a method or constructor that's more than one line long, you may be able to move it onto a local variable declaration. You may have to declare a new local variable, but it's worth it. For example, consider this toArray method, which comes from ArrayList:

```
public <T> T[] toArray(T[] a) {
    if (a.length < size)
        return (T[]) Arrays.copyOf(elements, size, a.getClass());
    System.arraycopy(elements, 0, a, 0, size);
    if (a.length > size)
        a[size] = null;
    return a;
}
```

If you compile ArrayList, the method generates this warning:

```
ArrayList.java:305: warning: [unchecked] unchecked cast
        return (T[]) Arrays.copyOf(elements, size, a.getClass());
                           ^
    required: T[]
    found:    Object[]
```

It is illegal to put a SuppressWarnings annotation on the return statement, because it isn't a declaration [JLS, 9.7]. You might be tempted to put the annotation on the entire method, but don't. Instead, declare a local variable to hold the return value and annotate its declaration, like so:

```
// Adding local variable to reduce scope of @SuppressWarnings
public <T> T[] toArray(T[] a) {
    if (a.length < size) {
        // This cast is correct because the array we're creating
        // is of the same type as the one passed in, which is T[].
        @SuppressWarnings("unchecked") T[] result =
            (T[]) Arrays.copyOf(elements, size, a.getClass());
        return result;
    }
    System.arraycopy(elements, 0, a, 0, size);
    if (a.length > size)
        a[size] = null;
    return a;
}
```

The resulting method compiles cleanly and minimizes the scope in which unchecked warnings are suppressed.

Every time you use a @SuppressWarnings("unchecked") annotation, add a comment saying why it is safe to do so. This will help others understand the code, and more importantly, it will decrease the odds that someone will modify the code so as to make the computation unsafe. If you find it hard to write such a comment, keep thinking. You may end up figuring out that the unchecked operation isn't safe after all.

In summary, unchecked warnings are important. Don't ignore them. Every unchecked warning represents the potential for a ClassCastException at runtime. Do your best to eliminate these warnings. If you can't eliminate an unchecked warning and you can prove that the code that provoked it is typesafe, suppress the warning with a @SuppressWarnings("unchecked") annotation in the narrowest possible scope. Record the rationale for your decision to suppress the warning in a comment.

Item 28: Prefer lists to arrays

Arrays differ from generic types in two important ways. First, arrays are *covariant*. This scary-sounding word means simply that if Sub is a subtype of Super, then the array type Sub[] is a subtype of the array type Super[]. Generics, by contrast, are *invariant*: for any two distinct types Type1 and Type2, List<Type1> is neither a subtype nor a supertype of List<Type2> [JLS, 4.10; Naftalin07, 2.5]. You might think this means that generics are deficient, but arguably it is arrays that are deficient. This code fragment is legal:

```
// Fails at runtime!
Object[] objectArray = new Long[1];
objectArray[0] = "I don't fit in"; // Throws ArrayStoreException
```

but this one is not:

```
// Won't compile!
List<Object> ol = new ArrayList<Long>(); // Incompatible types
ol.add("I don't fit in");
```

Either way you can't put a String into a Long container, but with an array you find out that you've made a mistake at runtime; with a list, you find out at compile time. Of course, you'd rather find out at compile time.

The second major difference between arrays and generics is that arrays are *reified* [JLS, 4.7]. This means that arrays know and enforce their element type at runtime. As noted earlier, if you try to put a String into an array of Long, you'll get an ArrayStoreException. Generics, by contrast, are implemented by *erasure* [JLS, 4.6]. This means that they enforce their type constraints only at compile time and discard (or *erase*) their element type information at runtime. Erasure is what allowed generic types to interoperate freely with legacy code that didn't use generics (Item 26), ensuring a smooth transition to generics in Java 5.

Because of these fundamental differences, arrays and generics do not mix well. For example, it is illegal to create an array of a generic type, a parameterized type, or a type parameter. Therefore, none of these array creation expressions are legal: new List<E>[], new List<String>[], new E[]. All will result in *generic array creation* errors at compile time.

Why is it illegal to create a generic array? Because it isn't typesafe. If it were legal, casts generated by the compiler in an otherwise correct program could fail at runtime with a ClassCastException. This would violate the fundamental guarantee provided by the generic type system.

To make this more concrete, consider the following code fragment:

```
// Why generic array creation is illegal - won't compile!
List<String>[] stringLists = new List<String>[1];  // (1)
List<Integer> intList = List.of(42);               // (2)
Object[] objects = stringLists;                    // (3)
objects[0] = intList;                              // (4)
String s = stringLists[0].get(0);                 // (5)
```

Let's pretend that line 1, which creates a generic array, is legal. Line 2 creates and initializes a List<Integer> containing a single element. Line 3 stores the List<String> array into an Object array variable, which is legal because arrays are covariant. Line 4 stores the List<Integer> into the sole element of the Object array, which succeeds because generics are implemented by erasure: the runtime type of a List<Integer> instance is simply List, and the runtime type of a List<String>[] instance is List[], so this assignment doesn't generate an ArrayStoreException. Now we're in trouble. We've stored a List<Integer> instance into an array that is declared to hold only List<String> instances. In line 5, we retrieve the sole element from the sole list in this array. The compiler automatically casts the retrieved element to String, but it's an Integer, so we get a ClassCastException at runtime. In order to prevent this from happening, line 1 (which creates a generic array) must generate a compile-time error.

Types such as E, List<E>, and List<String> are technically known as *non-reifiable* types [JLS, 4.7]. Intuitively speaking, a non-reifiable type is one whose runtime representation contains less information than its compile-time representation. Because of erasure, the only parameterized types that are reifiable are unbounded wildcard types such as List<?> and Map<?,?> (Item 26). It is legal, though rarely useful, to create arrays of unbounded wildcard types.

The prohibition on generic array creation can be annoying. It means, for example, that it's not generally possible for a generic collection to return an array of its element type (but see Item 33 for a partial solution). It also means that you get confusing warnings when using varargs methods (Item 53) in combination with generic types. This is because every time you invoke a varargs method, an array is created to hold the varargs parameters. If the element type of this array is not reifiable, you get a warning. The SafeVarargs annotation can be used to address this issue (Item 32).

When you get a generic array creation error or an unchecked cast warning on a cast to an array type, the best solution is often to use the collection type List<E> in preference to the array type E[]. You might sacrifice some conciseness or performance, but in exchange you get better type safety and interoperability.

For example, suppose you want to write a Chooser class with a constructor that takes a collection, and a single method that returns an element of the collection chosen at random. Depending on what collection you pass to the constructor, you could use a chooser as a game die, a magic 8-ball, or a data source for a Monte Carlo simulation. Here's a simplistic implementation without generics:

```java
// Chooser - a class badly in need of generics!
public class Chooser {
    private final Object[] choiceArray;

    public Chooser(Collection choices) {
        choiceArray = choices.toArray();
    }

    public Object choose() {
        Random rnd = ThreadLocalRandom.current();
        return choiceArray[rnd.nextInt(choiceArray.length)];
    }
}
```

To use this class, you have to cast the choose method's return value from Object to the desired type every time you use invoke the method, and the cast will fail at runtime if you get the type wrong. Taking the advice of Item 29 to heart, we attempt to modify Chooser to make it generic. Changes are shown in boldface:

```java
// A first cut at making Chooser generic - won't compile
public class Chooser<T> {
    private final T[] choiceArray;

    public Chooser(Collection<T> choices) {
        choiceArray = choices.toArray();
    }

    // choose method unchanged
}
```

If you try to compile this class, you'll get this error message:

```
Chooser.java:9: error: incompatible types: Object[] cannot be
converted to T[]
        choiceArray = choices.toArray();
                                       ^
  where T is a type-variable:
    T extends Object declared in class Chooser
```

No big deal, you say, I'll cast the Object array to a T array:

```
choiceArray = (T[]) choices.toArray();
```

This gets rid of the error, but instead you get a warning:

```
Chooser.java:9: warning: [unchecked] unchecked cast
        choiceArray = (T[]) choices.toArray();
                                           ^
    required: T[], found: Object[]
    where T is a type-variable:
T extends Object declared in class Chooser
```

The compiler is telling you that it can't vouch for the safety of the cast at runtime because the program won't know what type T represents—remember, element type information is erased from generics at runtime. Will the program work? Yes, but the compiler can't prove it. You could prove it to yourself, put the proof in a comment and suppress the warning with an annotation, but you're better off eliminating the cause of warning (Item 27).

To eliminate the unchecked cast warning, use a list instead of an array. Here is a version of the Chooser class that compiles without error or warning:

```
// List-based Chooser - typesafe
public class Chooser<T> {
    private final List<T> choiceList;

    public Chooser(Collection<T> choices) {
        choiceList = new ArrayList<>(choices);
    }

    public T choose() {
        Random rnd = ThreadLocalRandom.current();
        return choiceList.get(rnd.nextInt(choiceList.size()));
    }
}
```

This version is a tad more verbose, and perhaps a tad slower, but it's worth it for the peace of mind that you won't get a ClassCastException at runtime.

In summary, arrays and generics have very different type rules. Arrays are covariant and reified; generics are invariant and erased. As a consequence, arrays provide runtime type safety but not compile-time type safety, and vice versa for generics. As a rule, arrays and generics don't mix well. If you find yourself mixing them and getting compile-time errors or warnings, your first impulse should be to replace the arrays with lists.

Item 29: Favor generic types

It is generally not too difficult to parameterize your declarations and make use of the generic types and methods provided by the JDK. Writing your own generic types is a bit more difficult, but it's worth the effort to learn how.

Consider the simple (toy) stack implementation from Item 7:

```
// Object-based collection - a prime candidate for generics
public class Stack {
    private Object[] elements;
    private int size = 0;
    private static final int DEFAULT_INITIAL_CAPACITY = 16;

    public Stack() {
        elements = new Object[DEFAULT_INITIAL_CAPACITY];
    }

    public void push(Object e) {
        ensureCapacity();
        elements[size++] = e;
    }

    public Object pop() {
        if (size == 0)
            throw new EmptyStackException();
        Object result = elements[--size];
        elements[size] = null; // Eliminate obsolete reference
        return result;
    }

    public boolean isEmpty() {
        return size == 0;
    }

    private void ensureCapacity() {
        if (elements.length == size)
            elements = Arrays.copyOf(elements, 2 * size + 1);
    }
}
```

This class should have been parameterized to begin with, but since it wasn't, we can *generify* it after the fact. In other words, we can parameterize it without harming clients of the original non-parameterized version. As it stands, the client has to cast objects that are popped off the stack, and those casts might fail at runtime. The first step in generifying a class is to add one or more type parameters to its declaration. In this case there is one type parameter, representing the element type of the stack, and the conventional name for this type parameter is E (Item 68).

The next step is to replace all the uses of the type Object with the appropriate type parameter and then try to compile the resulting program:

```
// Initial attempt to generify Stack - won't compile!
public class Stack<E> {
    private E[] elements;
    private int size = 0;
    private static final int DEFAULT_INITIAL_CAPACITY = 16;

    public Stack() {
        elements = new E[DEFAULT_INITIAL_CAPACITY];
    }

    public void push(E e) {
        ensureCapacity();
        elements[size++] = e;
    }

    public E pop() {
        if (size == 0)
            throw new EmptyStackException();
        E result = elements[--size];
        elements[size] = null; // Eliminate obsolete reference
        return result;
    }
    ... // no changes in isEmpty or ensureCapacity
}
```

You'll generally get at least one error or warning, and this class is no exception. Luckily, this class generates only one error:

```
Stack.java:8: generic array creation
        elements = new E[DEFAULT_INITIAL_CAPACITY];
                   ^
```

As explained in Item 28, you can't create an array of a non-reifiable type, such as E. This problem arises every time you write a generic type that is backed by an array. There are two reasonable ways to solve it. The first solution directly circumvents the prohibition on generic array creation: create an array of Object and cast it to the generic array type. Now in place of an error, the compiler will emit a warning. This usage is legal, but it's not (in general) typesafe:

```
Stack.java:8: warning: [unchecked] unchecked cast
found: Object[], required: E[]
        elements = (E[]) new Object[DEFAULT_INITIAL_CAPACITY];
                   ^
```

The compiler may not be able to prove that your program is typesafe, but you can. You must convince yourself that the unchecked cast will not compromise the type safety of the program. The array in question (elements) is stored in a private field and never returned to the client or passed to any other method. The only elements stored in the array are those passed to the push method, which are of type E, so the unchecked cast can do no harm.

Once you've proved that an unchecked cast is safe, suppress the warning in as narrow a scope as possible (Item 27). In this case, the constructor contains only the unchecked array creation, so it's appropriate to suppress the warning in the entire constructor. With the addition of an annotation to do this, Stack compiles cleanly, and you can use it without explicit casts or fear of a ClassCastException:

```
// The elements array will contain only E instances from push(E).
// This is sufficient to ensure type safety, but the runtime
// type of the array won't be E[]; it will always be Object[]!
@SuppressWarnings("unchecked")
public Stack() {
    elements = (E[]) new Object[DEFAULT_INITIAL_CAPACITY];
}
```

The second way to eliminate the generic array creation error in Stack is to change the type of the field elements from E[] to Object[]. If you do this, you'll get a different error:

```
Stack.java:19: incompatible types
found: Object, required: E
        E result = elements[--size];
                   ^
```

You can change this error into a warning by casting the element retrieved from the array to E, but you will get a warning:

```
Stack.java:19: warning: [unchecked] unchecked cast
found: Object, required: E
        E result = (E) elements[--size];
                   ^
```

Because E is a non-reifiable type, there's no way the compiler can check the cast at runtime. Again, you can easily prove to yourself that the unchecked cast is safe, so it's appropriate to suppress the warning. In line with the advice of Item 27, we suppress the warning only on the assignment that contains the unchecked cast, not on the entire pop method:

```
// Appropriate suppression of unchecked warning
public E pop() {
    if (size == 0)
        throw new EmptyStackException();

    // push requires elements to be of type E, so cast is correct
    @SuppressWarnings("unchecked") E result =
        (E) elements[--size];

    elements[size] = null; // Eliminate obsolete reference
    return result;
}
```

Both techniques for eliminating the generic array creation have their adherents. The first is more readable: the array is declared to be of type E[], clearly indicating that it contains only E instances. It is also more concise: in a typical generic class, you read from the array at many points in the code; the first technique requires only a single cast (where the array is created), while the second requires a separate cast each time an array element is read. Thus, the first technique is preferable and more commonly used in practice. It does, however, cause *heap pollution* (Item 32): the runtime type of the array does not match its compile-time type (unless E happens to be Object). This makes some programmers sufficiently queasy that they opt for the second technique, though the heap pollution is harmless in this situation.

The following program demonstrates the use of our generic Stack class. The program prints its command line arguments in reverse order and converted to uppercase. No explicit cast is necessary to invoke String's toUpperCase method on the elements popped from the stack, and the automatically generated cast is guaranteed to succeed:

```
// Little program to exercise our generic Stack
public static void main(String[] args) {
    Stack<String> stack = new Stack<>();
    for (String arg : args)
        stack.push(arg);
    while (!stack.isEmpty())
        System.out.println(stack.pop().toUpperCase());
}
```

The foregoing example may appear to contradict Item 28, which encourages the use of lists in preference to arrays. It is not always possible or desirable to use lists inside your generic types. Java doesn't support lists natively, so some generic types, such as ArrayList, *must* be implemented atop arrays. Other generic types, such as HashMap, are implemented atop arrays for performance.

The great majority of generic types are like our Stack example in that their type parameters have no restrictions: you can create a Stack<Object>, Stack<int[]>, Stack<List<String>>, or Stack of any other object reference type. Note that you can't create a Stack of a primitive type: trying to create a Stack<int> or Stack<double> will result in a compile-time error. This is a fundamental limitation of Java's generic type system. You can work around this restriction by using boxed primitive types (Item 61).

There are some generic types that restrict the permissible values of their type parameters. For example, consider java.util.concurrent.DelayQueue, whose declaration looks like this:

```
class DelayQueue<E extends Delayed> implements BlockingQueue<E>
```

The type parameter list (<E extends Delayed>) requires that the actual type parameter E be a subtype of java.util.concurrent.Delayed. This allows the DelayQueue implementation and its clients to take advantage of Delayed methods on the elements of a DelayQueue, without the need for explicit casting or the risk of a ClassCastException. The type parameter E is known as a *bounded type parameter*. Note that the subtype relation is defined so that every type is a subtype of itself [JLS, 4.10], so it is legal to create a DelayQueue<Delayed>.

In summary, generic types are safer and easier to use than types that require casts in client code. When you design new types, make sure that they can be used without such casts. This will often mean making the types generic. If you have any existing types that should be generic but aren't, generify them. This will make life easier for new users of these types without breaking existing clients (Item 26).

Item 30: Favor generic methods

Just as classes can be generic, so can methods. Static utility methods that operate on parameterized types are usually generic. All of the "algorithm" methods in `Collections` (such as `binarySearch` and `sort`) are generic.

Writing generic methods is similar to writing generic types. Consider this deficient method, which returns the union of two sets:

```
// Uses raw types - unacceptable! (Item 26)
public static Set union(Set s1, Set s2) {
    Set result = new HashSet(s1);
    result.addAll(s2);
    return result;
}
```

This method compiles but with two warnings:

```
Union.java:5: warning: [unchecked] unchecked call to
HashSet(Collection<? extends E>) as a member of raw type HashSet
        Set result = new HashSet(s1);
                     ^
Union.java:6: warning: [unchecked] unchecked call to
addAll(Collection<? extends E>) as a member of raw type Set
        result.addAll(s2);
               ^
```

To fix these warnings and make the method typesafe, modify its declaration to declare a *type parameter* representing the element type for the three sets (the two arguments and the return value) and use this type parameter throughout the method. **The type parameter list, which declares the type parameters, goes between a method's modifiers and its return type.** In this example, the type parameter list is <E>, and the return type is Set<E>. The naming conventions for type parameters are the same for generic methods and generic types (Items 29, 68):

```
// Generic method
public static <E> Set<E> union(Set<E> s1, Set<E> s2) {
    Set<E> result = new HashSet<>(s1);
    result.addAll(s2);
    return result;
}
```

At least for simple generic methods, that's all there is to it. This method compiles without generating any warnings and provides type safety as well as ease of use. Here's a simple program to exercise the method. This program contains no casts and compiles without errors or warnings:

```
// Simple program to exercise generic method
public static void main(String[] args) {
    Set<String> guys = Set.of("Tom", "Dick", "Harry");
    Set<String> stooges = Set.of("Larry", "Moe", "Curly");
    Set<String> aflCio = union(guys, stooges);
    System.out.println(aflCio);
}
```

When you run the program, it prints [Moe, Tom, Harry, Larry, Curly, Dick]. (The order of the elements in the output is implementation-dependent.)

A limitation of the union method is that the types of all three sets (both input parameters and the return value) have to be exactly the same. You can make the method more flexible by using *bounded wildcard types* (Item 31).

On occasion, you will need to create an object that is immutable but applicable to many different types. Because generics are implemented by erasure (Item 28), you can use a single object for all required type parameterizations, but you need to write a static factory method to repeatedly dole out the object for each requested type parameterization. This pattern, called the *generic singleton factory*, is used for function objects (Item 42) such as Collections.reverseOrder, and occasionally for collections such as Collections.emptySet.

Suppose that you want to write an identity function dispenser. The libraries provide Function.identity, so there's no reason to write your own (Item 59), but it is instructive. It would be wasteful to create a new identity function object time one is requested, because it's stateless. If Java's generics were reified, you would need one identity function per type, but since they're erased a generic singleton will suffice. Here's how it looks:

```
// Generic singleton factory pattern
private static UnaryOperator<Object> IDENTITY_FN = (t) -> t;

@SuppressWarnings("unchecked")
public static <T> UnaryOperator<T> identityFunction() {
    return (UnaryOperator<T>) IDENTITY_FN;
}
```

The cast of IDENTITY_FN to (UnaryFunction<T>) generates an unchecked cast warning, as UnaryOperator<Object> is not a UnaryOperator<T> for every T. But the identity function is special: it returns its argument unmodified, so we know that it is typesafe to use it as a UnaryFunction<T>, whatever the value of T.

Therefore, we can confidently suppress the unchecked cast warning generated by this cast. Once we've done this, the code compiles without error or warning.

Here is a sample program that uses our generic singleton as a UnaryOperator<String> and a UnaryOperator<Number>. As usual, it contains no casts and compiles without errors or warnings:

```
// Sample program to exercise generic singleton
public static void main(String[] args) {
    String[] strings = { "jute", "hemp", "nylon" };
    UnaryOperator<String> sameString = identityFunction();
    for (String s : strings)
        System.out.println(sameString.apply(s));

    Number[] numbers = { 1, 2.0, 3L };
    UnaryOperator<Number> sameNumber = identityFunction();
    for (Number n : numbers)
        System.out.println(sameNumber.apply(n));
}
```

It is permissible, though relatively rare, for a type parameter to be bounded by some expression involving that type parameter itself. This is what's known as a *recursive type bound*. A common use of recursive type bounds is in connection with the Comparable interface, which defines a type's natural ordering (Item 14). This interface is shown here:

```
public interface Comparable<T> {
    int compareTo(T o);
}
```

The type parameter T defines the type to which elements of the type implementing Comparable<T> can be compared. In practice, nearly all types can be compared only to elements of their own type. So, for example, String implements Comparable<String>, Integer implements Comparable<Integer>, and so on.

Many methods take a collection of elements implementing Comparable to sort it, search within it, calculate its minimum or maximum, and the like. To do these things, it is required that every element in the collection be comparable to every other element in it, in other words, that the elements of the list be *mutually comparable*. Here is how to express that constraint:

```
// Using a recursive type bound to express mutual comparability
public static <E extends Comparable<E>> E max(Collection<E> c);
```

The type bound <E extends Comparable<E>> may be read as "any type E that can be compared to itself," which corresponds more or less precisely to the notion of mutual comparability.

Here is a method to go with the previous declaration. It calculates the maximum value in a collection according to its elements' natural order, and it compiles without errors or warnings:

```
// Returns max value in a collection - uses recursive type bound
public static <E extends Comparable<E>> E max(Collection<E> c) {
    if (c.isEmpty())
        throw new IllegalArgumentException("Empty collection");

    E result = null;
    for (E e : c)
        if (result == null || e.compareTo(result) > 0)
            result = Objects.requireNonNull(e);

    return result;
}
```

Note that this method throws IllegalArgumentException if the list is empty. A better alternative would be to return an Optional<E> (Item 55).

Recursive type bounds can get much more complex, but luckily they rarely do. If you understand this idiom, its wildcard variant (Item 31), and the *simulated self-type* idiom (Item 2), you'll be able to deal with most of the recursive type bounds you encounter in practice.

In summary, generic methods, like generic types, are safer and easier to use than methods requiring their clients to put explicit casts on input parameters and return values. Like types, you should make sure that your methods can be used without casts, which often means making them generic. And like types, you should generify existing methods whose use requires casts. This makes life easier for new users without breaking existing clients (Item 26).

Item 31: Use bounded wildcards to increase API flexibility

As noted in Item 28, parameterized types are *invariant*. In other words, for any two distinct types Type1 and Type2, List<Type1> is neither a subtype nor a supertype of List<Type2>. Although it is counterintuitive that List<String> is not a subtype of List<Object>, it really does make sense. You can put any object into a List<Object>, but you can put only strings into a List<String>. Since a List<String> can't do everything a List<Object> can, it isn't a subtype (by the Liskov substitution principal, Item 10).

Sometimes you need more flexibility than invariant typing can provide. Consider the Stack class from Item 29. To refresh your memory, here is its public API:

```
public class Stack<E> {
    public Stack();
    public void push(E e);
    public E pop();
    public boolean isEmpty();
}
```

Suppose we want to add a method that takes a sequence of elements and pushes them all onto the stack. Here's a first attempt:

```
// pushAll method without wildcard type - deficient!
public void pushAll(Iterable<E> src) {
    for (E e : src)
        push(e);
}
```

This method compiles cleanly, but it isn't entirely satisfactory. If the element type of the Iterable src exactly matches that of the stack, it works fine. But suppose you have a Stack<Number> and you invoke push(intVal), where intVal is of type Integer. This works because Integer is a subtype of Number. So logically, it seems that this should work, too:

```
Stack<Number> numberStack = new Stack<>();
Iterable<Integer> integers = ... ;
numberStack.pushAll(integers);
```

If you try it, however, you'll get this error message because parameterized types are invariant:

```
StackTest.java:7: error: incompatible types: Iterable<Integer>
cannot be converted to Iterable<Number>
        numberStack.pushAll(integers);
                    ^
```

Luckily, there's a way out. The language provides a special kind of parameterized type call a *bounded wildcard type* to deal with situations like this. The type of the input parameter to pushAll should not be "Iterable of E" but "Iterable of some subtype of E," and there is a wildcard type that means precisely that: Iterable<? extends E>. (The use of the keyword extends is slightly misleading: recall from Item 29 that *subtype* is defined so that every type is a subtype of itself, even though it does not extend itself.) Let's modify pushAll to use this type:

```
// Wildcard type for a parameter that serves as an E producer
public void pushAll(Iterable<? extends E> src) {
    for (E e : src)
        push(e);
}
```

With this change, not only does Stack compile cleanly, but so does the client code that wouldn't compile with the original pushAll declaration. Because Stack and its client compile cleanly, you know that everything is typesafe.

Now suppose you want to write a popAll method to go with pushAll. The popAll method pops each element off the stack and adds the elements to the given collection. Here's how a first attempt at writing the popAll method might look:

```
// popAll method without wildcard type - deficient!
public void popAll(Collection<E> dst) {
    while (!isEmpty())
        dst.add(pop());
}
```

Again, this compiles cleanly and works fine if the element type of the destination collection exactly matches that of the stack. But again, it isn't entirely satisfactory. Suppose you have a Stack<Number> and variable of type Object. If you pop an element from the stack and store it in the variable, it compiles and runs without error. So shouldn't you be able to do this, too?

```
Stack<Number> numberStack = new Stack<Number>();
Collection<Object> objects = ... ;
numberStack.popAll(objects);
```

If you try to compile this client code against the version of popAll shown earlier, you'll get an error very similar to the one that we got with our first version of pushAll: Collection<Object> is not a subtype of Collection<Number>. Once again, wildcard types provide a way out. The type of the input parameter to popAll should not be "collection of E" but "collection of some supertype of E" (where supertype is defined such that E is a supertype of itself [JLS, 4.10]). Again, there is a wildcard type that means precisely that: Collection<? super E>. Let's modify popAll to use it:

```
// Wildcard type for parameter that serves as an E consumer
public void popAll(Collection<? super E> dst) {
    while (!isEmpty())
        dst.add(pop());
}
```

With this change, both Stack and the client code compile cleanly.

The lesson is clear. **For maximum flexibility, use wildcard types on input parameters that represent producers or consumers.** If an input parameter is both a producer and a consumer, then wildcard types will do you no good: you need an exact type match, which is what you get without any wildcards.

Here is a mnemonic to help you remember which wildcard type to use:

PECS stands for producer-extends, consumer-super.

In other words, if a parameterized type represents a T producer, use <? extends T>; if it represents a T consumer, use <? super T>. In our Stack example, pushAll's src parameter produces E instances for use by the Stack, so the appropriate type for src is Iterable<? extends E>; popAll's dst parameter consumes E instances from the Stack, so the appropriate type for dst is Collection<? super E>. The PECS mnemonic captures the fundamental principle that guides the use of wildcard types. Naftalin and Wadler call it the *Get and Put Principle* [Naftalin07, 2.4].

With this mnemonic in mind, let's take a look at some method and constructor declarations from previous items in this chapter. The Chooser constructor in Item 28 has this declaration:

```
public Chooser(Collection<T> choices)
```

This constructor uses the collection choices only to **produce** values of type T (and stores them for later use), so its declaration should use a wildcard type that **extends** T. Here's the resulting constructor declaration:

```
// Wildcard type for parameter that serves as an T producer
public Chooser(Collection<? extends T> choices)
```

And would this change make any difference in practice? Yes, it would. Suppose you have a List<Integer>, and you want to pass it in to the constructor for a Chooser<Number>. This would not compile with the original declaration, but it does once you add the bounded wildcard type to the declaration.

Now let's look at the union method from Item 30. Here is the declaration:

```
public static <E> Set<E> union(Set<E> s1, Set<E> s2)
```

Both parameters, s1 and s2, are E producers, so the PECS mnemonic tells us that the declaration should be as follows:

```
public static <E> Set<E> union(Set<? extends E> s1,
                               Set<? extends E> s2)
```

Note that the return type is still Set<E>. **Do not use bounded wildcard types as return types.** Rather than providing additional flexibility for your users, it would force them to use wildcard types in client code. With the revised declaration, this code will compile cleanly:

```
Set<Integer> integers = Set.of(1, 3, 5);
Set<Double>  doubles  = Set.of(2.0, 4.0, 6.0);
Set<Number>  numbers  = union(integers, doubles);
```

Properly used, wildcard types are nearly invisible to the users of a class. They cause methods to accept the parameters they should accept and reject those they should reject. **If the user of a class has to think about wildcard types, there is probably something wrong with its API.**

Prior to Java 8, the type inference rules were not clever enough to handle the previous code fragment, which requires the compiler to use the contextually specified return type (or *target type*) to infer the type of E. The target type of the union invocation shown earlier is Set<Number>. If you try to compile the fragment in an earlier version of Java (with an appropriate replacement for the Set.of factory), you'll get a long, convoluted error message like this:

```
Union.java:14: error: incompatible types
        Set<Number> numbers = union(integers, doubles);
                                   ^
  required: Set<Number>
  found:    Set<INT#1>
  where INT#1,INT#2 are intersection types:
    INT#1 extends Number,Comparable<? extends INT#2>
    INT#2 extends Number,Comparable<?>
```

Luckily there is a way to deal with this sort of error. If the compiler doesn't infer the correct type, you can always tell it what type to use with an *explicit type argument* [JLS, 15.12]. Even prior to the introduction of target typing in Java 8, this isn't something that you had to do often, which is good because explicit type arguments aren't very pretty. With the addition of an explicit type argument, as shown here, the code fragment compiles cleanly in versions prior to Java 8:

```
// Explicit type parameter - required prior to Java 8
Set<Number> numbers = Union.<Number>union(integers, doubles);
```

Next let's turn our attention to the max method in Item 30. Here is the original declaration:

```
public static <T extends Comparable<T>> T max(List<T> list)
```

Here is a revised declaration that uses wildcard types:

```
public static <T extends Comparable<? super T>> T max(
        List<? extends T> list)
```

To get the revised declaration from the original, we applied the PECS heuristic twice. The straightforward application is to the parameter list. It produces T instances, so we change the type from List<T> to List<? extends T>. The tricky application is to the type parameter T. This is the first time we've seen a wildcard applied to a type parameter. Originally, T was specified to extend Comparable<T>, but a comparable of T consumes T instances (and produces integers indicating order relations). Therefore, the parameterized type Comparable<T> is replaced by the bounded wildcard type Comparable<? super T>. Comparables are always consumers, so you should generally **use Comparable<? super T> in preference to Comparable<T>.** The same is true of comparators; therefore, you should generally **use Comparator<? super T> in preference to Comparator<T>.**

The revised max declaration is probably the most complex method declaration in this book. Does the added complexity really buy you anything? Again, it does. Here is a simple example of a list that would be excluded by the original declaration but is permitted by the revised one:

```
List<ScheduledFuture<?>> scheduledFutures = ... ;
```

The reason that you can't apply the original method declaration to this list is that ScheduledFuture does not implement Comparable<ScheduledFuture>. Instead, it is a subinterface of Delayed, which extends Comparable<Delayed>. In other words, a ScheduledFuture instance isn't merely comparable to other

ScheduledFuture instances; it is comparable to any Delayed instance, and that's enough to cause the original declaration to reject it. More generally, the wildcard is required to support types that do not implement Comparable (or Comparator) directly but extend a type that does.

There is one more wildcard-related topic that bears discussing. There is a duality between type parameters and wildcards, and many methods can be declared using one or the other. For example, here are two possible declarations for a static method to swap two indexed items in a list. The first uses an unbounded type parameter (Item 30) and the second an unbounded wildcard:

```
// Two possible declarations for the swap method
public static <E> void swap(List<E> list, int i, int j);
public static void swap(List<?> list, int i, int j);
```

Which of these two declarations is preferable, and why? In a public API, the second is better because it's simpler. You pass in a list—any list—and the method swaps the indexed elements. There is no type parameter to worry about. As a rule, **if a type parameter appears only once in a method declaration, replace it with a wildcard.** If it's an unbounded type parameter, replace it with an unbounded wildcard; if it's a bounded type parameter, replace it with a bounded wildcard.

There's one problem with the second declaration for swap. The straightforward implementation won't compile:

```
public static void swap(List<?> list, int i, int j) {
    list.set(i, list.set(j, list.get(i)));
}
```

Trying to compile it produces this less-than-helpful error message:

```
Swap.java:5: error: incompatible types: Object cannot be
converted to CAP#1
        list.set(i, list.set(j, list.get(i)));
                                             ^
  where CAP#1 is a fresh type-variable:
    CAP#1 extends Object from capture of ?
```

It doesn't seem right that we can't put an element back into the list that we just took it out of. The problem is that the type of list is List<?>, and you can't put any value except null into a List<?>. Fortunately, there is a way to implement this method without resorting to an unsafe cast or a raw type. The idea is to write a private helper method to *capture* the wildcard type. The helper method must be a generic method in order to capture the type. Here's how it looks:

```
public static void swap(List<?> list, int i, int j) {
    swapHelper(list, i, j);
}

// Private helper method for wildcard capture
private static <E> void swapHelper(List<E> list, int i, int j) {
    list.set(i, list.set(j, list.get(i)));
}
```

The swapHelper method knows that list is a List<E>. Therefore, it knows that any value it gets out of this list is of type E and that it's safe to put any value of type E into the list. This slightly convoluted implementation of swap compiles cleanly. It allows us to export the nice wildcard-based declaration, while taking advantage of the more complex generic method internally. Clients of the swap method don't have to confront the more complex swapHelper declaration, but they do benefit from it. It is worth noting that the helper method has precisely the signature that we dismissed as too complex for the public method.

In summary, using wildcard types in your APIs, while tricky, makes the APIs far more flexible. If you write a library that will be widely used, the proper use of wildcard types should be considered mandatory. Remember the basic rule: producer-extends, consumer-super (PECS). Also remember that all comparables and comparators are consumers.

Item 32: Combine generics and varargs judiciously

Varargs methods (Item 53) and generics were both added to the platform in Java 5, so you might expect them to interact gracefully; sadly, they do not. The purpose of varargs is to allow clients to pass a variable number of arguments to a method, but it is a *leaky abstraction*: when you invoke a varargs method, an array is created to hold the varargs parameters; that array, which should be an implementation detail, is visible. As a consequence, you get confusing compiler warnings when varargs parameters have generic or parameterized types.

Recall from Item 28 that a non-reifiable type is one whose runtime representation has less information than its compile-time representation, and that nearly all generic and parameterized types are non-reifiable. If a method declares its varargs parameter to be of a non-reifiable type, the compiler generates a warning on the declaration. If the method is invoked on varargs parameters whose inferred type is non-reifiable, the compiler generates a warning on the invocation too. The warnings look something like this:

```
warning: [unchecked] Possible heap pollution from
    parameterized vararg type List<String>
```

Heap pollution occurs when a variable of a parameterized type refers to an object that is not of that type [JLS, 4.12.2]. It can cause the compiler's automatically generated casts to fail, violating the fundamental guarantee of the generic type system.

For example, consider this method, which is a thinly disguised variant of the code fragment on page 127:

```
// Mixing generics and varargs can violate type safety!
static void dangerous(List<String>... stringLists) {
    List<Integer> intList = List.of(42);
    Object[] objects = stringLists;
    objects[0] = intList;              // Heap pollution
    String s = stringLists[0].get(0); // ClassCastException
}
```

This method has no visible casts yet throws a ClassCastException when invoked with one or more arguments. Its last line has an invisible cast that is generated by the compiler. This cast fails, demonstrating that type safety has been compromised, and **it is unsafe to store a value in a generic varargs array parameter.**

This example raises an interesting question: Why is it even legal to declare a method with a generic varargs parameter, when it is illegal to create a generic array explicitly? In other words, why does the method shown previously generate only a warning, while the code fragment on page 127 generates an error? The answer is that methods with varargs parameters of generic or parameterized types can be very useful in practice, so the language designers opted to live with this inconsistency. In fact, the Java libraries export several such methods, including `Arrays.asList(T... a)`, `Collections.addAll(Collection<? super T> c, T... elements)`, and `EnumSet.of(E first, E... rest)`. Unlike the dangerous method shown earlier, these library methods are typesafe.

Prior to Java 7, there was nothing the author of a method with a generic varargs parameter could do about the warnings at the call sites. This made these APIs unpleasant to use. Users had to put up with the warnings or, preferably, to eliminate them with `@SuppressWarnings("unchecked")` annotations at every call site (Item 27). This was tedious, harmed readability, and hid warnings that flagged real issues.

In Java 7, the `SafeVarargs` annotation was added to the platform, to allow the author of a method with a generic varargs parameter to suppress client warnings automatically. In essence, **the `SafeVarargs` annotation constitutes a promise by the author of a method that it is typesafe.** In exchange for this promise, the compiler agrees not to warn the users of the method that calls may be unsafe.

It is critical that you do not annotate a method with `@SafeVarargs` unless it actually *is* safe. So what does it take to ensure this? Recall that a generic array is created when the method is invoked, to hold the varargs parameters. If the method doesn't store anything into the array (which would overwrite the parameters) and doesn't allow a reference to the array to escape (which would enable untrusted code to access the array), then it's safe. In other words, if the varargs parameter array is used only to transmit a variable number of arguments from the caller to the method—which is, after all, the purpose of varargs—then the method is safe.

It is worth noting that you can violate type safety without ever storing anything in the varargs parameter array. Consider the following generic varargs method, which returns an array containing its parameters. At first glance, it may look like a handy little utility:

```
// UNSAFE - Exposes a reference to its generic parameter array!
static <T> T[] toArray(T... args) {
    return args;
}
```

This method simply returns its varargs parameter array. The method may not look dangerous, but it is! The type of this array is determined by the compile-time types of the arguments passed in to the method, and the compiler may not have enough information to make an accurate determination. Because this method returns its varargs parameter array, it can propagate heap pollution up the call stack.

To make this concrete, consider the following generic method, which takes three arguments of type T and returns an array containing two of the arguments, chosen at random:

```
static <T> T[] pickTwo(T a, T b, T c) {
    switch(ThreadLocalRandom.current().nextInt(3)) {
      case 0: return toArray(a, b);
      case 1: return toArray(a, c);
      case 2: return toArray(b, c);
    }
    throw new AssertionError(); // Can't get here
}
```

This method is not, in and of itself, dangerous and would not generate a warning except that it invokes the toArray method, which has a generic varargs parameter.

When compiling this method, the compiler generates code to create a varargs parameter array in which to pass two T instances to toArray. This code allocates an array of type Object[], which is the most specific type that is guaranteed to hold these instances, no matter what types of objects are passed to pickTwo at the call site. The toArray method simply returns this array to pickTwo, which in turn returns it to its caller, so pickTwo will always return an array of type Object[].

Now consider this main method, which exercises pickTwo:

```
public static void main(String[] args) {
    String[] attributes = pickTwo("Good", "Fast", "Cheap");
}
```

There is nothing at all wrong with this method, so it compiles without generating any warnings. But when you run it, it throws a ClassCastException, though it contains no visible casts. What you don't see is that the compiler has generated a hidden cast to String[] on the value returned by pickTwo so that it can be stored in attributes. The cast fails, because Object[] is not a subtype of String[]. This failure is quite disconcerting because it is two levels removed from the method that actually causes the heap pollution (toArray), and the varargs parameter array is not modified after the actual parameters are stored in it.

This example is meant to drive home the point that **it is unsafe to give another method access to a generic varargs parameter array,** with two exceptions: it is safe to pass the array to another varargs method that is correctly annotated with @SafeVarargs, and it is safe to pass the array to a non-varargs method that merely computes some function of the contents of the array.

Here is a typical example of a safe use of a generic varargs parameter. This method takes an arbitrary number of lists as arguments and returns a single list containing the elements of all of the input lists in sequence. Because the method is annotated with @SafeVarargs, it doesn't generate any warnings, on the declaration or at its call sites:

```
// Safe method with a generic varargs parameter
@SafeVarargs
static <T> List<T> flatten(List<? extends T>... lists) {
    List<T> result = new ArrayList<>();
    for (List<? extends T> list : lists)
        result.addAll(list);
    return result;
}
```

The rule for deciding when to use the SafeVarargs annotation is simple: **Use @SafeVarargs on every method with a varargs parameter of a generic or parameterized type,** so its users won't be burdened by needless and confusing compiler warnings. This implies that you should *never* write unsafe varargs methods like dangerous or toArray. Every time the compiler warns you of possible heap pollution from a generic varargs parameter in a method you control, check that the method is safe. As a reminder, a generic varargs methods is safe if:

1. it doesn't store anything in the varargs parameter array, and

2. it doesn't make the array (or a clone) visible to untrusted code.

If either of these prohibitions is violated, fix it.

Note that the SafeVarargs annotation is legal only on methods that can't be overridden, because it is impossible to guarantee that every possible overriding method will be safe. In Java 8, the annotation was legal only on static methods and final instance methods; in Java 9, it became legal on private instance methods as well.

An alternative to using the SafeVarargs annotation is to take the advice of Item 28 and replace the varargs parameter (which is an array in disguise) with a List parameter. Here's how this approach looks when applied to our flatten method. Note that only the parameter declaration has changed:

```
// List as a typesafe alternative to a generic varargs parameter
static <T> List<T> flatten(List<List<? extends T>> lists) {
    List<T> result = new ArrayList<>();
    for (List<? extends T> list : lists)
        result.addAll(list);
    return result;
}
```

This method can then be used in conjunction with the static factory method
List.of to allow for a variable number of arguments. Note that this approach
relies on the fact that the List.of declaration is annotated with @SafeVarargs:

```
audience = flatten(List.of(friends, romans, countrymen));
```

The advantage of this approach is that the compiler can *prove* that the method
is typesafe. You don't have to vouch for its safety with a SafeVarargs annotation,
and you don't have worry that you might have erred in determining that it was
safe. The main disadvantage is that the client code is a bit more verbose and may
be a bit slower.

This trick can also be used in situations where it is impossible to write a safe
varargs method, as is the case with the toArray method on page 147. Its List analogue *is* the List.of method, so we don't even have to write it; the Java libraries
authors have done the work for us. The pickTwo method then becomes this:

```
static <T> List<T> pickTwo(T a, T b, T c) {
    switch(rnd.nextInt(3)) {
      case 0: return List.of(a, b);
      case 1: return List.of(a, c);
      case 2: return List.of(b, c);
    }
    throw new AssertionError();
}
```

and the main method becomes this:

```
public static void main(String[] args) {
    List<String> attributes = pickTwo("Good", "Fast", "Cheap");
}
```

The resulting code is typesafe because it uses only generics, and not arrays.

In summary, varargs and generics do not interact well because the varargs
facility is a leaky abstraction built atop arrays, and arrays have different type rules
from generics. Though generic varargs parameters are not typesafe, they are legal.
If you choose to write a method with a generic (or parameterized) varargs parameter, first ensure that the method is typesafe, and then annotate it with @Safe-
Varargs so it is not unpleasant to use.

Item 33: Consider typesafe heterogeneous containers

Common uses of generics include collections, such as Set<E> and Map<K,V>, and single-element containers, such as ThreadLocal<T> and AtomicReference<T>. In all of these uses, it is the container that is parameterized. This limits you to a fixed number of type parameters per container. Normally that is exactly what you want. A Set has a single type parameter, representing its element type; a Map has two, representing its key and value types; and so forth.

Sometimes, however, you need more flexibility. For example, a database row can have arbitrarily many columns, and it would be nice to be able to access all of them in a typesafe manner. Luckily, there is an easy way to achieve this effect. The idea is to parameterize the *key* instead of the *container*. Then present the parameterized key to the container to insert or retrieve a value. The generic type system is used to guarantee that the type of the value agrees with its key.

As a simple example of this approach, consider a Favorites class that allows its clients to store and retrieve a favorite instance of arbitrarily many types. The Class object for the type will play the part of the parameterized key. The reason this works is that class Class is generic. The type of a class literal is not simply Class, but Class<T>. For example, String.class is of type Class<String>, and Integer.class is of type Class<Integer>. When a class literal is passed among methods to communicate both compile-time and runtime type information, it is called a *type token* [Bracha04].

The API for the Favorites class is simple. It looks just like a simple map, except that the key is parameterized instead of the map. The client presents a Class object when setting and getting favorites. Here is the API:

```
// Typesafe heterogeneous container pattern - API
public class Favorites {
    public <T> void putFavorite(Class<T> type, T instance);
    public <T> T getFavorite(Class<T> type);
}
```

Here is a sample program that exercises the Favorites class, storing, retrieving, and printing a favorite String, Integer, and Class instance:

```
// Typesafe heterogeneous container pattern - client
public static void main(String[] args) {
    Favorites f = new Favorites();
    f.putFavorite(String.class, "Java");
    f.putFavorite(Integer.class, 0xcafebabe);
    f.putFavorite(Class.class, Favorites.class);
```

```java
    String favoriteString = f.getFavorite(String.class);
    int favoriteInteger = f.getFavorite(Integer.class);
    Class<?> favoriteClass = f.getFavorite(Class.class);
    System.out.printf("%s %x %s%n", favoriteString,
        favoriteInteger, favoriteClass.getName());
}
```

As you would expect, this program prints Java cafebabe Favorites. Note, incidentally, that Java's printf method differs from C's in that you should use %n where you'd use \n in C. The %n generates the applicable platform-specific line separator, which is \n on many but not all platforms.

A Favorites instance is *typesafe*: it will never return an Integer when you ask it for a String. It is also *heterogeneous*: unlike an ordinary map, all the keys are of different types. Therefore, we call Favorites a *typesafe heterogeneous container.*

The implementation of Favorites is surprisingly tiny. Here it is, in its entirety:

```java
// Typesafe heterogeneous container pattern - implementation
public class Favorites {
    private Map<Class<?>, Object> favorites = new HashMap<>();

    public <T> void putFavorite(Class<T> type, T instance) {
        favorites.put(Objects.requireNonNull(type), instance);
    }

    public <T> T getFavorite(Class<T> type) {
        return type.cast(favorites.get(type));
    }
}
```

There are a few subtle things going on here. Each Favorites instance is backed by a private Map<Class<?>, Object> called favorites. You might think that you couldn't put anything into this Map because of the unbounded wildcard type, but the truth is quite the opposite. The thing to notice is that the wildcard type is nested: it's not the type of the map that's a wildcard type but the type of its key. This means that every key can have a *different* parameterized type: one can be Class<String>, the next Class<Integer>, and so on. That's where the heterogeneity comes from.

The next thing to notice is that the value type of the favorites Map is simply Object. In other words, the Map does not guarantee the type relationship between keys and values, which is that every value is of the type represented by its key. In fact, Java's type system is not powerful enough to express this. But we know that it's true, and we take advantage of it when the time comes to retrieve a favorite.

The putFavorite implementation is trivial: it simply puts into favorites a mapping from the given Class object to the given favorite instance. As noted, this discards the "type linkage" between the key and the value; it loses the knowledge that the value is an instance of the key. But that's OK, because the getFavorites method can and does reestablish this linkage.

The implementation of getFavorite is trickier than that of putFavorite. First, it gets from the favorites map the value corresponding to the given Class object. This is the correct object reference to return, but it has the wrong compile-time type: it is Object (the value type of the favorites map) and we need to return a T. So, the getFavorite implementation *dynamically casts* the object reference to the type represented by the Class object, using Class's cast method.

The cast method is the dynamic analogue of Java's cast operator. It simply checks that its argument is an instance of the type represented by the Class object. If so, it returns the argument; otherwise it throws a ClassCastException. We know that the cast invocation in getFavorite won't throw ClassCastException, assuming the client code compiled cleanly. That is to say, we know that the values in the favorites map always match the types of their keys.

So what does the cast method do for us, given that it simply returns its argument? The signature of the cast method takes full advantage of the fact that class Class is generic. Its return type is the type parameter of the Class object:

```
public class Class<T> {
    T cast(Object obj);
}
```

This is precisely what's needed by the getFavorite method. It is what allows us to make Favorites typesafe without resorting to an unchecked cast to T.

There are two limitations to the Favorites class that are worth noting. First, a malicious client could easily corrupt the type safety of a Favorites instance, by using a Class object in its raw form. But the resulting client code would generate an unchecked warning when it was compiled. This is no different from a normal collection implementations such as HashSet and HashMap. You can easily put a String into a HashSet<Integer> by using the raw type HashSet (Item 26). That said, you can have runtime type safety if you're willing to pay for it. The way to ensure that Favorites never violates its type invariant is to have the putFavorite method check that `instance` is actually an instance of the type represented by type, and we already know how to do this. Just use a dynamic cast:

```
// Achieving runtime type safety with a dynamic cast
public <T> void putFavorite(Class<T> type, T instance) {
    favorites.put(type, type.cast(instance));
}
```

There are collection wrappers in `java.util.Collections` that play the same trick. They are called `checkedSet`, `checkedList`, `checkedMap`, and so forth. Their static factories take a `Class` object (or two) in addition to a collection (or map). The static factories are generic methods, ensuring that the compile-time types of the `Class` object and the collection match. The wrappers add reification to the collections they wrap. For example, the wrapper throws a `ClassCastException` at runtime if someone tries to put a `Coin` into your `Collection<Stamp>`. These wrappers are useful for tracking down client code that adds an incorrectly typed element to a collection, in an application that mixes generic and raw types.

The second limitation of the `Favorites` class is that it cannot be used on a non-reifiable type (Item 28). In other words, you can store your favorite `String` or `String[]`, but not your favorite `List<String>`. If you try to store your favorite `List<String>`, your program won't compile. The reason is that you can't get a `Class` object for `List<String>`. The class literal `List<String>.class` is a syntax error, and it's a good thing, too. `List<String>` and `List<Integer>` share a single `Class` object, which is `List.class`. It would wreak havoc with the internals of a `Favorites` object if the "type literals" `List<String>.class` and `List<Integer>.class` were legal and returned the same object reference. There is no entirely satisfactory workaround for this limitation.

The type tokens used by `Favorites` are unbounded: `getFavorite` and `putFavorite` accept any `Class` object. Sometimes you may need to limit the types that can be passed to a method. This can be achieved with a *bounded type token*, which is simply a type token that places a bound on what type can be represented, using a bounded type parameter (Item 30) or a bounded wildcard (Item 31).

The annotations API (Item 39) makes extensive use of bounded type tokens. For example, here is the method to read an annotation at runtime. This method comes from the `AnnotatedElement` interface, which is implemented by the reflective types that represent classes, methods, fields, and other program elements:

```
public <T extends Annotation>
    T getAnnotation(Class<T> annotationType);
```

The argument, annotationType, is a bounded type token representing an annotation type. The method returns the element's annotation of that type, if it has one, or null, if it doesn't. In essence, an annotated element is a typesafe heterogeneous container whose keys are annotation types.

Suppose you have an object of type Class<?> and you want to pass it to a method that requires a bounded type token, such as getAnnotation. You could cast the object to Class<? extends Annotation>, but this cast is unchecked, so it would generate a compile-time warning (Item 27). Luckily, class Class provides an instance method that performs this sort of cast safely (and dynamically). The method is called asSubclass, and it casts the Class object on which it is called to represent a subclass of the class represented by its argument. If the cast succeeds, the method returns its argument; if it fails, it throws a ClassCastException.

Here's how you use the asSubclass method to read an annotation whose type is unknown at compile time. This method compiles without error or warning:

```
// Use of asSubclass to safely cast to a bounded type token
static Annotation getAnnotation(AnnotatedElement element,
                                String annotationTypeName) {
    Class<?> annotationType = null; // Unbounded type token
    try {
        annotationType = Class.forName(annotationTypeName);
    } catch (Exception ex) {
        throw new IllegalArgumentException(ex);
    }
    return element.getAnnotation(
        annotationType.asSubclass(Annotation.class));
}
```

In summary, the normal use of generics, exemplified by the collections APIs, restricts you to a fixed number of type parameters per container. You can get around this restriction by placing the type parameter on the key rather than the container. You can use Class objects as keys for such typesafe heterogeneous containers. A Class object used in this fashion is called a type token. You can also use a custom key type. For example, you could have a DatabaseRow type representing a database row (the container), and a generic type Column<T> as its key.

Enums and Annotations

JAVA supports two special-purpose families of reference types: a kind of class called an *enum type,* and a kind of interface called an *annotation type*. This chapter discusses best practices for using these type families.

Item 34: Use enums instead of `int` constants

An *enumerated type* is a type whose legal values consist of a fixed set of constants, such as the seasons of the year, the planets in the solar system, or the suits in a deck of playing cards. Before enum types were added to the language, a common pattern for representing enumerated types was to declare a group of named `int` constants, one for each member of the type:

```
// The int enum pattern - severely deficient!
public static final int APPLE_FUJI         = 0;
public static final int APPLE_PIPPIN       = 1;
public static final int APPLE_GRANNY_SMITH = 2;

public static final int ORANGE_NAVEL  = 0;
public static final int ORANGE_TEMPLE = 1;
public static final int ORANGE_BLOOD  = 2;
```

This technique, known as the *int enum pattern,* has many shortcomings. It provides nothing in the way of type safety and little in the way of expressive power. The compiler won't complain if you pass an apple to a method that expects an orange, compare apples to oranges with the == operator, or worse:

```
// Tasty citrus flavored applesauce!
int i = (APPLE_FUJI - ORANGE_TEMPLE) / APPLE_PIPPIN;
```

Note that the name of each apple constant is prefixed with APPLE_ and the name of each orange constant is prefixed with ORANGE_. This is because Java doesn't provide namespaces for int enum groups. Prefixes prevent name clashes when two int enum groups have identically named constants, for example between ELEMENT_MERCURY and PLANET_MERCURY.

Programs that use int enums are brittle. Because int enums are *constant variables* [JLS, 4.12.4], their int values are compiled into the clients that use them [JLS, 13.1]. If the value associated with an int enum is changed, its clients must be recompiled. If not, the clients will still run, but their behavior will be incorrect.

There is no easy way to translate int enum constants into printable strings. If you print such a constant or display it from a debugger, all you see is a number, which isn't very helpful. There is no reliable way to iterate over all the int enum constants in a group, or even to obtain the size of an int enum group.

You may encounter a variant of this pattern in which String constants are used in place of int constants. This variant, known as the *String enum pattern*, is even less desirable. While it does provide printable strings for its constants, it can lead naive users to hard-code string constants into client code instead of using field names. If such a hard-coded string constant contains a typographical error, it will escape detection at compile time and result in bugs at runtime. Also, it might lead to performance problems, because it relies on string comparisons.

Luckily, Java provides an alternative that avoids all the shortcomings of the int and string enum patterns and provides many added benefits. It is the *enum type* [JLS, 8.9]. Here's how it looks in its simplest form:

```
public enum Apple  { FUJI, PIPPIN, GRANNY_SMITH }
public enum Orange { NAVEL, TEMPLE, BLOOD }
```

On the surface, these enum types may appear similar to those of other languages, such as C, C++, and C#, but appearances are deceiving. Java's enum types are full-fledged classes, far more powerful than their counterparts in these other languages, where enums are essentially int values.

The basic idea behind Java's enum types is simple: they are classes that export one instance for each enumeration constant via a public static final field. Enum types are effectively final, by virtue of having no accessible constructors. Because clients can neither create instances of an enum type nor extend it, there can be no instances but the declared enum constants. In other words, enum types are instance-controlled (page 6). They are a generalization of singletons (Item 3), which are essentially single-element enums.

Enums provide compile-time type safety. If you declare a parameter to be of type Apple, you are guaranteed that any non-null object reference passed to the parameter is one of the three valid Apple values. Attempts to pass values of the wrong type will result in compile-time errors, as will attempts to assign an expression of one enum type to a variable of another, or to use the == operator to compare values of different enum types.

Enum types with identically named constants coexist peacefully because each type has its own namespace. You can add or reorder constants in an enum type without recompiling its clients because the fields that export the constants provide a layer of insulation between an enum type and its clients: constant values are not compiled into the clients as they are in the int enum patterns. Finally, you can translate enums into printable strings by calling their toString method.

In addition to rectifying the deficiencies of int enums, enum types let you add arbitrary methods and fields and implement arbitrary interfaces. They provide high-quality implementations of all the Object methods (Chapter 3), they implement Comparable (Item 14) and Serializable (Chapter 12), and their serialized form is designed to withstand most changes to the enum type.

So why would you want to add methods or fields to an enum type? For starters, you might want to associate data with its constants. Our Apple and Orange types, for example, might benefit from a method that returns the color of the fruit, or one that returns an image of it. You can augment an enum type with any method that seems appropriate. An enum type can start life as a simple collection of enum constants and evolve over time into a full-featured abstraction.

For a nice example of a rich enum type, consider the eight planets of our solar system. Each planet has a mass and a radius, and from these two attributes you can compute its surface gravity. This in turn lets you compute the weight of an object on the planet's surface, given the mass of the object. Here's how this enum looks. The numbers in parentheses after each enum constant are parameters that are passed to its constructor. In this case, they are the planet's mass and radius:

```
// Enum type with data and behavior
public enum Planet {
    MERCURY(3.302e+23, 2.439e6),
    VENUS  (4.869e+24, 6.052e6),
    EARTH  (5.975e+24, 6.378e6),
    MARS   (6.419e+23, 3.393e6),
    JUPITER(1.899e+27, 7.149e7),
    SATURN (5.685e+26, 6.027e7),
    URANUS (8.683e+25, 2.556e7),
    NEPTUNE(1.024e+26, 2.477e7);

    private final double mass;          // In kilograms
    private final double radius;        // In meters
    private final double surfaceGravity; // In m / s^2
```

```
    // Universal gravitational constant in m^3 / kg s^2
    private static final double G = 6.67300E-11;

    // Constructor
    Planet(double mass, double radius) {
        this.mass = mass;
        this.radius = radius;
        surfaceGravity = G * mass / (radius * radius);
    }

    public double mass()           { return mass; }
    public double radius()         { return radius; }
    public double surfaceGravity() { return surfaceGravity; }

    public double surfaceWeight(double mass) {
        return mass * surfaceGravity;   // F = ma
    }
}
```

It is easy to write a rich enum type such as Planet. **To associate data with enum constants, declare instance fields and write a constructor that takes the data and stores it in the fields.** Enums are by their nature immutable, so all fields should be final (Item 17). Fields can be public, but it is better to make them private and provide public accessors (Item 16). In the case of Planet, the constructor also computes and stores the surface gravity, but this is just an optimization. The gravity could be recomputed from the mass and radius each time it was used by the surfaceWeight method, which takes an object's mass and returns its weight on the planet represented by the constant.

While the Planet enum is simple, it is surprisingly powerful. Here is a short program that takes the earth weight of an object (in any unit) and prints a nice table of the object's weight on all eight planets (in the same unit):

```
public class WeightTable {
    public static void main(String[] args) {
        double earthWeight = Double.parseDouble(args[0]);
        double mass = earthWeight / Planet.EARTH.surfaceGravity();
        for (Planet p : Planet.values())
            System.out.printf("Weight on %s is %f%n",
                              p, p.surfaceWeight(mass));
    }
}
```

Note that Planet, like all enums, has a static values method that returns an array of its values in the order they were declared. Note also that the toString method returns the declared name of each enum value, enabling easy printing by println and printf. If you're dissatisfied with this string representation, you can change it by overriding the `toString` method. Here is the result of running our `WeightTable` program (which doesn't override `toString`) with the command line argument 185:

```
Weight on MERCURY is 69.912739
Weight on VENUS is 167.434436
Weight on EARTH is 185.000000
Weight on MARS is 70.226739
Weight on JUPITER is 467.990696
Weight on SATURN is 197.120111
Weight on URANUS is 167.398264
Weight on NEPTUNE is 210.208751
```

Until 2006, two years after enums were added to Java, Pluto was a planet. This raises the question "what happens when you remove an element from an enum type?" The answer is that any client program that doesn't refer to the removed element will continue to work fine. So, for example, our `WeightTable` program would simply print a table with one fewer row. And what of a client program that refers to the removed element (in this case, `Planet.Pluto`)? If you recompile the client program, the compilation will fail with a helpful error message at the line that refers to the erstwhile planet; if you fail to recompile the client, it will throw a helpful exception from this line at runtime. This is the best behavior you could hope for, far better than what you'd get with the int enum pattern.

Some behaviors associated with enum constants may need to be used only from within the class or package in which the enum is defined. Such behaviors are best implemented as private or package-private methods. Each constant then carries with it a hidden collection of behaviors that allows the class or package containing the enum to react appropriately when presented with the constant. Just as with other classes, unless you have a compelling reason to expose an enum method to its clients, declare it private or, if need be, package-private (Item 15).

If an enum is generally useful, it should be a top-level class; if its use is tied to a specific top-level class, it should be a member class of that top-level class (Item 24). For example, the `java.math.RoundingMode` enum represents a rounding mode for decimal fractions. These rounding modes are used by the `BigDecimal` class, but they provide a useful abstraction that is not fundamentally tied to `BigDecimal`. By making `RoundingMode` a top-level enum, the library designers encourage any programmer who needs rounding modes to reuse this enum, leading to increased consistency across APIs.

The techniques demonstrated in the `Planet` example are sufficient for most enum types, but sometimes you need more. There is different data associated with each `Planet` constant, but sometimes you need to associate fundamentally different *behavior* with each constant. For example, suppose you are writing an enum type to represent the operations on a basic four-function calculator and you want to provide a method to perform the arithmetic operation represented by each constant. One way to achieve this is to switch on the value of the enum:

```java
// Enum type that switches on its own value - questionable
public enum Operation {
    PLUS, MINUS, TIMES, DIVIDE;

    // Do the arithmetic operation represented by this constant
    public double apply(double x, double y) {
        switch(this) {
            case PLUS:   return x + y;
            case MINUS:  return x - y;
            case TIMES:  return x * y;
            case DIVIDE: return x / y;
        }
        throw new AssertionError("Unknown op: " + this);
    }
}
```

This code works, but it isn't very pretty. It won't compile without the `throw` statement because the end of the method is technically reachable, even though it will never be reached [JLS, 14.21]. Worse, the code is fragile. If you add a new enum constant but forget to add a corresponding case to the `switch`, the enum will still compile, but it will fail at runtime when you try to apply the new operation.

Luckily, there is a better way to associate a different behavior with each enum constant: declare an abstract `apply` method in the enum type, and override it with a concrete method for each constant in a *constant-specific class body*. Such methods are known as *constant-specific method implementations*:

```java
// Enum type with constant-specific method implementations
public enum Operation {
    PLUS   {public double apply(double x, double y){return x + y;}},
    MINUS  {public double apply(double x, double y){return x - y;}},
    TIMES  {public double apply(double x, double y){return x * y;}},
    DIVIDE {public double apply(double x, double y){return x / y;}};

    public abstract double apply(double x, double y);
}
```

If you add a new constant to the second version of `Operation`, it is unlikely that you'll forget to provide an `apply` method, because the method immediately follows each constant declaration. In the unlikely event that you do forget, the compiler will remind you because abstract methods in an enum type must be overridden with concrete methods in all of its constants.

Constant-specific method implementations can be combined with constant-specific data. For example, here is a version of Operation that overrides the toString method to return the symbol commonly associated with the operation:

```
// Enum type with constant-specific class bodies and data
public enum Operation {
    PLUS("+") {
        public double apply(double x, double y) { return x + y; }
    },
    MINUS("-") {
        public double apply(double x, double y) { return x - y; }
    },
    TIMES("*") {
        public double apply(double x, double y) { return x * y; }
    },
    DIVIDE("/") {
        public double apply(double x, double y) { return x / y; }
    };

    private final String symbol;

    Operation(String symbol) { this.symbol = symbol; }

    @Override public String toString() { return symbol; }

    public abstract double apply(double x, double y);
}
```

The toString implementation shown makes it easy to print arithmetic expressions, as demonstrated by this little program:

```
public static void main(String[] args) {
    double x = Double.parseDouble(args[0]);
    double y = Double.parseDouble(args[1]);
    for (Operation op : Operation.values())
        System.out.printf("%f %s %f = %f%n",
                          x, op, y, op.apply(x, y));
}
```

Running this program with 2 and 4 as command line arguments produces the following output:

```
2.000000 + 4.000000 = 6.000000
2.000000 - 4.000000 = -2.000000
2.000000 * 4.000000 = 8.000000
2.000000 / 4.000000 = 0.500000
```

Enum types have an automatically generated `valueOf(String)` method that translates a constant's name into the constant itself. If you override the `toString` method in an enum type, consider writing a `fromString` method to translate the custom string representation back to the corresponding enum. The following code (with the type name changed appropriately) will do the trick for any enum, so long as each constant has a unique string representation:

```
// Implementing a fromString method on an enum type
private static final Map<String, Operation> stringToEnum =
        Stream.of(values()).collect(
            toMap(Object::toString, e -> e));

// Returns Operation for string, if any
public static Optional<Operation> fromString(String symbol) {
    return Optional.ofNullable(stringToEnum.get(symbol));
}
```

Note that the `Operation` constants are put into the `stringToEnum` map from a static field initialization that runs after the enum constants have been created. The previous code uses a stream (Chapter 7) over the array returned by the `values()` method; prior to Java 8, we would have created an empty hash map and iterated over the values array inserting the string-to-enum mappings into the map, and you can still do it that way if you prefer. But note that attempting to have each constant put itself into a map from its own constructor does *not* work. It would cause a compilation error, which is good thing because if it were legal, it would cause a `NullPointerException` at runtime. Enum constructors aren't permitted to access the enum's static fields, with the exception of constant variables (Item 34). This restriction is necessary because static fields have not yet been initialized when enum constructors run. A special case of this restriction is that enum constants cannot access one another from their constructors.

Also note that the `fromString` method returns an `Optional<String>`. This allows the method to indicate that the string that was passed in does not represent a valid operation, and it forces the client to confront this possibility (Item 55).

A disadvantage of constant-specific method implementations is that they make it harder to share code among enum constants. For example, consider an enum representing the days of the week in a payroll package. This enum has a method that calculates a worker's pay for that day given the worker's base salary (per hour) and the number of minutes worked on that day. On the five weekdays, any time worked in excess of a normal shift generates overtime pay; on the two weekend days, all work generates overtime pay. With a `switch` statement, it's easy to do this calculation by applying multiple case labels to each of two code fragments:

```
// Enum that switches on its value to share code - questionable
enum PayrollDay {
    MONDAY, TUESDAY, WEDNESDAY, THURSDAY, FRIDAY,
    SATURDAY, SUNDAY;

    private static final int MINS_PER_SHIFT = 8 * 60;

    int pay(int minutesWorked, int payRate) {
        int basePay = minutesWorked * payRate;

        int overtimePay;
        switch(this) {
          case SATURDAY: case SUNDAY: // Weekend
            overtimePay = basePay / 2;
            break;
          default: // Weekday
            overtimePay = minutesWorked <= MINS_PER_SHIFT ?
              0 : (minutesWorked - MINS_PER_SHIFT) * payRate / 2;
        }

        return basePay + overtimePay;
    }
}
```

This code is undeniably concise, but it is dangerous from a maintenance perspective. Suppose you add an element to the enum, perhaps a special value to represent a vacation day, but forget to add a corresponding case to the switch statement. The program will still compile, but the pay method will silently pay the worker the same amount for a vacation day as for an ordinary weekday.

To perform the pay calculation safely with constant-specific method implementations, you would have to duplicate the overtime pay computation for each constant, or move the computation into two helper methods, one for weekdays and one for weekend days, and invoke the appropriate helper method from each constant. Either approach would result in a fair amount of boilerplate code, substantially reducing readability and increasing the opportunity for error.

The boilerplate could be reduced by replacing the abstract overtimePay method on PayrollDay with a concrete method that performs the overtime calculation for weekdays. Then only the weekend days would have to override the method. But this would have the same disadvantage as the switch statement: if you added another day without overriding the overtimePay method, you would silently inherit the weekday calculation.

What you really want is to be *forced* to choose an overtime pay strategy each time you add an enum constant. Luckily, there is a nice way to achieve this. The idea is to move the overtime pay computation into a private nested enum, and to pass an instance of this *strategy enum* to the constructor for the Payroll Day enum. The PayrollDay enum then delegates the overtime pay calculation to the strategy enum, eliminating the need for a switch statement or constant-specific method implementation in PayrollDay. While this pattern is less concise than the switch statement, it is safer and more flexible:

```java
// The strategy enum pattern
enum PayrollDay {
    MONDAY, TUESDAY, WEDNESDAY, THURSDAY, FRIDAY,
    SATURDAY(PayType.WEEKEND), SUNDAY(PayType.WEEKEND);

    private final PayType payType;

    PayrollDay(PayType payType) { this.payType = payType; }
    PayrollDay() { this(PayType.WEEKDAY); }  // Default

    int pay(int minutesWorked, int payRate) {
        return payType.pay(minutesWorked, payRate);
    }

    // The strategy enum type
    private enum PayType {
        WEEKDAY {
            int overtimePay(int minsWorked, int payRate) {
                return minsWorked <= MINS_PER_SHIFT ? 0 :
                    (minsWorked - MINS_PER_SHIFT) * payRate / 2;
            }
        },
        WEEKEND {
            int overtimePay(int minsWorked, int payRate) {
                return minsWorked * payRate / 2;
            }
        };

        abstract int overtimePay(int mins, int payRate);
        private static final int MINS_PER_SHIFT = 8 * 60;

        int pay(int minsWorked, int payRate) {
            int basePay = minsWorked * payRate;
            return basePay + overtimePay(minsWorked, payRate);
        }
    }
}
```

If `switch` statements on enums are not a good choice for implementing constant-specific behavior on enums, what *are* they good for? **Switches on enums are good for augmenting enum types with constant-specific behavior.** For example, suppose the `Operation` enum is not under your control and you wish it had an instance method to return the inverse of each operation. You could simulate the effect with the following static method:

```
// Switch on an enum to simulate a missing method
public static Operation inverse(Operation op) {
    switch(op) {
        case PLUS:   return Operation.MINUS;
        case MINUS:  return Operation.PLUS;
        case TIMES:  return Operation.DIVIDE;
        case DIVIDE: return Operation.TIMES;

        default: throw new AssertionError("Unknown op: " + op);
    }
}
```

You should also use this technique on enum types that *are* under your control if a method simply doesn't belong in the enum type. The method may be required for some use but is not generally useful enough to merit inclusion in the enum type.

Enums are, generally speaking, comparable in performance to `int` constants. A minor performance disadvantage of enums is that there is a space and time cost to load and initialize enum types, but it is unlikely to be noticeable in practice.

So when should you use enums? **Use enums any time you need a set of constants whose members are known at compile time.** Of course, this includes "natural enumerated types," such as the planets, the days of the week, and the chess pieces. But it also includes other sets for which you know all the possible values at compile time, such as choices on a menu, operation codes, and command line flags. **It is not necessary that the set of constants in an enum type stay fixed for all time.** The enum feature was specifically designed to allow for binary compatible evolution of enum types.

In summary, the advantages of enum types over `int` constants are compelling. Enums are more readable, safer, and more powerful. Many enums require no explicit constructors or members, but others benefit from associating data with each constant and providing methods whose behavior is affected by this data. Fewer enums benefit from associating multiple behaviors with a single method. In this relatively rare case, prefer constant-specific methods to enums that switch on their own values. Consider the strategy enum pattern if some, but not all, enum constants share common behaviors.

Item 35: Use instance fields instead of ordinals

Many enums are naturally associated with a single int value. All enums have an ordinal method, which returns the numerical position of each enum constant in its type. You may be tempted to derive an associated int value from the ordinal:

```
// Abuse of ordinal to derive an associated value - DON'T DO THIS
public enum Ensemble {
    SOLO,   DUET,   TRIO, QUARTET, QUINTET,
    SEXTET, SEPTET, OCTET, NONET,  DECTET;

    public int numberOfMusicians() { return ordinal() + 1; }
}
```

While this enum works, it is a maintenance nightmare. If the constants are reordered, the numberOfMusicians method will break. If you want to add a second enum constant associated with an int value that you've already used, you're out of luck. For example, it might be nice to add a constant for *double quartet*, which, like an octet, consists of eight musicians, but there is no way to do it.

Also, you can't add a constant for an int value without adding constants for all intervening int values. For example, suppose you want to add a constant representing a *triple quartet*, which consists of twelve musicians. There is no standard term for an ensemble consisting of eleven musicians, so you are forced to add a dummy constant for the unused int value (11). At best, this is ugly. If many int values are unused, it's impractical.

Luckily, there is a simple solution to these problems. **Never derive a value associated with an enum from its ordinal; store it in an instance field instead:**

```
public enum Ensemble {
    SOLO(1), DUET(2), TRIO(3), QUARTET(4), QUINTET(5),
    SEXTET(6), SEPTET(7), OCTET(8), DOUBLE_QUARTET(8),
    NONET(9), DECTET(10), TRIPLE_QUARTET(12);

    private final int numberOfMusicians;
    Ensemble(int size) { this.numberOfMusicians = size; }
    public int numberOfMusicians() { return numberOfMusicians; }
}
```

The Enum specification has this to say about ordinal: "Most programmers will have no use for this method. It is designed for use by general-purpose enum-based data structures such as EnumSet and EnumMap." Unless you are writing code with this character, you are best off avoiding the ordinal method entirely.

Item 36: Use `EnumSet` instead of bit fields

If the elements of an enumerated type are used primarily in sets, it is traditional to use the `int` enum pattern (Item 34), assigning a different power of 2 to each constant:

```
// Bit field enumeration constants - OBSOLETE!
public class Text {
    public static final int STYLE_BOLD          = 1 << 0;  // 1
    public static final int STYLE_ITALIC        = 1 << 1;  // 2
    public static final int STYLE_UNDERLINE     = 1 << 2;  // 4
    public static final int STYLE_STRIKETHROUGH = 1 << 3;  // 8

    // Parameter is bitwise OR of zero or more STYLE_ constants
    public void applyStyles(int styles) { ... }
}
```

This representation lets you use the bitwise OR operation to combine several constants into a set, known as a *bit field*:

```
text.applyStyles(STYLE_BOLD | STYLE_ITALIC);
```

The bit field representation also lets you perform set operations such as union and intersection efficiently using bitwise arithmetic. But bit fields have all the disadvantages of `int` enum constants and more. It is even harder to interpret a bit field than a simple `int` enum constant when it is printed as a number. There is no easy way to iterate over all of the elements represented by a bit field. Finally, you have to predict the maximum number of bits you'll ever need at the time you're writing the API and choose a type for the bit field (typically `int` or `long`) accordingly. Once you've picked a type, you can't exceed its width (32 or 64 bits) without changing the API.

Some programmers who use enums in preference to `int` constants still cling to the use of bit fields when they need to pass around sets of constants. There is no reason to do this, because a better alternative exists. The `java.util` package provides the `EnumSet` class to efficiently represent sets of values drawn from a single enum type. This class implements the `Set` interface, providing all of the richness, type safety, and interoperability you get with any other `Set` implementation. But internally, each `EnumSet` is represented as a bit vector. If the underlying enum type has sixty-four or fewer elements—and most do—the entire `EnumSet` is represented with a single `long`, so its performance is comparable to that of a bit field. Bulk operations, such as `removeAll` and `retainAll`, are implemented using bitwise arithmetic, just as you'd do manually for bit fields. But you are insulated from the ugliness and error-proneness of manual bit twiddling: the EnumSet does the hard work for you.

Here is how the previous example looks when modified to use enums and enum sets instead of bit fields. It is shorter, clearer, and safer:

```
// EnumSet - a modern replacement for bit fields
public class Text {
    public enum Style { BOLD, ITALIC, UNDERLINE, STRIKETHROUGH }

    // Any Set could be passed in, but EnumSet is clearly best
    public void applyStyles(Set<Style> styles) { ... }
}
```

Here is client code that passes an EnumSet instance to the applyStyles method. The EnumSet class provides a rich set of static factories for easy set creation, one of which is illustrated in this code:

```
text.applyStyles(EnumSet.of(Style.BOLD, Style.ITALIC));
```

Note that the applyStyles method takes a Set<Style> rather than an EnumSet<Style>. While it seems likely that all clients would pass an EnumSet to the method, it is generally good practice to accept the interface type rather than the implementation type (Item 64). This allows for the possibility of an unusual client to pass in some other Set implementation.

In summary, **just because an enumerated type will be used in sets, there is no reason to represent it with bit fields.** The EnumSet class combines the conciseness and performance of bit fields with all the many advantages of enum types described in Item 34. The one real disadvantage of EnumSet is that it is not, as of Java 9, possible to create an immutable EnumSet, but this will likely be remedied in an upcoming release. In the meantime, you can wrap an EnumSet with Collections.unmodifiableSet, but conciseness and performance will suffer.

Item 37: Use EnumMap instead of ordinal indexing

Occasionally you may see code that uses the `ordinal` method (Item 35) to index into an array or list. For example, consider this simplistic class meant to represent a plant:

```
class Plant {
    enum LifeCycle { ANNUAL, PERENNIAL, BIENNIAL }

    final String name;
    final LifeCycle lifeCycle;

    Plant(String name, LifeCycle lifeCycle) {
        this.name = name;
        this.lifeCycle = lifeCycle;
    }

    @Override public String toString() {
        return name;
    }
}
```

Now suppose you have an array of plants representing a garden, and you want to list these plants organized by life cycle (annual, perennial, or biennial). To do this, you construct three sets, one for each life cycle, and iterate through the garden, placing each plant in the appropriate set. Some programmers would do this by putting the sets into an array indexed by the life cycle's ordinal:

```
// Using ordinal() to index into an array - DON'T DO THIS!
Set<Plant>[] plantsByLifeCycle =
    (Set<Plant>[]) new Set[Plant.LifeCycle.values().length];
for (int i = 0; i < plantsByLifeCycle.length; i++)
    plantsByLifeCycle[i] = new HashSet<>();

for (Plant p : garden)
    plantsByLifeCycle[p.lifeCycle.ordinal()].add(p);

// Print the results
for (int i = 0; i < plantsByLifeCycle.length; i++) {
    System.out.printf("%s: %s%n",
        Plant.LifeCycle.values()[i], plantsByLifeCycle[i]);
}
```

This technique works, but it is fraught with problems. Because arrays are not compatible with generics (Item 28), the program requires an unchecked cast and will not compile cleanly. Because the array does not know what its index represents, you have to label the output manually. But the most serious problem with this technique is that when you access an array that is indexed by an enum's ordinal, it is your responsibility to use the correct `int` value; `int`s do not provide the type safety of enums. If you use the wrong value, the program will silently do the wrong thing or—if you're lucky—throw an `ArrayIndexOutOfBoundsException`.

There is a much better way to achieve the same effect. The array is effectively serving as a map from the enum to a value, so you might as well use a Map. More specifically, there is a very fast Map implementation designed for use with enum keys, known as `java.util.EnumMap`. Here is how the program looks when it is rewritten to use EnumMap:

```
// Using an EnumMap to associate data with an enum
Map<Plant.LifeCycle, Set<Plant>> plantsByLifeCycle =
    new EnumMap<>(Plant.LifeCycle.class);
for (Plant.LifeCycle lc : Plant.LifeCycle.values())
    plantsByLifeCycle.put(lc, new HashSet<>());
for (Plant p : garden)
    plantsByLifeCycle.get(p.lifeCycle).add(p);
System.out.println(plantsByLifeCycle);
```

This program is shorter, clearer, safer, and comparable in speed to the original version. There is no unsafe cast; no need to label the output manually because the map keys are enums that know how to translate themselves to printable strings; and no possibility for error in computing array indices. The reason that EnumMap is comparable in speed to an ordinal-indexed array is that EnumMap uses such an array internally, but it hides this implementation detail from the programmer, combining the richness and type safety of a Map with the speed of an array. Note that the EnumMap constructor takes the Class object of the key type: this is a *bounded type token*, which provides runtime generic type information (Item 33).

The previous program can be further shortened by using a stream (Item 45) to manage the map. Here is the simplest stream-based code that largely duplicates the behavior of the previous example:

```
// Naive stream-based approach - unlikely to produce an EnumMap!
System.out.println(Arrays.stream(garden)
        .collect(groupingBy(p -> p.lifeCycle)));
```

The problem with this code is that it chooses its own map implementation, and in practice it won't be an EnumMap, so it won't match the space and time performance of the version with the explicit EnumMap. To rectify this problem, use the three-parameter form of `Collectors.groupingBy`, which allows the caller to specify the map implementation using the `mapFactory` parameter:

```
// Using a stream and an EnumMap to associate data with an enum
System.out.println(Arrays.stream(garden)
        .collect(groupingBy(p -> p.lifeCycle,
            () -> new EnumMap<>(LifeCycle.class), toSet()))));
```

This optimization would not be worth doing in a toy program like this one but could be critical in a program that made heavy use of the map.

The behavior of the stream-based versions differs slightly from that of the EmumMap version. The EnumMap version always makes a nested map for each plant lifecycle, while the stream-based versions only make a nested map if the garden contains one or more plants with that lifecycle. So, for example, if the garden contains annuals and perennials but no biennials, the size of `plantsByLifeCycle` will be three in the EnumMap version and two in both of the stream-based versions.

You may see an array of arrays indexed (twice!) by ordinals used to represent a mapping from two enum values. For example, this program uses such an array to map two phases to a phase transition (liquid to solid is freezing, liquid to gas is boiling, and so forth):

```
// Using ordinal() to index array of arrays - DON'T DO THIS!
public enum Phase {
    SOLID, LIQUID, GAS;

    public enum Transition {
        MELT, FREEZE, BOIL, CONDENSE, SUBLIME, DEPOSIT;

        // Rows indexed by from-ordinal, cols by to-ordinal
        private static final Transition[][] TRANSITIONS = {
            { null,    MELT,     SUBLIME },
            { FREEZE,  null,     BOIL    },
            { DEPOSIT, CONDENSE, null    }
        };

        // Returns the phase transition from one phase to another
        public static Transition from(Phase from, Phase to) {
            return TRANSITIONS[from.ordinal()][to.ordinal()];
        }
    }
}
```

This program works and may even appear elegant, but appearances can be deceiving. Like the simpler garden example shown earlier, the compiler has no way of knowing the relationship between ordinals and array indices. If you make a mistake in the transition table or forget to update it when you modify the Phase or Phase.Transition enum type, your program will fail at runtime. The failure may be an ArrayIndexOutOfBoundsException, a NullPointerException, or (worse) silent erroneous behavior. And the size of the table is quadratic in the number of phases, even if the number of non-null entries is smaller.

Again, you can do much better with EnumMap. Because each phase transition is indexed by a *pair* of phase enums, you are best off representing the relationship as a map from one enum (the "from" phase) to a map from the second enum (the "to" phase) to the result (the phase transition). The two phases associated with a phase transition are best captured by associating them with the phase transition enum, which can then be used to initialize the nested EnumMap:

```
// Using a nested EnumMap to associate data with enum pairs
public enum Phase {
    SOLID, LIQUID, GAS;

    public enum Transition {
        MELT(SOLID, LIQUID), FREEZE(LIQUID, SOLID),
        BOIL(LIQUID, GAS),   CONDENSE(GAS, LIQUID),
        SUBLIME(SOLID, GAS), DEPOSIT(GAS, SOLID);

        private final Phase from;
        private final Phase to;

        Transition(Phase from, Phase to) {
            this.from = from;
            this.to = to;
        }

        // Initialize the phase transition map
        private static final Map<Phase, Map<Phase, Transition>>
          m = Stream.of(values()).collect(groupingBy(t -> t.from,
          () -> new EnumMap<>(Phase.class),
          toMap(t -> t.to, t -> t,
              (x, y) -> y, () -> new EnumMap<>(Phase.class))));

        public static Transition from(Phase from, Phase to) {
            return m.get(from).get(to);
        }
    }
}
```

The code to initialize the phase transition map is a bit complicated. The type of the map is Map<Phase, Map<Phase, Transition>>, which means "map from (source) phase to map from (destination) phase to transition." This map-of-maps is initialized using a cascaded sequence of two collectors. The first collector groups the transitions by source phase, and the second creates an EnumMap with mappings from destination phase to transition. The merge function in the second collector ((x, y) -> y)) is unused; it is required only because we need to specify a map factory in order to get an EnumMap, and Collectors provides telescoping factories. The previous edition of this book used explicit iteration to initialize the phase transition map. The code was more verbose but arguably easier to understand.

Now suppose you want to add a new phase to the system: *plasma,* or ionized gas. There are only two transitions associated with this phase: *ionization*, which takes a gas to a plasma; and *deionization*, which takes a plasma to a gas. To update the array-based program, you would have to add one new constant to Phase and two to Phase.Transition, and replace the original nine-element array of arrays with a new sixteen-element version. If you add too many or too few elements to the array or place an element out of order, you are out of luck: the program will compile, but it will fail at runtime. To update the EnumMap-based version, all you have to do is add PLASMA to the list of phases, and IONIZE(GAS, PLASMA) and DEIONIZE(PLASMA, GAS) to the list of phase transitions:

```
// Adding a new phase using the nested EnumMap implementation
public enum Phase {
    SOLID, LIQUID, GAS, PLASMA;

    public enum Transition {
        MELT(SOLID, LIQUID),  FREEZE(LIQUID, SOLID),
        BOIL(LIQUID, GAS),    CONDENSE(GAS, LIQUID),
        SUBLIME(SOLID, GAS), DEPOSIT(GAS, SOLID),
        IONIZE(GAS, PLASMA), DEIONIZE(PLASMA, GAS);
        ... // Remainder unchanged
    }
}
```

The program takes care of everything else and leaves you virtually no opportunity for error. Internally, the map of maps is implemented with an array of arrays, so you pay little in space or time cost for the added clarity, safety, and ease of maintenance.

In the interest of brevity, the above examples use null to indicate the absence of a state change (wherein to and from are identical). This is not good practice and is likely to result in a NullPointerException at runtime. Designing a clean, elegant solution to this problem is surprisingly tricky, and the resulting programs are sufficiently long that they would detract from the primary material in this item.

In summary, **it is rarely appropriate to use ordinals to index into arrays: use EnumMap instead.** If the relationship you are representing is multidimensional, use EnumMap<..., EnumMap<...>>. This is a special case of the general principle that application programmers should rarely, if ever, use Enum.ordinal (Item 35).

Item 38: Emulate extensible enums with interfaces

In almost all respects, enum types are superior to the typesafe enum pattern described in the first edition of this book [Bloch01]. On the face of it, one exception concerns extensibility, which was possible under the original pattern but is not supported by the language construct. In other words, using the pattern, it was possible to have one enumerated type extend another; using the language feature, it is not. This is no accident. For the most part, extensibility of enums turns out to be a bad idea. It is confusing that elements of an extension type are instances of the base type and not vice versa. There is no good way to enumerate over all of the elements of a base type and its extensions. Finally, extensibility would complicate many aspects of the design and implementation.

That said, there is at least one compelling use case for extensible enumerated types, which is *operation codes,* also known as *opcodes.* An opcode is an enumerated type whose elements represent operations on some machine, such as the Operation type in Item 34, which represents the functions on a simple calculator. Sometimes it is desirable to let the users of an API provide their own operations, effectively extending the set of operations provided by the API.

Luckily, there is a nice way to achieve this effect using enum types. The basic idea is to take advantage of the fact that enum types can implement arbitrary interfaces by defining an interface for the opcode type and an enum that is the standard implementation of the interface. For example, here is an extensible version of the Operation type from Item 34:

```java
// Emulated extensible enum using an interface
public interface Operation {
    double apply(double x, double y);
}

public enum BasicOperation implements Operation {
    PLUS("+") {
        public double apply(double x, double y) { return x + y; }
    },
    MINUS("-") {
        public double apply(double x, double y) { return x - y; }
    },
    TIMES("*") {
        public double apply(double x, double y) { return x * y; }
    },
    DIVIDE("/") {
        public double apply(double x, double y) { return x / y; }
    };
```

```java
    private final String symbol;

    BasicOperation(String symbol) {
        this.symbol = symbol;
    }

    @Override public String toString() {
        return symbol;
    }
}
```

While the enum type (BasicOperation) is not extensible, the interface type (Operation) is, and it is the interface type that is used to represent operations in APIs. You can define another enum type that implements this interface and use instances of this new type in place of the base type. For example, suppose you want to define an extension to the operation type shown earlier, consisting of the exponentiation and remainder operations. All you have to do is write an enum type that implements the Operation interface:

```java
// Emulated extension enum
public enum ExtendedOperation implements Operation {
    EXP("^") {
        public double apply(double x, double y) {
            return Math.pow(x, y);
        }
    },
    REMAINDER("%") {
        public double apply(double x, double y) {
            return x % y;
        }
    };

    private final String symbol;

    ExtendedOperation(String symbol) {
        this.symbol = symbol;
    }

    @Override public String toString() {
        return symbol;
    }
}
```

You can now use your new operations anywhere you could use the basic operations, provided that APIs are written to take the interface type (Operation), not the implementation (BasicOperation). Note that you don't have to declare the abstract `apply` method in the enum as you do in a nonextensible enum with instance-specific method implementations (page 162). This is because the abstract method (`apply`) is a member of the interface (`Operation`).

Not only is it possible to pass a single instance of an "extension enum" anywhere a "base enum" is expected, but it is possible to pass in an entire extension enum type and use its elements in addition to or instead of those of the base type. For example, here is a version of the test program on page 163 that exercises all of the extended operations defined previously:

```
public static void main(String[] args) {
    double x = Double.parseDouble(args[0]);
    double y = Double.parseDouble(args[1]);
    test(ExtendedOperation.class, x, y);
}

private static <T extends Enum<T> & Operation> void test(
        Class<T> opEnumType, double x, double y) {
    for (Operation op : opEnumType.getEnumConstants())
        System.out.printf("%f %s %f = %f%n",
                          x, op, y, op.apply(x, y));
}
```

Note that the class literal for the extended operation type (`ExtendedOperation.class`) is passed from `main` to `test` to describe the set of extended operations. The class literal serves as a *bounded type token* (Item 33). The admittedly complex declaration for the `opEnumType` parameter (`<T extends Enum<T> & Operation> Class<T>`) ensures that the `Class` object represents both an enum and a subtype of `Operation`, which is exactly what is required to iterate over the elements and perform the operation associated with each one.

A second alternative is to pass a `Collection<? extends Operation>`, which is a *bounded wildcard type* (Item 31), instead of passing a class object:

```
public static void main(String[] args) {
    double x = Double.parseDouble(args[0]);
    double y = Double.parseDouble(args[1]);
    test(Arrays.asList(ExtendedOperation.values()), x, y);
}

private static void test(Collection<? extends Operation> opSet,
        double x, double y) {
    for (Operation op : opSet)
        System.out.printf("%f %s %f = %f%n",
                          x, op, y, op.apply(x, y));
}
```

The resulting code is a bit less complex, and the `test` method is a bit more flexible: it allows the caller to combine operations from multiple implementation types. On the other hand, you forgo the ability to use `EnumSet` (Item 36) and `EnumMap` (Item 37) on the specified operations.

Both programs shown previously will produce this output when run with command line arguments 4 and 2:

```
4.000000 ^ 2.000000 = 16.000000
4.000000 % 2.000000 = 0.000000
```

A minor disadvantage of the use of interfaces to emulate extensible enums is that implementations cannot be inherited from one enum type to another. If the implementation code does not rely on any state, it can be placed in the interface, using default implementations (Item 20). In the case of our `Operation` example, the logic to store and retrieve the symbol associated with an operation must be duplicated in `BasicOperation` and `ExtendedOperation`. In this case it doesn't matter because very little code is duplicated. If there were a larger amount of shared functionality, you could encapsulate it in a helper class or a static helper method to eliminate the code duplication.

The pattern described in this item is used in the Java libraries. For example, the `java.nio.file.LinkOption` enum type implements the `CopyOption` and `OpenOption` interfaces.

In summary, **while you cannot write an extensible enum type, you can emulate it by writing an interface to accompany a basic enum type that implements the interface.** This allows clients to write their own enums (or other types) that implement the interface. Instances of these types can then be used wherever instances of the basic enum type can be used, assuming APIs are written in terms of the interface.

Item 39: Prefer annotations to naming patterns

Historically, it was common to use *naming patterns* to indicate that some program elements demanded special treatment by a tool or framework. For example, prior to release 4, the JUnit testing framework required its users to designate test methods by beginning their names with the characters `test` [Beck04]. This technique works, but it has several big disadvantages. First, typographical errors result in silent failures. For example, suppose you accidentally named a test method `tsetSafetyOverride` instead of `testSafetyOverride`. JUnit 3 wouldn't complain, but it wouldn't execute the test either, leading to a false sense of security.

A second disadvantage of naming patterns is that there is no way to ensure that they are used only on appropriate program elements. For example, suppose you called a class `TestSafetyMechanisms` in hopes that JUnit 3 would automatically test all of its methods, regardless of their names. Again, JUnit 3 wouldn't complain, but it wouldn't execute the tests either.

A third disadvantage of naming patterns is that they provide no good way to associate parameter values with program elements. For example, suppose you want to support a category of test that succeeds only if it throws a particular exception. The exception type is essentially a parameter of the test. You could encode the exception type name into the test method name using some elaborate naming pattern, but this would be ugly and fragile (Item 62). The compiler would have no way of knowing to check that the string that was supposed to name an exception actually did. If the named class didn't exist or wasn't an exception, you wouldn't find out until you tried to run the test.

Annotations [JLS, 9.7] solve all of these problems nicely, and JUnit adopted them starting with release 4. In this item, we'll write our own toy testing framework to show how annotations work. Suppose you want to define an annotation type to designate simple tests that are run automatically and fail if they throw an exception. Here's how such an annotation type, named `Test`, might look:

```
// Marker annotation type declaration
import java.lang.annotation.*;

/**
 * Indicates that the annotated method is a test method.
 * Use only on parameterless static methods.
 */
@Retention(RetentionPolicy.RUNTIME)
@Target(ElementType.METHOD)
public @interface Test {
}
```

The declaration for the `Test` annotation type is itself annotated with `Retention` and `Target` annotations. Such annotations on annotation type declarations are known as *meta-annotations*. The `@Retention(RetentionPolicy.RUN-TIME)` meta-annotation indicates that `Test` annotations should be retained at runtime. Without it, `Test` annotations would be invisible to the test tool. The `@Target.get(ElementType.METHOD)` meta-annotation indicates that the `Test` annotation is legal only on method declarations: it cannot be applied to class declarations, field declarations, or other program elements.

The comment before the `Test` annotation declaration says, "Use only on parameterless static methods." It would be nice if the compiler could enforce this, but it can't, unless you write an *annotation processor* to do so. For more on this topic, see the documentation for `javax.annotation.processing`. In the absence of such an annotation processor, if you put a `Test` annotation on the declaration of an instance method or on a method with one or more parameters, the test program will still compile, leaving it to the testing tool to deal with the problem at runtime.

Here is how the `Test` annotation looks in practice. It is called a *marker annotation* because it has no parameters but simply "marks" the annotated element. If the programmer were to misspell `Test` or to apply the `Test` annotation to a program element other than a method declaration, the program wouldn't compile:

```
// Program containing marker annotations
public class Sample {
    @Test public static void m1() { }  // Test should pass
    public static void m2() { }
    @Test public static void m3() {    // Test should fail
        throw new RuntimeException("Boom");
    }
    public static void m4() { }
    @Test public void m5() { } // INVALID USE: nonstatic method
    public static void m6() { }
    @Test public static void m7() {    // Test should fail
        throw new RuntimeException("Crash");
    }
    public static void m8() { }
}
```

The `Sample` class has seven static methods, four of which are annotated as tests. Two of these, `m3` and `m7`, throw exceptions, and two, `m1` and `m5`, do not. But one of the annotated methods that does not throw an exception, `m5`, is an instance method, so it is not a valid use of the annotation. In sum, `Sample` contains four tests: one will pass, two will fail, and one is invalid. The four methods that are not annotated with the `Test` annotation will be ignored by the testing tool.

The Test annotations have no direct effect on the semantics of the Sample class. They serve only to provide information for use by interested programs. More generally, annotations don't change the semantics of the annotated code but enable it for special treatment by tools such as this simple test runner:

```
// Program to process marker annotations
import java.lang.reflect.*;

public class RunTests {
    public static void main(String[] args) throws Exception {
        int tests = 0;
        int passed = 0;
        Class<?> testClass = Class.forName(args[0]);
        for (Method m : testClass.getDeclaredMethods()) {
            if (m.isAnnotationPresent(Test.class)) {
                tests++;
                try {
                    m.invoke(null);
                    passed++;
                } catch (InvocationTargetException wrappedExc) {
                    Throwable exc = wrappedExc.getCause();
                    System.out.println(m + " failed: " + exc);
                } catch (Exception exc) {
                    System.out.println("Invalid @Test: " + m);
                }
            }
        }
        System.out.printf("Passed: %d, Failed: %d%n",
                          passed, tests - passed);
    }
}
```

The test runner tool takes a fully qualified class name on the command line and runs all of the class's Test-annotated methods reflectively, by calling Method.invoke. The isAnnotationPresent method tells the tool which methods to run. If a test method throws an exception, the reflection facility wraps it in an InvocationTargetException. The tool catches this exception and prints a failure report containing the original exception thrown by the test method, which is extracted from the InvocationTargetException with the getCause method.

If an attempt to invoke a test method by reflection throws any exception other than InvocationTargetException, it indicates an invalid use of the Test annotation that was not caught at compile time. Such uses include annotation of an instance method, of a method with one or more parameters, or of an inaccessible method. The second catch block in the test runner catches these Test usage errors and prints an appropriate error message. Here is the output that is printed if RunTests is run on Sample:

```
public static void Sample.m3() failed: RuntimeException: Boom
Invalid @Test: public void Sample.m5()
public static void Sample.m7() failed: RuntimeException: Crash
Passed: 1, Failed: 3
```

Now let's add support for tests that succeed only if they throw a particular exception. We'll need a new annotation type for this:

```
// Annotation type with a parameter
import java.lang.annotation.*;
/**
 * Indicates that the annotated method is a test method that
 * must throw the designated exception to succeed.
 */
@Retention(RetentionPolicy.RUNTIME)
@Target(ElementType.METHOD)
public @interface ExceptionTest {
    Class<? extends Throwable> value();
}
```

The type of the parameter for this annotation is Class<? extends Throwable>. This wildcard type is, admittedly, a mouthful. In English, it means "the Class object for some class that extends Throwable," and it allows the user of the annotation to specify any exception (or error) type. This usage is an example of a *bounded type token* (Item 33). Here's how the annotation looks in practice. Note that class literals are used as the values for the annotation parameter:

```
// Program containing annotations with a parameter
public class Sample2 {
    @ExceptionTest(ArithmeticException.class)
    public static void m1() {  // Test should pass
        int i = 0;
        i = i / i;
    }
    @ExceptionTest(ArithmeticException.class)
    public static void m2() {  // Should fail (wrong exception)
        int[] a = new int[0];
        int i = a[1];
    }
    @ExceptionTest(ArithmeticException.class)
    public static void m3() { }  // Should fail (no exception)
}
```

Now let's modify the test runner tool to process the new annotation. Doing so consists of adding the following code to the main method:

```
if (m.isAnnotationPresent(ExceptionTest.class)) {
    tests++;
    try {
        m.invoke(null);
        System.out.printf("Test %s failed: no exception%n", m);
    } catch (InvocationTargetException wrappedEx) {
        Throwable exc = wrappedEx.getCause();
        Class<? extends Throwable> excType =
            m.getAnnotation(ExceptionTest.class).value();
        if (excType.isInstance(exc)) {
            passed++;
        } else {
            System.out.printf(
                "Test %s failed: expected %s, got %s%n",
                m, excType.getName(), exc);
        }
    } catch (Exception exc) {
        System.out.println("Invalid @Test: " + m);
    }
}
```

This code is similar to the code we used to process Test annotations, with one exception: this code extracts the value of the annotation parameter and uses it to check if the exception thrown by the test is of the right type. There are no explicit casts, and hence no danger of a ClassCastException. The fact that the test program compiled guarantees that its annotation parameters represent valid exception types, with one caveat: if the annotation parameters were valid at compile time but the class file representing a specified exception type is no longer present at runtime, the test runner will throw TypeNotPresentException.

Taking our exception testing example one step further, it is possible to envision a test that passes if it throws any one of several specified exceptions. The annotation mechanism has a facility that makes it easy to support this usage. Suppose we change the parameter type of the ExceptionTest annotation to be an array of Class objects:

```
// Annotation type with an array parameter
@Retention(RetentionPolicy.RUNTIME)
@Target(ElementType.METHOD)
public @interface ExceptionTest {
    Class<? extends Exception>[] value();
}
```

The syntax for array parameters in annotations is flexible. It is optimized for single-element arrays. All of the previous ExceptionTest annotations are still valid with the new array-parameter version of ExceptionTest and result in single-element arrays. To specify a multiple-element array, surround the elements with curly braces and separate them with commas:

```java
// Code containing an annotation with an array parameter
@ExceptionTest({ IndexOutOfBoundsException.class,
                 NullPointerException.class })
public static void doublyBad() {
    List<String> list = new ArrayList<>();

    // The spec permits this method to throw either
    // IndexOutOfBoundsException or NullPointerException
    list.addAll(5, null);
}
```

It is reasonably straightforward to modify the test runner tool to process the new version of ExceptionTest. This code replaces the original version:

```java
if (m.isAnnotationPresent(ExceptionTest.class)) {
    tests++;
    try {
        m.invoke(null);
        System.out.printf("Test %s failed: no exception%n", m);
    } catch (Throwable wrappedExc) {
        Throwable exc = wrappedExc.getCause();
        int oldPassed = passed;
        Class<? extends Exception>[] excTypes =
            m.getAnnotation(ExceptionTest.class).value();
        for (Class<? extends Exception> excType : excTypes) {
            if (excType.isInstance(exc)) {
                passed++;
                break;
            }
        }
        if (passed == oldPassed)
            System.out.printf("Test %s failed: %s %n", m, exc);
    }
}
```

As of Java 8, there is another way to do multivalued annotations. Instead of declaring an annotation type with an array parameter, you can annotate the declaration of an annotation with the @Repeatable meta-annotation, to indicate that the annotation may be applied repeatedly to a single element. This meta-annotation takes a single parameter, which is the class object of a *containing annotation type*, whose sole parameter is an array of the annotation type [JLS, 9.6.3]. Here's how the annotation declarations look if we take this approach with our ExceptionTest annotation. Note that the containing annotation type must be annotated with an appropriate retention policy and target, or the declarations won't compile:

```
// Repeatable annotation type
@Retention(RetentionPolicy.RUNTIME)
@Target(ElementType.METHOD)
@Repeatable(ExceptionTestContainer.class)
public @interface ExceptionTest {
    Class<? extends Exception> value();
}

@Retention(RetentionPolicy.RUNTIME)
@Target(ElementType.METHOD)
public @interface ExceptionTestContainer {
    ExceptionTest[] value();
}
```

Here's how our doublyBad test looks with a repeated annotation in place of an array-valued annotation:

```
// Code containing a repeated annotation
@ExceptionTest(IndexOutOfBoundsException.class)
@ExceptionTest(NullPointerException.class)
public static void doublyBad() { ... }
```

Processing repeatable annotations requires care. A repeated annotation generates a synthetic annotation of the containing annotation type. The getAnnotationsByType method glosses over this fact, and can be used to access both repeated and non-repeated annotations of a repeatable annotation type. But isAnnotationPresent makes it explicit that repeated annotations are not of the annotation type, but of the containing annotation type. If an element has a repeated annotation of some type and you use the isAnnotationPresent method to check if the element has an annotation of that type, you'll find that it does not. Using this method to check for the presence of an annotation type will therefore cause your program to silently ignore repeated annotations. Similarly, using this method to check for the containing annotation type will cause the program to silently ignore non-repeated annotations. To detect repeated and non-repeated annotations with isAnnotationPresent, you much check for both the annotation type and its containing annotation type. Here's how the relevant part of our

RunTests program looks when modified to use the repeatable version of the ExceptionTest annotation:

```
// Processing repeatable annotations
if (m.isAnnotationPresent(ExceptionTest.class)
    || m.isAnnotationPresent(ExceptionTestContainer.class)) {
    tests++;
    try {
        m.invoke(null);
        System.out.printf("Test %s failed: no exception%n", m);
    } catch (Throwable wrappedExc) {
        Throwable exc = wrappedExc.getCause();
        int oldPassed = passed;
        ExceptionTest[] excTests =
                m.getAnnotationsByType(ExceptionTest.class);
        for (ExceptionTest excTest : excTests) {
            if (excTest.value().isInstance(exc)) {
                passed++;
                break;
            }
        }
        if (passed == oldPassed)
            System.out.printf("Test %s failed: %s %n", m, exc);
    }
}
```

Repeatable annotations were added to improve the readability of source code that logically applies multiple instances of the same annotation type to a given program element. If you feel they enhance the readability of your source code, use them, but remember that there is more boilerplate in declaring and processing repeatable annotations, and that processing repeatable annotations is error-prone.

The testing framework in this item is just a toy, but it clearly demonstrates the superiority of annotations over naming patterns, and it only scratches the surface of what you can do with them. If you write a tool that requires programmers to add information to source code, define appropriate annotation types. **There is simply no reason to use naming patterns when you can use annotations instead.**

That said, with the exception of toolsmiths, most programmers will have no need to define annotation types. But **all programmers should use the predefined annotation types that Java provides** (Items 40, 27). Also, consider using the annotations provided by your IDE or static analysis tools. Such annotations can improve the quality of the diagnostic information provided by these tools. Note, however, that these annotations have yet to be standardized, so you may have some work to do if you switch tools or if a standard emerges.

Item 40: Consistently use the Override annotation

The Java libraries contain several annotation types. For the typical programmer, the most important of these is @Override. This annotation can be used only on method declarations, and it indicates that the annotated method declaration overrides a declaration in a supertype. If you consistently use this annotation, it will protect you from a large class of nefarious bugs. Consider this program, in which the class Bigram represents a *bigram*, or ordered pair of letters:

```
// Can you spot the bug?
public class Bigram {
    private final char first;
    private final char second;

    public Bigram(char first, char second) {
        this.first  = first;
        this.second = second;
    }
    public boolean equals(Bigram b) {
        return b.first == first && b.second == second;
    }
    public int hashCode() {
        return 31 * first + second;
    }

    public static void main(String[] args) {
        Set<Bigram> s = new HashSet<>();
        for (int i = 0; i < 10; i++)
            for (char ch = 'a'; ch <= 'z'; ch++)
                s.add(new Bigram(ch, ch));
        System.out.println(s.size());
    }
}
```

The main program repeatedly adds twenty-six bigrams, each consisting of two identical lowercase letters, to a set. Then it prints the size of the set. You might expect the program to print 26, as sets cannot contain duplicates. If you try running the program, you'll find that it prints not 26 but 260. What is wrong with it?

Clearly, the author of the Bigram class intended to override the equals method (Item 10) and even remembered to override hashCode in tandem (Item 11). Unfortunately, our hapless programmer failed to override equals, overloading it instead (Item 52). To override Object.equals, you must define an equals method whose parameter is of type Object, but the parameter of Bigram's equals method is not of type Object, so Bigram inherits the equals method from Object. This equals method tests for object *identity*, just like the == operator. Each of the ten copies of each bigram is distinct from the other nine, so they are deemed unequal by Object.equals, which explains why the program prints 260.

Luckily, the compiler can help you find this error, but only if you help it by telling it that you intend to override Object.equals. To do this, annotate Bigram.equals with @Override, as shown here:

```
@Override public boolean equals(Bigram b) {
    return b.first == first && b.second == second;
}
```

If you insert this annotation and try to recompile the program, the compiler will generate an error message like this:

```
Bigram.java:10: method does not override or implement a method
from a supertype
    @Override public boolean equals(Bigram b) {
    ^
```

You will immediately realize what you did wrong, slap yourself on the forehead, and replace the broken equals implementation with a correct one (Item 10):

```
@Override public boolean equals(Object o) {
    if (!(o instanceof Bigram))
        return false;
    Bigram b = (Bigram) o;
    return b.first == first && b.second == second;
}
```

Therefore, you should **use the Override annotation on every method declaration that you believe to override a superclass declaration.** There is one minor exception to this rule. If you are writing a class that is not labeled abstract and you believe that it overrides an abstract method in its superclass, you needn't bother putting the Override annotation on that method. In a class that is not declared abstract, the compiler will emit an error message if you fail to override an abstract superclass method. However, you might wish to draw attention to all of the methods in your class that override superclass methods, in which case you should feel free to annotate these methods too. Most IDEs can be set to insert Override annotations automatically when you elect to override a method.

Most IDEs provide another reason to use the Override annotation consistently. If you enable the appropriate check, the IDE will generate a warning if you have a method that doesn't have an Override annotation but does override a superclass method. If you use the Override annotation consistently, these warnings will alert you to unintentional overriding. They complement the compiler's error messages, which alert you to unintentional failure to override. Between the IDE and the compiler, you can be sure that you're overriding methods everywhere you want to and nowhere else.

The Override annotation may be used on method declarations that override declarations from interfaces as well as classes. With the advent of default methods, it is good practice to use Override on concrete implementations of interface methods to ensure that the signature is correct. If you know that an interface does not have default methods, you may choose to omit Override annotations on concrete implementations of interface methods to reduce clutter.

In an abstract class or an interface, however, it *is* worth annotating *all* methods that you believe to override superclass or superinterface methods, whether concrete or abstract. For example, the Set interface adds no new methods to the Collection interface, so it should include Override annotations on all of its method declarations to ensure that it does not accidentally add any new methods to the Collection interface.

In summary, the compiler can protect you from a great many errors if you use the Override annotation on every method declaration that you believe to override a supertype declaration, with one exception. In concrete classes, you need not annotate methods that you believe to override abstract method declarations (though it is not harmful to do so).

Item 41: Use marker interfaces to define types

A *marker interface* is an interface that contains no method declarations but merely designates (or "marks") a class that implements the interface as having some property. For example, consider the `Serializable` interface (Chapter 12). By implementing this interface, a class indicates that its instances can be written to an `ObjectOutputStream` (or "serialized").

You may hear it said that marker annotations (Item 39) make marker interfaces obsolete. This assertion is incorrect. Marker interfaces have two advantages over marker annotations. First and foremost, **marker interfaces define a type that is implemented by instances of the marked class; marker annotations do not.** The existence of a marker interface type allows you to catch errors at compile time that you couldn't catch until runtime if you used a marker annotation.

Java's serialization facility (Chapter 6) uses the `Serializable` marker interface to indicate that a type is serializable. The `ObjectOutputStream.writeObject` method, which serializes the object that is passed to it, requires that its argument be serializable. Had the argument of this method been of type `Serializable`, an attempt to serialize an inappropriate object would have been detected at compile time (by type checking). Compile-time error detection is the intent of marker interfaces, but unfortunately, the `ObjectOutputStream.write` API does not take advantage of the `Serializable` interface: its argument is declared to be of type `Object`, so attempts to serialize an unserializable object won't fail until runtime.

Another advantage of marker interfaces over marker annotations is that they can be targeted more precisely. If an annotation type is declared with target `ElementType.TYPE`, it can be applied to *any* class or interface. Suppose you have a marker that is applicable only to implementations of a particular interface. If you define it as a marker interface, you can have it extend the sole interface to which it is applicable, guaranteeing that all marked types are also subtypes of the sole interface to which it is applicable.

Arguably, the `Set` interface is just such a *restricted marker interface*. It is applicable only to `Collection` subtypes, but it adds no methods beyond those defined by `Collection`. It is not generally considered to be a marker interface because it refines the contracts of several `Collection` methods, including `add`, `equals`, and `hashCode`. But it is easy to imagine a marker interface that is applicable only to subtypes of some particular interface and does *not* refine the contracts of any of the interface's methods. Such a marker interface might describe some invariant of the entire object or indicate that instances are eligible for processing by a method of some other class (in the way that the Serializable interface indicates that instances are eligible for processing by ObjectOutputStream).

The chief advantage of marker annotations over marker interfaces is that they are part of the larger annotation facility. Therefore, marker annotations allow for consistency in annotation-based frameworks.

So when should you use a marker annotation and when should you use a marker interface? Clearly you must use an annotation if the marker applies to any program element other than a class or interface, because only classes and interfaces can be made to implement or extend an interface. If the marker applies only to classes and interfaces, ask yourself the question "Might I want to write one or more methods that accept only objects that have this marking?" If so, you should use a marker interface in preference to an annotation. This will make it possible for you to use the interface as a parameter type for the methods in question, which will result in the benefit of compile-time type checking. If you can convince yourself that you'll never want to write a method that accepts only objects with the marking, then you're probably better off using a marker annotation. If, additionally, the marking is part of a framework that makes heavy use of annotations, then a marker annotation is the clear choice.

In summary, marker interfaces and marker annotations both have their uses. If you want to define a type that does not have any new methods associated with it, a marker interface is the way to go. If you want to mark program elements other than classes and interfaces or to fit the marker into a framework that already makes heavy use of annotation types, then a marker annotation is the correct choice. **If you find yourself writing a marker annotation type whose target is ElementType.TYPE, take the time to figure out whether it really should be an annotation type or whether a marker interface would be more appropriate.**

In a sense, this item is the inverse of Item 22, which says, "If you don't want to define a type, don't use an interface." To a first approximation, this item says, "If you do want to define a type, do use an interface."

CHAPTER 7

Lambdas and Streams

In Java 8, functional interfaces, lambdas, and method references were added to make it easier to create function objects. The streams API was added in tandem with these language changes to provide library support for processing sequences of data elements. In this chapter, we discuss how to make best use of these facilities.

Item 42: Prefer lambdas to anonymous classes

Historically, interfaces (or, rarely, abstract classes) with a single abstract method were used as *function types*. Their instances, known as *function objects*, represent functions or actions. Since JDK 1.1 was released in 1997, the primary means of creating a function object was the *anonymous class* (Item 24). Here's a code snippet to sort a list of strings in order of length, using an anonymous class to create the sort's comparison function (which imposes the sort order):

```
// Anonymous class instance as a function object - obsolete!
Collections.sort(words, new Comparator<String>() {
    public int compare(String s1, String s2) {
        return Integer.compare(s1.length(), s2.length());
    }
});
```

Anonymous classes were adequate for the classic objected-oriented design patterns requiring function objects, notably the *Strategy* pattern [Gamma95]. The Comparator interface represents an *abstract strategy* for sorting; the anonymous class above is a *concrete strategy* for sorting strings. The verbosity of anonymous classes, however, made functional programming in Java an unappealing prospect.

In Java 8, the language formalized the notion that interfaces with a single abstract method are special and deserve special treatment. These interfaces are now known as *functional interfaces*, and the language allows you to create instances of these interfaces using *lambda expressions*, or *lambdas* for short.

Lambdas are similar in function to anonymous classes, but far more concise. Here's how the code snippet above looks with the anonymous class replaced by a lambda. The boilerplate is gone, and the behavior is clearly evident:

```
// Lambda expression as function object (replaces anonymous class)
Collections.sort(words,
        (s1, s2) -> Integer.compare(s1.length(), s2.length()));
```

Note that the types of the lambda (Comparator<String>), of its parameters (s1 and s2, both String), and of its return value (int) are not present in the code. The compiler deduces these types from context, using a process known as *type inference*. In some cases, the compiler won't be able to determine the types, and you'll have to specify them. The rules for type inference are complex: they take up an entire chapter in the JLS [JLS, 18]. Few programmers understand these rules in detail, but that's OK. **Omit the types of all lambda parameters unless their presence makes your program clearer.** If the compiler generates an error telling you it can't infer the type of a lambda parameter, *then* specify it. Sometimes you may have to cast the return value or the entire lambda expression, but this is rare.

One caveat should be added concerning type inference. Item 26 tells you not to use raw types, Item 29 tells you to favor generic types, and Item 30 tells you to favor generic methods. This advice is doubly important when you're using lambdas, because the compiler obtains most of the type information that allows it to perform type inference from generics. If you don't provide this information, the compiler will be unable to do type inference, and you'll have to specify types manually in your lambdas, which will greatly increase their verbosity. By way of example, the code snippet above won't compile if the variable words is declared to be of the raw type List instead of the parameterized type List<String>.

Incidentally, the comparator in the snippet can be made even more succinct if a *comparator construction method* is used in place of a lambda (Items 14. 43):

```
Collections.sort(words, comparingInt(String::length));
```

In fact, the snippet can be made still shorter by taking advantage of the sort method that was added to the List interface in Java 8:

```
words.sort(comparingInt(String::length));
```

The addition of lambdas to the language makes it practical to use function objects where it would not previously have made sense. For example, consider the Operation enum type in Item 34. Because each enum required different behavior for its apply method, we used constant-specific class bodies and overrode the apply method in each enum constant. To refresh your memory, here is the code:

```java
// Enum type with constant-specific class bodies & data (Item 34)
public enum Operation {
    PLUS("+") {
        public double apply(double x, double y) { return x + y; }
    },
    MINUS("-") {
        public double apply(double x, double y) { return x - y; }
    },
    TIMES("*") {
        public double apply(double x, double y) { return x * y; }
    },
    DIVIDE("/") {
        public double apply(double x, double y) { return x / y; }
    };

    private final String symbol;
    Operation(String symbol) { this.symbol = symbol; }
    @Override public String toString() { return symbol; }

    public abstract double apply(double x, double y);
}
```

Item 34 says that enum instance fields are preferable to constant-specific class bodies. Lambdas make it easy to implement constant-specific behavior using the former instead of the latter. Merely pass a lambda implementing each enum constant's behavior to its constructor. The constructor stores the lambda in an instance field, and the `apply` method forwards invocations to the lambda. The resulting code is simpler and clearer than the original version:

```java
// Enum with function object fields & constant-specific behavior
public enum Operation {
    PLUS  ("+", (x, y) -> x + y),
    MINUS ("-", (x, y) -> x - y),
    TIMES ("*", (x, y) -> x * y),
    DIVIDE("/", (x, y) -> x / y);

    private final String symbol;
    private final DoubleBinaryOperator op;

    Operation(String symbol, DoubleBinaryOperator op) {
        this.symbol = symbol;
        this.op = op;
    }

    @Override public String toString() { return symbol; }

    public double apply(double x, double y) {
        return op.applyAsDouble(x, y);
    }
}
```

Note that we're using the DoubleBinaryOperator interface for the lambdas that represent the enum constant's behavior. This is one of the many predefined functional interfaces in java.util.function (Item 44). It represents a function that takes two double arguments and returns a double result.

Looking at the lambda-based Operation enum, you might think constant-specific method bodies have outlived their usefulness, but this is not the case. Unlike methods and classes, **lambdas lack names and documentation; if a computation isn't self-explanatory, or exceeds a few lines, don't put it in a lambda.** One line is ideal for a lambda, and three lines is a reasonable maximum. If you violate this rule, it can cause serious harm to the readability of your programs. If a lambda is long or difficult to read, either find a way to simplify it or refactor your program to eliminate it. Also, the arguments passed to enum constructors are evaluated in a static context. Thus, lambdas in enum constructors can't access instance members of the enum. Constant-specific class bodies are still the way to go if an enum type has constant-specific behavior that is difficult to understand, that can't be implemented in a few lines, or that requires access to instance fields or methods.

Likewise, you might think that anonymous classes are obsolete in the era of lambdas. This is closer to the truth, but there are a few things you can do with anonymous classes that you can't do with lambdas. Lambdas are limited to functional interfaces. If you want to create an instance of an abstract class, you can do it with an anonymous class, but not a lambda. Similarly, you can use anonymous classes to create instances of interfaces with multiple abstract methods. Finally, a lambda cannot obtain a reference to itself. In a lambda, the this keyword refers to the enclosing instance, which is typically what you want. In an anonymous class, the this keyword refers to the anonymous class instance. If you need access to the function object from within its body, then you must use an anonymous class.

Lambdas share with anonymous classes the property that you can't reliably serialize and deserialize them across implementations. Therefore, **you should rarely, if ever, serialize a lambda** (or an anonymous class instance). If you have a function object that you want to make serializable, such as a Comparator, use an instance of a private static nested class (Item 24).

In summary, as of Java 8, lambdas are by far the best way to represent small function objects. **Don't use anonymous classes for function objects unless you have to create instances of types that aren't functional interfaces.** Also, remember that lambdas make it so easy to represent small function objects that it opens the door to functional programming techniques that were not previously practical in Java.

Item 43: Prefer method references to lambdas

The primary advantage of lambdas over anonymous classes is that they are more succinct. Java provides a way to generate function objects even more succinct than lambdas: *method references*. Here is a code snippet from a program that maintains a map from arbitrary keys to Integer values. If the value is interpreted as a count of the number of instances of the key, then the program is a multiset implementation. The function of the code snippet is to associate the number 1 with the key if it is not in the map and to increment the associated value if the key is already present:

```
map.merge(key, 1, (count, incr) -> count + incr);
```

Note that this code uses the merge method, which was added to the Map interface in Java 8. If no mapping is present for the given key, the method simply inserts the given value; if a mapping is already present, merge applies the given function to the current value and the given value and overwrites the current value with the result. This code represents a typical use case for the merge method.

The code reads nicely, but there's still some boilerplate. The parameters count and incr don't add much value, and they take up a fair amount of space. Really, all the lambda tells you is that the function returns the sum of its two arguments. As of Java 8, Integer (and all the other boxed numerical primitive types) provides a static method sum that does exactly the same thing. We can simply pass a reference to this method and get the same result with less visual clutter:

```
map.merge(key, 1, Integer::sum);
```

The more parameters a method has, the more boilerplate you can eliminate with a method reference. In some lambdas, however, the parameter names you choose provide useful documentation, making the lambda more readable and maintainable than a method reference, even if the lambda is longer.

There's nothing you can do with a method reference that you can't also do with a lambda (with one obscure exception—see JLS, 9.9-2 if you're curious). That said, method references usually result in shorter, clearer code. They also give you an out if a lambda gets too long or complex: You can extract the code from the lambda into a new method and replace the lambda with a reference to that method. You can give the method a good name and document it to your heart's content.

If you're programming with an IDE, it will offer to replace a lambda with a method reference wherever it can. You should usually, but not always, take the IDE up on the offer. Occasionally, a lambda will be more succinct than a method reference. This happens most often when the method is in the same class as the lambda. For example, consider this snippet, which is presumed to occur in a class named GoshThisClassNameIsHumongous:

```
service.execute(GoshThisClassNameIsHumongous::action);
```

The lambda equivalent looks like this:

```
service.execute(() -> action());
```

The snippet using the method reference is neither shorter nor clearer than the snippet using the lambda, so prefer the latter. Along similar lines, the Function interface provides a generic static factory method to return the identity function, Function.identity(). It's typically shorter and cleaner *not* to use this method but to code the equivalent lambda inline: x -> x.

Many method references refer to static methods, but there are four kinds that do not. Two of them are *bound* and *unbound* instance method references. In bound references, the receiving object is specified in the method reference. Bound references are similar in nature to static references: the function object takes the same arguments as the referenced method. In unbound references, the receiving object is specified when the function object is applied, via an additional parameter before the method's declared parameters. Unbound references are often used as mapping and filter functions in stream pipelines (Item 45). Finally, there are two kinds of *constructor* references, for classes and arrays. Constructor references serve as factory objects. All five kinds of method references are summarized in the table below:

Method Ref Type	Example	Lambda Equivalent
Static	Integer::parseInt	str -> Integer.parseInt(str)
Bound	Instant.now()::isAfter	Instant then = Instant.now(); t -> then.isAfter(t)
Unbound	String::toLowerCase	str -> str.toLowerCase()
Class Constructor	TreeMap<K,V>::new	() -> new TreeMap<K,V>
Array Constructor	int[]::new	len -> new int[len]

In summary, method references often provide a more succinct alternative to lambdas. **Where method references are shorter and clearer, use them; where they aren't, stick with lambdas.**

Item 44: Favor the use of standard functional interfaces

Now that Java has lambdas, best practices for writing APIs have changed considerably. For example, the *Template Method* pattern [Gamma95], wherein a subclass overrides a *primitive method* to specialize the behavior of its superclass, is far less attractive. The modern alternative is to provide a static factory or constructor that accepts a function object to achieve the same effect. More generally, you'll be writing more constructors and methods that take function objects as parameters. Choosing the right functional parameter type demands care.

Consider `LinkedHashMap.` You can use this class as a cache by overriding its protected `removeEldestEntry` method, which is invoked by `put` each time a new key is added to the map. When this method returns `true`, the map removes its eldest entry, which is passed to the method. The following override allows the map to grow to one hundred entries and then deletes the eldest entry each time a new key is added, maintaining the hundred most recent entries:

```
protected boolean removeEldestEntry(Map.Entry<K,V> eldest) {
    return size() > 100;
}
```

This technique works fine, but you can do much better with lambdas. If `LinkedHashMap` were written today, it would have a static factory or constructor that took a function object. Looking at the declaration for `removeEldestEntry`, you might think that the function object should take a `Map.Entry<K,V>` and return a `boolean`, but that wouldn't quite do it: The `removeEldestEntry` method calls `size()` to get the number of entries in the map, which works because `removeEldestEntry` is an instance method on the map. The function object that you pass to the constructor is not an instance method on the map and can't capture it because the map doesn't exist yet when its factory or constructor is invoked. Thus, the map must pass itself to the function object, which must therefore take the map on input as well as its eldest entry. If you were to declare such a functional interface, it would look something like this:

```
// Unnecessary functional interface; use a standard one instead.
@FunctionalInterface interface EldestEntryRemovalFunction<K,V>{
    boolean remove(Map<K,V> map, Map.Entry<K,V> eldest);
}
```

This interface would work fine, but you shouldn't use it, because you don't need to declare a new interface for this purpose. The `java.util.function` package provides a large collection of standard functional interfaces for your use.

If one of the standard functional interfaces does the job, you should generally use it in preference to a purpose-built functional interface. This will make your API easier to learn, by reducing its conceptual surface area, and will provide significant interoperability benefits, as many of the standard functional interfaces provide useful default methods. The `Predicate` interface, for instance, provides methods to combine predicates. In the case of our `LinkedHashMap` example, the standard `BiPredicate<Map<K,V>, Map.Entry<K,V>>` interface should be used in preference to a custom `EldestEntryRemovalFunction` interface.

There are forty-three interfaces in `java.util.Function`. You can't be expected to remember them all, but if you remember six basic interfaces, you can derive the rest when you need them. The basic interfaces operate on object reference types. The `Operator` interfaces represent functions whose result and argument types are the same. The `Predicate` interface represents a function that takes an argument and returns a `boolean`. The `Function` interface represents a function whose argument and return types differ. The `Supplier` interface represents a function that takes no arguments and returns (or "supplies") a value. Finally, `Consumer` represents a function that takes an argument and returns nothing, essentially consuming its argument. The six basic functional interfaces are summarized below:

Interface	Function Signature	Example
UnaryOperator<T>	T apply(T t)	String::toLowerCase
BinaryOperator<T>	T apply(T t1, T t2)	BigInteger::add
Predicate<T>	boolean test(T t)	Collection::isEmpty
Function<T,R>	R apply(T t)	Arrays::asList
Supplier<T>	T get()	Instant::now
Consumer<T>	void accept(T t)	System.out::println

There are also three variants of each of the six basic interfaces to operate on the primitive types `int`, `long`, and `double`. Their names are derived from the basic interfaces by prefixing them with a primitive type. So, for example, a predicate that takes an `int` is an `IntPredicate`, and a binary operator that takes two `long` values and returns a `long` is a `LongBinaryOperator`. None of these variant types is parameterized except for the `Function` variants, which are parameterized by return type. For example, `LongFunction<int[]>` takes a `long` and returns an `int[]`.

There are nine additional variants of the `Function` interface, for use when the result type is primitive. The source and result types always differ, because a function from a type to itself is a `UnaryOperator`. If both the source and result types are primitive, prefix `Function` with *SrcToResult*, for example `LongToIntFunction` (six variants). If the source is a primitive and the result is an object reference, prefix `Function` with `<Src>ToObj`, for example `DoubleToObjFunction` (three variants).

There are two-argument versions of the three basic functional interfaces for which it makes sense to have them: `BiPredicate<T,U>`, `BiFunction<T,U,R>`, and `BiConsumer<T,U>`. There are also `BiFunction` variants returning the three relevant primitive types: `ToIntBiFunction<T,U>`, `ToLongBiFunction<T,U>`, and `ToDoubleBiFunction<T,U>`. There are two-argument variants of `Consumer` that take one object reference and one primitive type: `ObjDoubleConsumer<T>`, `ObjIntConsumer<T>`, and `ObjLongConsumer<T>`. In total, there are nine two-argument versions of the basic interfaces.

Finally, there is the `BooleanSupplier` interface, a variant of `Supplier` that returns `boolean` values. This is the only explicit mention of the `boolean` type in any of the standard functional interface names, but `boolean` return values are supported via `Predicate` and its four variant forms. The `BooleanSupplier` interface and the forty-two interfaces described in the previous paragraphs account for all forty-three standard functional interfaces. Admittedly, this is a lot to swallow, and not terribly orthogonal. On the other hand, the bulk of the functional interfaces that you'll need have been written for you and their names are regular enough that you shouldn't have too much trouble coming up with one when you need it.

Most of the standard functional interfaces exist only to provide support for primitive types. **Don't be tempted to use basic functional interfaces with boxed primitives instead of primitive functional interfaces.** While it works, it violates the advice of Item 61, "prefer primitive types to boxed primitives." The performance consequences of using boxed primitives for bulk operations can be deadly.

Now you know that you should typically use standard functional interfaces in preference to writing your own. But when *should* you write your own? Of course you need to write your own if none of the standard ones does what you need, for example if you require a predicate that takes three parameters, or one that throws a checked exception. But there are times you should write your own functional interface even when one of the standard ones is structurally identical.

Consider our old friend `Comparator<T>`, which is structurally identical to the `ToIntBiFunction<T,T>` interface. Even if the latter interface had existed when the former was added to the libraries, it would have been wrong to use it. There are several reasons that Comparator deserves its own interface. First, its name provides excellent documentation every time it is used in an API, and it's used a lot. Second, the Comparator interface has strong requirements on what constitutes a valid instance, which comprise its *general contract*. By implementing the interface, you are pledging to adhere to its contract. Third, the interface is heavily outfitted with useful default methods to transform and combine comparators.

You should seriously consider writing a purpose-built functional interface in preference to using a standard one if you need a functional interface that shares one or more of the following characteristics with Comparator:

- It will be commonly used and could benefit from a descriptive name.
- It has a strong contract associated with it.
- It would benefit from custom default methods.

If you elect to write your own functional interface, remember that it's an interface and hence should be designed with great care (Item 21).

Notice that the EldestEntryRemovalFunction interface (page 199) is labeled with the @FunctionalInterface annotation. This annotation type is similar in spirit to @Override. It is a statement of programmer intent that serves three purposes: it tells readers of the class and its documentation that the interface was designed to enable lambdas; it keeps you honest because the interface won't compile unless it has exactly one abstract method; and it prevents maintainers from accidentally adding abstract methods to the interface as it evolves. **Always annotate your functional interfaces with the @FunctionalInterface annotation.**

A final point should be made concerning the use of functional interfaces in APIs. Do not provide a method with multiple overloadings that take different functional interfaces in the same argument position if it could create a possible ambiguity in the client. This is not just a theoretical problem. The submit method of ExecutorService can take either a Callable<T> or a Runnable, and it is possible to write a client program that requires a cast to indicate the correct overloading (Item 52). The easiest way to avoid this problem is not to write overloadings that take different functional interfaces in the same argument position. This is a special case of the advice in Item 52, "use overloading judiciously."

In summary, now that Java has lambdas, it is imperative that you design your APIs with lambdas in mind. Accept functional interface types on input and return them on output. It is generally best to use the standard interfaces provided in java.util.function.Function, but keep your eyes open for the relatively rare cases where you would be better off writing your own functional interface.

Item 45: Use streams judiciously

The streams API was added in Java 8 to ease the task of performing bulk operations, sequentially or in parallel. This API provides two key abstractions: the *stream*, which represents a finite or infinite sequence of data elements, and the *stream pipeline*, which represents a multistage computation on these elements. The elements in a stream can come from anywhere. Common sources include collections, arrays, files, regular expression pattern matchers, pseudorandom number generators, and other streams. The data elements in a stream can be object references or primitive values. Three primitive types are supported: int, long, and double.

A stream pipeline consists of a source stream followed by zero or more *intermediate operations* and one *terminal operation*. Each intermediate operation transforms the stream in some way, such as mapping each element to a function of that element or filtering out all elements that do not satisfy some condition. Intermediate operations all transform one stream into another, whose element type may be the same as the input stream or different from it. The terminal operation performs a final computation on the stream resulting from the last intermediate operation, such as storing its elements into a collection, returning a certain element, or printing all of its elements.

Stream pipelines are evaluated *lazily*: evaluation doesn't start until the terminal operation is invoked, and data elements that aren't required in order to complete the terminal operation are never computed. This lazy evaluation is what makes it possible to work with infinite streams. Note that a stream pipeline without a terminal operation is a silent no-op, so don't forget to include one.

The streams API is *fluent*: it is designed to allow all of the calls that comprise a pipeline to be chained into a single expression. In fact, multiple pipelines can be chained together into a single expression.

By default, stream pipelines run sequentially. Making a pipeline execute in parallel is as simple as invoking the parallel method on any stream in the pipeline, but it is seldom appropriate to do so (Item 48).

The streams API is sufficiently versatile that practically any computation can be performed using streams, but just because you can doesn't mean you should. When used appropriately, streams can make programs shorter and clearer; when used inappropriately, they can make programs difficult to read and maintain. There are no hard and fast rules for when to use streams, but there are heuristics.

Consider the following program, which reads the words from a dictionary file and prints all the anagram groups whose size meets a user-specified minimum. Recall that two words are anagrams if they consist of the same letters in a different order. The program reads each word from a user-specified dictionary file and places the words into a map. The map key is the word with its letters alphabetized, so the key for "staple" is "aelpst", and the key for "petals" is also "aelpst": the two words are anagrams, and all anagrams share the same alphabetized form (or *alphagram*, as it is sometimes known). The map value is a list containing all of the words that share an alphabetized form. After the dictionary has been processed, each list is a complete anagram group. The program then iterates through the map's values() view and prints each list whose size meets the threshold:

```java
// Prints all large anagram groups in a dictionary iteratively
public class Anagrams {
    public static void main(String[] args) throws IOException {
        File dictionary = new File(args[0]);
        int minGroupSize = Integer.parseInt(args[1]);

        Map<String, Set<String>> groups = new HashMap<>();
        try (Scanner s = new Scanner(dictionary)) {
            while (s.hasNext()) {
                String word = s.next();
                groups.computeIfAbsent(alphabetize(word),
                    (unused) -> new TreeSet<>()).add(word);
            }
        }

        for (Set<String> group : groups.values())
            if (group.size() >= minGroupSize)
                System.out.println(group.size() + ": " + group);
    }

    private static String alphabetize(String s) {
        char[] a = s.toCharArray();
        Arrays.sort(a);
        return new String(a);
    }
}
```

One step in this program is worthy of note. The insertion of each word into the map, which is shown in bold, uses the computeIfAbsent method, which was added in Java 8. This method looks up a key in the map: If the key is present, the method simply returns the value associated with it. If not, the method computes a value by applying the given function object to the key, associates this value with the key, and returns the computed value. The computeIfAbsent method simplifies the implementation of maps that associate multiple values with each key.

Now consider the following program, which solves the same problem, but makes heavy use of streams. Note that the entire program, with the exception of the code that opens the dictionary file, is contained in a single expression. The only reason the dictionary is opened in a separate expression is to allow the use of the try-with-resources statement, which ensures that the dictionary file is closed:

```java
// Overuse of streams - don't do this!
public class Anagrams {
  public static void main(String[] args) throws IOException {
    Path dictionary = Paths.get(args[0]);
    int minGroupSize = Integer.parseInt(args[1]);

    try (Stream<String> words = Files.lines(dictionary)) {
      words.collect(
        groupingBy(word -> word.chars().sorted()
                     .collect(StringBuilder::new,
                       (sb, c) -> sb.append((char) c),
                       StringBuilder::append).toString()))
        .values().stream()
          .filter(group -> group.size() >= minGroupSize)
          .map(group -> group.size() + ": " + group)
          .forEach(System.out::println);
    }
  }
}
```

If you find this code hard to read, don't worry; you're not alone. It is shorter, but it is also less readable, especially to programmers who are not experts in the use of streams. **Overusing streams makes programs hard to read and maintain.**

Luckily, there is a happy medium. The following program solves the same problem, using streams without overusing them. The result is a program that's both shorter and clearer than the original:

```java
// Tasteful use of streams enhances clarity and conciseness
public class Anagrams {
    public static void main(String[] args) throws IOException {
        Path dictionary = Paths.get(args[0]);
        int minGroupSize = Integer.parseInt(args[1]);

        try (Stream<String> words = Files.lines(dictionary)) {
            words.collect(groupingBy(word -> alphabetize(word)))
                .values().stream()
                .filter(group -> group.size() >= minGroupSize)
                .forEach(g -> System.out.println(g.size() + ": " + g));
        }
    }

    // alphabetize method is the same as in original version
}
```

Even if you have little previous exposure to streams, this program is not hard to understand. It opens the dictionary file in a try-with-resources block, obtaining a stream consisting of all the lines in the file. The stream variable is named words to suggest that each element in the stream is a word. The pipeline on this stream has no intermediate operations; its terminal operation collects all the words into a map that groups the words by their alphabetized form (Item 46). This is exactly the same map that was constructed in both previous versions of the program. Then a new Stream<List<String>> is opened on the values() view of the map. The elements in this stream are, of course, the anagram groups. The stream is filtered so that all of the groups whose size is less than minGroupSize are ignored, and finally, the remaining groups are printed by the terminal operation forEach.

Note that the lambda parameter names were chosen carefully. The parameter g should really be named group, but the resulting line of code would be too wide for the book. **In the absence of explicit types, careful naming of lambda parameters is essential to the readability of stream pipelines.**

Note also that word alphabetization is done in a separate alphabetize method. This enhances readability by providing a name for the operation and keeping implementation details out of the main program. **Using helper methods is even more important for readability in stream pipelines than in iterative code** because pipelines lack explicit type information and named temporary variables.

The alphabetize method could have been reimplemented to use streams, but a stream-based alphabetize method would have been less clear, more difficult to write correctly, and probably slower. These deficiencies result from Java's lack of support for primitive char streams (which is not to imply that Java should have supported char streams; it would have been infeasible to do so). To demonstrate the hazards of processing char values with streams, consider the following code:

```
"Hello world!".chars().forEach(System.out::print);
```

You might expect it to print Hello world!, but if you run it, you'll find that it prints 721011081081113211911111410810033. This happens because the elements of the stream returned by "Hello world!".chars() are not char values but int values, so the int overloading of print is invoked. It is admittedly confusing that a method named chars returns a stream of int values. You *could* fix the program by using a cast to force the invocation of the correct overloading:

```
"Hello world!".chars().forEach(x -> System.out.print((char) x));
```

but ideally you should **refrain from using streams to process char values.**

When you start using streams, you may feel the urge to convert all your loops into streams, but resist the urge. While it may be possible, it will likely harm the readability and maintainability of your code base. As a rule, even moderately complex tasks are best accomplished using some combination of streams and iteration, as illustrated by the Anagrams programs above. So **refactor existing code to use streams and use them in new code only where it makes sense to do so.**

As shown in the programs in this item, stream pipelines express repeated computation using function objects (typically lambdas or method references), while iterative code expresses repeated computation using code blocks. There are some things you can do from code blocks that you can't do from function objects:

- From a code block, you can read or modify any local variable in scope; from a lambda, you can only read final or effectively final variables [JLS 4.12.4], and you can't modify any local variables.

- From a code block, you can return from the enclosing method, break or continue an enclosing loop, or throw any checked exception that this method is declared to throw; from a lambda you can do none of these things.

If a computation is best expressed using these techniques, then it's probably not a good match for streams. Conversely, streams make it very easy to do some things:

- Uniformly transform sequences of elements
- Filter sequences of elements
- Combine sequences of elements using a single operation (for example to add them, concatenate them, or compute their minimum)
- Accumulate sequences of elements into a collection, perhaps grouping them by some common attribute
- Search a sequence of elements for an element satisfying some criterion

If a computation is best expressed using these techniques, then it is a good candidate for streams.

One thing that is hard to do with streams is to access corresponding elements from multiple stages of a pipeline simultaneously: once you map a value to some other value, the original value is lost. One workaround is to map each value to a *pair object* containing the original value and the new value, but this is not a satisfying solution, especially if the pair objects are required for multiple stages of a pipeline. The resulting code is messy and verbose, which defeats a primary purpose of streams. When it is applicable, a better workaround is to invert the mapping when you need access to the earlier-stage value.

For example, let's write a program to print the first twenty *Mersenne primes*. To refresh your memory, a *Mersenne number* is a number of the form $2^p - 1$. If p is prime, the corresponding Mersenne number *may* be prime; if so, it's a Mersenne prime. As the initial stream in our pipeline, we want all the prime numbers. Here's a method to return that (infinite) stream. We assume a static import has been used for easy access to the static members of `BigInteger`:

```
static Stream<BigInteger> primes() {
    return Stream.iterate(TWO, BigInteger::nextProbablePrime);
}
```

The name of the method (`primes`) is a plural noun describing the elements of the stream. This naming convention is highly recommended for all methods that return streams because it enhances the readability of stream pipelines. The method uses the static factory `Stream.iterate`, which takes two parameters: the first element in the stream, and a function to generate the next element in the stream from the previous one. Here is the program to print the first twenty Mersenne primes:

```
public static void main(String[] args) {
    primes().map(p -> TWO.pow(p.intValueExact()).subtract(ONE))
        .filter(mersenne -> mersenne.isProbablePrime(50))
        .limit(20)
        .forEach(System.out::println);
}
```

This program is a straightforward encoding of the prose description above: it starts with the primes, computes the corresponding Mersenne numbers, filters out all but the primes (the magic number 50 controls the probabilistic primality test), limits the resulting stream to twenty elements, and prints them out.

Now suppose that we want to precede each Mersenne prime with its exponent (p). This value is present only in the initial stream, so it is inaccessible in the terminal operation, which prints the results. Luckily, it's easy to compute the exponent of a Mersenne number by inverting the mapping that took place in the first intermediate operation. The exponent is simply the number of bits in the binary representation, so this terminal operation generates the desired result:

```
.forEach(mp -> System.out.println(mp.bitLength() + ": " + mp));
```

There are plenty of tasks where it is not obvious whether to use streams or iteration. For example, consider the task of initializing a new deck of cards. Assume that `Card` is an immutable value class that encapsulates a `Rank` and a `Suit`, both of which are enum types. This task is representative of any task that requires computing all the pairs of elements that can be chosen from two sets. Mathematicians call this the *Cartesian product* of the two sets. Here's an iterative implementation with a nested for-each loop that should look very familiar to you:

```
// Iterative Cartesian product computation
private static List<Card> newDeck() {
    List<Card> result = new ArrayList<>();
    for (Suit suit : Suit.values())
        for (Rank rank : Rank.values())
            result.add(new Card(suit, rank));
    return result;
}
```

And here is a stream-based implementation that makes use of the intermediate operation flatMap. This operation maps each element in a stream to a stream and then concatenates all of these new streams into a single stream (or *flattens* them). Note that this implementation contains a nested lambda, shown in boldface:

```
// Stream-based Cartesian product computation
private static List<Card> newDeck() {
    return Stream.of(Suit.values())
        .flatMap(suit ->
            Stream.of(Rank.values())
                .map(rank -> new Card(suit, rank)))
        .collect(toList());
}
```

Which of the two versions of newDeck is better? It boils down to personal preference and the environment in which you're programming. The first version is simpler and perhaps feels more natural. A larger fraction of Java programmers will be able to understand and maintain it, but some programmers will feel more comfortable with the second (stream-based) version. It's a bit more concise and not too difficult to understand if you're reasonably well-versed in streams and functional programming. If you're not sure which version you prefer, the iterative version is probably the safer choice. If you prefer the stream version and you believe that other programmers who will work with the code will share your preference, then you should use it.

In summary, some tasks are best accomplished with streams, and others with iteration. Many tasks are best accomplished by combining the two approaches. There are no hard and fast rules for choosing which approach to use for a task, but there are some useful heuristics. In many cases, it will be clear which approach to use; in some cases, it won't. **If you're not sure whether a task is better served by streams or iteration, try both and see which works better.**

Item 46: Prefer side-effect-free functions in streams

If you're new to streams, it can be difficult to get the hang of them. Merely expressing your computation as a stream pipeline can be hard. When you succeed, your program will run, but you may realize little if any benefit. Streams isn't just an API, it's a paradigm based on functional programming. In order to obtain the expressiveness, speed, and in some cases parallelizability that streams have to offer, you have to adopt the paradigm as well as the API.

The most important part of the streams paradigm is to structure your computation as a sequence of transformations where the result of each stage is as close as possible to a *pure function* of the result of the previous stage. A pure function is one whose result depends only on its input: it does not depend on any mutable state, nor does it update any state. In order to achieve this, any function objects that you pass into stream operations, both intermediate and terminal, should be free of side-effects.

Occasionally, you may see streams code that looks like this snippet, which builds a frequency table of the words in a text file:

```
// Uses the streams API but not the paradigm--Don't do this!
Map<String, Long> freq = new HashMap<>();
try (Stream<String> words = new Scanner(file).tokens()) {
    words.forEach(word -> {
        freq.merge(word.toLowerCase(), 1L, Long::sum);
    });
}
```

What's wrong with this code? After all, it uses streams, lambdas, and method references, and gets the right answer. Simply put, it's not streams code at all; it's iterative code masquerading as streams code. It derives no benefits from the streams API, and it's (a bit) longer, harder to read, and less maintainable than the corresponding iterative code. The problem stems from the fact that this code is doing all its work in a terminal forEach operation, using a lambda that mutates external state (the frequency table). A forEach operation that does anything more than present the result of the computation performed by a stream is a "bad smell in code," as is a lambda that mutates state. So how should this code look?

```
// Proper use of streams to initialize a frequency table
Map<String, Long> freq;
try (Stream<String> words = new Scanner(file).tokens()) {
    freq = words
        .collect(groupingBy(String::toLowerCase, counting()));
}
```

This snippet does the same thing as the previous one but makes proper use of the streams API. It's shorter and clearer. So why would anyone write it the other way? Because it uses tools they're already familiar with. Java programmers know how to use for-each loops, and the forEach terminal operation is similar. But the forEach operation is among the least powerful of the terminal operations and the least stream-friendly. It's explicitly iterative, and hence not amenable to parallelization. **The forEach operation should be used only to report the result of a stream computation, not to perform the computation.** Occasionally, it makes sense to use forEach for some other purpose, such as adding the results of a stream computation to a preexisting collection.

The improved code uses a *collector*, which is a new concept that you have to learn in order to use streams. The Collectors API is intimidating: it has thirty-nine methods, some of which have as many as five type parameters. The good news is that you can derive most of the benefit from this API without delving into its full complexity. For starters, you can ignore the Collector interface and think of a collector as an opaque object that encapsulates a *reduction* strategy. In this context, reduction means combining the elements of a stream into a single object. The object produced by a collector is typically a collection (which accounts for the name collector).

The collectors for gathering the elements of a stream into a true Collection are straightforward. There are three such collectors: toList(), toSet(), and toCollection(collectionFactory). They return, respectively, a set, a list, and a programmer-specified collection type. Armed with this knowledge, we can write a stream pipeline to extract a top-ten list from our frequency table.

```
// Pipeline to get a top-ten list of words from a frequency table
List<String> topTen = freq.keySet().stream()
    .sorted(comparing(freq::get).reversed())
    .limit(10)
    .collect(toList());
```

Note that we haven't qualified the toList method with its class, Collectors. **It is customary and wise to statically import all members of Collectors because it makes stream pipelines more readable.**

The only tricky part of this code is the comparator that we pass to sorted, comparing(freq::get).reversed(). The comparing method is a comparator construction method (Item 14) that takes a key extraction function. The function takes a word, and the "extraction" is actually a table lookup: the bound method reference freq::get looks up the word in the frequency table and returns the number of times the word appears in the file. Finally, we call reversed on the comparator, so we're sorting the words from most frequent to least frequent. Then it's a simple matter to limit the stream to ten words and collect them into a list.

The previous code snippets use Scanner's stream method to get a stream over the scanner. This method was added in Java 9. If you're using an earlier release, you can translate the scanner, which implements Iterator, into a stream using an adapter similar to the one in Item 47 (streamOf(Iterable<E>)).

So what about the other thirty-six methods in Collectors? Most of them exist to let you collect streams into maps, which is far more complicated than collecting them into true collections. Each stream element is associated with a key *and a value*, and multiple stream elements can be associated with the same key.

The simplest map collector is toMap(keyMapper, valueMapper), which takes two functions, one of which maps a stream element to a key, the other, to a value. We used this collector in our fromString implementation in Item 34 to make a map from the string form of an enum to the enum itself:

```
// Using a toMap collector to make a map from string to enum
private static final Map<String, Operation> stringToEnum =
    Stream.of(values()).collect(
        toMap(Object::toString, e -> e));
```

This simple form of toMap is perfect if each element in the stream maps to a unique key. If multiple stream elements map to the same key, the pipeline will terminate with an IllegalStateException.

The more complicated forms of toMap, as well as the groupingBy method, give you various ways to provide strategies for dealing with such collisions. One way is to provide the toMap method with a *merge function* in addition to its key and value mappers. The merge function is a BinaryOperator<V>, where V is the value type of the map. Any additional values associated with a key are combined with the existing value using the merge function, so, for example, if the merge function is multiplication, you end up with a value that is the product of all the values associated with the key by the value mapper.

The three-argument form of toMap is also useful to make a map from a key to a chosen element associated with that key. For example, suppose we have a stream of record albums by various artists, and we want a map from recording artist to best-selling album. This collector will do the job.

```
// Collector to generate a map from key to chosen element for key
Map<Artist, Album> topHits = albums.collect(
    toMap(Album::artist, a->a, maxBy(comparing(Album::sales))));
```

Note that the comparator uses the static factory method maxBy, which is statically imported from BinaryOperator. This method converts a Comparator<T> into a BinaryOperator<T> that computes the maximum implied by the specified comparator. In this case, the comparator is returned by the comparator construction method comparing, which takes the key extractor function Album::sales. This may seem a bit convoluted, but the code reads nicely. Loosely speaking, it says, "convert the stream of albums to a map, mapping each artist to the album that has the best album by sales." This is surprisingly close to the problem statement.

Another use of the three-argument form of toMap is to produce a collector that imposes a last-write-wins policy when there are collisions. For many streams, the results will be nondeterministic, but if all the values that may be associated with a key by the mapping functions are identical, or if they are all acceptable, this collector's s behavior may be just what you want:

```
// Collector to impose last-write-wins policy
toMap(keyMapper, valueMapper, (v1, v2) -> v2)
```

The third and final version of toMap takes a fourth argument, which is a map factory, for use when you want to specify a particular map implementation such as an EnumMap or a TreeMap.

There are also variant forms of the first three versions of toMap, named toConcurrentMap, that run efficiently in parallel and produce ConcurrentHashMap instances.

In addition to the toMap method, the Collectors API provides the groupingBy method, which returns collectors to produce maps that group elements into categories based on a *classifier function*. The classifier function takes an element and returns the category into which it falls. This category serves as the element's map key. The simplest version of the groupingBy method takes only a classifier and returns a map whose values are lists of all the elements in each category. This is the collector that we used in the Anagram program in Item 45 to generate a map from alphabetized word to a list of the words sharing the alphabetization:

```
words.collect(groupingBy(word -> alphabetize(word)))
```

If you want groupingBy to return a collector that produces a map with values other than lists, you can specify a *downstream collector* in addition to a classifier. A downstream collector produces a value from a stream containing all the elements in a category. The simplest use of this parameter is to pass `toSet()`, which results in a map whose values are sets of elements rather than lists.

Alternatively, you can pass `toCollection(collectionFactory)`, which lets you create the collections into which each category of elements is placed. This gives you the flexibility to choose any collection type you want. Another simple use of the two-argument form of `groupingBy` is to pass `counting()` as the downstream collector. This results in a map that associates each category with the *number* of elements in the category, rather than a collection containing the elements. That's what you saw in the frequency table example at the beginning of this item:

```
Map<String, Long> freq = words
        .collect(groupingBy(String::toLowerCase, counting()));
```

The third version of `groupingBy` lets you specify a map factory in addition to a downstream collector. Note that this method violates the standard telescoping argument list pattern: the `mapFactory` parameter precedes, rather than follows, the `downStream` parameter. This version of `groupingBy` gives you control over the containing map as well as the contained collections, so, for example, you can specify a collector that returns a `TreeMap` whose values are `TreeSets`.

The `groupingByConcurrent` method provides variants of all three overloadings of `groupingBy`. These variants run efficiently in parallel and produce `ConcurrentHashMap` instances. There is also a rarely used relative of `groupingBy` called `partitioningBy`. In lieu of a classifier method, it takes a predicate and returns a map whose key is a `Boolean`. There are two overloadings of this method, one of which takes a downstream collector in addition to a predicate.

The collectors returned by the `counting` method are intended *only* for use as downstream collectors. The same functionality is available directly on `Stream`, via the `count` method, so **there is never a reason to say `collect(counting())`**. There are fifteen more `Collectors` methods with this property. They include the nine methods whose names begin with `summing`, `averaging`, and `summarizing` (whose functionality is available on the corresponding primitive stream types). They also include all overloadings of the `reducing` method, and the `filtering`, `mapping`, `flatMapping`, and `collectingAndThen` methods. Most programmers can safely ignore the majority of these methods. From a design perspective, these collectors represent an attempt to partially duplicate the functionality of streams in collectors so that downstream collectors can act as "ministreams."

There are three `Collectors` methods we have yet to mention. Though they are in `Collectors`, they don't involve collections. The first two are `minBy` and `maxBy`, which take a comparator and return the minimum or maximum element in the stream as determined by the comparator. They are minor generalizations of the `min` and `max` methods in the `Stream` interface and are the collector analogues of the binary operators returned by the like-named methods in `BinaryOperator`. Recall that we used `BinaryOperator.maxBy` in our best-selling album example.

The final `Collectors` method is `joining`, which operates only on streams of `CharSequence` instances such as strings. In its parameterless form, it returns a collector that simply concatenates the elements. Its one argument form takes a single `CharSequence` parameter named `delimiter` and returns a collector that joins the stream elements, inserting the delimiter between adjacent elements. If you pass in a comma as the delimiter, the collector returns a comma-separated values string (but beware that the string will be ambiguous if any of the elements in the stream contain commas). The three argument form takes a prefix and suffix in addition to the delimiter. The resulting collector generates strings like the ones that you get when you print a collection, for example `[came, saw, conquered]`.

In summary, the essence of programming stream pipelines is side-effect-free function objects. This applies to all of the many function objects passed to streams and related objects. The terminal operation `forEach` should only be used to report the result of a computation performed by a stream, not to perform the computation. In order to use streams properly, you have to know about collectors. The most important collector factories are `toList`, `toSet`, `toMap`, `groupingBy`, and `joining`.

Item 47: Prefer Collection to Stream as a return type

Many methods return sequences of elements. Prior to Java 8, the obvious return types for such methods were the collection interfaces Collection, Set, and List; Iterable; and the array types. Usually, it was easy to decide which of these types to return. The norm was a collection interface. If the method existed solely to enable for-each loops or the returned sequence couldn't be made to implement some Collection method (typically, contains(Object)), the Iterable interface was used. If the returned elements were primitive values or there were stringent performance requirements, arrays were used. In Java 8, streams were added to the platform, substantially complicating the task of choosing the appropriate return type for a sequence-returning method.

You may hear it said that streams are now the obvious choice to return a sequence of elements, but as discussed in Item 45, streams do not make iteration obsolete: writing good code requires combining streams and iteration judiciously. If an API returns only a stream and some users want to iterate over the returned sequence with a for-each loop, those users will be justifiably upset. It is especially frustrating because the Stream interface contains the sole abstract method in the Iterable interface, and Stream's specification for this method is compatible with Iterable's. The only thing preventing programmers from using a for-each loop to iterate over a stream is Stream's failure to extend Iterable.

Sadly, there is no good workaround for this problem. At first glance, it might appear that passing a method reference to Stream's iterator method would work. The resulting code is perhaps a bit noisy and opaque, but not unreasonable:

```
// Won't compile, due to limitations on Java's type inference
for (ProcessHandle ph : ProcessHandle.allProcesses()::iterator) {
    // Process the process
}
```

Unfortunately, if you attempt to compile this code, you'll get an error message:

```
Test.java:6: error: method reference not expected here
for (ProcessHandle ph : ProcessHandle.allProcesses()::iterator) {
                        ^
```

In order to make the code compile, you have to cast the method reference to an appropriately parameterized Iterable:

```
// Hideous workaround to iterate over a stream
for (ProcessHandle ph : (Iterable<ProcessHandle>)
                    ProcessHandle.allProcesses()::iterator)
```

This client code works, but it is too noisy and opaque to use in practice. A better workaround is to use an adapter method. The JDK does not provide such a method, but it's easy to write one, using the same technique used in-line in the snippets above. Note that no cast is necessary in the adapter method because Java's type inference works properly in this context:

```
// Adapter from  Stream<E> to Iterable<E>
public static <E> Iterable<E> iterableOf(Stream<E> stream) {
    return stream::iterator;
}
```

With this adapter, you can iterate over any stream with a for-each statement:

```
for (ProcessHandle p : iterableOf(ProcessHandle.allProcesses())) {
    // Process the process
}
```

Note that the stream versions of the Anagrams program in Item 34 use the Files.lines method to read the dictionary, while the iterative version uses a scanner. The Files.lines method is superior to a scanner, which silently swallows any exceptions encountered while reading the file. Ideally, we would have used Files.lines in the iterative version too. This is the sort of compromise that programmers will make if an API provides only stream access to a sequence and they want to iterate over the sequence with a for-each statement.

Conversely, a programmer who wants to process a sequence using a stream pipeline will be justifiably upset by an API that provides only an Iterable. Again the JDK does not provide an adapter, but it's easy enough to write one:

```
// Adapter from Iterable<E> to Stream<E>
public static <E> Stream<E> streamOf(Iterable<E> iterable) {
    return StreamSupport.stream(iterable.spliterator(), false);
}
```

If you're writing a method that returns a sequence of objects and you know that it will only be used in a stream pipeline, then of course you should feel free to return a stream. Similarly, a method returning a sequence that will only be used for iteration should return an Iterable. But if you're writing a public API that returns a sequence, you should provide for users who want to write stream pipelines as well as those who want to write for-each statements, unless you have a good reason to believe that most of your users will want to use the same mechanism.

The Collection interface is a subtype of Iterable and has a stream method, so it provides for both iteration and stream access. Therefore, **Collection or an appropriate subtype is generally the best return type for a public, sequence-returning method.** Arrays also provide for easy iteration and stream access with the Arrays.asList and Stream.of methods. If the sequence you're returning is small enough to fit easily in memory, you're probably best off returning one of the standard collection implementations, such as ArrayList or HashSet. But **do not store a large sequence in memory just to return it as a collection.**

If the sequence you're returning is large but can be represented concisely, consider implementing a special-purpose collection. For example, suppose you want to return the *power set* of a given set, which consists of all of its subsets. The power set of $\{a, b, c\}$ is $\{\{\}, \{a\}, \{b\}, \{c\}, \{a, b\}, \{a, c\}, \{b, c\}, \{a, b, c\}\}$. If a set has n elements, its power set has 2^n. Therefore, you shouldn't even consider storing the power set in a standard collection implementation. It is, however, easy to implement a custom collection for the job with the help of AbstractList.

The trick is to use the index of each element in the power set as a bit vector, where the nth bit in the index indicates the presence or absence of the nth element from the source set. In essence, there is a natural mapping between the binary numbers from 0 to $2^n - 1$ and the power set of an n-element set. Here's the code:

```java
// Returns the power set of an input set as custom collection
public class PowerSet {
    public static final <E> Collection<Set<E>> of(Set<E> s) {
        List<E> src = new ArrayList<>(s);
        if (src.size() > 30)
            throw new IllegalArgumentException("Set too big " + s);
        return new AbstractList<Set<E>>() {
            @Override public int size() {
                return 1 << src.size(); // 2 to the power srcSize
            }

            @Override public boolean contains(Object o) {
                return o instanceof Set && src.containsAll((Set)o);
            }

            @Override public Set<E> get(int index) {
                Set<E> result = new HashSet<>();
                for (int i = 0; index != 0; i++, index >>= 1)
                    if ((index & 1) == 1)
                        result.add(src.get(i));
                return result;
            }
        };
    }
}
```

Note that PowerSet.of throws an exception if the input set has more than 30 elements. This highlights a disadvantage of using Collection as a return type rather than Stream or Iterable: Collection has an int-returning size method, which limits the length of the returned sequence to Integer.MAX_VALUE, or $2^{31} - 1$. The Collection specification does allow the size method to return $2^{31} - 1$ if the collection is larger, even infinite, but this is not a wholly satisfying solution.

In order to write a Collection implementation atop AbstractCollection, you need implement only two methods beyond the one required for Iterable: contains and size. Often it's easy to write efficient implementations of these methods. If it isn't feasible, perhaps because the contents of the sequence aren't predetermined before iteration takes place, return a stream or iterable, whichever feels more natural. If you choose, you can return both using two separate methods.

There are times when you'll choose the return type based solely on ease of implementation. For example, suppose you want to write a method that returns all of the (contiguous) sublists of an input list. It takes only three lines of code to generate these sublists and put them in a standard collection, but the memory required to hold this collection is quadratic in the size of the source list. While this is not as bad as the power set, which is exponential, it is clearly unacceptable. Implementing a custom collection, as we did for the power set, would be tedious, more so because the JDK lacks a skeletal Iterator implementation to help us.

It is, however, straightforward to implement a stream of all the sublists of an input list, though it does require a minor insight. Let's call a sublist that contains the first element of a list a *prefix* of the list. For example, the prefixes of (a, b, c) are (a), (a, b), and (a, b, c). Similarly, let's call a sublist that contains the last element a *suffix*, so the suffixes of (a, b, c) are (a, b, c), (b, c), and (c). The insight is that the sublists of a list are simply the suffixes of the prefixes (or identically, the prefixes of the suffixes) and the empty list. This observation leads directly to a clear, reasonably concise implementation:

```
// Returns a stream of all the sublists of its input list
public class SubLists {
    public static <E> Stream<List<E>> of(List<E> list) {
        return Stream.concat(Stream.of(Collections.emptyList()),
            prefixes(list).flatMap(SubLists::suffixes));
    }

    private static <E> Stream<List<E>> prefixes(List<E> list) {
        return IntStream.rangeClosed(1, list.size())
            .mapToObj(end -> list.subList(0, end));
    }
```

```java
    private static <E> Stream<List<E>> suffixes(List<E> list) {
        return IntStream.range(0, list.size())
            .mapToObj(start -> list.subList(start, list.size()));
    }
}
```

Note that the `Stream.concat` method is used to add the empty list into the returned stream. Also note that the `flatMap` method (Item 45) is used to generate a single stream consisting of all the suffixes of all the prefixes. Finally, note that we generate the prefixes and suffixes by mapping a stream of consecutive `int` values returned by `IntStream.range` and `IntStream.rangeClosed`. This idiom is, roughly speaking, the stream equivalent of the standard for-loop on integer indices. Thus, our sublist implementation is similar in spirit to the obvious nested for-loop:

```java
for (int start = 0; start < src.size(); start++)
    for (int end = start + 1; end <= src.size(); end++)
        System.out.println(src.subList(start, end));
```

It is possible to translate this for-loop directly into a stream. The result is more concise than our previous implementation, but perhaps a bit less readable. It is similar in spirit to the streams code for the Cartesian product in Item 45:

```java
// Returns a stream of all the sublists of its input list
public static <E> Stream<List<E>> of(List<E> list) {
    return IntStream.range(0, list.size())
        .mapToObj(start ->
            IntStream.rangeClosed(start + 1, list.size())
                .mapToObj(end -> list.subList(start, end)))
        .flatMap(x -> x);
}
```

Like the for-loop that precedes it, this code does *not* emit the empty list. In order to fix this deficiency, you could either use `concat`, as we did in the previous version, or replace 1 by `(int) Math.signum(start)` in the `rangeClosed` call.

Either of these stream implementations of sublists is fine, but both will require some users to employ a `Stream-to-Iterable` adapter or to use a stream in places where iteration would be more natural. Not only does the `Stream-to-Iterable` adapter clutter up client code, but it slows down the loop by a factor of 2.3 on my machine. A purpose-built `Collection` implementation (not shown here) is considerably more verbose but runs about 1.4 times as fast as our stream-based implementation on my machine.

In summary, when writing a method that returns a sequence of elements, remember that some of your users may want to process them as a stream while others may want to iterate over them. Try to accommodate both groups. If it's feasible to return a collection, do so. If you already have the elements in a collection or the number of elements in the sequence is small enough to justify creating a new one, return a standard collection such as `ArrayList`. Otherwise, consider implementing a custom collection as we did for the power set. If it isn't feasible to return a collection, return a stream or iterable, whichever seems more natural. If, in a future Java release, the `Stream` interface declaration is modified to extend `Iterable`, then you should feel free to return streams because they will allow for both stream processing and iteration.

Item 48: Use caution when making streams parallel

Among mainstream languages, Java has always been at the forefront of providing facilities to ease the task of concurrent programming. When Java was released in 1996, it had built-in support for threads, with synchronization and wait/notify. Java 5 introduced the java.util.concurrent library, with concurrent collections and the executor framework. Java 7 introduced the fork-join package, a high-performance framework for parallel decomposition. Java 8 introduced streams, which can be parallelized with a single call to the parallel method. Writing concurrent programs in Java keeps getting easier, but writing concurrent programs that are correct and fast is as difficult as it ever was. Safety and liveness violations are a fact of life in concurrent programming, and parallel stream pipelines are no exception.

Consider this program from Item 45:

```
// Stream-based program to generate the first 20 Mersenne primes
public static void main(String[] args) {
    primes().map(p -> TWO.pow(p.intValueExact()).subtract(ONE))
        .filter(mersenne -> mersenne.isProbablePrime(50))
        .limit(20)
        .forEach(System.out::println);
}

static Stream<BigInteger> primes() {
    return Stream.iterate(TWO, BigInteger::nextProbablePrime);
}
```

On my machine, this program immediately starts printing primes and takes 12.5 seconds to run to completion. Suppose I naively try to speed it up by adding a call to parallel() to the stream pipeline. What do you think will happen to its performance? Will it get a few percent faster? A few percent slower? Sadly, what happens is that it doesn't print anything, but CPU usage spikes to 90 percent and stays there indefinitely (a *liveness failure*). The program might terminate eventually, but I was unwilling to find out; I stopped it forcibly after half an hour.

What's going on here? Simply put, the streams library has no idea how to parallelize this pipeline and the heuristics fail. Even under the best of circumstances, **parallelizing a pipeline is unlikely to increase its performance if the source is from Stream.iterate, or the intermediate operation limit is used.** This pipeline has to contend with *both* of these issues. Worse, the default parallelization strategy deals with the unpredictability of limit by assuming there's no harm in processing a few extra elements and discarding any unneeded results. In this case, it takes roughly twice as long to find each Mersenne prime as it did to find the previous one. Thus, the cost of computing a single extra element is roughly equal to the cost of computing all previous elements combined, and this innocuous-looking pipeline brings the automatic parallelization algorithm to its knees. The moral of this story is simple: **Do not parallelize stream pipelines indiscriminately.** The performance consequences may be disastrous.

As a rule, **performance gains from parallelism are best on streams over ArrayList, HashMap, HashSet, and ConcurrentHashMap instances; arrays; int ranges; and long ranges.** What these data structures have in common is that they can all be accurately and cheaply split into subranges of any desired sizes, which makes it easy to divide work among parallel threads. The abstraction used by the streams library to perform this task is the *spliterator*, which is returned by the spliterator method on Stream and Iterable.

Another important factor that all of these data structures have in common is that they provide good-to-excellent *locality of reference* when processed sequentially: sequential element references are stored together in memory. The objects referred to by those references may not be close to one another in memory, which reduces locality-of-reference. Locality-of-reference turns out to be critically important for parallelizing bulk operations: without it, threads spend much of their time idle, waiting for data to be transferred from memory into the processor's cache. The data structures with the best locality of reference are primitive arrays because the data itself is stored contiguously in memory.

The nature of a stream pipeline's terminal operation also affects the effectiveness of parallel execution. If a significant amount of work is done in the terminal operation compared to the overall work of the pipeline and that operation is inherently sequential, then parallelizing the pipeline will have limited effectiveness. The best terminal operations for parallelism are *reductions*, where all of the elements emerging from the pipeline are combined using one of Stream's reduce methods, or prepackaged reductions such as min, max, count, and sum. The *short-circuiting* operations anyMatch, allMatch, and noneMatch are also amenable to parallelism. The operations performed by Stream's collect method, which are known as *mutable reductions*, are not good candidates for parallelism because the overhead of combining collections is costly.

If you write your own Stream, Iterable, or Collection implementation and you want decent parallel performance, you must override the spliterator method and test the parallel performance of the resulting streams extensively. Writing high-quality spliterators is difficult and beyond the scope of this book.

Not only can parallelizing a stream lead to poor performance, including liveness failures; it can lead to incorrect results and unpredictable behavior (*safety failures*). Safety failures may result from parallelizing a pipeline that uses mappers, filters, and other programmer-supplied function objects that fail to adhere to their specifications. The Stream specification places stringent requirements on these function objects. For example, the accumulator and combiner functions passed to Stream's reduce operation must be associative, non-interfering, and stateless. If you violate these requirements (some of which are discussed in Item 46) but run your pipeline sequentially, it will likely yield correct results; if you parallelize it, it will likely fail, perhaps catastrophically.

Along these lines, it's worth noting that even if the parallelized Mersenne primes program had run to completion, it would not have printed the primes in the correct (ascending) order. To preserve the order displayed by the sequential version, you'd have to replace the forEach terminal operation with forEachOrdered, which is guaranteed to traverse parallel streams in *encounter order*.

Even assuming that you're using an efficiently splittable source stream, a parallelizable or cheap terminal operation, and non-interfering function objects, you won't get a good speedup from parallelization unless the pipeline is doing enough real work to offset the costs associated with parallelism. As a *very* rough estimate, the number of elements in the stream times the number of lines of code executed per element should be at least a hundred thousand [Lea14].

It's important to remember that parallelizing a stream is strictly a performance optimization. As is the case for any optimization, you must test the performance before and after the change to ensure that it is worth doing (Item 67). Ideally, you should perform the test in a realistic system setting. Normally, all parallel stream pipelines in a program run in a common fork-join pool. A single misbehaving pipeline can harm the performance of others in unrelated parts of the system.

If it sounds like the odds are stacked against you when parallelizing stream pipelines, it's because they are. An acquaintance who maintains a multimillion-line codebase that makes heavy use of streams found only a handful of places where parallel streams were effective. This does *not* mean that you should refrain from parallelizing streams. **Under the right circumstances, it *is* possible to achieve near-linear speedup in the number of processor cores simply by adding a parallel call to a stream pipeline.** Certain domains, such as machine learning and data processing, are particularly amenable to these speedups.

As a simple example of a stream pipeline where parallelism is effective, consider this function for computing $\pi(n)$, the number of primes less than or equal to n:

```
// Prime-counting stream pipeline - benefits from parallelization
static long pi(long n) {
    return LongStream.rangeClosed(2, n)
        .mapToObj(BigInteger::valueOf)
        .filter(i -> i.isProbablePrime(50))
        .count();
}
```

On my machine, it takes 31 seconds to compute $\pi(10^8)$ using this function. Simply adding a parallel() call reduces the time to 9.2 seconds:

```
// Prime-counting stream pipeline - parallel version
static long pi(long n) {
    return LongStream.rangeClosed(2, n)
        .parallel()
        .mapToObj(BigInteger::valueOf)
        .filter(i -> i.isProbablePrime(50))
        .count();
}
```

In other words, parallelizing the computation speeds it up by a factor of 3.7 on my quad-core machine. It's worth noting that this is *not* how you'd compute $\pi(n)$ for large values of n in practice. There are far more efficient algorithms, notably Lehmer's formula.

If you are going to parallelize a stream of random numbers, start with a SplittableRandom instance rather than a ThreadLocalRandom (or the essentially obsolete Random). SplittableRandom is designed for precisely this use, and has the potential for linear speedup. ThreadLocalRandom is designed for use by a single thread, and will adapt itself to function as a parallel stream source, but won't be as fast as SplittableRandom. Random synchronizes on every operation, so it will result in excessive, parallelism-killing contention.

In summary, do not even attempt to parallelize a stream pipeline unless you have good reason to believe that it will preserve the correctness of the computation and increase its speed. The cost of inappropriately parallelizing a stream can be a program failure or performance disaster. If you believe that parallelism may be justified, ensure that your code remains correct when run in parallel, and do careful performance measurements under realistic conditions. If your code remains correct and these experiments bear out your suspicion of increased performance, then and only then parallelize the stream in production code.

CHAPTER 8

Methods

THIS chapter discusses several aspects of method design: how to treat parameters and return values, how to design method signatures, and how to document methods. Much of the material in this chapter applies to constructors as well as to methods. Like Chapter 4, this chapter focuses on usability, robustness, and flexibility.

Item 49: Check parameters for validity

Most methods and constructors have some restrictions on what values may be passed into their parameters. For example, it is not uncommon that index values must be non-negative and object references must be non-null. You should clearly document all such restrictions and enforce them with checks at the beginning of the method body. This is a special case of the general principle that you should attempt to detect errors as soon as possible after they occur. Failing to do so makes it less likely that an error will be detected and makes it harder to determine the source of an error once it has been detected.

If an invalid parameter value is passed to a method and the method checks its parameters before execution, it will fail quickly and cleanly with an appropriate exception. If the method fails to check its parameters, several things could happen. The method could fail with a confusing exception in the midst of processing. Worse, the method could return normally but silently compute the wrong result. Worst of all, the method could return normally but leave some object in a compromised state, causing an error at some unrelated point in the code at some undetermined time in the future. In other words, failure to validate parameters, can result in a violation of *failure atomicity* (Item 76).

For public and protected methods, use the Javadoc @throws tag to document the exception that will be thrown if a restriction on parameter values is violated

(Item 74). Typically, the resulting exception will be IllegalArgumentException, IndexOutOfBoundsException, or NullPointerException (Item 72). Once you've documented the restrictions on a method's parameters and you've documented the exceptions that will be thrown if these restrictions are violated, it is a simple matter to enforce the restrictions. Here's a typical example:

```java
/**
 * Returns a BigInteger whose value is (this mod m).  This method
 * differs from the remainder method in that it always returns a
 * non-negative BigInteger.
 *
 * @param  m the modulus, which must be positive
 * @return this mod m
 * @throws ArithmeticException if m is less than or equal to 0
 */
public BigInteger mod(BigInteger m) {
    if (m.signum() <= 0)
        throw new ArithmeticException("Modulus <= 0: " + m);
    ... // Do the computation
}
```

Note that the doc comment does *not* say "mod throws NullPointerException if m is null," even though the method does exactly that, as a byproduct of invoking m.signum(). This exception *is* documented in the class-level doc comment for the enclosing BigInteger class. The class-level comment applies to all parameters in all of the class's public methods. This is a good way to avoid the clutter of documenting every NullPointerException on every method individually. It may be combined with the use of @Nullable or a similar annotation to indicate that a particular parameter may be null, but this practice is not standard, and multiple annotations are in use for this purpose.

The Objects.requireNonNull method, added in Java 7, is flexible and convenient, so there's no reason to perform null checks manually anymore. You can specify your own exception detail message if you wish. The method returns its input, so you can perform a null check at the same time as you use a value:

```java
// Inline use of Java's null-checking facility
this.strategy = Objects.requireNonNull(strategy, "strategy");
```

You can also ignore the return value and use Objects.requireNonNull as a freestanding null check where that suits your needs.

In Java 9, a range-checking facility was added to java.util.Objects. This facility consists of three methods: checkFromIndexSize, checkFromToIndex, and checkIndex. This facility is not as flexible as the null-checking method. It doesn't let you specify your own exception detail message, and it is designed solely for use on list and array indices. It does not handle closed ranges (which contain both of their endpoints). But if it does what you need, it's a useful convenience.

For an unexported method, you, as the package author, control the circumstances under which the method is called, so you can and should ensure that only valid parameter values are ever passed in. Therefore, nonpublic methods can check their parameters using *assertions,* as shown below:

```
// Private helper function for a recursive sort
private static void sort(long a[], int offset, int length) {
    assert a != null;
    assert offset >= 0 && offset <= a.length;
    assert length >= 0 && length <= a.length - offset;
    ... // Do the computation
}
```

In essence, these assertions are claims that the asserted condition *will* be true, regardless of how the enclosing package is used by its clients. Unlike normal validity checks, assertions throw AssertionError if they fail. And unlike normal validity checks, they have no effect and essentially no cost unless you enable them, which you do by passing the -ea (or -enableassertions) flag to the java command. For more information on assertions, see the tutorial [Asserts].

It is particularly important to check the validity of parameters that are not used by a method, but stored for later use. For example, consider the static factory method on page 101, which takes an int array and returns a List view of the array. If a client were to pass in null, the method would throw a NullPointerException because the method has an explicit check (the call to Objects.requireNonNull). Had the check been omitted, the method would return a reference to a newly created List instance that would throw a NullPointerException as soon as a client attempted to use it. By that time, the origin of the List instance might be difficult to determine, which could greatly complicate the task of debugging.

Constructors represent a special case of the principle that you should check the validity of parameters that are to be stored away for later use. It is critical to check the validity of constructor parameters to prevent the construction of an object that violates its class invariants.

There are exceptions to the rule that you should explicitly check a method's parameters before performing its computation. An important exception is the case in which the validity check would be expensive or impractical *and* the check is performed implicitly in the process of doing the computation. For example, consider a method that sorts a list of objects, such as `Collections.sort(List)`. All of the objects in the list must be mutually comparable. In the process of sorting the list, every object in the list will be compared to some other object in the list. If the objects aren't mutually comparable, one of these comparisons will throw a `ClassCastException`, which is exactly what the `sort` method should do. Therefore, there would be little point in checking ahead of time that the elements in the list were mutually comparable. Note, however, that indiscriminate reliance on implicit validity checks can result in the loss of *failure atomicity* (Item 76).

Occasionally, a computation implicitly performs a required validity check but throws the wrong exception if the check fails. In other words, the exception that the computation would naturally throw as the result of an invalid parameter value doesn't match the exception that the method is documented to throw. Under these circumstances, you should use the *exception translation* idiom, described in Item 73, to translate the natural exception into the correct one.

Do not infer from this item that arbitrary restrictions on parameters are a good thing. On the contrary, you should design methods to be as general as it is practical to make them. The fewer restrictions that you place on parameters, the better, assuming the method can do something reasonable with all of the parameter values that it accepts. Often, however, some restrictions are intrinsic to the abstraction being implemented.

To summarize, each time you write a method or constructor, you should think about what restrictions exist on its parameters. You should document these restrictions and enforce them with explicit checks at the beginning of the method body. It is important to get into the habit of doing this. The modest work that it entails will be paid back with interest the first time a validity check fails.

Item 50: Make defensive copies when needed

One thing that makes Java a pleasure to use is that it is a *safe language*. This means that in the absence of native methods it is immune to buffer overruns, array overruns, wild pointers, and other memory corruption errors that plague unsafe languages such as C and C++. In a safe language, it is possible to write classes and to know with certainty that their invariants will hold, no matter what happens in any other part of the system. This is not possible in languages that treat all of memory as one giant array.

Even in a safe language, you aren't insulated from other classes without some effort on your part. **You must program defensively, with the assumption that clients of your class will do their best to destroy its invariants.** This is increasingly true as people try harder to break the security of systems, but more commonly, your class will have to cope with unexpected behavior resulting from the honest mistakes of well-intentioned programmers. Either way, it is worth taking the time to write classes that are robust in the face of ill-behaved clients.

While it is impossible for another class to modify an object's internal state without some assistance from the object, it is surprisingly easy to provide such assistance without meaning to do so. For example, consider the following class, which purports to represent an immutable time period:

```java
// Broken "immutable" time period class
public final class Period {
    private final Date start;
    private final Date end;

    /**
     * @param  start the beginning of the period
     * @param  end the end of the period; must not precede start
     * @throws IllegalArgumentException if start is after end
     * @throws NullPointerException if start or end is null
     */
    public Period(Date start, Date end) {
        if (start.compareTo(end) > 0)
            throw new IllegalArgumentException(
                start + " after " + end);
        this.start = start;
        this.end   = end;
    }

    public Date start() {
        return start;
    }
```

```java
        public Date end() {
            return end;
        }

        ...  // Remainder omitted
}
```

At first glance, this class may appear to be immutable and to enforce the invariant that the start of a period does not follow its end. It is, however, easy to violate this invariant by exploiting the fact that Date is mutable:

```java
// Attack the internals of a Period instance
Date start = new Date();
Date end = new Date();
Period p = new Period(start, end);
end.setYear(78);   // Modifies internals of p!
```

As of Java 8, the obvious way to fix this problem is to use Instant (or Local-DateTime or ZonedDateTime) in place of a Date because Instant (and the other java.time classes) are immutable (Item 17). **Date is obsolete and should no longer be used in new code.** That said, the problem still exists: there are times when you'll have to use mutable value types in your APIs and internal representations, and the techniques discussed in this item are appropriate for those times.

To protect the internals of a Period instance from this sort of attack, **it is essential to make a *defensive copy* of each mutable parameter to the constructor** and to use the copies as components of the Period instance in place of the originals:

```java
// Repaired constructor - makes defensive copies of parameters
public Period(Date start, Date end) {
    this.start = new Date(start.getTime());
    this.end   = new Date(end.getTime());

    if (this.start.compareTo(this.end) > 0)
      throw new IllegalArgumentException(
          this.start + " after " + this.end);
}
```

With the new constructor in place, the previous attack will have no effect on the Period instance. Note that **defensive copies are made *before* checking the validity of the parameters (Item 49), and the validity check is performed on the copies rather than on the originals.** While this may seem unnatural, it is necessary. It protects the class against changes to the parameters from another thread during the *window of vulnerability* between the time the parameters are checked and the time they are copied. In the computer security community, this is known as a *time-of-check/time-of-use* or *TOCTOU* attack [Viega01].

Note also that we did not use Date's clone method to make the defensive copies. Because Date is nonfinal, the clone method is not guaranteed to return an object whose class is java.util.Date: it could return an instance of an untrusted subclass that is specifically designed for malicious mischief. Such a subclass could, for example, record a reference to each instance in a private static list at the time of its creation and allow the attacker to access this list. This would give the attacker free rein over all instances. To prevent this sort of attack, **do not use the clone method to make a defensive copy of a parameter whose type is subclassable by untrusted parties.**

While the replacement constructor successfully defends against the previous attack, it is still possible to mutate a Period instance, because its accessors offer access to its mutable internals:

```
// Second attack on the internals of a Period instance
Date start = new Date();
Date end = new Date();
Period p = new Period(start, end);
p.end().setYear(78);  // Modifies internals of p!
```

To defend against the second attack, merely modify the accessors to **return defensive copies of mutable internal fields:**

```
// Repaired accessors - make defensive copies of internal fields
public Date start() {
    return new Date(start.getTime());
}

public Date end() {
    return new Date(end.getTime());
}
```

With the new constructor and the new accessors in place, Period is truly immutable. No matter how malicious or incompetent a programmer, there is simply no way to violate the invariant that the start of a period does not follow its end (without resorting to extralinguistic means such as native methods and reflection). This is true because there is no way for any class other than Period itself to gain access to either of the mutable fields in a Period instance. These fields are truly encapsulated within the object.

In the accessors, unlike the constructor, it would be permissible to use the `clone` method to make the defensive copies. This is so because we know that the class of `Period`'s internal `Date` objects is `java.util.Date`, and not some untrusted subclass. That said, you are generally better off using a constructor or static factory to copy an instance, for reasons outlined in Item 13.

Defensive copying of parameters is not just for immutable classes. Any time you write a method or constructor that stores a reference to a client-provided object in an internal data structure, think about whether the client-provided object is potentially mutable. If it is, think about whether your class could tolerate a change in the object after it was entered into the data structure. If the answer is no, you must defensively copy the object and enter the copy into the data structure in place of the original. For example, if you are considering using a client-provided object reference as an element in an internal `Set` instance or as a key in an internal `Map` instance, you should be aware that the invariants of the set or map would be corrupted if the object were modified after it is inserted.

The same is true for defensive copying of internal components prior to returning them to clients. Whether or not your class is immutable, you should think twice before returning a reference to an internal component that is mutable. Chances are, you should return a defensive copy. Remember that nonzero-length arrays are always mutable. Therefore, you should always make a defensive copy of an internal array before returning it to a client. Alternatively, you could return an immutable view of the array. Both of these techniques are shown in Item 15.

Arguably, the real lesson in all of this is that you should, where possible, use immutable objects as components of your objects so that you that don't have to worry about defensive copying (Item 17). In the case of our `Period` example, use `Instant` (or `LocalDateTime` or `ZonedDateTime`), unless you're using a release prior to Java 8. If you are using an earlier release, one option is to store the primitive `long` returned by `Date.getTime()` in place of a `Date` reference.

There may be a performance penalty associated with defensive copying and it isn't always justified. If a class trusts its caller not to modify an internal component, perhaps because the class and its client are both part of the same package, then it may be appropriate to dispense with defensive copying. Under these circumstances, the class documentation should make it clear that the caller must not modify the affected parameters or return values.

Even across package boundaries, it is not always appropriate to make a defensive copy of a mutable parameter before integrating it into an object. There are some methods and constructors whose invocation indicates an explicit *handoff* of the object referenced by a parameter. When invoking such a method, the client promises that it will no longer modify the object directly. A method or constructor that expects to take ownership of a client-provided mutable object must make this clear in its documentation.

Classes containing methods or constructors whose invocation indicates a transfer of control cannot defend themselves against malicious clients. Such classes are acceptable only when there is mutual trust between a class and its client or when damage to the class's invariants would harm no one but the client. An example of the latter situation is the wrapper class pattern (Item 18). Depending on the nature of the wrapper class, the client could destroy the class's invariants by directly accessing an object after it has been wrapped, but this typically would harm only the client.

In summary, if a class has mutable components that it gets from or returns to its clients, the class must defensively copy these components. If the cost of the copy would be prohibitive *and* the class trusts its clients not to modify the components inappropriately, then the defensive copy may be replaced by documentation outlining the client's responsibility not to modify the affected components.

Item 51: Design method signatures carefully

This item is a grab bag of API design hints that don't quite deserve items of their own. Taken together, they'll help make your API easier to learn and use and less prone to errors.

Choose method names carefully. Names should always obey the standard naming conventions (Item 68). Your primary goal should be to choose names that are understandable and consistent with other names in the same package. Your secondary goal should be to choose names consistent with the broader consensus, where it exists. Avoid long method names. When in doubt, look to the Java library APIs for guidance. While there are plenty of inconsistencies—inevitable, given the size and scope of these libraries—there is also a fair amount of consensus.

Don't go overboard in providing convenience methods. Every method should "pull its weight." Too many methods make a class difficult to learn, use, document, test, and maintain. This is doubly true for interfaces, where too many methods complicate life for implementors as well as users. For each action supported by your class or interface, provide a fully functional method. Consider providing a "shorthand" only if it will be used often. **When in doubt, leave it out.**

Avoid long parameter lists. Aim for four parameters or fewer. Most programmers can't remember longer parameter lists. If many of your methods exceed this limit, your API won't be usable without constant reference to its documentation. Modern IDEs help, but you are still much better off with short parameter lists. **Long sequences of identically typed parameters are especially harmful.** Not only won't users be able to remember the order of the parameters, but when they transpose parameters accidentally, their programs will still compile and run. They just won't do what their authors intended.

There are three techniques for shortening overly long parameter lists. One is to break the method up into multiple methods, each of which requires only a subset of the parameters. If done carelessly, this can lead to too many methods, but it can also help *reduce* the method count by increasing orthogonality. For example, consider the `java.util.List` interface. It does not provide methods to find the first or last index of an element in a sublist, both of which would require three parameters. Instead it provides the `subList` method, which takes two parameters and returns a *view* of a sublist. This method can be combined with the `indexOf` or `lastIndexOf` method, each of which has a single parameter, to yield the desired functionality. Moreover, the `subList` method can be combined with *any* method that operates on a `List` instance to perform arbitrary computations on sublists. The resulting API has a very high power-to-weight ratio.

A second technique for shortening long parameter lists is to create *helper classes* to hold groups of parameters. Typically these helper classes are static member classes (Item 24). This technique is recommended if a frequently occurring sequence of parameters is seen to represent some distinct entity. For example, suppose you are writing a class representing a card game, and you find yourself constantly passing a sequence of two parameters representing a card's rank and its suit. Your API, as well as the internals of your class, would probably benefit if you added a helper class to represent a card and replaced every occurrence of the parameter sequence with a single parameter of the helper class.

A third technique that combines aspects of the first two is to adapt the Builder pattern (Item 2) from object construction to method invocation. If you have a method with many parameters, especially if some of them are optional, it can be beneficial to define an object that represents all of the parameters and to allow the client to make multiple "setter" calls on this object, each of which sets a single parameter or a small, related group. Once the desired parameters have been set, the client invokes the object's "execute" method, which does any final validity checks on the parameters and performs the actual computation.

For parameter types, favor interfaces over classes (Item 64). If there is an appropriate interface to define a parameter, use it in favor of a class that implements the interface. For example, there is no reason to ever write a method that takes HashMap on input—use Map instead. This lets you pass in a HashMap, a TreeMap, a ConcurrentHashMap, a submap of a TreeMap, or any Map implementation yet to be written. By using a class instead of an interface, you restrict your client to a particular implementation and force an unnecessary and potentially expensive copy operation if the input data happens to exist in some other form.

Prefer two-element enum types to boolean parameters, unless the meaning of the boolean is clear from the method name. Enums make your code easier to read and to write. Also, they make it easy to add more options later. For example, you might have a Thermometer type with a static factory that takes this enum:

```
public enum TemperatureScale { FAHRENHEIT, CELSIUS }
```

Not only does Thermometer.newInstance(TemperatureScale.CELSIUS) make a lot more sense than Thermometer.newInstance(true), but you can add KELVIN to TemperatureScale in a future release without having to add a new static factory to Thermometer. Also, you can refactor temperature-scale dependencies into methods on the enum constants (Item 34). For example, each scale constant could have a method that took a double value and converted it to Celsius.

Item 52: Use overloading judiciously

The following program is a well-intentioned attempt to classify collections according to whether they are sets, lists, or some other kind of collection:

```
// Broken! - What does this program print?
public class CollectionClassifier {
    public static String classify(Set<?> s) {
        return "Set";
    }

    public static String classify(List<?> lst) {
        return "List";
    }

    public static String classify(Collection<?> c) {
        return "Unknown Collection";
    }

    public static void main(String[] args) {
        Collection<?>[] collections = {
            new HashSet<String>(),
            new ArrayList<BigInteger>(),
            new HashMap<String, String>().values()
        };

        for (Collection<?> c : collections)
            System.out.println(classify(c));
    }
}
```

You might expect this program to print Set, followed by List and Unknown Collection, but it doesn't. It prints Unknown Collection three times. Why does this happen? Because the classify method is *overloaded*, and **the choice of which overloading to invoke is made at compile time.** For all three iterations of the loop, the compile-time type of the parameter is the same: Collection<?>. The runtime type is different in each iteration, but this does not affect the choice of overloading. Because the compile-time type of the parameter is Collection<?>, the only applicable overloading is the third one, classify(Collection<?>), and this overloading is invoked in each iteration of the loop.

The behavior of this program is counterintuitive because **selection among overloaded methods is static, while selection among overridden methods is dynamic.** The correct version of an *overridden* method is chosen at runtime, based on the runtime type of the object on which the method is invoked. As a reminder, a method is overridden when a subclass contains a method declaration with the same signature as a method declaration in an ancestor. If an instance method is overridden in a subclass and this method is invoked on an instance of the subclass, the subclass's *overriding method* executes, regardless of the compile-time type of the subclass instance. To make this concrete, consider the following program:

```
class Wine {
    String name() { return "wine"; }
}

class SparklingWine extends Wine {
    @Override String name() { return "sparkling wine"; }
}

class Champagne extends SparklingWine {
    @Override String name() { return "champagne"; }
}

public class Overriding {
    public static void main(String[] args) {
        List<Wine> wineList = List.of(
            new Wine(), new SparklingWine(), new Champagne());

        for (Wine wine : wineList)
            System.out.println(wine.name());
    }
}
```

The name method is declared in class Wine and overridden in subclasses SparklingWine and Champagne. As you would expect, this program prints out wine, sparkling wine, and champagne, even though the compile-time type of the instance is Wine in each iteration of the loop. The compile-time type of an object has no effect on which method is executed when an overridden method is invoked; the "most specific" overriding method always gets executed. Compare this to overloading, where the runtime type of an object has no effect on which overloading is executed; the selection is made at compile time, based entirely on the compile-time types of the parameters.

In the CollectionClassifier example, the intent of the program was to discern the type of the parameter by dispatching automatically to the appropriate method overloading based on the runtime type of the parameter, just as the name method did in the Wine example. Method overloading simply does not provide this

functionality. Assuming a static method is required, the best way to fix the
CollectionClassifier program is to replace all three overloadings of classify
with a single method that does explicit instanceof tests:

```
public static String classify(Collection<?> c) {
    return c instanceof Set  ? "Set" :
           c instanceof List ? "List" : "Unknown Collection";
}
```

Because overriding is the norm and overloading is the exception, overriding
sets people's expectations for the behavior of method invocation. As demonstrated
by the CollectionClassifier example, overloading can easily confound these
expectations. It is bad practice to write code whose behavior is likely to confuse
programmers. This is especially true for APIs. If the typical user of an API does
not know which of several method overloadings will get invoked for a given set of
parameters, use of the API is likely to result in errors. These errors will likely
manifest themselves as erratic behavior at runtime, and many programmers will
have a hard time diagnosing them. Therefore you should **avoid confusing uses of
overloading.**

Exactly what constitutes a confusing use of overloading is open to some
debate. **A safe, conservative policy is never to export two overloadings with
the same number of parameters.** If a method uses varargs, a conservative policy
is not to overload it at all, except as described in Item 53. If you adhere to these
restrictions, programmers will never be in doubt as to which overloading applies
to any set of actual parameters. These restrictions are not terribly onerous because
you can always give methods different names instead of overloading them.

For example, consider the ObjectOutputStream class. It has a variant of its
write method for every primitive type and for several reference types. Rather than
overloading the write method, these variants all have different names, such as
writeBoolean(boolean), writeInt(int), and writeLong(long). An added
benefit of this naming pattern, when compared to overloading, is that it is possible
to provide read methods with corresponding names, for example, readBoolean(),
readInt(), and readLong(). The ObjectInputStream class does, in fact,
provide such read methods.

For constructors, you don't have the option of using different names: multiple
constructors for a class are *always* overloaded. You do, in many cases, have the
option of exporting static factories instead of constructors (Item 1). Also, with
constructors you don't have to worry about interactions between overloading and
overriding, because constructors can't be overridden. You will probably have

occasion to export multiple constructors with the same number of parameters, so it pays to know how to do it safely.

Exporting multiple overloadings with the same number of parameters is unlikely to confuse programmers *if* it is always clear which overloading will apply to any given set of actual parameters. This is the case when at least one corresponding formal parameter in each pair of overloadings has a "radically different" type in the two overloadings. Two types are radically different if it is clearly impossible to cast any non-null expression to both types. Under these circumstances, which overloading applies to a given set of actual parameters is fully determined by the runtime types of the parameters and cannot be affected by their compile-time types, so a major source of confusion goes away. For example, `ArrayList` has one constructor that takes an `int` and a second constructor that takes a `Collection`. It is hard to imagine any confusion over which of these two constructors will be invoked under any circumstances.

Prior to Java 5, all primitive types were radically different from all reference types, but this is not true in the presence of autoboxing, and it has caused real trouble. Consider the following program:

```
public class SetList {
    public static void main(String[] args) {
        Set<Integer> set = new TreeSet<>();
        List<Integer> list = new ArrayList<>();

        for (int i = -3; i < 3; i++) {
            set.add(i);
            list.add(i);
        }
        for (int i = 0; i < 3; i++) {
            set.remove(i);
            list.remove(i);
        }
        System.out.println(set + " " + list);
    }
}
```

First, the program adds the integers from -3 to 2, inclusive, to a sorted set and a list. Then, it makes three identical calls to `remove` on the set and the list. If you're like most people, you'd expect the program to remove the non-negative values (0, 1, and 2) from the set and the list and to print `[-3, -2, -1]` `[-3, -2, -1]`. In fact, the program removes the non-negative values from the set and the odd values from the list and prints `[-3, -2, -1]` `[-2, 0, 2]`. It is an understatement to call this behavior confusing.

Here's what's happening: The call to set.remove(i) selects the overloading remove(E), where E is the element type of the set (Integer), and autoboxes i from int to Integer. This is the behavior you'd expect, so the program ends up removing the positive values from the set. The call to list.remove(i), on the other hand, selects the overloading remove(int i), which removes the element at the specified *position* in the list. If you start with the list [-3, -2, -1, 0, 1, 2] and remove the zeroth element, then the first, and then the second, you're left with [-2, 0, 2], and the mystery is solved. To fix the problem, cast list.remove's argument to Integer, forcing the correct overloading to be selected. Alternatively, you could invoke Integer.valueOf on i and pass the result to list.remove. Either way, the program prints [-3, -2, -1] [-3, -2, -1], as expected:

```
for (int i = 0; i < 3; i++) {
    set.remove(i);
    list.remove((Integer) i);  // or remove(Integer.valueOf(i))
}
```

The confusing behavior demonstrated by the previous example came about because the List<E> interface has two overloadings of the remove method: remove(E) and remove(int). Prior to Java 5 when the List interface was "generified," it had a remove(Object) method in place of remove(E), and the corresponding parameter types, Object and int, were radically different. But in the presence of generics and autoboxing, the two parameter types are no longer radically different. In other words, adding generics and autoboxing to the language damaged the List interface. Luckily, few if any other APIs in the Java libraries were similarly damaged, but this tale makes it clear that autoboxing and generics increased the importance of caution when overloading.

The addition of lambdas and method references in Java 8 further increased the potential for confusion in overloading. For example, consider these two snippets:

```
new Thread(System.out::println).start();

ExecutorService exec = Executors.newCachedThreadPool();
exec.submit(System.out::println);
```

While the Thread constructor invocation and the submit method invocation look similar, the former compiles while the latter does not. The arguments are identical (System.out::println), and both the constructor and the method have an overloading that takes a Runnable. What's going on here? The surprising answer is that the submit method has an overloading that takes a Callable<T>, while the Thread constructor does not. You might think that this shouldn't make any difference because all overloadings of `println` return `void`, so the method reference couldn't possibly be a `Callable`. This makes perfect sense, but it's not the way the overload resolution algorithm works. Perhaps equally surprising is that the `submit` method invocation would be legal if the `println` method weren't also overloaded. It is the combination of the overloading of the referenced method (`println`) and the invoked method (`submit`) that prevents the overload resolution algorithm from behaving as you'd expect.

Technically speaking, the problem is that `System.out::println` is an *inexact method reference* [JLS, 15.13.1] and that "certain argument expressions that contain implicitly typed lambda expressions or inexact method references are ignored by the applicability tests, because their meaning cannot be determined until a target type is selected [JLS, 15.12.2]." Don't worry if you don't understand this passage; it is aimed at compiler writers. The key point is that overloading methods or constructors with different functional interfaces in the same argument position causes confusion. Therefore, **do not overload methods to take different functional interfaces in the same argument position.** In the parlance of this item, different functional interfaces are not radically different. The Java compiler will warn you about this sort of problematic overload if you pass the command line switch `-Xlint:overloads`.

Array types and class types other than `Object` are radically different. Also, array types and interface types other than `Serializable` and `Cloneable` are radically different. Two distinct classes are said to be *unrelated* if neither class is a descendant of the other [JLS, 5.5]. For example, `String` and `Throwable` are unrelated. It is impossible for any object to be an instance of two unrelated classes, so unrelated classes are radically different, too.

There are other pairs of types that can't be converted in either direction [JLS, 5.1.12], but once you go beyond the simple cases described above, it becomes very difficult for most programmers to discern which, if any, overloading applies to a set of actual parameters. The rules that determine which overloading is selected are extremely complex and grow more complex with every release. Few programmers understand all of their subtleties.

There may be times when you feel the need to violate the guidelines in this item, especially when evolving existing classes. For example, consider `String`, which has had a `contentEquals(StringBuffer)` method since Java 4. In Java 5, `CharSequence` was added to provide a common interface for `StringBuffer`, `StringBuilder`, `String`, `CharBuffer`, and other similar types. At the same time that `CharSequence` was added, `String` was outfitted with an overloading of the `contentEquals` method that takes a `CharSequence`.

While the resulting overloading clearly violates the guidelines in this item, it causes no harm because both overloaded methods do exactly the same thing when they are invoked on the same object reference. The programmer may not know which overloading will be invoked, but it is of no consequence so long as they behave identically. The standard way to ensure this behavior is to have the more specific overloading forward to the more general:

```
// Ensuring that 2 methods have identical behavior by forwarding
public boolean contentEquals(StringBuffer sb) {
    return contentEquals((CharSequence) sb);
}
```

While the Java libraries largely adhere to the spirit of the advice in this item, there are a number of classes that violate it. For example, String exports two overloaded static factory methods, valueOf(char[]) and valueOf(Object), that do completely different things when passed the same object reference. There is no real justification for this, and it should be regarded as an anomaly with the potential for real confusion.

To summarize, just because you can overload methods doesn't mean you should. It is generally best to refrain from overloading methods with multiple signatures that have the same number of parameters. In some cases, especially where constructors are involved, it may be impossible to follow this advice. In these cases, you should at least avoid situations where the same set of parameters can be passed to different overloadings by the addition of casts. If this cannot be avoided, for example, because you are retrofitting an existing class to implement a new interface, you should ensure that all overloadings behave identically when passed the same parameters. If you fail to do this, programmers will be hard pressed to make effective use of the overloaded method or constructor, and they won't understand why it doesn't work.

Item 53: Use varargs judiciously

Varargs methods, formally known as *variable arity* methods [JLS, 8.4.1], accept zero or more arguments of a specified type. The varargs facility works by first creating an array whose size is the number of arguments passed at the call site, then putting the argument values into the array, and finally passing the array to the method.

For example, here is a varargs method that takes a sequence of int arguments and returns their sum. As you would expect, the value of sum(1, 2, 3) is 6, and the value of sum() is 0:

```
// Simple use of varargs
static int sum(int... args) {
    int sum = 0;
    for (int arg : args)
        sum += arg;
    return sum;
}
```

Sometimes it's appropriate to write a method that requires *one* or more arguments of some type, rather than *zero* or more. For example, suppose you want to write a function that computes the minimum of its arguments. This function is not well defined if the client passes no arguments. You could check the array length at runtime:

```
// The WRONG way to use varargs to pass one or more arguments!
static int min(int... args) {
    if (args.length == 0)
        throw new IllegalArgumentException("Too few arguments");
    int min = args[0];
    for (int i = 1; i < args.length; i++)
        if (args[i] < min)
            min = args[i];
    return min;
}
```

This solution has several problems. The most serious is that if the client invokes this method with no arguments, it fails at runtime rather than compile time. Another problem is that it is ugly. You have to include an explicit validity check on args, and you can't use a for-each loop unless you initialize min to Integer.MAX_VALUE, which is also ugly.

Luckily there's a much better way to achieve the desired effect. Declare the method to take two parameters, one normal parameter of the specified type and one varargs parameter of this type. This solution corrects all the deficiencies of the previous one:

```
// The right way to use varargs to pass one or more arguments
static int min(int firstArg, int... remainingArgs) {
    int min = firstArg;
    for (int arg : remainingArgs)
        if (arg < min)
            min = arg;
    return min;
}
```

As you can see from this example, varargs are effective in circumstances where you want a method with a variable number of arguments. Varargs were designed for printf, which was added to the platform at the same time as varargs, and for the core reflection facility (Item 65), which was retrofitted. Both printf and reflection benefited enormously from varargs.

Exercise care when using varargs in performance-critical situations. Every invocation of a varargs method causes an array allocation and initialization. If you have determined empirically that you can't afford this cost but you need the flexibility of varargs, there is a pattern that lets you have your cake and eat it too. Suppose you've determined that 95 percent of the calls to a method have three or fewer parameters. Then declare five overloadings of the method, one each with zero through three ordinary parameters, and a single varargs method for use when the number of arguments exceeds three:

```
public void foo() { }
public void foo(int a1) { }
public void foo(int a1, int a2) { }
public void foo(int a1, int a2, int a3) { }
public void foo(int a1, int a2, int a3, int... rest) { }
```

Now you know that you'll pay the cost of the array creation only in the 5 percent of all invocations where the number of parameters exceeds three. Like most performance optimizations, this technique usually isn't appropriate, but when it is, it's a lifesaver.

The static factories for EnumSet use this technique to reduce the cost of creating enum sets to a minimum. This was appropriate because it was critical that enum sets provide a performance-competitive replacement for bit fields (Item 36).

In summary, varargs are invaluable when you need to define methods with a variable number of arguments. Precede the varargs parameter with any required parameters, and be aware of the performance consequences of using varargs.

Item 54: Return empty collections or arrays, not nulls

It is not uncommon to see methods that look something like this:

```
// Returns null to indicate an empty collection. Don't do this!
private final List<Cheese> cheesesInStock = ...;

/**
 * @return a list containing all of the cheeses in the shop,
 *     or null if no cheeses are available for purchase.
 */
public List<Cheese> getCheeses() {
    return cheesesInStock.isEmpty() ? null
        : new ArrayList<>(cheesesInStock);
}
```

There is no reason to special-case the situation where no cheeses are available for purchase. Doing so requires extra code in the client to handle the possibly null return value, for example:

```
List<Cheese> cheeses = shop.getCheeses();
if (cheeses != null && cheeses.contains(Cheese.STILTON))
    System.out.println("Jolly good, just the thing.");
```

This sort of circumlocution is required in nearly every use of a method that returns null in place of an empty collection or array. It is error-prone, because the programmer writing the client might forget to write the special-case code to handle a null return. Such an error may go unnoticed for years because such methods usually return one or more objects. Also, returning null in place of an empty container complicates the implementation of the method returning the container.

It is sometimes argued that a null return value is preferable to an empty collection or array because it avoids the expense of allocating the empty container. This argument fails on two counts. First, it is inadvisable to worry about performance at this level unless measurements have shown that the allocation in question is a real contributor to performance problems (Item 67). Second, it *is* possible to return empty collections and arrays without allocating them. Here is the typical code to return a possibly empty collection. Usually, this is all you need:

```
//The right way to return a possibly empty collection
public List<Cheese> getCheeses() {
    return new ArrayList<>(cheesesInStock);
}
```

In the unlikely event that you have evidence suggesting that allocating empty collections is harming performance, you can avoid the allocations by returning the same *immutable* empty collection repeatedly, as immutable objects may be shared freely (Item 17). Here is the code to do it, using the Collections.emptyList method. If you were returning a set, you'd use Collections.emptySet; if you were returning a map, you'd use Collections.emptyMap. But remember, this is an optimization, and it's seldom called for. If you think you need it, measure performance before and after, to ensure that it's actually helping:

```
// Optimization - avoids allocating empty collections
public List<Cheese> getCheeses() {
    return cheesesInStock.isEmpty() ? Collections.emptyList()
        : new ArrayList<>(cheesesInStock);
}
```

The situation for arrays is identical to that for collections. Never return null instead of a zero-length array. Normally, you should simply return an array of the correct length, which may be zero. Note that we're passing a zero-length array into the toArray method to indicate the desired return type, which is Cheese[]:

```
//The right way to return a possibly empty array
public Cheese[] getCheeses() {
    return cheesesInStock.toArray(new Cheese[0]);
}
```

If you believe that allocating zero-length arrays is harming performance, you can return the same zero-length array repeatedly because all zero-length arrays are immutable:

```
// Optimization - avoids allocating empty arrays
private static final Cheese[] EMPTY_CHEESE_ARRAY = new Cheese[0];

public Cheese[] getCheeses() {
    return cheesesInStock.toArray(EMPTY_CHEESE_ARRAY);
}
```

In the optimized version, we pass *the same* empty array into every toArray call, and this array will be returned from getCheeses whenever cheesesInStock is empty. Do *not* preallocate the array passed to toArray in hopes of improving performance. Studies have shown that it is counterproductive [Shipilëv16]:

```
// Don't do this - preallocating the array harms performance!
return cheesesInStock.toArray(new Cheese[cheesesInStock.size()]);
```

In summary, **never return null in place of an empty array or collection.** It makes your API more difficult to use and more prone to error, and it has no performance advantages.

Item 55: Return optionals judiciously

Prior to Java 8, there were two approaches you could take when writing a method that was unable to return a value under certain circumstances. Either you could throw an exception, or you could return `null` (assuming the return type was an object reference type). Neither of these approaches is perfect. Exceptions should be reserved for exceptional conditions (Item 69), and throwing an exception is expensive because the entire stack trace is captured when an exception is created. Returning `null` doesn't have these shortcomings, but it has its own. If a method returns `null`, clients must contain special-case code to deal with the possibility of a null return, unless the programmer can *prove* that a null return is impossible. If a client neglects to check for a null return and stores a null return value away in some data structure, a `NullPointerException` may result at some arbitrary time in the future, at some place in the code that has nothing to do with the problem.

In Java 8, there is a third approach to writing methods that may not be able to return a value. The `Optional<T>` class represents an immutable container that can hold either a single non-null `T` reference or nothing at all. An optional that contains nothing is said to be *empty*. A value is said to be *present* in an optional that is not empty. An optional is essentially an immutable collection that can hold at most one element. `Optional<T>` does not implement `Collection<T>`, but it could in principle.

A method that conceptually returns a `T` but may be unable to do so under certain circumstances can instead be declared to return an `Optional<T>`. This allows the method to return an empty result to indicate that it couldn't return a valid result. An `Optional`-returning method is more flexible and easier to use than one that throws an exception, and it is less error-prone than one that returns `null`.

In Item 30, we showed this method to calculate the maximum value in a collection, according to its elements' natural order.

```java
// Returns maximum value in collection - throws exception if empty
public static <E extends Comparable<E>> E max(Collection<E> c) {
    if (c.isEmpty())
        throw new IllegalArgumentException("Empty collection");

    E result = null;
    for (E e : c)
        if (result == null || e.compareTo(result) > 0)
            result = Objects.requireNonNull(e);

    return result;
}
```

This method throws an IllegalArgumentException if the given collection is empty. We mentioned in Item 30 that a better alternative would be to return Optional<E>. Here's how the method looks when it is modified to do so:

```
// Returns maximum value in collection as an Optional<E>
public static <E extends Comparable<E>>
        Optional<E> max(Collection<E> c) {
    if (c.isEmpty())
        return Optional.empty();

    E result = null;
    for (E e : c)
        if (result == null || e.compareTo(result) > 0)
            result = Objects.requireNonNull(e);

    return Optional.of(result);
}
```

As you can see, it is straightforward to return an optional. All you have to do is to create the optional with the appropriate static factory. In this program, we use two: Optional.empty() returns an empty optional, and Optional.of(value) returns an optional containing the given non-null value. It is a programming error to pass null to Optional.of(value). If you do this, the method responds by throwing a NullPointerException. The Optional.ofNullable(value) method accepts a possibly null value and returns an empty optional if null is passed in. **Never return a null value from an Optional-returning method:** it defeats the entire purpose of the facility.

Many terminal operations on streams return optionals. If we rewrite the max method to use a stream, Stream's max operation does the work of generating an optional for us (though we do have to pass in an explicit comparator):

```
// Returns max val in collection as Optional<E> - uses stream
public static <E extends Comparable<E>>
        Optional<E> max(Collection<E> c) {
    return c.stream().max(Comparator.naturalOrder());
}
```

So how do you choose to return an optional instead of returning a null or throwing an exception? **Optionals are similar in spirit to checked exceptions** (Item 71), in that they *force* the user of an API to confront the fact that there may be no value returned. Throwing an unchecked exception or returning a null allows the user to ignore this eventuality, with potentially dire consequences. However, throwing a checked exception requires additional boilerplate code in the client.

If a method returns an optional, the client gets to choose what action to take if the method can't return a value. You can specify a default value:

```
// Using an optional to provide a chosen default value
String lastWordInLexicon = max(words).orElse("No words...");
```

or you can throw any exception that is appropriate. Note that we pass in an exception factory rather than an actual exception. This avoids the expense of creating the exception unless it will actually be thrown:

```
// Using an optional to throw a chosen exception
Toy myToy = max(toys).orElseThrow(TemperTantrumException::new);
```

If you can *prove* that an optional is nonempty, you can get the value from the optional without specifying an action to take if the optional is empty, but if you're wrong, your code will throw a NoSuchElementException:

```
// Using optional when you know there's a return value
Element lastNobleGas = max(Elements.NOBLE_GASES).get();
```

Occasionally you may be faced with a situation where it's expensive to get the default value, and you want to avoid that cost unless it's necessary. For these situations, Optional provides a method that takes a Supplier<T> and invokes it only when necessary. This method is called orElseGet, but perhaps it should have been called orElseCompute because it is closely related to the three Map methods whose names begin with compute. There are several Optional methods for dealing with more specialized use cases: filter, map, flatMap, and ifPresent. In Java 9, two more of these methods were added: or and ifPresentOrElse. If the basic methods described above aren't a good match for your use case, look at the documentation for these more advanced methods and see if they do the job.

In case none of these methods meets your needs, Optional provides the isPresent() method, which may be viewed as a safety valve. It returns true if the optional contains a value, false if it's empty. You can use this method to perform any processing you like on an optional result, but make sure to use it wisely. Many uses of isPresent can profitably be replaced by one of the methods mentioned above. The resulting code will typically be shorter, clearer, and more idiomatic.

For example, consider this code snippet, which prints the process ID of the parent of a process, or N/A if the process has no parent. The snippet uses the ProcessHandle class, introduced in Java 9:

```
Optional<ProcessHandle> parentProcess = ph.parent();
System.out.println("Parent PID: " + (parentProcess.isPresent() ?
    String.valueOf(parentProcess.get().pid()) : "N/A"));
```

The code snippet above can be replaced by this one, which uses Optional's map function:

```
System.out.println("Parent PID: " +
    ph.parent().map(h -> String.valueOf(h.pid())).orElse("N/A"));
```

When programming with streams, it is not uncommon to find yourself with a Stream<Optional<T>> and to require a Stream<T> containing all the elements in the nonempty optionals in order to proceed. If you're using Java 8, here's how to bridge the gap:

```
streamOfOptionals
    .filter(Optional::isPresent)
    .map(Optional::get)
```

In Java 9, Optional was outfitted with a stream() method. This method is an adapter that turns an Optional into a Stream containing an element if one is present in the optional, or none if it is empty. In conjunction with Stream's flatMap method (Item 45), this method provides a concise replacement for the code snippet above:

```
streamOfOptionals.
    .flatMap(Optional::stream)
```

Not all return types benefit from the optional treatment. **Container types, including collections, maps, streams, arrays, and optionals should not be wrapped in optionals.** Rather than returning an empty Optional<List<T>>, you should simply return an empty List<T> (Item 54). Returning the empty container will eliminate the need for client code to process an optional. The ProcessHandle class does have the arguments method, which returns Optional<String[]>, but this method should be regarded as an anomaly that is not to be emulated.

So when should you declare a method to return Optional<T> rather than T? As a rule, **you should declare a method to return Optional<T> if it might not be able to return a result *and* clients will have to perform special processing if no result is returned.** That said, returning an Optional<T> is not without cost.

An `Optional` is an object that has to be allocated and initialized, and reading the value out of the optional requires an extra indirection. This makes optionals inappropriate for use in some performance-critical situations. Whether a particular method falls into this category can only be determined by careful measurement (Item 67).

Returning an optional that contains a boxed primitive type is prohibitively expensive compared to returning a primitive type because the optional has two levels of boxing instead of zero. Therefore, the library designers saw fit to provide analogues of `Optional<T>` for the primitive types `int`, `long`, and `double`. These optional types are `OptionalInt`, `OptionalLong`, and `OptionalDouble`. They contain most, but not all, of the methods on `Optional<T>`. Therefore, **you should never return an optional of a boxed primitive type,** with the possible exception of the "minor primitive types," `Boolean`, `Byte`, `Character`, `Short`, and `Float`.

Thus far, we have discussed returning optionals and processing them after they are returned. We have not discussed other possible uses, and that is because most other uses of optionals are suspect. For example, you should never use optionals as map values. If you do, you have two ways of expressing a key's logical absence from the map: either the key can be absent from the map, or it can be present and map to an empty optional. This represents needless complexity with great potential for confusion and errors. More generally, **it is almost never appropriate to use an optional as a key, value, or element in a collection or array.**

This leaves a big question unanswered. Is it ever appropriate to store an optional in an instance field? Often it's a "bad smell": it suggests that perhaps you should have a subclass containing the optional fields. But sometimes it may be justified. Consider the case of our `NutritionFacts` class in Item 2. A `NutritionFacts` instance contains many fields that are not required. You can't have a subclass for every possible combination of these fields. Also, the fields have primitive types, which make it awkward to express absence directly. The best API for `NutritionFacts` would return an optional from the getter for each optional field, so it makes good sense to simply store those optionals as fields in the object.

In summary, if you find yourself writing a method that can't always return a value and you believe it is important that users of the method consider this possibility every time they call it, then you should probably return an optional. You should, however, be aware that there are real performance consequences associated with returning optionals; for performance-critical methods, it may be better to return a `null` or throw an exception. Finally, you should rarely use an optional in any other capacity than as a return value.

Item 56: Write doc comments for all exposed API elements

If an API is to be usable, it must be documented. Traditionally, API documentation was generated manually, and keeping it in sync with code was a chore. The Java programming environment eases this task with the *Javadoc* utility. Javadoc generates API documentation automatically from source code with specially formatted *documentation comments*, more commonly known as *doc comments*.

While the doc comment conventions are not officially part of the language, they constitute a de facto API that every Java programmer should know. These conventions are described in the *How to Write Doc Comments* web page [Javadoc-guide]. While this page has not been updated since Java 4 was released, it is still an invaluable resource. One important doc tag was added in Java 9, {@index}; one in Java 8, {@implSpec}; and two in Java 5, {@literal} and {@code}. These tags are missing from the aforementioned web page, but are discussed in this item.

To document your API properly, you must precede *every* exported class, interface, constructor, method, and field declaration with a doc comment. If a class is serializable, you should also document its serialized form (Item 87). In the absence of a doc comment, the best that Javadoc can do is to reproduce the declaration as the sole documentation for the affected API element. It is frustrating and error-prone to use an API with missing documentation comments. Public classes should not use default constructors because there is no way to provide doc comments for them. To write maintainable code, you should also write doc comments for most unexported classes, interfaces, constructors, methods, and fields, though these comments needn't be as thorough as those for exported API elements.

The doc comment for a method should describe succinctly the contract between the method and its client. With the exception of methods in classes designed for inheritance (Item 19), the contract should say *what* the method does rather than *how* it does its job. The doc comment should enumerate all of the method's *preconditions*, which are the things that have to be true in order for a client to invoke it, and its *postconditions*, which are the things that will be true after the invocation has completed successfully. Typically, preconditions are described implicitly by the @throws tags for unchecked exceptions; each unchecked exception corresponds to a precondition violation. Also, preconditions can be specified along with the affected parameters in their @param tags.

In addition to preconditions and postconditions, methods should document any *side effects*. A side effect is an observable change in the state of the system that is not obviously required in order to achieve the postcondition. For example, if a method starts a background thread, the documentation should make note of it.

To describe a method's contract fully, the doc comment should have an @param tag for every parameter, an @return tag unless the method has a void return type, and an @throws tag for every exception thrown by the method, whether checked or unchecked (Item 74). If the text in the @return tag would be identical to the description of the method, it may be permissible to omit it, depending on the coding standards you are following.

By convention, the text following an @param tag or @return tag should be a noun phrase describing the value represented by the parameter or return value. Rarely, arithmetic expressions are used in place of noun phrases; see BigInteger for examples. The text following an @throws tag should consist of the word "if," followed by a clause describing the conditions under which the exception is thrown. By convention, the phrase or clause following an @param, @return, or @throws tag is not terminated by a period. All of these conventions are illustrated by the following doc comment:

```
/**
 * Returns the element at the specified position in this list.
 *
 * <p>This method is <i>not</i> guaranteed to run in constant
 * time. In some implementations it may run in time proportional
 * to the element position.
 *
 * @param  index index of element to return; must be
 *         non-negative and less than the size of this list
 * @return the element at the specified position in this list
 * @throws IndexOutOfBoundsException if the index is out of range
 *         ({@code index < 0 || index >= this.size()})
 */
E get(int index);
```

Notice the use of HTML tags in this doc comment (<p> and <i>). The Javadoc utility translates doc comments into HTML, and arbitrary HTML elements in doc comments end up in the resulting HTML document. Occasionally, programmers go so far as to embed HTML tables in their doc comments, although this is rare.

Also notice the use of the Javadoc {@code} tag around the code fragment in the @throws clause. This tag serves two purposes: it causes the code fragment to be rendered in code font, and it suppresses processing of HTML markup and nested Javadoc tags in the code fragment. The latter property is what allows us to use the less-than sign (<) in the code fragment even though it's an HTML metacharacter. To include a multiline code example in a doc comment, use a Javadoc {@code} tag wrapped inside an HTML <pre> tag. In other words, precede the code example with the characters <pre>{@code and follow it with }</pre>. This preserves line breaks in the code, and eliminates the need to escape HTML metacharacters, but *not* the at sign (@), which must be escaped if the code sample uses annotations.

Finally, notice the use of the words "this list" in the doc comment. By convention, the word "this" refers to the object on which a method is invoked when it is used in the doc comment for an instance method.

As mentioned in Item 15, when you design a class for inheritance, you must document its *self-use patterns,* so programmers know the semantics of overriding its methods. These self-use patterns should be documented using the @implSpec tag, added in Java 8. Recall that ordinary doc comments describe the contract between a method and its client; @implSpec comments, by contrast, describe the contract between a method and its subclass, allowing subclasses to rely on implementation behavior if they inherit the method or call it via super. Here's how it looks in practice:

```
/**
 * Returns true if this collection is empty.
 *
 * @implSpec
 * This implementation returns {@code this.size() == 0}.
 *
 * @return true if this collection is empty
 */
public boolean isEmpty() { ... }
```

As of Java 9, the Javadoc utility still ignores the @implSpec tag unless you pass the command line switch -tag "implSpec:a:Implementation Requirements:". Hopefully this will be remedied in a subsequent release.

Don't forget that you must take special action to generate documentation that contains HTML metacharacters, such as the less-than sign (<), the greater-than sign (>), and the ampersand (&). The best way to get these characters into documentation is to surround them with the {@literal} tag, which suppress processing of HTML markup and nested Javadoc tags. It is like the {@code} tag, except that it doesn't render the text in code font. For example, this Javadoc fragment:

```
 * A geometric series converges if {@literal |r| < 1}.
```

generates the documentation: "A geometric series converges if $|r| < 1$." The {@literal} tag could have been placed around just the less-than sign rather than the entire inequality with the same resulting documentation, but the doc comment would have been less readable in the source code. This illustrates the general principle that **doc comments should be readable both in the source code and in the generated documentation.** If you can't achieve both, the readability of the generated documentation trumps that of the source code.

The first "sentence" of each doc comment (as defined below) becomes the *summary description* of the element to which the comment pertains. For example, the summary description in the doc comment on page 255 is "Returns the element at the specified position in this list." The summary description must stand on its own to describe the functionality of the element it summarizes. To avoid confusion, **no two members or constructors in a class or interface should have the same summary description.** Pay particular attention to overloadings, for which it is often natural to use the same first sentence (but unacceptable in doc comments).

Be careful if the intended summary description contains a period, because the period can prematurely terminate the description. For example, a doc comment that begins with the phrase "A college degree, such as B.S., M.S. or Ph.D." will result in the summary description "A college degree, such as B.S., M.S." The problem is that the summary description ends at the first period that is followed by a space, tab, or line terminator (or at the first block tag) [Javadoc-ref]. Here, the second period in the abbreviation "M.S." is followed by a space. The best solution is to surround the offending period and any associated text with an {@literal} tag, so the period is no longer followed by a space in the source code:

```
/**
 * A college degree, such as B.S., {@literal M.S.} or Ph.D.
 */
public class Degree { ... }
```

It is a bit misleading to say that the summary description is the first *sentence* in a doc comment. Convention dictates that it should seldom be a complete sentence. For methods and constructors, the summary description should be a verb phrase (including any object) describing the action performed by the method. For example:

- `ArrayList(int initialCapacity)`—Constructs an empty list with the specified initial capacity.

- `Collection.size()`—Returns the number of elements in this collection.

As shown in these examples, use the third person declarative tense ("returns the number") rather than the second person imperative ("return the number").

For classes, interfaces, and fields, the summary description should be a noun phrase describing the thing represented by an instance of the class or interface or by the field itself. For example:

- `Instant`—An instantaneous point on the time-line.

- `Math.PI`—The `double` value that is closer than any other to pi, the ratio of the circumference of a circle to its diameter.

In Java 9, a client-side index was added to the HTML generated by Javadoc. This index, which eases the task of navigating large API documentation sets, takes the form of a search box in the upper-right corner of the page. When you type into the box, you get a drop-down menu of matching pages. API elements, such as classes, methods, and fields, are indexed automatically. Occasionally you may wish to index additional terms that are important to your API. The {@index} tag was added for this purpose. Indexing a term that appears in a doc comment is as simple as wrapping it in this tag, as shown in this fragment:

```
* This method complies with the {@index IEEE 754} standard.
```

Generics, enums, and annotations require special care in doc comments. **When documenting a generic type or method, be sure to document all type parameters:**

```
/**
 * An object that maps keys to values.  A map cannot contain
 * duplicate keys; each key can map to at most one value.
 *
 * (Remainder omitted)
 *
 * @param <K> the type of keys maintained by this map
 * @param <V> the type of mapped values
 */
public interface Map<K, V> { ... }
```

When documenting an enum type, be sure to document the constants as well as the type and any public methods. Note that you can put an entire doc comment on one line if it's short:

```
/**
 * An instrument section of a symphony orchestra.
 */
public enum OrchestraSection {
    /** Woodwinds, such as flute, clarinet, and oboe. */
    WOODWIND,

    /** Brass instruments, such as french horn and trumpet. */
    BRASS,

    /** Percussion instruments, such as timpani and cymbals. */
    PERCUSSION,

    /** Stringed instruments, such as violin and cello. */
    STRING;
}
```

When documenting an annotation type, be sure to document any members as well as the type itself. Document members with noun phrases, as if they were fields. For the summary description of the type, use a verb phrase that says what it means when a program element has an annotation of this type:

```
/**
 * Indicates that the annotated method is a test method that
 * must throw the designated exception to pass.
 */
@Retention(RetentionPolicy.RUNTIME)
@Target(ElementType.METHOD)
public @interface ExceptionTest {
    /**
     * The exception that the annotated test method must throw
     * in order to pass. (The test is permitted to throw any
     * subtype of the type described by this class object.)
     */
    Class<? extends Throwable> value();
}
```

Package-level doc comments should be placed in a file named package-info.java. In addition to these comments, package-info.java must contain a package declaration and may contain annotations on this declaration. Similarly, if you elect to use the module system (Item 15), module-level comments should be placed in the module-info.java file.

Two aspects of APIs that are often neglected in documentation are thread-safety and serializability. **Whether or not a class or static method is thread-safe, you should document its thread-safety** level, as described in Item 82. If a class is serializable, you should document its serialized form, as described in Item 87.

Javadoc has the ability to "inherit" method comments. If an API element does not have a doc comment, Javadoc searches for the most specific applicable doc comment, giving preference to interfaces over superclasses. The details of the search algorithm can be found in *The Javadoc Reference Guide* [Javadoc-ref]. You can also inherit *parts* of doc comments from supertypes using the {@inheritDoc} tag. This means, among other things, that classes can reuse doc comments from interfaces they implement, rather than copying these comments. This facility has the potential to reduce the burden of maintaining multiple sets of nearly identical doc comments, but it is tricky to use and has some limitations. The details are beyond the scope of this book.

One caveat should be added concerning documentation comments. While it is necessary to provide documentation comments for all exported API elements, it is not always sufficient. For complex APIs consisting of multiple interrelated classes, it is often necessary to supplement the documentation comments with an external document describing the overall architecture of the API. If such a document exists, the relevant class or package documentation comments should include a link to it.

Javadoc automatically checks for adherence to many of the recommendations in this item. In Java 7, the command line switch -Xdoclint was required to get this behavior. In Java 8 and 9, checking is enabled by default. IDE plug-ins such as checkstyle go further in checking for adherence to these recommendations [Burn01]. You can also reduce the likelihood of errors in doc comments by running the HTML files generated by Javadoc through an *HTML validity checker*. This will detect many incorrect uses of HTML tags. Several such checkers are available for download, and you can validate HTML on the web using the W3C markup validation service [W3C-validator]. When validating generated HTML, keep in mind that as of Java 9, Javadoc is capable of generating HTML5 as well as HTML 4.01, though it still generates HTML 4.01 by default. Use the -html5 command line switch if you want Javadoc to generate HTML5.

The conventions described in this item cover the basics. Though it is fifteen years old at the time of this writing, the definitive guide to writing doc comments is still *How to Write Doc Comments* [Javadoc-guide].

If you adhere to the guidelines in this item, the generated documentation should provide a clear description of your API. The only way to know for sure, however, is to **read the web pages generated by the Javadoc utility.** It is worth doing this for every API that will be used by others. Just as testing a program almost inevitably results in some changes to the code, reading the documentation generally results in at least a few minor changes to the doc comments.

To summarize, documentation comments are the best, most effective way to document your API. Their use should be considered mandatory for all exported API elements. Adopt a consistent style that adheres to standard conventions. Remember that arbitrary HTML is permissible in documentation comments and that HTML metacharacters must be escaped.

CHAPTER 9

General Programming

THIS chapter is devoted to the nuts and bolts of the language. It discusses local variables, control structures, libraries, data types, and two extralinguistic facilities: *reflection* and *native methods*. Finally, it discusses optimization and naming conventions.

Item 57: Minimize the scope of local variables

This item is similar in nature to Item 15, "Minimize the accessibility of classes and members." By minimizing the scope of local variables, you increase the readability and maintainability of your code and reduce the likelihood of error.

Older programming languages, such as C, mandated that local variables must be declared at the head of a block, and some programmers continue to do this out of habit. It's a habit worth breaking. As a gentle reminder, Java lets you declare variables anywhere a statement is legal (as does C, since C99).

The most powerful technique for minimizing the scope of a local variable is to declare it where it is first used. If a variable is declared before it is used, it's just clutter—one more thing to distract the reader who is trying to figure out what the program does. By the time the variable is used, the reader might not remember the variable's type or initial value.

Declaring a local variable prematurely can cause its scope not only to begin too early but also to end too late. The scope of a local variable extends from the point where it is declared to the end of the enclosing block. If a variable is declared outside of the block in which it is used, it remains visible after the program exits that block. If a variable is used accidentally before or after its region of intended use, the consequences can be disastrous.

Nearly every local variable declaration should contain an initializer. If you don't yet have enough information to initialize a variable sensibly, you should postpone the declaration until you do. One exception to this rule concerns `try-catch` statements. If a variable is initialized to an expression whose evaluation can throw a checked exception, the variable must be initialized inside a `try` block (unless the enclosing method can propagate the exception). If the value must be used outside of the `try` block, then it must be declared before the `try` block, where it cannot yet be "sensibly initialized." For an example, see page 283.

Loops present a special opportunity to minimize the scope of variables. The `for` loop, in both its traditional and for-each forms, allows you to declare *loop variables*, limiting their scope to the exact region where they're needed. (This region consists of the body of the loop and the code in parentheses between the `for` keyword and the body.) Therefore, **prefer for loops to while loops**, assuming the contents of the loop variable aren't needed after the loop terminates.

For example, here is the preferred idiom for iterating over a collection (Item 58):

```
// Preferred idiom for iterating over a collection or array
for (Element e : c) {
    ... // Do Something with e
}
```

If you need access to the iterator, perhaps to call its remove method, the preferred idiom uses a traditional `for` loop in place of the for-each loop:

```
// Idiom for iterating when you need the iterator
for (Iterator<Element> i = c.iterator(); i.hasNext(); ) {
    Element e = i.next();
    ... // Do something with e and i
}
```

To see why these `for` loops are preferable to a `while` loop, consider the following code fragment, which contains two `while` loops and one bug:

```
Iterator<Element> i = c.iterator();
while (i.hasNext()) {
    doSomething(i.next());
}
...

Iterator<Element> i2 = c2.iterator();
while (i.hasNext()) {                    // BUG!
    doSomethingElse(i2.next());
}
```

The second loop contains a copy-and-paste error: it initializes a new loop variable, i2, but uses the old one, i, which is, unfortunately, still in scope. The resulting code compiles without error and runs without throwing an exception, but it does the wrong thing. Instead of iterating over c2, the second loop terminates immediately, giving the false impression that c2 is empty. Because the program errs silently, the error can remain undetected for a long time.

If a similar copy-and-paste error were made in conjunction with either of the for loops (for-each or traditional), the resulting code wouldn't even compile. The element (or iterator) variable from the first loop would not be in scope in the second loop. Here's how it looks with the traditional for loop:

```
for (Iterator<Element> i = c.iterator(); i.hasNext(); ) {
    Element e = i.next();
    ... // Do something with e and i
}
...

// Compile-time error - cannot find symbol i
for (Iterator<Element> i2 = c2.iterator(); i.hasNext(); ) {
    Element e2 = i2.next();
    ... // Do something with e2 and i2
}
```

Moreover, if you use a for loop, it's much less likely that you'll make the copy-and-paste error because there's no incentive to use different variable names in the two loops. The loops are completely independent, so there's no harm in reusing the element (or iterator) variable name. In fact, it's often stylish to do so.

The for loop has one more advantage over the while loop: it is shorter, which enhances readability.

Here is another loop idiom that minimizes the scope of local variables:

```
for (int i = 0, n = expensiveComputation(); i < n; i++) {
    ... // Do something with i;
}
```

The important thing to notice about this idiom is that it has *two* loop variables, i and n, both of which have exactly the right scope. The second variable, n, is used to store the limit of the first, thus avoiding the cost of a redundant computation in every iteration. As a rule, you should use this idiom if the loop test involves a method invocation that is guaranteed to return the same result on each iteration.

A final technique to minimize the scope of local variables is to **keep methods small and focused.** If you combine two activities in the same method, local variables relevant to one activity may be in the scope of the code performing the other activity. To prevent this from happening, simply separate the method into two: one for each activity.

Item 58: Prefer for-each loops to traditional for loops

As discussed in Item 45, some tasks are best accomplished with streams, others with iteration. Here is a traditional for loop to iterate over a collection:

```
// Not the best way to iterate over a collection!
for (Iterator<Element> i = c.iterator(); i.hasNext(); ) {
    Element e = i.next();
    ... // Do something with e
}
```

and here is a traditional for loop to iterate over an array:

```
// Not the best way to iterate over an array!
for (int i = 0; i < a.length; i++) {
    ... // Do something with a[i]
}
```

These idioms are better than while loops (Item 57), but they aren't perfect. The iterator and the index variables are both just clutter—all you need are the elements. Furthermore, they represent opportunities for error. The iterator occurs three times in each loop and the index variable four, which gives you many chances to use the wrong variable. If you do, there is no guarantee that the compiler will catch the problem. Finally, the two loops are quite different, drawing unnecessary attention to the type of the container and adding a (minor) hassle to changing that type.

The for-each loop (officially known as the "enhanced for statement") solves all of these problems. It gets rid of the clutter and the opportunity for error by hiding the iterator or index variable. The resulting idiom applies equally to collections and arrays, easing the process of switching the implementation type of a container from one to the other:

```
// The preferred idiom for iterating over collections and arrays
for (Element e : elements) {
    ... // Do something with e
}
```

When you see the colon (:), read it as "in." Thus, the loop above reads as "for each element *e* in *elements*." There is no performance penalty for using for-each loops, even for arrays: the code they generate is essentially identical to the code you would write by hand.

The advantages of the for-each loop over the traditional for loop are even greater when it comes to nested iteration. Here is a common mistake that people make when doing nested iteration:

```java
// Can you spot the bug?
enum Suit { CLUB, DIAMOND, HEART, SPADE }
enum Rank { ACE, DEUCE, THREE, FOUR, FIVE, SIX, SEVEN, EIGHT,
            NINE, TEN, JACK, QUEEN, KING }
...
static Collection<Suit> suits = Arrays.asList(Suit.values());
static Collection<Rank> ranks = Arrays.asList(Rank.values());

List<Card> deck = new ArrayList<>();
for (Iterator<Suit> i = suits.iterator(); i.hasNext(); )
    for (Iterator<Rank> j = ranks.iterator(); j.hasNext(); )
        deck.add(new Card(i.next(), j.next()));
```

Don't feel bad if you didn't spot the bug. Many expert programmers have made this mistake at one time or another. The problem is that the next method is called too many times on the iterator for the outer collection (suits). It should be called from the outer loop so that it is called once per suit, but instead it is called from the inner loop, so it is called once per card. After you run out of suits, the loop throws a NoSuchElementException.

If you're really unlucky and the size of the outer collection is a multiple of the size of the inner collection—perhaps because they're the same collection—the loop will terminate normally, but it won't do what you want. For example, consider this ill-conceived attempt to print all the possible rolls of a pair of dice:

```java
// Same bug, different symptom!
enum Face { ONE, TWO, THREE, FOUR, FIVE, SIX }
...
Collection<Face> faces = EnumSet.allOf(Face.class);

for (Iterator<Face> i = faces.iterator(); i.hasNext(); )
    for (Iterator<Face> j = faces.iterator(); j.hasNext(); )
        System.out.println(i.next() + " " + j.next());
```

The program doesn't throw an exception, but it prints only the six "doubles" (from "ONE ONE" to "SIX SIX"), instead of the expected thirty-six combinations.

To fix the bugs in these examples, you must add a variable in the scope of the outer loop to hold the outer element:

```java
// Fixed, but ugly - you can do better!
for (Iterator<Suit> i = suits.iterator(); i.hasNext(); ) {
    Suit suit = i.next();
    for (Iterator<Rank> j = ranks.iterator(); j.hasNext(); )
        deck.add(new Card(suit, j.next()));
}
```

If instead you use a nested for-each loop, the problem simply disappears. The resulting code is as succinct as you could wish for:

```
// Preferred idiom for nested iteration on collections and arrays
for (Suit suit : suits)
    for (Rank rank : ranks)
        deck.add(new Card(suit, rank));
```

Unfortunately, there are three common situations where you *can't* use for-each:

- **Destructive filtering**—If you need to traverse a collection removing selected elements, then you need to use an explicit iterator so that you can call its remove method. You can often avoid explicit traversal by using Collection's removeIf method, added in Java 8.

- **Transforming**—If you need to traverse a list or array and replace some or all of the values of its elements, then you need the list iterator or array index in order to replace the value of an element.

- **Parallel iteration**—If you need to traverse multiple collections in parallel, then you need explicit control over the iterator or index variable so that all iterators or index variables can be advanced in lockstep (as demonstrated unintentionally in the buggy card and dice examples above).

If you find yourself in any of these situations, use an ordinary for loop and be wary of the traps mentioned in this item.

Not only does the for-each loop let you iterate over collections and arrays, it lets you iterate over any object that implements the Iterable interface, which consists of a single method. Here is how the interface looks:

```
public interface Iterable<E> {
    // Returns an iterator over the elements in this iterable
    Iterator<E> iterator();
}
```

It is a bit tricky to implement Iterable if you have to write your own Iterator implementation from scratch, but if you are writing a type that represents a group of elements, you should strongly consider having it implement Iterable, even if you choose not to have it implement Collection. This will allow your users to iterate over your type using the for-each loop, and they will be forever grateful.

In summary, the for-each loop provides compelling advantages over the traditional for loop in clarity, flexibility, and bug prevention, with no performance penalty. Use for-each loops in preference to for loops wherever you can.

Item 59: Know and use the libraries

Suppose you want to generate random integers between zero and some upper bound. Faced with this common task, many programmers would write a little method that looks something like this:

```
// Common but deeply flawed!
static Random rnd = new Random();

static int random(int n) {
    return Math.abs(rnd.nextInt()) % n;
}
```

This method may look good, but it has three flaws. The first is that if n is a small power of two, the sequence of random numbers will repeat itself after a fairly short period. The second flaw is that if n is not a power of two, some numbers will, on average, be returned more frequently than others. If n is large, this effect can be quite pronounced. This is powerfully demonstrated by the following program, which generates a million random numbers in a carefully chosen range and then prints out how many of the numbers fell in the lower half of the range:

```
public static void main(String[] args) {
    int n = 2 * (Integer.MAX_VALUE / 3);
    int low = 0;
    for (int i = 0; i < 1000000; i++)
        if (random(n) < n/2)
            low++;
    System.out.println(low);
}
```

If the random method worked properly, the program would print a number close to half a million, but if you run it, you'll find that it prints a number close to 666,666. Two-thirds of the numbers generated by the random method fall in the lower half of its range!

The third flaw in the random method is that it can, on rare occasions, fail catastrophically, returning a number outside the specified range. This is so because the method attempts to map the value returned by rnd.nextInt() to a non-negative int by calling Math.abs. If nextInt() returns Integer.MIN_VALUE, Math.abs will also return Integer.MIN_VALUE, and the remainder operator (%) will return a negative number, assuming n is not a power of two. This will almost certainly cause your program to fail, and the failure may be difficult to reproduce.

To write a version of the random method that corrects these flaws, you'd have to know a fair amount about pseudorandom number generators, number theory, and two's complement arithmetic. Luckily, you don't have to do this—it's been done for you. It's called `Random.nextInt(int)`. You needn't concern yourself with the details of how it does its job (although you can study the documentation or the source code if you're curious). A senior engineer with a background in algorithms spent a good deal of time designing, implementing, and testing this method and then showed it to several experts in the field to make sure it was right. Then the library was beta tested, released, and used extensively by millions of programmers for almost two decades. No flaws have yet been found in the method, but if a flaw were to be discovered, it would be fixed in the next release. **By using a standard library, you take advantage of the knowledge of the experts who wrote it and the experience of those who used it before you.**

As of Java 7, you should no longer use `Random`. For most uses, **the random number generator of choice is now `ThreadLocalRandom`.** It produces higher quality random numbers, and it's very fast. On my machine, it is 3.6 times faster than `Random`. For fork join pools and parallel streams, use `SplittableRandom`.

A second advantage of using the libraries is that you don't have to waste your time writing ad hoc solutions to problems that are only marginally related to your work. If you are like most programmers, you'd rather spend your time working on your application than on the underlying plumbing.

A third advantage of using standard libraries is that their performance tends to improve over time, with no effort on your part. Because many people use them and because they're used in industry-standard benchmarks, the organizations that supply these libraries have a strong incentive to make them run faster. Many of the Java platform libraries have been rewritten over the years, sometimes repeatedly, resulting in dramatic performance improvements.

A fourth advantage of using libraries is that they tend to gain functionality over time. If a library is missing something, the developer community will make it known, and the missing functionality may get added in a subsequent release.

A final advantage of using the standard libraries is that you place your code in the mainstream. Such code is more easily readable, maintainable, and reusable by the multitude of developers.

Given all these advantages, it seems only logical to use library facilities in preference to ad hoc implementations, yet many programmers don't. Why not? Perhaps they don't know the library facilities exist. **Numerous features are added to the libraries in every major release, and it pays to keep abreast of these additions.** Each time there is a major release of the Java platform, a web page is published describing its new features. These pages are well worth reading [Java8-feat, Java9-feat]. To reinforce this point, suppose you wanted to write a program to print the contents of a URL specified on the command line (which is roughly what the Linux `curl` command does). Prior to Java 9, this code was a bit tedious, but in Java 9 the `transferTo` method was added to `InputStream`. Here is a complete program to perform this task using this new method:

```
// Printing the contents of a URL with transferTo, added in Java 9
public static void main(String[] args) throws IOException {
    try (InputStream in = new URL(args[0]).openStream()) {
        in.transferTo(System.out);
    }
}
```

The libraries are too big to study all the documentation [Java9-api], but **every programmer should be familiar with the basics of `java.lang`, `java.util`, and `java.io`, and their subpackages.** Knowledge of other libraries can be acquired on an as-needed basis. It is beyond the scope of this item to summarize the facilities in the libraries, which have grown immense over the years.

Several libraries bear special mention. The collections framework and the streams library (Items 45–48) should be part of every programmer's basic toolkit, as should parts of the concurrency utilities in `java.util.concurrent`. This package contains both high-level utilities to simplify the task of multithreaded programming and low-level primitives to allow experts to write their own higher-level concurrent abstractions. The high-level parts of `java.util.concurrent` are discussed in Items 80 and 81.

Occasionally, a library facility can fail to meet your needs. The more specialized your needs, the more likely this is to happen. While your first impulse should be to use the libraries, if you've looked at what they have to offer in some area and it doesn't meet your needs, then use an alternate implementation. There will always be holes in the functionality provided by any finite set of libraries. If you can't find what you need in Java platform libraries, your next choice should be to look in high-quality third-party libraries, such as Google's excellent, open source Guava library [Guava]. If you can't find the functionality that you need in any appropriate library, you may have no choice but to implement it yourself.

To summarize, don't reinvent the wheel. If you need to do something that seems like it should be reasonably common, there may already be a facility in the libraries that does what you want. If there is, use it; if you don't know, check. Generally speaking, library code is likely to be better than code that you'd write yourself and is likely to improve over time. This is no reflection on your abilities as a programmer. Economies of scale dictate that library code receives far more attention than most developers could afford to devote to the same functionality.

Item 60: Avoid `float` and `double` if exact answers are required

The `float` and `double` types are designed primarily for scientific and engineering calculations. They perform *binary floating-point arithmetic*, which was carefully designed to furnish accurate approximations quickly over a broad range of magnitudes. They do not, however, provide exact results and should not be used where exact results are required. **The `float` and `double` types are particularly ill-suited for monetary calculations** because it is impossible to represent 0.1 (or any other negative power of ten) as a `float` or `double` exactly.

For example, suppose you have $1.03 in your pocket, and you spend 42¢. How much money do you have left? Here's a naive program fragment that attempts to answer this question:

```
System.out.println(1.03 - 0.42);
```

Unfortunately, it prints out `0.6100000000000001`. This is not an isolated case. Suppose you have a dollar in your pocket, and you buy nine washers priced at ten cents each. How much change do you get?

```
System.out.println(1.00 - 9 * 0.10);
```

According to this program fragment, you get $`0.09999999999999998`.

You might think that the problem could be solved merely by rounding results prior to printing, but unfortunately this does not always work. For example, suppose you have a dollar in your pocket, and you see a shelf with a row of delicious candies priced at 10¢, 20¢, 30¢, and so forth, up to a dollar. You buy one of each candy, starting with the one that costs 10¢, until you can't afford to buy the next candy on the shelf. How many candies do you buy, and how much change do you get? Here's a naive program designed to solve this problem:

```
// Broken - uses floating point for monetary calculation!
public static void main(String[] args) {
    double funds = 1.00;
    int itemsBought = 0;
    for (double price = 0.10; funds >= price; price += 0.10) {
        funds -= price;
        itemsBought++;
    }
    System.out.println(itemsBought + " items bought.");
    System.out.println("Change: $" + funds);
}
```

If you run the program, you'll find that you can afford three pieces of candy, and you have $0.3999999999999999 left. This is the wrong answer! The right way to solve this problem is to **use BigDecimal, int, or long for monetary calculations**.

Here's a straightforward transformation of the previous program to use the BigDecimal type in place of double. Note that BigDecimal's String constructor is used rather than its double constructor. This is required in order to avoid introducing inaccurate values into the computation [Bloch05, Puzzle 2]:

```
public static void main(String[] args) {
    final BigDecimal TEN_CENTS = new BigDecimal(".10");

    int itemsBought = 0;
    BigDecimal funds = new BigDecimal("1.00");
    for (BigDecimal price = TEN_CENTS;
            funds.compareTo(price) >= 0;
            price = price.add(TEN_CENTS)) {
        funds = funds.subtract(price);
        itemsBought++;
    }
    System.out.println(itemsBought + " items bought.");
    System.out.println("Money left over: $" + funds);
}
```

If you run the revised program, you'll find that you can afford four pieces of candy, with $0.00 left over. This is the correct answer.

There are, however, two disadvantages to using BigDecimal: it's a lot less convenient than using a primitive arithmetic type, and it's a lot slower. The latter disadvantage is irrelevant if you're solving a single short problem, but the former may annoy you.

An alternative to using BigDecimal is to use int or long, depending on the amounts involved, and to keep track of the decimal point yourself. In this example, the obvious approach is to do all computation in cents instead of dollars. Here's a straightforward transformation that takes this approach:

```
public static void main(String[] args) {
    int itemsBought = 0;
    int funds = 100;
    for (int price = 10; funds >= price; price += 10) {
        funds -= price;
        itemsBought++;
    }
    System.out.println(itemsBought + " items bought.");
    System.out.println("Cash left over: " + funds + " cents");
}
```

In summary, don't use `float` or `double` for any calculations that require an exact answer. Use `BigDecimal` if you want the system to keep track of the decimal point and you don't mind the inconvenience and cost of not using a primitive type. Using `BigDecimal` has the added advantage that it gives you full control over rounding, letting you select from eight rounding modes whenever an operation that entails rounding is performed. This comes in handy if you're performing business calculations with legally mandated rounding behavior. If performance is of the essence, you don't mind keeping track of the decimal point yourself, and the quantities aren't too big, use `int` or `long`. If the quantities don't exceed nine decimal digits, you can use `int`; if they don't exceed eighteen digits, you can use `long`. If the quantities might exceed eighteen digits, use `BigDecimal`.

Item 61: Prefer primitive types to boxed primitives

Java has a two-part type system, consisting of *primitives*, such as int, double, and boolean, and *reference types*, such as String and List. Every primitive type has a corresponding reference type, called a *boxed primitive*. The boxed primitives corresponding to int, double, and boolean are Integer, Double, and Boolean.

As mentioned in Item 6, autoboxing and auto-unboxing blur but do not erase the distinction between the primitive and boxed primitive types. There are real differences between the two, and it's important that you remain aware of which you are using and that you choose carefully between them.

There are three major differences between primitives and boxed primitives. First, primitives have only their values, whereas boxed primitives have identities distinct from their values. In other words, two boxed primitive instances can have the same value and different identities. Second, primitive types have only fully functional values, whereas each boxed primitive type has one nonfunctional value, which is null, in addition to all the functional values of the corresponding primitive type. Last, primitives are more time- and space-efficient than boxed primitives. All three of these differences can get you into real trouble if you aren't careful.

Consider the following comparator, which is designed to represent ascending numerical order on Integer values. (Recall that a comparator's compare method returns a number that is negative, zero, or positive, depending on whether its first argument is less than, equal to, or greater than its second.) You wouldn't need to write this comparator in practice because it implements the natural ordering on Integer, but it makes for an interesting example:

```
// Broken comparator - can you spot the flaw?
Comparator<Integer> naturalOrder =
    (i, j) -> (i < j) ? -1 : (i == j ? 0 : 1);
```

This comparator looks like it ought to work, and it will pass many tests. For example, it can be used with Collections.sort to correctly sort a million-element list, whether or not the list contains duplicate elements. But the comparator is deeply flawed. To convince yourself of this, merely print the value of naturalOrder.compare(new Integer(42), new Integer(42)). Both Integer instances represent the same value (42), so the value of this expression should be 0, but it's 1, which indicates that the first Integer value is greater than the second!

So what's the problem? The first test in naturalOrder works fine. Evaluating the expression i < j causes the Integer instances referred to by i and j to be *auto-unboxed*; that is, it extracts their primitive values. The evaluation proceeds to check if the first of the resulting int values is less than the second. But suppose it is not. Then the next test evaluates the expression i == j, which performs an *identity comparison* on the two object references. If i and j refer to distinct Integer instances that represent the same int value, this comparison will return false, and the comparator will incorrectly return 1, indicating that the first Integer value is greater than the second. **Applying the == operator to boxed primitives is almost always wrong.**

In practice, if you need a comparator to describe a type's natural order, you should simply call Comparator.naturalOrder(), and if you write a comparator yourself, you should use the comparator construction methods, or the static compare methods on primitive types (Item 14). That said, you could fix the problem in the broken comparator by adding two local variables to store the primitive int values corresponding to the boxed Integer parameters, and performing all of the comparisons on these variables. This avoids the erroneous identity comparison:

```
Comparator<Integer> naturalOrder = (iBoxed, jBoxed) -> {
    int i = iBoxed, j = jBoxed; // Auto-unboxing
    return i < j ? -1 : (i == j ? 0 : 1);
};
```

Next, consider this delightful little program:

```
public class Unbelievable {
    static Integer i;

    public static void main(String[] args) {
        if (i == 42)
            System.out.println("Unbelievable");
    }
}
```

No, it doesn't print Unbelievable—but what it does is almost as strange. It throws a NullPointerException when evaluating the expression i == 42. The problem is that i is an Integer, not an int, and like all nonconstant object reference fields, its initial value is null. When the program evaluates the expression i == 42, it is comparing an Integer to an int. In nearly every case **when you mix primitives and boxed primitives in an operation, the boxed primitive is auto-unboxed.** If a null object reference is auto-unboxed, you get a NullPointerException. As this program demonstrates, it can happen almost anywhere. Fixing the problem is as simple as declaring i to be an int instead of an Integer.

Finally, consider the program from page 24 in Item 6:

```
// Hideously slow program! Can you spot the object creation?
public static void main(String[] args) {
    Long sum = 0L;
    for (long i = 0; i < Integer.MAX_VALUE; i++) {
        sum += i;
    }
    System.out.println(sum);
}
```

This program is much slower than it should be because it accidentally declares a local variable (sum) to be of the boxed primitive type Long instead of the primitive type long. The program compiles without error or warning, and the variable is repeatedly boxed and unboxed, causing the observed performance degradation.

In all three of the programs discussed in this item, the problem was the same: the programmer ignored the distinction between primitives and boxed primitives and suffered the consequences. In the first two programs, the consequences were outright failure; in the third, severe performance problems.

So when should you use boxed primitives? They have several legitimate uses. The first is as elements, keys, and values in collections. You can't put primitives in collections, so you're forced to use boxed primitives. This is a special case of a more general one. You must use boxed primitives as type parameters in parameterized types and methods (Chapter 5), because the language does not permit you to use primitives. For example, you cannot declare a variable to be of type ThreadLocal<int>, so you must use ThreadLocal<Integer> instead. Finally, you must use boxed primitives when making reflective method invocations (Item 65).

In summary, use primitives in preference to boxed primitives whenever you have the choice. Primitive types are simpler and faster. If you must use boxed primitives, be careful! **Autoboxing reduces the verbosity, but not the danger, of using boxed primitives.** When your program compares two boxed primitives with the == operator, it does an identity comparison, which is almost certainly *not* what you want. When your program does mixed-type computations involving boxed and unboxed primitives, it does unboxing, and **when your program does unboxing, it can throw a NullPointerException.** Finally, when your program boxes primitive values, it can result in costly and unnecessary object creations.

Item 62: Avoid strings where other types are more appropriate

Strings are designed to represent text, and they do a fine job of it. Because strings are so common and so well supported by the language, there is a natural tendency to use strings for purposes other than those for which they were designed. This item discusses a few things that you shouldn't do with strings.

Strings are poor substitutes for other value types. When a piece of data comes into a program from a file, from the network, or from keyboard input, it is often in string form. There is a natural tendency to leave it that way, but this tendency is justified only if the data really is textual in nature. If it's numeric, it should be translated into the appropriate numeric type, such as `int`, `float`, or `BigInteger`. If it's the answer to a yes-or-no question, it should be translated into an appropriate enum type or a `boolean`. More generally, if there's an appropriate value type, whether primitive or object reference, you should use it; if there isn't, you should write one. While this advice may seem obvious, it is often violated.

Strings are poor substitutes for enum types. As discussed in Item 34, enums make far better enumerated type constants than strings.

Strings are poor substitutes for aggregate types. If an entity has multiple components, it is usually a bad idea to represent it as a single string. For example, here's a line of code that comes from a real system—identifier names have been changed to protect the guilty:

```
// Inappropriate use of string as aggregate type
String compoundKey = className + "#" + i.next();
```

This approach has many disadvantages. If the character used to separate fields occurs in one of the fields, chaos may result. To access individual fields, you have to parse the string, which is slow, tedious, and error-prone. You can't provide `equals`, `toString`, or `compareTo` methods but are forced to accept the behavior that `String` provides. A better approach is simply to write a class to represent the aggregate, often a private static member class (Item 24).

Strings are poor substitutes for capabilities. Occasionally, strings are used to grant access to some functionality. For example, consider the design of a thread-local variable facility. Such a facility provides variables for which each thread has its own value. The Java libraries have had a thread-local variable facility since release 1.2, but prior to that, programmers had to roll their own. When confronted with the task of designing such a facility many years ago, several people independently came up with the same design, in which client-provided string keys are used to identify each thread-local variable:

```
// Broken - inappropriate use of string as capability!
public class ThreadLocal {
    private ThreadLocal() { } // Noninstantiable

    // Sets the current thread's value for the named variable.
    public static void set(String key, Object value);

    // Returns the current thread's value for the named variable.
    public static Object get(String key);
}
```

The problem with this approach is that the string keys represent a shared global namespace for thread-local variables. In order for the approach to work, the client-provided string keys have to be unique: if two clients independently decide to use the same name for their thread-local variable, they unintentionally share a single variable, which will generally cause both clients to fail. Also, the security is poor. A malicious client could intentionally use the same string key as another client to gain illicit access to the other client's data.

This API can be fixed by replacing the string with an unforgeable key (sometimes called a *capability*):

```
public class ThreadLocal {
    private ThreadLocal() { }  // Noninstantiable

    public static class Key {  // (Capability)
        Key() { }
    }

    // Generates a unique, unforgeable key
    public static Key getKey() {
        return new Key();
    }

    public static void set(Key key, Object value);
    public static Object get(Key key);
}
```

While this solves both of the problems with the string-based API, you can do much better. You don't really need the static methods anymore. They can instead become instance methods on the key, at which point the key is no longer a key for a thread-local variable: it *is* a thread-local variable. At this point, the top-level class isn't doing anything for you anymore, so you might as well get rid of it and rename the nested class to ThreadLocal:

```
public final class ThreadLocal {
    public ThreadLocal();
    public void set(Object value);
    public Object get();
}
```

This API isn't typesafe, because you have to cast the value from Object to its actual type when you retrieve it from a thread-local variable. It is impossible to make the original String-based API typesafe and difficult to make the Key-based API typesafe, but it is a simple matter to make this API typesafe by making ThreadLocal a parameterized class (Item 29):

```
public final class ThreadLocal<T> {
    public ThreadLocal();
    public void set(T value);
    public T get();
}
```

This is, roughly speaking, the API that java.lang.ThreadLocal provides. In addition to solving the problems with the string-based API, it is faster and more elegant than either of the key-based APIs.

To summarize, avoid the natural tendency to represent objects as strings when better data types exist or can be written. Used inappropriately, strings are more cumbersome, less flexible, slower, and more error-prone than other types. Types for which strings are commonly misused include primitive types, enums, and aggregate types.

Item 63: Beware the performance of string concatenation

The string concatenation operator (+) is a convenient way to combine a few strings into one. It is fine for generating a single line of output or constructing the string representation of a small, fixed-size object, but it does not scale. **Using the string concatenation operator repeatedly to concatenate n strings requires time quadratic in n.** This is an unfortunate consequence of the fact that strings are *immutable* (Item 17). When two strings are concatenated, the contents of both are copied.

For example, consider this method, which constructs the string representation of a billing statement by repeatedly concatenating a line for each item:

```
// Inappropriate use of string concatenation - Performs poorly!
public String statement() {
    String result = "";
    for (int i = 0; i < numItems(); i++)
        result += lineForItem(i);  // String concatenation
    return result;
}
```

The method performs abysmally if the number of items is large. **To achieve acceptable performance, use a `StringBuilder` in place of a `String`** to store the statement under construction:

```
public String statement() {
    StringBuilder b = new StringBuilder(numItems() * LINE_WIDTH);
    for (int i = 0; i < numItems(); i++)
        b.append(lineForItem(i));
    return b.toString();
}
```

A lot of work has gone into making string concatenation faster since Java 6, but the difference in the performance of the two methods is still dramatic: If `numItems` returns 100 and `lineForItem` returns an 80-character string, the second method runs 6.5 times faster than the first on my machine. Because the first method is quadratic in the number of items and the second is linear, the performance difference gets much larger as the number of items grows. Note that the second method preallocates a `StringBuilder` large enough to hold the entire result, eliminating the need for automatic growth. Even if it is detuned to use a default-sized `StringBuilder`, it is still 5.5 times faster than the first method.

The moral is simple: **Don't use the string concatenation operator to combine more than a few strings** unless performance is irrelevant. Use `StringBuilder`'s append method instead. Alternatively, use a character array, or process the strings one at a time instead of combining them.

Item 64: Refer to objects by their interfaces

Item 51 says that you should use interfaces rather than classes as parameter types. More generally, you should favor the use of interfaces over classes to refer to objects. **If appropriate interface types exist, then parameters, return values, variables, and fields should all be declared using interface types.** The only time you really need to refer to an object's class is when you're creating it with a constructor. To make this concrete, consider the case of `LinkedHashSet`, which is an implementation of the `Set` interface. Get in the habit of typing this:

```
// Good - uses interface as type
Set<Son> sonSet = new LinkedHashSet<>();
```

not this:

```
// Bad - uses class as type!
LinkedHashSet<Son> sonSet = new LinkedHashSet<>();
```

If you get into the habit of using interfaces as types, your program will be much more flexible. If you decide that you want to switch implementations, all you have to do is change the class name in the constructor (or use a different static factory). For example, the first declaration could be changed to read:

```
Set<Son> sonSet = new HashSet<>();
```

and all of the surrounding code would continue to work. The surrounding code was unaware of the old implementation type, so it would be oblivious to the change.

There is one caveat: if the original implementation offered some special functionality not required by the general contract of the interface and the code depended on that functionality, then it is critical that the new implementation provide the same functionality. For example, if the code surrounding the first declaration depended on `LinkedHashSet`'s ordering policy, then it would be incorrect to substitute `HashSet` for `LinkedHashSet` in the declaration, because `HashSet` makes no guarantee concerning iteration order.

So why would you want to change an implementation type? Because the second implementation offers better performance than the original, or because it offers desirable functionality that the original implementation lacks. For example, suppose a field contains a `HashMap` instance. Changing it to an `EnumMap` will provide better performance and iteration order consistent with the natural order of the keys, but you can only use an `EnumMap` if the key type is an enum type.

Changing the HashMap to a LinkedHashMap will provide predictable iteration order with performance comparable to that of HashMap, without making any special demands on the key type.

You might think it's OK to declare a variable using its implementation type, because you can change the declaration type and the implementation type at the same time, but there is no guarantee that this change will result in a program that compiles. If the client code used methods on the original implementation type that are not also present on its replacement or if the client code passed the instance to a method that requires the original implementation type, then the code will no longer compile after making this change. Declaring the variable with the interface type keeps you honest.

It is entirely appropriate to refer to an object by a class rather than an interface if no appropriate interface exists. For example, consider *value classes,* such as String and BigInteger. Value classes are rarely written with multiple implementations in mind. They are often final and rarely have corresponding interfaces. It is perfectly appropriate to use such a value class as a parameter, variable, field, or return type.

A second case in which there is no appropriate interface type is that of objects belonging to a framework whose fundamental types are classes rather than interfaces. If an object belongs to such a *class-based framework*, it is preferable to refer to it by the relevant *base class*, which is often abstract, rather than by its implementation class. Many java.io classes such as OutputStream fall into this category.

A final case in which there is no appropriate interface type is that of classes that implement an interface but also provide extra methods not found in the interface—for example, PriorityQueue has a comparator method that is not present on the Queue interface. Such a class should be used to refer to its instances *only* if the program relies on the extra methods, and this should be very rare.

These three cases are not meant to be exhaustive but merely to convey the flavor of situations where it is appropriate to refer to an object by its class. In practice, it should be apparent whether a given object has an appropriate interface. If it does, your program will be more flexible and stylish if you use the interface to refer to the object. **If there is no appropriate interface, just use the least specific class in the class hierarchy that provides the required functionality.**

Item 65: Prefer interfaces to reflection

The *core reflection facility*, java.lang.reflect, offers programmatic access to arbitrary classes. Given a Class object, you can obtain Constructor, Method, and Field instances representing the constructors, methods, and fields of the class represented by the Class instance. These objects provide programmatic access to the class's member names, field types, method signatures, and so on.

Moreover, Constructor, Method, and Field instances let you manipulate their underlying counterparts *reflectively*: you can construct instances, invoke methods, and access fields of the underlying class by invoking methods on the Constructor, Method, and Field instances. For example, Method.invoke lets you invoke any method on any object of any class (subject to the usual security constraints). Reflection allows one class to use another, even if the latter class did not exist when the former was compiled. This power, however, comes at a price:

- **You lose all the benefits of compile-time type checking,** including exception checking. If a program attempts to invoke a nonexistent or inaccessible method reflectively, it will fail at runtime unless you've taken special precautions.

- **The code required to perform reflective access is clumsy and verbose.** It is tedious to write and difficult to read.

- **Performance suffers.** Reflective method invocation is much slower than normal method invocation. Exactly how much slower is hard to say, as there are many factors at work. On my machine, invoking a method with no input parameters and an int return was eleven times slower when done reflectively.

There are a few sophisticated applications that require reflection. Examples include code analysis tools and dependency injection frameworks. Even such tools have been moving away from reflection of late, as its disadvantages become clearer. If you have any doubts as to whether your application requires reflection, it probably doesn't.

You can obtain many of the benefits of reflection while incurring few of its costs by using it only in a very limited form. For many programs that must use a class that is unavailable at compile time, there exists at compile time an appropriate interface or superclass by which to refer to the class (Item 64). If this is the case, you can **create instances reflectively and access them normally via their interface or superclass.**

For example, here is a program that creates a Set<String> instance whose class is specified by the first command line argument. The program inserts the remaining command line arguments into the set and prints it. Regardless of the first argument, the program prints the remaining arguments with duplicates eliminated. The order in which these arguments are printed, however, depends on the class specified in the first argument. If you specify java.util.HashSet, they're printed in apparently random order; if you specify java.util.TreeSet, they're printed in alphabetical order because the elements in a TreeSet are sorted:

```java
// Reflective instantiation with interface access
public static void main(String[] args) {
    // Translate the class name into a Class object
    Class<? extends Set<String>> cl = null;
    try {
        cl = (Class<? extends Set<String>>)  // Unchecked cast!
                Class.forName(args[0]);
    } catch (ClassNotFoundException e) {
        fatalError("Class not found.");
    }

    // Get the constructor
    Constructor<? extends Set<String>> cons = null;
    try {
        cons = cl.getDeclaredConstructor();
    } catch (NoSuchMethodException e) {
        fatalError("No parameterless constructor");
    }

    // Instantiate the set
    Set<String> s = null;
    try {
        s = cons.newInstance();
    } catch (IllegalAccessException e) {
        fatalError("Constructor not accessible");
    } catch (InstantiationException e) {
        fatalError("Class not instantiable.");
    } catch (InvocationTargetException e) {
        fatalError("Constructor threw " + e.getCause());
    } catch (ClassCastException e) {
        fatalError("Class doesn't implement Set");
    }

    // Exercise the set
    s.addAll(Arrays.asList(args).subList(1, args.length));
    System.out.println(s);
}

private static void fatalError(String msg) {
    System.err.println(msg);
    System.exit(1);
}
```

While this program is just a toy, the technique it demonstrates is quite powerful. The toy program could easily be turned into a generic set tester that validates the specified Set implementation by aggressively manipulating one or more instances and checking that they obey the Set contract. Similarly, it could be turned into a generic set performance analysis tool. In fact, this technique is sufficiently powerful to implement a full-blown *service provider framework* (Item 1). Usually, this technique is all that you need in the way of reflection.

This example demonstrates two disadvantages of reflection. First, the example can generate six different exceptions at runtime, all of which would have been compile-time errors if reflective instantiation were not used. (For fun, you can cause the program to generate each of the six exceptions by passing in appropriate command line arguments.) The second disadvantage is that it takes twenty-five lines of tedious code to generate an instance of the class from its name, whereas a constructor invocation would fit neatly on a single line. The length of the program could be reduced by catching ReflectiveOperationException, a superclass of the various reflective exceptions that was introduced in Java 7. Both disadvantages are restricted to the part of the program that instantiates the object. Once instantiated, the set is indistinguishable from any other Set instance. In a real program, the great bulk of the code is thus unaffected by this limited use of reflection.

If you compile this program, you'll get an unchecked cast warning. This warning is legitimate, in that the cast to Class<? extends Set<String>> will succeed even if the named class is not a Set implementation, in which case the program with throw a ClassCastException when it instantiates the class. To learn about suppressing the warning, read Item 27.

A legitimate, if rare, use of reflection is to manage a class's dependencies on other classes, methods, or fields that may be absent at runtime. This can be useful if you are writing a package that must run against multiple versions of some other package. The technique is to compile your package against the minimal environment required to support it, typically the oldest version, and to access any newer classes or methods reflectively. To make this work, you have to take appropriate action if a newer class or method that you are attempting to access does not exist at runtime. Appropriate action might consist of using some alternate means to accomplish the same goal or operating with reduced functionality.

In summary, reflection is a powerful facility that is required for certain sophisticated system programming tasks, but it has many disadvantages. If you are writing a program that has to work with classes unknown at compile time, you should, if at all possible, use reflection only to instantiate objects, and access the objects using some interface or superclass that is known at compile time.

Item 66: Use native methods judiciously

The Java Native Interface (JNI) allows Java programs to call *native methods*, which are methods written in *native programming languages* such as C or C++. Historically, native methods have had three main uses. They provide access to platform-specific facilities such as registries. They provide access to existing libraries of native code, including legacy libraries that provide access to legacy data. Finally, native methods are used to write performance-critical parts of applications in native languages for improved performance.

It is legitimate to use native methods to access platform-specific facilities, but it is seldom necessary: as the Java platform matured, it provided access to many features previously found only in host platforms. For example, the process API, added in Java 9, provides access to OS processes. It is also legitimate to use native methods to use native libraries when no equivalent libraries are available in Java.

It is rarely advisable to use native methods for improved performance. In early releases (prior to Java 3), it was often necessary, but JVMs have gotten *much* faster since then. For most tasks, it is now possible to obtain comparable performance in Java. For example, when java.math was added in release 1.1, BigInteger relied on a then-fast multiprecision arithmetic library written in C. In Java 3, BigInteger was reimplemented in Java, and carefully tuned to the point where it ran faster than the original native implementation.

A sad coda to this story is that BigInteger has changed little since then, with the exception of faster multiplication for large numbers in Java 8. In that time, work continued apace on native libraries, notably GNU Multiple Precision arithmetic library (GMP). Java programmers in need of truly high-performance multiprecision arithmetic are now justified in using GMP via native methods [Blum14].

The use of native methods has *serious* disadvantages. Because native languages are not *safe* (Item 50), applications using native methods are no longer immune to memory corruption errors. Because native languages are more platform-dependent than Java, programs using native methods are less portable. They are also harder to debug. If you aren't careful, native methods can *decrease* performance because the garbage collector can't automate, or even track, native memory usage (Item 8), and there is a cost associated with going into and out of native code. Finally, native methods require "glue code" that is difficult to read and tedious to write.

In summary, think twice before using native methods. It is rare that you need to use them for improved performance. If you must use native methods to access low-level resources or native libraries, use as little native code as possible and test it thoroughly. A single bug in the native code can corrupt your entire application.

Item 67: Optimize judiciously

There are three aphorisms concerning optimization that everyone should know:

> More computing sins are committed in the name of efficiency (without necessarily achieving it) than for any other single reason—including blind stupidity.
> —William A. Wulf [Wulf72]

> We *should* forget about small efficiencies, say about 97% of the time: premature optimization is the root of all evil.
> —Donald E. Knuth [Knuth74]

> We follow two rules in the matter of optimization:
> Rule 1. Don't do it.
> Rule 2 (for experts only). Don't do it yet—that is, not until you have a perfectly clear and unoptimized solution.
> —M. A. Jackson [Jackson75]

All of these aphorisms predate the Java programming language by two decades. They tell a deep truth about optimization: it is easy to do more harm than good, especially if you optimize prematurely. In the process, you may produce software that is neither fast nor correct and cannot easily be fixed.

Don't sacrifice sound architectural principles for performance. **Strive to write good programs rather than fast ones.** If a good program is not fast enough, its architecture will allow it to be optimized. Good programs embody the principle of *information hiding*: where possible, they localize design decisions within individual components, so individual decisions can be changed without affecting the remainder of the system (Item 15).

This does *not* mean that you can ignore performance concerns until your program is complete. Implementation problems can be fixed by later optimization, but pervasive architectural flaws that limit performance can be impossible to fix without rewriting the system. Changing a fundamental facet of your design after the fact can result in an ill-structured system that is difficult to maintain and evolve. Therefore you must think about performance during the design process.

Strive to avoid design decisions that limit performance. The components of a design that are most difficult to change after the fact are those specifying interactions between components and with the outside world. Chief among these design components are APIs, wire-level protocols, and persistent data formats. Not only are these design components difficult or impossible to change after the fact, but all of them can place significant limitations on the performance that a system can ever achieve.

Consider the performance consequences of your API design decisions. Making a public type mutable may require a lot of needless defensive copying (Item 50). Similarly, using inheritance in a public class where composition would have been appropriate ties the class forever to its superclass, which can place artificial limits on the performance of the subclass (Item 18). As a final example, using an implementation type rather than an interface in an API ties you to a specific implementation, even though faster implementations may be written in the future (Item 64).

The effects of API design on performance are very real. Consider the `getSize` method in the `java.awt.Component` class. The decision that this performance-critical method was to return a `Dimension` instance, coupled with the decision that `Dimension` instances are mutable, forces any implementation of this method to allocate a new `Dimension` instance on every invocation. Even though allocating small objects is inexpensive on a modern VM, allocating millions of objects needlessly can do real harm to performance.

Several API design alternatives existed. Ideally, `Dimension` should have been immutable (Item 17); alternatively, `getSize` could have been replaced by two methods returning the individual primitive components of a `Dimension` object. In fact, two such methods were added to `Component` in Java 2 for performance reasons. Preexisting client code, however, still uses the `getSize` method and still suffers the performance consequences of the original API design decisions.

Luckily, it is generally the case that good API design is consistent with good performance. **It is a very bad idea to warp an API to achieve good performance.** The performance issue that caused you to warp the API may go away in a future release of the platform or other underlying software, but the warped API and the support headaches that come with it will be with you forever.

Once you've carefully designed your program and produced a clear, concise, and well-structured implementation, *then* it may be time to consider optimization, assuming you're not already satisfied with the performance of the program.

Recall that Jackson's two rules of optimization were "Don't do it," and "(for experts only). Don't do it yet." He could have added one more: **measure performance before and after each attempted optimization.** You may be surprised by what you find. Often, attempted optimizations have no measurable effect on performance; sometimes, they make it worse. The main reason is that it's difficult to guess where your program is spending its time. The part of the program that you think is slow may not be at fault, in which case you'd be wasting your time trying to optimize it. Common wisdom says that programs spend 90 percent of their time in 10 percent of their code.

Profiling tools can help you decide where to focus your optimization efforts. These tools give you runtime information, such as roughly how much time each method is consuming and how many times it is invoked. In addition to focusing your tuning efforts, this can alert you to the need for algorithmic changes. If a quadratic (or worse) algorithm lurks inside your program, no amount of tuning will fix the problem. You must replace the algorithm with one that is more efficient. The more code in the system, the more important it is to use a profiler. It's like looking for a needle in a haystack: the bigger the haystack, the more useful it is to have a metal detector. Another tool that deserves special mention is jmh, which is not a profiler but a *microbenchmarking framework* that provides unparalleled visibility into the detailed performance of Java code [JMH].

The need to measure the effects of attempted optimization is even greater in Java than in more traditional languages such as C and C++, because Java has a weaker *performance model*: The relative cost of the various primitive operations is less well defined. The "abstraction gap" between what the programmer writes and what the CPU executes is greater, which makes it even more difficult to reliably predict the performance consequences of optimizations. There are plenty of performance myths floating around that turn out to be half-truths or outright lies.

Not only is Java's performance model ill-defined, but it varies from implementation to implementation, from release to release, and from processor to processor. If you will be running your program on multiple implementations or multiple hardware platforms, it is important that you measure the effects of your optimization on each. Occasionally you may be forced to make trade-offs between performance on different implementations or hardware platforms.

In the nearly two decades since this item was first written, every component of the Java software stack has grown in complexity, from processors to VMs to libraries, and the variety of hardware on which Java runs has grown immensely. All of this has combined to make the performance of Java programs even less predictable now than it was in 2001, with a corresponding increase in the need to measure it.

To summarize, do not strive to write fast programs—strive to write good ones; speed will follow. But do think about performance while you're designing systems, especially while you're designing APIs, wire-level protocols, and persistent data formats. When you've finished building the system, measure its performance. If it's fast enough, you're done. If not, locate the source of the problem with the aid of a profiler and go to work optimizing the relevant parts of the system. The first step is to examine your choice of algorithms: no amount of low-level optimization can make up for a poor choice of algorithm. Repeat this process as necessary, measuring the performance after every change, until you're satisfied.

Item 68: Adhere to generally accepted naming conventions

The Java platform has a well-established set of *naming conventions*, many of which are contained in *The Java Language Specification* [JLS, 6.1]. Loosely speaking, naming conventions fall into two categories: typographical and grammatical.

There are only a handful of typographical naming conventions, covering packages, classes, interfaces, methods, fields, and type variables. You should rarely violate them and never without a very good reason. If an API violates these conventions, it may be difficult to use. If an implementation violates them, it may be difficult to maintain. In both cases, violations have the potential to confuse and irritate other programmers who work with the code and can cause faulty assumptions that lead to errors. The conventions are summarized in this item.

Package and module names should be hierarchical with the components separated by periods. Components should consist of lowercase alphabetic characters and, rarely, digits. The name of any package that will be used outside your organization should begin with your organization's Internet domain name with the components reversed, for example, `edu.cmu`, `com.google`, `org.eff`. The standard libraries and optional packages, whose names begin with `java` and `javax`, are exceptions to this rule. Users must not create packages or modules whose names begin with `java` or `javax`. Detailed rules for converting Internet domain names to package name prefixes can be found in the JLS [JLS, 6.1].

The remainder of a package name should consist of one or more components describing the package. Components should be short, generally eight or fewer characters. Meaningful abbreviations are encouraged, for example, `util` rather than `utilities`. Acronyms are acceptable, for example, `awt`. Components should generally consist of a single word or abbreviation.

Many packages have names with just one component in addition to the Internet domain name. Additional components are appropriate for large facilities whose size demands that they be broken up into an informal hierarchy. For example, the `javax.util` package has a rich hierarchy of packages with names such as `java.util.concurrent.atomic`. Such packages are known as *subpackages*, although there is almost no linguistic support for package hierarchies.

Class and interface names, including enum and annotation type names, should consist of one or more words, with the first letter of each word capitalized, for example, `List` or `FutureTask`. Abbreviations are to be avoided, except for acronyms and certain common abbreviations like `max` and `min`. There is some disagreement as to whether acronyms should be uppercase or have only their first letter capitalized. While some programmers still use uppercase, a strong argument can be made in favor of capitalizing only the first letter: even if multiple acronyms occur back-to-back, you can still tell where one word starts and the next word ends. Which class name would you rather see, HTTPURL or HttpUrl?

Method and field names follow the same typographical conventions as class and interface names, except that the first letter of a method or field name should be lowercase, for example, remove or ensureCapacity. If an acronym occurs as the first word of a method or field name, it should be lowercase.

The sole exception to the previous rule concerns "constant fields," whose names should consist of one or more uppercase words separated by the underscore character, for example, VALUES or NEGATIVE_INFINITY. A constant field is a static final field whose value is immutable. If a static final field has a primitive type or an immutable reference type (Item 17), then it is a constant field. For example, enum constants are constant fields. If a static final field has a mutable reference type, it can still be a constant field if the referenced object is immutable. Note that constant fields constitute the *only* recommended use of underscores.

Local variable names have similar typographical naming conventions to member names, except that abbreviations are permitted, as are individual characters and short sequences of characters whose meaning depends on the context in which they occur, for example, i, denom, houseNum. Input parameters are a special kind of local variable. They should be named much more carefully than ordinary local variables, as their names are an integral part of their method's documentation.

Type parameter names usually consist of a single letter. Most commonly it is one of these five: T for an arbitrary type, E for the element type of a collection, K and V for the key and value types of a map, and X for an exception. The return type of a function is usually R. A sequence of arbitrary types can be T, U, V or T1, T2, T3.

For quick reference, the following table shows examples of typographical conventions.

Identifier Type	Examples
Package or module	org.junit.jupiter.api, com.google.common.collect
Class or Interface	Stream, FutureTask, LinkedHashMap, HttpClient
Method or Field	remove, groupingBy, getCrc
Constant Field	MIN_VALUE, NEGATIVE_INFINITY
Local Variable	i, denom, houseNum
Type Parameter	T, E, K, V, X, R, U, V, T1, T2

Grammatical naming conventions are more flexible and more controversial than typographical conventions. There are no grammatical naming conventions to speak of for packages. Instantiable classes, including enum types, are generally named with a singular noun or noun phrase, such as `Thread`, `PriorityQueue`, or `ChessPiece`. Non-instantiable utility classes (Item 4) are often named with a plural noun, such as `Collectors` or `Collections`. Interfaces are named like classes, for example, `Collection` or `Comparator`, or with an adjective ending in `able` or `ible`, for example, `Runnable`, `Iterable`, or `Accessible`. Because annotation types have so many uses, no part of speech predominates. Nouns, verbs, prepositions, and adjectives are all common, for example, `BindingAnnotation`, `Inject`, `ImplementedBy`, or `Singleton`.

Methods that perform some action are generally named with a verb or verb phrase (including object), for example, `append` or `drawImage`. Methods that return a `boolean` value usually have names that begin with the word `is` or, less commonly, `has`, followed by a noun, noun phrase, or any word or phrase that functions as an adjective, for example, `isDigit`, `isProbablePrime`, `isEmpty`, `isEnabled`, or `hasSiblings`.

Methods that return a non-`boolean` function or attribute of the object on which they're invoked are usually named with a noun, a noun phrase, or a verb phrase beginning with the verb `get`, for example, `size`, `hashCode`, or `getTime`. There is a vocal contingent that claims that only the third form (beginning with `get`) is acceptable, but there is little basis for this claim. The first two forms usually lead to more readable code, for example:

```
if (car.speed() > 2 * SPEED_LIMIT)
    generateAudibleAlert("Watch out for cops!");
```

The form beginning with `get` has its roots in the largely obsolete *Java Beans* specification, which formed the basis of an early reusable component architecture. There are modern tools that continue to rely on the Beans naming convention, and you should feel free to use it in any code that is to be used in conjunction with these tools. There is also a strong precedent for following this naming convention if a class contains both a setter and a getter for the same attribute. In this case, the two methods are typically named get*Attribute* and set*Attribute*.

A few method names deserve special mention. Instance methods that convert the type of an object, returning an independent object of a different type, are often called to*Type*, for example, `toString` or `toArray`. Methods that return a *view* (Item 6) whose type differs from that of the receiving object are often called as*Type*, for example, asList. Methods that return a primitive with the same value as the object on which they're invoked are often called *type*Value, for example, intValue. Common names for static factories include from, of, valueOf, instance, getInstance, newInstance, get*Type*, and new*Type* (Item 1, page 9).

Grammatical conventions for field names are less well established and less important than those for class, interface, and method names because well-designed APIs contain few if any exposed fields. Fields of type boolean are often named like boolean accessor methods with the initial is omitted, for example, initialized, composite. Fields of other types are usually named with nouns or noun phrases, such as height, digits, or bodyStyle. Grammatical conventions for local variables are similar to those for fields but even weaker.

To summarize, internalize the standard naming conventions and learn to use them as second nature. The typographical conventions are straightforward and largely unambiguous; the grammatical conventions are more complex and looser. To quote from *The Java Language Specification* [JLS, 6.1], "These conventions should not be followed slavishly if long-held conventional usage dictates otherwise." Use common sense.

CHAPTER 10

Exceptions

WHEN used to best advantage, exceptions can improve a program's readability, reliability, and maintainability. When used improperly, they can have the opposite effect. This chapter provides guidelines for using exceptions effectively.

Item 69: Use exceptions only for exceptional conditions

Someday, if you are unlucky, you may stumble across a piece of code that looks something like this:

```
// Horrible abuse of exceptions. Don't ever do this!
try {
    int i = 0;
    while(true)
        range[i++].climb();
} catch (ArrayIndexOutOfBoundsException e) {
}
```

What does this code do? It's not at all obvious from inspection, and that's reason enough not to use it (Item 67). It turns out to be a horribly ill-conceived idiom for looping through the elements of an array. The infinite loop terminates by throwing, catching, and ignoring an ArrayIndexOutOfBoundsException when it attempts to access the first array element outside the bounds of the array. It's supposed to be equivalent to the standard idiom for looping through an array, which is instantly recognizable to any Java programmer:

```
for (Mountain m : range)
    m.climb();
```

So why would anyone use the exception-based loop in preference to the tried and true? It's a misguided attempt to improve performance based on the faulty reasoning that, since the VM checks the bounds of all array accesses, the normal loop termination test—hidden by the compiler but still present in the for-each loop—is redundant and should be avoided. There are three things wrong with this reasoning:

- Because exceptions are designed for exceptional circumstances, there is little incentive for JVM implementors to make them as fast as explicit tests.

- Placing code inside a `try-catch` block inhibits certain optimizations that JVM implementations might otherwise perform.

- The standard idiom for looping through an array doesn't necessarily result in redundant checks. Many JVM implementations optimize them away.

In fact, the exception-based idiom is far slower than the standard one. On my machine, the exception-based idiom is about twice as slow as the standard one for arrays of one hundred elements.

Not only does the exception-based loop obfuscate the purpose of the code and reduce its performance, but it's not guaranteed to work. If there is a bug in the loop, the use of exceptions for flow control can mask the bug, greatly complicating the debugging process. Suppose the computation in the body of the loop invokes a method that performs an out-of-bounds access to some unrelated array. If a reasonable loop idiom were used, the bug would generate an uncaught exception, resulting in immediate thread termination with a full stack trace. If the misguided exception-based loop were used, the bug-related exception would be caught and misinterpreted as a normal loop termination.

The moral of this story is simple: **Exceptions are, as their name implies, to be used only for exceptional conditions; they should never be used for ordinary control flow.** More generally, use standard, easily recognizable idioms in preference to overly clever techniques that purport to offer better performance. Even if the performance advantage is real, it may not remain in the face of steadily improving platform implementations. The subtle bugs and maintenance headaches that come from overly clever techniques, however, are sure to remain.

This principle also has implications for API design. **A well-designed API must not force its clients to use exceptions for ordinary control flow.** A class with a "state-dependent" method that can be invoked only under certain unpredictable conditions should generally have a separate "state-testing" method indicating whether it is appropriate to invoke the state-dependent method. For example, the `Iterator` interface has the state-dependent method next and the corresponding state-testing method `hasNext`. This enables the standard idiom for iterating over a collection with a traditional `for` loop (as well as the for-each loop, where the `hasNext` method is used internally):

```
for (Iterator<Foo> i = collection.iterator(); i.hasNext(); ) {
    Foo foo = i.next();
    ...
}
```

If `Iterator` lacked the `hasNext` method, clients would be forced to do this instead:

```
// Do not use this hideous code for iteration over a collection!
try {
    Iterator<Foo> i = collection.iterator();
    while(true) {
        Foo foo = i.next();
        ...
    }
} catch (NoSuchElementException e) {
}
```

This should look very familiar after the array iteration example that began this item. In addition to being wordy and misleading, the exception-based loop is likely to perform poorly and can mask bugs in unrelated parts of the system.

An alternative to providing a separate state-testing method is to have the state-dependent method return an empty optional (Item 55) or a distinguished value such as `null` if it cannot perform the desired computation.

Here are some guidelines to help you choose between a state-testing method and an optional or distinguished return value. If an object is to be accessed concurrently without external synchronization or is subject to externally induced state transitions, you must use an optional or distinguished return value, as the object's state could change in the interval between the invocation of a state-testing method and its state-dependent method. Performance concerns may dictate that an optional or distinguished return value be used if a separate state-testing method would duplicate the work of the state-dependent method. All other things being equal, a state-testing method is mildly preferable to a distinguished return value. It offers slightly better readability, and incorrect use may be easier to detect: if you forget to call a state-testing method, the state-dependent method will throw an exception, making the bug obvious; if you forget to check for a distinguished return value, the bug may be subtle. This is not an issue for optional return values.

In summary, exceptions are designed for exceptional conditions. Don't use them for ordinary control flow, and don't write APIs that force others to do so.

Item 70: Use checked exceptions for recoverable conditions and runtime exceptions for programming errors

Java provides three kinds of throwables: *checked exceptions*, *runtime exceptions*, and *errors*. There is some confusion among programmers as to when it is appropriate to use each kind of throwable. While the decision is not always clear-cut, there are some general rules that provide strong guidance.

The cardinal rule in deciding whether to use a checked or an unchecked exception is this: **use checked exceptions for conditions from which the caller can reasonably be expected to recover.** By throwing a checked exception, you force the caller to handle the exception in a catch clause or to propagate it outward. Each checked exception that a method is declared to throw is therefore a potent indication to the API user that the associated condition is a possible outcome of invoking the method.

By confronting the user with a checked exception, the API designer presents a mandate to recover from the condition. The user can disregard the mandate by catching the exception and ignoring it, but this is usually a bad idea (Item 77).

There are two kinds of unchecked throwables: runtime exceptions and errors. They are identical in their behavior: both are throwables that needn't, and generally shouldn't, be caught. If a program throws an unchecked exception or an error, it is generally the case that recovery is impossible and continued execution would do more harm than good. If a program does not catch such a throwable, it will cause the current thread to halt with an appropriate error message.

Use runtime exceptions to indicate programming errors. The great majority of runtime exceptions indicate *precondition violations*. A precondition violation is simply a failure by the client of an API to adhere to the contract established by the API specification. For example, the contract for array access specifies that the array index must be between zero and the array length minus one, inclusive. ArrayIndexOutOfBoundsException indicates that this precondition was violated.

One problem with this advice is that it is not always clear whether you're dealing with a recoverable conditions or a programming error. For example, consider the case of resource exhaustion, which can be caused by a programming error such as allocating an unreasonably large array, or by a genuine shortage of resources. If resource exhaustion is caused by a temporary shortage or by temporarily heightened demand, the condition may well be recoverable. It is a matter of judgment on the part of the API designer whether a given instance of resource exhaustion is likely to allow for recovery. If you believe a condition is likely to allow for recovery, use a checked exception; if not, use a runtime exception. If it isn't clear whether recovery is possible, you're probably better off using an unchecked exception, for reasons discussed in Item 71.

While the Java Language Specification does not require it, there is a strong convention that *errors* are reserved for use by the JVM to indicate resource deficiencies, invariant failures, or other conditions that make it impossible to continue execution. Given the almost universal acceptance of this convention, it's best not to implement any new Error subclasses. Therefore, **all of the unchecked throwables you implement should subclass RuntimeException** (directly or indirectly). Not only shouldn't you define Error subclasses, but with the exception of AssertionError, you shouldn't throw them either.

It is possible to define a throwable that is not a subclass of Exception, RuntimeException, or Error. The JLS doesn't address such throwables directly but specifies implicitly that they behave as ordinary checked exceptions (which are subclasses of Exception but not RuntimeException). So when should you use such a beast? In a word, never. They have no benefits over ordinary checked exceptions and would serve merely to confuse the user of your API.

API designers often forget that exceptions are full-fledged objects on which arbitrary methods can be defined. The primary use of such methods is to provide code that catches the exception with additional information concerning the condition that caused the exception to be thrown. In the absence of such methods, programmers have been known to parse the string representation of an exception to ferret out additional information. This is extremely bad practice (Item 12). Throwable classes seldom specify the details of their string representations, so string representations can differ from implementation to implementation and release to release. Therefore, code that parses the string representation of an exception is likely to be nonportable and fragile.

Because checked exceptions generally indicate recoverable conditions, it's especially important for them to provide methods that furnish information to help the caller recover from the exceptional condition. For example, suppose a checked exception is thrown when an attempt to make a purchase with a gift card fails due to insufficient funds. The exception should provide an accessor method to query the amount of the shortfall. This will enable the caller to relay the amount to the shopper. See Item 75 for more on this topic.

To summarize, throw checked exceptions for recoverable conditions and unchecked exceptions for programming errors. When in doubt, throw unchecked exceptions. Don't define any throwables that are neither checked exceptions nor runtime exceptions. Provide methods on your checked exceptions to aid in recovery.

Item 71: Avoid unnecessary use of checked exceptions

Many Java programmers dislike checked exceptions, but used properly, they can improve APIs and programs. Unlike return codes and unchecked exceptions, they *force* programmers to deal with problems, enhancing reliability. That said, overuse of checked exceptions in APIs can make them far less pleasant to use. If a method throws checked exceptions, the code that invokes it must handle them in one or more catch blocks, or declare that it throws them and let them propagate outward. Either way, it places a burden on the user of the API. The burden increased in Java 8, as methods throwing checked exceptions can't be used directly in streams (Items 45–48).

This burden may be justified if the exceptional condition cannot be prevented by proper use of the API *and* the programmer using the API can take some useful action once confronted with the exception. Unless both of these conditions are met, an unchecked exception is appropriate. As a litmus test, ask yourself how the programmer will handle the exception. Is this the best that can be done?

```
} catch (TheCheckedException e) {
    throw new AssertionError(); // Can't happen!
}
```

Or this?

```
} catch (TheCheckedException e) {
    e.printStackTrace();        // Oh well, we lose.
    System.exit(1);
}
```

If the programmer can do no better, an unchecked exception is called for.

The additional burden on the programmer caused by a checked exception is substantially higher if it is the *sole* checked exception thrown by a method. If there are others, the method must already appear in a try block, and this exception requires, at most, another catch block. If a method throws a single checked exception, this exception is the sole reason the method must appear in a try block and can't be used directly in streams. Under these circumstances, it pays to ask yourself if there is a way to avoid the checked exception.

The easiest way to eliminate a checked exception is to return an *optional* of the desired result type (Item 55). Instead of throwing a checked exception, the method simply returns an empty optional. The disadvantage of this technique is that the method can't return any additional information detailing its inability to perform the desired computation. Exceptions, by contrast, have descriptive types, and can export methods to provide additional information (Item 70).

You can also turn a checked exception into an unchecked exception by breaking the method that throws the exception into two methods, the first of which returns a `boolean` indicating whether the exception would be thrown. This API refactoring transforms the calling sequence from this:

```
// Invocation with checked exception
try {
    obj.action(args);
} catch (TheCheckedException e) {
    ... // Handle exceptional condition
}
```

into this:

```
// Invocation with state-testing method and unchecked exception
if (obj.actionPermitted(args)) {
    obj.action(args);
} else {
    ... // Handle exceptional condition
}
```

This refactoring is not always appropriate, but where it is, it can make an API more pleasant to use. While the latter calling sequence is no prettier than the former, the refactored API is more flexible. If the programmer knows the call will succeed, or is content to let the thread terminate if it fails, the refactoring also allows this trivial calling sequence:

```
obj.action(args);
```

If you suspect that the trivial calling sequence will be the norm, then the API refactoring may be appropriate. The resulting API is essentially the state-testing method API in Item 69 and the same caveats apply: if an object is to be accessed concurrently without external synchronization or it is subject to externally induced state transitions, this refactoring is inappropriate because the object's state may change between the calls to `actionPermitted` and `action`. If a separate `actionPermitted` method would duplicate the work of the `action` method, the refactoring may be ruled out on performance grounds.

In summary, when used sparingly, checked exceptions can increase the reliability of programs; when overused, they make APIs painful to use. If callers won't be able to recover from failures, throw unchecked exceptions. If recovery may be possible and you want to *force* callers to handle exceptional conditions, first consider returning an optional. Only if this would provide insufficient information in the case of failure should you throw a checked exception.

Item 72: Favor the use of standard exceptions

An attribute that distinguishes expert programmers from less experienced ones is that experts strive for and usually achieve a high degree of code reuse. Exceptions are no exception to the rule that code reuse is a good thing. The Java libraries provide a set of exceptions that covers most of the exception-throwing needs of most APIs.

Reusing standard exceptions has several benefits. Chief among them is that it makes your API easier to learn and use because it matches the established conventions that programmers are already familiar with. A close second is that programs using your API are easier to read because they aren't cluttered with unfamiliar exceptions. Last (and least), fewer exception classes means a smaller memory footprint and less time spent loading classes.

The most commonly reused exception type is `IllegalArgumentException` (Item 49). This is generally the exception to throw when the caller passes in an argument whose value is inappropriate. For example, this would be the exception to throw if the caller passed a negative number in a parameter representing the number of times some action was to be repeated.

Another commonly reused exception is `IllegalStateException`. This is generally the exception to throw if the invocation is illegal because of the state of the receiving object. For example, this would be the exception to throw if the caller attempted to use some object before it had been properly initialized.

Arguably, every erroneous method invocation boils down to an illegal argument or state, but other exceptions are standardly used for certain kinds of illegal arguments and states. If a caller passes `null` in some parameter for which null values are prohibited, convention dictates that `NullPointerException` be thrown rather than `IllegalArgumentException`. Similarly, if a caller passes an out-of-range value in a parameter representing an index into a sequence, `IndexOutOfBoundsException` should be thrown rather than `IllegalArgumentException`.

Another reusable exception is `ConcurrentModificationException`. It should be thrown if an object that was designed for use by a single thread (or with external synchronization) detects that it is being modified concurrently. This exception is at best a hint because it is impossible to reliably detect concurrent modification.

A last standard exception of note is `UnsupportedOperationException`. This is the exception to throw if an object does not support an attempted operation. Its use is rare because most objects support all of their methods. This exception is used by classes that fail to implement one or more *optional operations* defined by an interface they implement. For example, an append-only `List` implementation would throw this exception if someone tried to delete an element from the list.

Do *not* reuse `Exception`, `RuntimeException`, `Throwable`, or `Error` directly. Treat these classes as if they were abstract. You can't reliably test for these exceptions because they are superclasses of other exceptions that a method may throw.

This table summarizes the most commonly reused exceptions:

Exception	Occasion for Use
`IllegalArgumentException`	Non-null parameter value is inappropriate
`IllegalStateException`	Object state is inappropriate for method invocation
`NullPointerException`	Parameter value is null where prohibited
`IndexOutOfBoundsException`	Index parameter value is out of range
`ConcurrentModificationException`	Concurrent modification of an object has been detected where it is prohibited
`UnsupportedOperationException`	Object does not support method

While these are by far the most commonly reused exceptions, others may be reused where circumstances warrant. For example, it would be appropriate to reuse `ArithmeticException` and `NumberFormatException` if you were implementing arithmetic objects such as complex numbers or rational numbers. If an exception fits your needs, go ahead and use it, but only if the conditions under which you would throw it are consistent with the exception's documentation: reuse must be based on documented semantics, not just on name. Also, feel free to subclass a standard exception if you want to add more detail (Item 75), but remember that exceptions are serializable (Chapter 12). That alone is reason not to write your own exception class without good reason.

Choosing which exception to reuse can be tricky because the "occasions for use" in the table above do not appear to be mutually exclusive. Consider the case of an object representing a deck of cards, and suppose there were a method to deal a hand from the deck that took as an argument the size of the hand. If the caller passed a value larger than the number of cards remaining in the deck, it could be construed as an `IllegalArgumentException` (the `handSize` parameter value is too high) or an `IllegalStateException` (the deck contains too few cards). Under these circumstances, the rule is to **throw `IllegalStateException` if no argument values would have worked, otherwise throw `IllegalArgumentException`.**

Item 73: Throw exceptions appropriate to the abstraction

It is disconcerting when a method throws an exception that has no apparent connection to the task that it performs. This often happens when a method propagates an exception thrown by a lower-level abstraction. Not only is it disconcerting, but it pollutes the API of the higher layer with implementation details. If the implementation of the higher layer changes in a later release, the exceptions it throws will change too, potentially breaking existing client programs.

To avoid this problem, **higher layers should catch lower-level exceptions and, in their place, throw exceptions that can be explained in terms of the higher-level abstraction.** This idiom is known as *exception translation*:

```
// Exception Translation
try {
    ... // Use lower-level abstraction to do our bidding
} catch (LowerLevelException e) {
    throw new HigherLevelException(...);
}
```

Here is an example of exception translation taken from the AbstractSequentialList class, which is a *skeletal implementation* (Item 20) of the List interface. In this example, exception translation is mandated by the specification of the get method in the List<E> interface:

```
/**
 * Returns the element at the specified position in this list.
 * @throws IndexOutOfBoundsException if the index is out of range
 *         ({@code index < 0 || index >= size()}).
 */
public E get(int index) {
    ListIterator<E> i = listIterator(index);
    try {
        return i.next();
    } catch (NoSuchElementException e) {
        throw new IndexOutOfBoundsException("Index: " + index);
    }
}
```

A special form of exception translation called *exception chaining* is called for in cases where the lower-level exception might be helpful to someone debugging the problem that caused the higher-level exception. The lower-level exception (the *cause*) is passed to the higher-level exception, which provides an accessor method (Throwable's getCause method) to retrieve the lower-level exception:

```
// Exception Chaining
try {
    ... // Use lower-level abstraction to do our bidding
} catch (LowerLevelException cause) {
    throw new HigherLevelException(cause);
}
```

The higher-level exception's constructor passes the cause to a *chaining-aware* superclass constructor, so it is ultimately passed to one of Throwable's chaining-aware constructors, such as Throwable(Throwable):

```
// Exception with chaining-aware constructor
class HigherLevelException extends Exception {
    HigherLevelException(Throwable cause) {
        super(cause);
    }
}
```

Most standard exceptions have chaining-aware constructors. For exceptions that don't, you can set the cause using Throwable's initCause method. Not only does exception chaining let you access the cause programmatically (with getCause), but it integrates the cause's stack trace into that of the higher-level exception.

While exception translation is superior to mindless propagation of exceptions from lower layers, it should not be overused. Where possible, the best way to deal with exceptions from lower layers is to avoid them, by ensuring that lower-level methods succeed. Sometimes you can do this by checking the validity of the higher-level method's parameters before passing them on to lower layers.

If it is impossible to prevent exceptions from lower layers, the next best thing is to have the higher layer silently work around these exceptions, insulating the caller of the higher-level method from lower-level problems. Under these circumstances, it may be appropriate to log the exception using some appropriate logging facility such as java.util.logging. This allows programmers to investigate the problem, while insulating client code and the users from it.

In summary, if it isn't feasible to prevent or to handle exceptions from lower layers, use exception translation, unless the lower-level method happens to guarantee that all of its exceptions are appropriate to the higher level. Chaining provides the best of both worlds: it allows you to throw an appropriate higher-level exception, while capturing the underlying cause for failure analysis (Item 75).

Item 74: Document all exceptions thrown by each method

A description of the exceptions thrown by a method is an important part of the documentation required to use the method properly. Therefore, it is critically important that you take the time to carefully document all of the exceptions thrown by each method (Item 56).

Always declare checked exceptions individually, and document precisely the conditions under which each one is thrown using the Javadoc @throws tag. Don't take the shortcut of declaring that a method throws some superclass of multiple exception classes that it can throw. As an extreme example, don't declare that a public method throws Exception or, worse, throws Throwable. In addition to denying any guidance to the method's user concerning the exceptions it is capable of throwing, such a declaration greatly hinders the use of the method because it effectively obscures any other exception that may be thrown in the same context. One exception to this advice is the main method, which can safely be declared to throw Exception because it is called only by VM.

While the language does not require programmers to declare the unchecked exceptions that a method is capable of throwing, it is wise to document them as carefully as the checked exceptions. Unchecked exceptions generally represent programming errors (Item 70), and familiarizing programmers with all of the errors they can make helps them avoid making these errors. A well-documented list of the unchecked exceptions that a method can throw effectively describes the *preconditions* for its successful execution. It is essential that every public method's documentation describe its preconditions (Item 56), and documenting its unchecked exceptions is the best way to satisfy this requirement.

It is particularly important that methods in interfaces document the unchecked exceptions they may throw. This documentation forms a part of the interface's *general contract* and enables common behavior among multiple implementations of the interface.

Use the Javadoc @throws tag to document each exception that a method can throw, but do *not* use the throws keyword on unchecked exceptions. It is important that programmers using your API are aware of which exceptions are checked and which are unchecked because the programmers' responsibilities differ in these two cases. The documentation generated by the Javadoc @throws tag without a corresponding throws clause in the method declaration provides a strong visual cue to the programmer that an exception is unchecked.

It should be noted that documenting all of the unchecked exceptions that each method can throw is an ideal, not always achievable in the real world. When a class undergoes revision, it is not a violation of source or binary compatibility if an exported method is modified to throw additional unchecked exceptions. Suppose a class invokes a method from another, independently written class. The authors of the former class may carefully document all of the unchecked exceptions that each method throws, but if the latter class is revised to throw additional unchecked exceptions, it is quite likely that the former class (which has not undergone revision) will propagate the new unchecked exceptions even though it does not document them.

If an exception is thrown by many methods in a class for the same reason, you can document the exception in the class's documentation comment rather than documenting it individually for each method. A common example is `NullPointerException`. It is fine for a class's documentation comment to say, "All methods in this class throw a `NullPointerException` if a null object reference is passed in any parameter," or words to that effect.

In summary, document every exception that can be thrown by each method that you write. This is true for unchecked as well as checked exceptions, and for abstract as well as concrete methods. This documentation should take the form of `@throws` tags in doc comments. Declare each checked exception individually in a method's `throws` clause, but do not declare unchecked exceptions. If you fail to document the exceptions that your methods can throw, it will be difficult or impossible for others to make effective use of your classes and interfaces.

Item 75: Include failure-capture information in detail messages

When a program fails due to an uncaught exception, the system automatically prints out the exception's stack trace. The stack trace contains the exception's *string representation*, the result of invoking its toString method. This typically consists of the exception's class name followed by its *detail message*. Frequently this is the only information that programmers or site reliability engineers will have when investigating a software failure. If the failure is not easily reproducible, it may be difficult or impossible to get any more information. Therefore, it is critically important that the exception's toString method return as much information as possible concerning the cause of the failure. In other words, the detail message of an exception should *capture the failure* for subsequent analysis.

To capture a failure, the detail message of an exception should contain the values of all parameters and fields that contributed to the exception. For example, the detail message of an IndexOutOfBoundsException should contain the lower bound, the upper bound, and the index value that failed to lie between the bounds. This information tells a lot about the failure. Any or all of the three values could be wrong. The index could be one less than the lower bound or equal to the upper bound (a "fencepost error"), or it could be a wild value, far too low or high. The lower bound could be greater than the upper bound (a serious internal invariant failure). Each of these situations points to a different problem, and it greatly aids in the diagnosis if you know what sort of error you're looking for.

One caveat concerns security-sensitive information. Because stack traces may be seen by many people in the process of diagnosing and fixing software issues, **do not include passwords, encryption keys, and the like in detail messages.**

While it is critical to include all of the pertinent data in the detail message of an exception, it is generally unimportant to include a lot of prose. The stack trace is intended to be analyzed in conjunction with the documentation and, if necessary, source code. It generally contains the exact file and line number from which the exception was thrown, as well as the files and line numbers of all other method invocations on the stack. Lengthy prose descriptions of the failure are superfluous; the information can be gleaned by reading the documentation and source code.

The detail message of an exception should not be confused with a user-level error message, which must be intelligible to end users. Unlike a user-level error message, the detail message is primarily for the benefit of programmers or site reliability engineers, when analyzing a failure. Therefore, information content is far more important than readability. User-level error messages are often *localized*, whereas exception detail messages rarely are.

One way to ensure that exceptions contain adequate failure-capture information in their detail messages is to require this information in their constructors instead of a string detail message. The detail message can then be generated automatically to include the information. For example, instead of a String constructor, IndexOutOfBoundsException could have had a constructor that looks like this:

```java
/**
 * Constructs an IndexOutOfBoundsException.
 *
 * @param lowerBound the lowest legal index value
 * @param upperBound the highest legal index value plus one
 * @param index      the actual index value
 */
public IndexOutOfBoundsException(int lowerBound, int upperBound,
                                 int index) {
    // Generate a detail message that captures the failure
    super(String.format(
            "Lower bound: %d, Upper bound: %d, Index: %d",
            lowerBound, upperBound, index));

    // Save failure information for programmatic access
    this.lowerBound = lowerBound;
    this.upperBound = upperBound;
    this.index = index;
}
```

As of Java 9, IndexOutOfBoundsException finally acquired a constructor that takes an int valued index parameter, but sadly it omits the lowerBound and upperBound parameters. More generally, the Java libraries don't make heavy use of this idiom, but it is highly recommended. It makes it easy for the programmer throwing an exception to capture the failure. In fact, it makes it hard for the programmer not to capture the failure! In effect, the idiom centralizes the code to generate a high-quality detail message in the exception class, rather than requiring each user of the class to generate the detail message redundantly.

As suggested in Item 70, it may be appropriate for an exception to provide accessor methods for its failure-capture information (lowerBound, upperBound, and index in the above example). It is more important to provide such accessor methods on checked exceptions than unchecked, because the failure-capture information could be useful in recovering from the failure. It is rare (although not inconceivable) that a programmer might want programmatic access to the details of an unchecked exception. Even for unchecked exceptions, however, it seems advisable to provide these accessors on general principle (Item 12, page 57).

Item 76: Strive for failure atomicity

After an object throws an exception, it is generally desirable that the object still be in a well-defined, usable state, even if the failure occurred in the midst of performing an operation. This is especially true for checked exceptions, from which the caller is expected to recover. **Generally speaking, a failed method invocation should leave the object in the state that it was in prior to the invocation**. A method with this property is said to be *failure-atomic*.

There are several ways to achieve this effect. The simplest is to design immutable objects (Item 17). If an object is immutable, failure atomicity is free. If an operation fails, it may prevent a new object from getting created, but it will never leave an existing object in an inconsistent state, because the state of each object is consistent when it is created and can't be modified thereafter.

For methods that operate on mutable objects, the most common way to achieve failure atomicity is to check parameters for validity before performing the operation (Item 49). This causes most exceptions to get thrown before object modification commences. For example, consider the Stack.pop method in Item 7:

```java
public Object pop() {
    if (size == 0)
        throw new EmptyStackException();
    Object result = elements[--size];
    elements[size] = null; // Eliminate obsolete reference
    return result;
}
```

If the initial size check were eliminated, the method would still throw an exception when it attempted to pop an element from an empty stack. It would, however, leave the size field in an inconsistent (negative) state, causing any future method invocations on the object to fail. Additionally, the ArrayIndexOutOf-BoundsException thrown by the pop method would be inappropriate to the abstraction (Item 73).

A closely related approach to achieving failure atomicity is to order the computation so that any part that may fail takes place before any part that modifies the object. This approach is a natural extension of the previous one when arguments cannot be checked without performing a part of the computation. For example, consider the case of TreeMap, whose elements are sorted according to some ordering. In order to add an element to a TreeMap, the element must be of a type that can be compared using the TreeMap's ordering. Attempting to add an incorrectly typed element will naturally fail with a `ClassCastException` as a result of searching for the element in the tree, before the tree has been modified in any way.

A third approach to achieving failure atomicity is to perform the operation on a temporary copy of the object and to replace the contents of the object with the temporary copy once the operation is complete. This approach occurs naturally when the computation can be performed more quickly once the data has been stored in a temporary data structure. For example, some sorting functions copy their input list into an array prior to sorting to reduce the cost of accessing elements in the inner loop of the sort. This is done for performance, but as an added benefit, it ensures that the input list will be untouched if the sort fails.

A last and far less common approach to achieving failure atomicity is to write *recovery code* that intercepts a failure that occurs in the midst of an operation, and causes the object to roll back its state to the point before the operation began. This approach is used mainly for durable (disk-based) data structures.

While failure atomicity is generally desirable, it is not always achievable. For example, if two threads attempt to modify the same object concurrently without proper synchronization, the object may be left in an inconsistent state. It would therefore be wrong to assume that an object was still usable after catching a `ConcurrentModificationException`. Errors are unrecoverable, so you need not even attempt to preserve failure atomicity when throwing `AssertionError`.

Even where failure atomicity is possible, it is not always desirable. For some operations, it would significantly increase the cost or complexity. That said, it is often both free and easy to achieve failure atomicity once you're aware of the issue.

In summary, as a rule, any generated exception that is part of a method's specification should leave the object in the same state it was in prior to the method invocation. Where this rule is violated, the API documentation should clearly indicate what state the object will be left in. Unfortunately, plenty of existing API documentation fails to live up to this ideal.

Item 77: Don't ignore exceptions

While this advice may seem obvious, it is violated often enough that it bears repeating. When the designers of an API declare a method to throw an exception, they are trying to tell you something. Don't ignore it! It is easy to ignore exceptions by surrounding a method invocation with a `try` statement whose `catch` block is empty:

```
// Empty catch block ignores exception - Highly suspect!
try {
    ...
} catch (SomeException e) {
}
```

An empty catch block defeats the purpose of exceptions, which is to force you to handle exceptional conditions. Ignoring an exception is analogous to ignoring a fire alarm—and turning it off so no one else gets a chance to see if there's a real fire. You may get away with it, or the results may be disastrous. Whenever you see an empty `catch` block, alarm bells should go off in your head.

There are situations where it is appropriate to ignore an exception. For example, it might be appropriate when closing a `FileInputStream`. You haven't changed the state of the file, so there's no need to perform any recovery action, and you've already read the information that you need from the file, so there's no reason to abort the operation in progress. It may be wise to log the exception, so that you can investigate the matter if these exceptions happen often. **If you choose to ignore an exception, the `catch` block should contain a comment explaining why it is appropriate to do so, and the variable should be named `ignored`:**

```
Future<Integer> f = exec.submit(planarMap::chromaticNumber);
int numColors = 4; // Default; guaranteed sufficient for any map
try {
    numColors = f.get(1L, TimeUnit.SECONDS);
} catch (TimeoutException | ExecutionException ignored) {
    // Use default: minimal coloring is desirable, not required
}
```

The advice in this item applies equally to checked and unchecked exceptions. Whether an exception represents a predictable exceptional condition or a programming error, ignoring it with an empty `catch` block will result in a program that continues silently in the face of error. The program might then fail at an arbitrary time in the future, at a point in the code that bears no apparent relation to the source of the problem. Properly handling an exception can avert failure entirely. Merely letting an exception propagate outward can at least cause the program to fail swiftly, preserving information to aid in debugging the failure.

CHAPTER 11

Concurrency

THREADS allow multiple activities to proceed concurrently. Concurrent programming is harder than single-threaded programming, because more things can go wrong, and failures can be hard to reproduce. You can't avoid concurrency. It is inherent in the platform and a requirement if you are to obtain good performance from multicore processors, which are now ubiquitous. This chapter contains advice to help you write clear, correct, well-documented concurrent programs.

Item 78: Synchronize access to shared mutable data

The synchronized keyword ensures that only a single thread can execute a method or block at one time. Many programmers think of synchronization solely as a means of *mutual exclusion*, to prevent an object from being seen in an inconsistent state by one thread while it's being modified by another. In this view, an object is created in a consistent state (Item 17) and locked by the methods that access it. These methods observe the state and optionally cause a *state transition*, transforming the object from one consistent state to another. Proper use of synchronization guarantees that no method will ever observe the object in an inconsistent state.

This view is correct, but it's only half the story. Without synchronization, one thread's changes might not be visible to other threads. Not only does synchronization prevent threads from observing an object in an inconsistent state, but it ensures that each thread entering a synchronized method or block sees the effects of all previous modifications that were guarded by the same lock.

The language specification guarantees that reading or writing a variable is *atomic* unless the variable is of type long or double [JLS, 17.4, 17.7]. In other words, reading a variable other than a long or double is guaranteed to return a value that was stored into that variable by some thread, even if multiple threads modify the variable concurrently and without synchronization.

311

You may hear it said that to improve performance, you should dispense with synchronization when reading or writing atomic data. This advice is dangerously wrong. While the language specification guarantees that a thread will not see an arbitrary value when reading a field, it does not guarantee that a value written by one thread will be visible to another. **Synchronization is required for reliable communication between threads as well as for mutual exclusion.** This is due to a part of the language specification known as the *memory model*, which specifies when and how changes made by one thread become visible to others [JLS, 17.4; Goetz06, 16].

The consequences of failing to synchronize access to shared mutable data can be dire even if the data is atomically readable and writable. Consider the task of stopping one thread from another. The libraries provide the Thread.stop method, but this method was deprecated long ago because it is inherently *unsafe*—its use can result in data corruption. **Do not use Thread.stop.** A recommended way to stop one thread from another is to have the first thread poll a boolean field that is initially false but can be set to true by the second thread to indicate that the first thread is to stop itself. Because reading and writing a boolean field is atomic, some programmers dispense with synchronization when accessing the field:

```java
// Broken! - How long would you expect this program to run?
public class StopThread {
    private static boolean stopRequested;

    public static void main(String[] args)
            throws InterruptedException {
        Thread backgroundThread = new Thread(() -> {
            int i = 0;
            while (!stopRequested)
                i++;
        });
        backgroundThread.start();

        TimeUnit.SECONDS.sleep(1);
        stopRequested = true;
    }
}
```

You might expect this program to run for about a second, after which the main thread sets stopRequested to true, causing the background thread's loop to terminate. On my machine, however, the program *never* terminates: the background thread loops forever!

The problem is that in the absence of synchronization, there is no guarantee as to when, if ever, the background thread will see the change in the value of `stopRequested` made by the main thread. In the absence of synchronization, it's quite acceptable for the virtual machine to transform this code:

```
while (!stopRequested)
    i++;
```

into this code:

```
if (!stopRequested)
    while (true)
        i++;
```

This optimization is known as *hoisting*, and it is precisely what the OpenJDK Server VM does. The result is a *liveness failure*: the program fails to make progress. One way to fix the problem is to synchronize access to the `stopRequested` field. This program terminates in about one second, as expected:

```
// Properly synchronized cooperative thread termination
public class StopThread {
    private static boolean stopRequested;

    private static synchronized void requestStop() {
        stopRequested = true;
    }

    private static synchronized boolean stopRequested() {
        return stopRequested;
    }

    public static void main(String[] args)
            throws InterruptedException {
        Thread backgroundThread = new Thread(() -> {
            int i = 0;
            while (!stopRequested())
                i++;
        });
        backgroundThread.start();

        TimeUnit.SECONDS.sleep(1);
        requestStop();
    }
}
```

Note that both the write method (requestStop) and the read method (stop-Requested) are synchronized. It is *not* sufficient to synchronize only the write method! **Synchronization is not guaranteed to work unless both read and write operations are synchronized.** Occasionally a program that synchronizes only writes (or reads) may *appear* to work on some machines, but in this case, appearances are deceiving.

The actions of the synchronized methods in StopThread would be atomic even without synchronization. In other words, the synchronization on these methods is used *solely* for its communication effects, not for mutual exclusion. While the cost of synchronizing on each iteration of the loop is small, there is a correct alternative that is less verbose and whose performance is likely to be better. The locking in the second version of StopThread can be omitted if stopRequested is declared volatile. While the volatile modifier performs no mutual exclusion, it guarantees that any thread that reads the field will see the most recently written value:

```java
// Cooperative thread termination with a volatile field
public class StopThread {
    private static volatile boolean stopRequested;

    public static void main(String[] args)
            throws InterruptedException {
        Thread backgroundThread = new Thread(() -> {
            int i = 0;
            while (!stopRequested)
                i++;
        });
        backgroundThread.start();

        TimeUnit.SECONDS.sleep(1);
        stopRequested = true;
    }
}
```

You do have to be careful when using volatile. Consider the following method, which is supposed to generate serial numbers:

```java
// Broken - requires synchronization!
private static volatile int nextSerialNumber = 0;

public static int generateSerialNumber() {
    return nextSerialNumber++;
}
```

The intent of the method is to guarantee that every invocation returns a unique value (so long as there are no more than 2^{32} invocations). The method's state consists of a single atomically accessible field, nextSerialNumber, and all possible values of this field are legal. Therefore, no synchronization is necessary to protect its invariants. Still, the method won't work properly without synchronization.

The problem is that the increment operator (++) is not atomic. It performs *two* operations on the nextSerialNumber field: first it reads the value, and then it writes back a new value, equal to the old value plus one. If a second thread reads the field between the time a thread reads the old value and writes back a new one, the second thread will see the same value as the first and return the same serial number. This is a *safety failure*: the program computes the wrong results.

One way to fix generateSerialNumber is to add the synchronized modifier to its declaration. This ensures that multiple invocations won't be interleaved and that each invocation of the method will see the effects of all previous invocations. Once you've done that, you can and should remove the volatile modifier from nextSerialNumber. To bulletproof the method, use long instead of int, or throw an exception if nextSerialNumber is about to wrap.

Better still, follow the advice in Item 59 and use the class AtomicLong, which is part of java.util.concurrent.atomic. This package provides primitives for lock-free, thread-safe programming on single variables. While volatile provides only the communication effects of synchronization, this package also provides atomicity. This is exactly what we want for generateSerialNumber, and it is likely to outperform the synchronized version:

```
// Lock-free synchronization with java.util.concurrent.atomic
private static final AtomicLong nextSerialNum = new AtomicLong();

public static long generateSerialNumber() {
    return nextSerialNum.getAndIncrement();
}
```

The best way to avoid the problems discussed in this item is not to share mutable data. Either share immutable data (Item 17) or don't share at all. In other words, **confine mutable data to a single thread.** If you adopt this policy, it is important to document it so that the policy is maintained as your program evolves. It is also important to have a deep understanding of the frameworks and libraries you're using because they may introduce threads that you are unaware of.

It is acceptable for one thread to modify a data object for a while and then to share it with other threads, synchronizing only the act of sharing the object reference. Other threads can then read the object without further synchronization, so long as it isn't modified again. Such objects are said to be *effectively immutable* [Goetz06, 3.5.4]. Transferring such an object reference from one thread to others is called *safe publication* [Goetz06, 3.5.3]. There are many ways to safely publish an object reference: you can store it in a static field as part of class initialization; you can store it in a volatile field, a final field, or a field that is accessed with normal locking; or you can put it into a concurrent collection (Item 81).

In summary, **when multiple threads share mutable data, each thread that reads or writes the data must perform synchronization.** In the absence of synchronization, there is no guarantee that one thread's changes will be visible to another thread. The penalties for failing to synchronize shared mutable data are liveness and safety failures. These failures are among the most difficult to debug. They can be intermittent and timing-dependent, and program behavior can vary radically from one VM to another. If you need only inter-thread communication, and not mutual exclusion, the `volatile` modifier is an acceptable form of synchronization, but it can be tricky to use correctly.

Item 79: Avoid excessive synchronization

Item 78 warns of the dangers of insufficient synchronization. This item concerns the opposite problem. Depending on the situation, excessive synchronization can cause reduced performance, deadlock, or even nondeterministic behavior.

To avoid liveness and safety failures, never cede control to the client within a synchronized method or block. In other words, inside a synchronized region, do not invoke a method that is designed to be overridden, or one provided by a client in the form of a function object (Item 24). From the perspective of the class with the synchronized region, such methods are *alien*. The class has no knowledge of what the method does and has no control over it. Depending on what an alien method does, calling it from a synchronized region can cause exceptions, deadlocks, or data corruption.

To make this concrete, consider the following class, which implements an *observable* set wrapper. It allows clients to subscribe to notifications when elements are added to the set. This is the *Observer* pattern [Gamma95]. For brevity's sake, the class does not provide notifications when elements are removed from the set, but it would be a simple matter to provide them. This class is implemented atop the reusable ForwardingSet from Item 18 (page 90):

```java
// Broken - invokes alien method from synchronized block!
public class ObservableSet<E> extends ForwardingSet<E> {
    public ObservableSet(Set<E> set) { super(set); }

    private final List<SetObserver<E>> observers
        = new ArrayList<>();

    public void addObserver(SetObserver<E> observer) {
        synchronized(observers) {
            observers.add(observer);
        }
    }

    public boolean removeObserver(SetObserver<E> observer) {
        synchronized(observers) {
            return observers.remove(observer);
        }
    }

    private void notifyElementAdded(E element) {
        synchronized(observers) {
            for (SetObserver<E> observer : observers)
                observer.added(this, element);
        }
    }
}
```

```
@Override public boolean add(E element) {
    boolean added = super.add(element);
    if (added)
        notifyElementAdded(element);
    return added;
}

@Override public boolean addAll(Collection<? extends E> c) {
    boolean result = false;
    for (E element : c)
        result |= add(element);   // Calls notifyElementAdded
    return result;
}
}
```

Observers subscribe to notifications by invoking the addObserver method and unsubscribe by invoking the removeObserver method. In both cases, an instance of this *callback* interface is passed to the method.

```
@FunctionalInterface public interface SetObserver<E> {
    // Invoked when an element is added to the observable set
    void added(ObservableSet<E> set, E element);
}
```

This interface is structurally identical to BiConsumer<ObservableSet<E>, E>. We chose to define a custom functional interface because the interface and method names make the code more readable and because the interface could evolve to incorporate multiple callbacks. That said, a reasonable argument could also be made for using BiConsumer (Item 44).

On cursory inspection, ObservableSet appears to work fine. For example, the following program prints the numbers from 0 through 99:

```
public static void main(String[] args) {
    ObservableSet<Integer> set =
            new ObservableSet<>(new HashSet<>());

    set.addObserver((s, e) -> System.out.println(e));

    for (int i = 0; i < 100; i++)
        set.add(i);
}
```

Now let's try something a bit fancier. Suppose we replace the addObserver call with one that passes an observer that prints the Integer value that was added to the set and removes itself if the value is 23:

```
set.addObserver(new SetObserver<>() {
    public void added(ObservableSet<Integer> s, Integer e) {
        System.out.println(e);
        if (e == 23)
            s.removeObserver(this);
    }
});
```

Note that this call uses an anonymous class instance in place of the lambda used in the previous call. That is because the function object needs to pass itself to s.removeObserver, and lambdas cannot access themselves (Item 42).

You might expect the program to print the numbers 0 through 23, after which the observer would unsubscribe and the program would terminate silently. In fact, it prints these numbers and then throws a ConcurrentModificationException. The problem is that notifyElementAdded is in the process of iterating over the observers list when it invokes the observer's added method. The added method calls the observable set's removeObserver method, which in turn calls the method observers.remove. Now we're in trouble. We are trying to remove an element from a list in the midst of iterating over it, which is illegal. The iteration in the notifyElementAdded method is in a synchronized block to prevent concurrent modification, but it doesn't prevent the iterating thread itself from calling back into the observable set and modifying its observers list.

Now let's try something odd: let's write an observer that tries to unsubscribe, but instead of calling removeObserver directly, it engages the services of another thread to do the deed. This observer uses an *executor service* (Item 80):

```
// Observer that uses a background thread needlessly
set.addObserver(new SetObserver<>() {
    public void added(ObservableSet<Integer> s, Integer e) {
        System.out.println(e);
        if (e == 23) {
            ExecutorService exec =
                Executors.newSingleThreadExecutor();
            try {
                exec.submit(() -> s.removeObserver(this)).get();
            } catch (ExecutionException | InterruptedException ex) {
                throw new AssertionError(ex);
            } finally {
                exec.shutdown();
            }
        }
    }
});
```

Incidentally, note that this program catches two different exception types in one catch clause. This facility, informally known as *multi-catch*, was added in Java 7. It can greatly increase the clarity and reduce the size of programs that behave the same way in response to multiple exception types.

When we run this program, we don't get an exception; we get a deadlock. The background thread calls s.removeObserver, which attempts to lock observers, but it can't acquire the lock, because the main thread already has the lock. All the while, the main thread is waiting for the background thread to finish removing the observer, which explains the deadlock.

This example is contrived because there is no reason for the observer to use a background thread to unsubscribe itself, but the problem is real. Invoking alien methods from within synchronized regions has caused many deadlocks in real systems, such as GUI toolkits.

In both of the previous examples (the exception and the deadlock) we were lucky. The resource that was guarded by the synchronized region (observers) was in a consistent state when the alien method (added) was invoked. Suppose you were to invoke an alien method from a synchronized region while the invariant protected by the synchronized region was temporarily invalid. Because locks in the Java programming language are *reentrant*, such calls won't deadlock. As in the first example, which resulted in an exception, the calling thread already holds the lock, so the thread will succeed when it tries to reacquire the lock, even though another conceptually unrelated operation is in progress on the data guarded by the lock. The consequences of such a failure can be catastrophic. In essence, the lock has failed to do its job. Reentrant locks simplify the construction of multithreaded object-oriented programs, but they can turn liveness failures into safety failures.

Luckily, it is usually not too hard to fix this sort of problem by moving alien method invocations out of synchronized blocks. For the notifyElementAdded method, this involves taking a "snapshot" of the observers list that can then be safely traversed without a lock. With this change, both of the previous examples run without exception or deadlock:

```
// Alien method moved outside of synchronized block - open calls
private void notifyElementAdded(E element) {
    List<SetObserver<E>> snapshot = null;
    synchronized(observers) {
        snapshot = new ArrayList<>(observers);
    }
    for (SetObserver<E> observer : snapshot)
        observer.added(this, element);
}
```

In fact, there's a better way to move the alien method invocations out of the synchronized block. The libraries provide a *concurrent collection* (Item 81) known as CopyOnWriteArrayList that is tailor-made for this purpose. This List implementation is a variant of ArrayList in which all modification operations are implemented by making a fresh copy of the entire underlying array. Because the internal array is never modified, iteration requires no locking and is very fast. For most uses, the performance of CopyOnWriteArrayList would be atrocious, but it's perfect for observer lists, which are rarely modified and often traversed.

The add and addAll methods of ObservableSet need not be changed if the list is modified to use CopyOnWriteArrayList. Here is how the remainder of the class looks. Notice that there is no explicit synchronization whatsoever:

```
// Thread-safe observable set with CopyOnWriteArrayList
private final List<SetObserver<E>> observers =
        new CopyOnWriteArrayList<>();

public void addObserver(SetObserver<E> observer) {
    observers.add(observer);
}

public boolean removeObserver(SetObserver<E> observer) {
    return observers.remove(observer);
}

private void notifyElementAdded(E element) {
    for (SetObserver<E> observer : observers)
        observer.added(this, element);
}
```

An alien method invoked outside of a synchronized region is known as an *open call* [Goetz06, 10.1.4]. Besides preventing failures, open calls can greatly increase concurrency. An alien method might run for an arbitrarily long period. If the alien method were invoked from a synchronized region, other threads would be denied access to the protected resource unnecessarily.

As a rule, you should do as little work as possible inside synchronized regions. Obtain the lock, examine the shared data, transform it as necessary, and drop the lock. If you must perform some time-consuming activity, find a way to move it out of the synchronized region without violating the guidelines in Item 78.

The first part of this item was about correctness. Now let's take a brief look at performance. While the cost of synchronization has plummeted since the early days of Java, it is more important than ever not to oversynchronize. In a multicore world, the real cost of excessive synchronization is not the CPU time spent getting locks; it is *contention*: the lost opportunities for parallelism and the delays imposed by the need to ensure that every core has a consistent view of memory. Another hidden cost of oversynchronization is that it can limit the VM's ability to optimize code execution.

If you are writing a mutable class, you have two options: you can omit all synchronization and allow the client to synchronize externally if concurrent use is desired, or you can synchronize internally, making the class *thread-safe* (Item 82). You should choose the latter option only if you can achieve significantly higher concurrency with internal synchronization than you could by having the client lock the entire object externally. The collections in `java.util` (with the exception of the obsolete `Vector` and `Hashtable`) take the former approach, while those in `java.util.concurrent` take the latter (Item 81).

In the early days of Java, many classes violated these guidelines. For example, `StringBuffer` instances are almost always used by a single thread, yet they perform internal synchronization. It is for this reason that `StringBuffer` was supplanted by `StringBuilder`, which is just an unsynchronized `StringBuffer`. Similarly, it's a large part of the reason that the thread-safe pseudorandom number generator in `java.util.Random` was supplanted by the unsynchronized implementation in `java.util.concurrent.ThreadLocalRandom`. When in doubt, do *not* synchronize your class, but document that it is not thread-safe.

If you do synchronize your class internally, you can use various techniques to achieve high concurrency, such as lock splitting, lock striping, and nonblocking concurrency control. These techniques are beyond the scope of this book, but they are discussed elsewhere [Goetz06, Herlihy08].

If a method modifies a static field and there is any possibility that the method will be called from multiple threads, you *must* synchronize access to the field internally (unless the class can tolerate nondeterministic behavior). It is not possible for a multithreaded client to perform external synchronization on such a method, because unrelated clients can invoke the method without synchronization. The field is essentially a global variable even if it is private because it can be read and modified by unrelated clients. The `nextSerialNumber` field used by the method `generateSerialNumber` in Item 78 exemplifies this situation.

In summary, to avoid deadlock and data corruption, never call an alien method from within a synchronized region. More generally, keep the amount of work that you do from within synchronized regions to a minimum. When you are designing a mutable class, think about whether it should do its own synchronization. In the multicore era, it is more important than ever not to oversynchronize. Synchronize your class internally only if there is a good reason to do so, and document your decision clearly (Item 82).

Item 80: Prefer executors, tasks, and streams to threads

The first edition of this book contained code for a simple *work queue* [Bloch01, Item 49]. This class allowed clients to enqueue work for asynchronous processing by a background thread. When the work queue was no longer needed, the client could invoke a method to ask the background thread to terminate itself gracefully after completing any work that was already on the queue. The implementation was little more than a toy, but even so, it required a full page of subtle, delicate code, of the sort that is prone to safety and liveness failures if you don't get it just right. Luckily, there is no reason to write this sort of code anymore.

By the time the second edition of this book came out, `java.util.concurrent` had been added to Java. This package contains an *Executor Framework*, which is a flexible interface-based task execution facility. Creating a work queue that is better in every way than the one in the first edition of this book requires but a single line of code:

```
ExecutorService exec = Executors.newSingleThreadExecutor();
```

Here is how to submit a runnable for execution:

```
exec.execute(runnable);
```

And here is how to tell the executor to terminate gracefully (if you fail to do this, it is likely that your VM will not exit):

```
exec.shutdown();
```

You can do *many* more things with an executor service. For example, you can wait for a particular task to complete (with the `get` method, as shown in Item 79, page 319), you can wait for any or all of a collection of tasks to complete (using the `invokeAny` or `invokeAll` methods), you can wait for the executor service to terminate (using the `awaitTermination` method), you can retrieve the results of tasks one by one as they complete (using an `ExecutorCompletionService`), you can schedule tasks to run at a particular time or to run periodically (using a `ScheduledThreadPoolExecutor`), and so on.

If you want more than one thread to process requests from the queue, simply call a different static factory that creates a different kind of executor service called a *thread pool*. You can create a thread pool with a fixed or variable number of threads. The `java.util.concurrent.Executors` class contains static factories that provide most of the executors you'll ever need. If, however, you want something out of the ordinary, you can use the ThreadPoolExecutor class directly. This class lets you configure nearly every aspect of a thread pool's operation.

Choosing the executor service for a particular application can be tricky. For a small program, or a lightly loaded server, Executors.newCachedThreadPool is generally a good choice because it demands no configuration and generally "does the right thing." But a cached thread pool is not a good choice for a heavily loaded production server! In a cached thread pool, submitted tasks are not queued but immediately handed off to a thread for execution. If no threads are available, a new one is created. If a server is so heavily loaded that all of its CPUs are fully utilized and more tasks arrive, more threads will be created, which will only make matters worse. Therefore, in a heavily loaded production server, you are much better off using Executors.newFixedThreadPool, which gives you a pool with a fixed number of threads, or using the ThreadPoolExecutor class directly, for maximum control.

Not only should you refrain from writing your own work queues, but you should generally refrain from working directly with threads. When you work directly with threads, a Thread serves as both a unit of work and the mechanism for executing it. In the executor framework, the unit of work and the execution mechanism are separate. The key abstraction is the unit of work, which is the *task*. There are two kinds of tasks: Runnable and its close cousin, Callable (which is like Runnable, except that it returns a value and can throw arbitrary exceptions). The general mechanism for executing tasks is the *executor service*. If you think in terms of tasks and let an executor service execute them for you, you gain the flexibility to select an appropriate execution policy to meet your needs and to change the policy if your needs change. In essence, the Executor Framework does for execution what the Collections Framework did for aggregation.

In Java 7, the Executor Framework was extended to support fork-join tasks, which are run by a special kind of executor service known as a fork-join pool. A fork-join task, represented by a ForkJoinTask instance, may be split up into smaller subtasks, and the threads comprising a ForkJoinPool not only process these tasks but "steal" tasks from one another to ensure that all threads remain busy, resulting in higher CPU utilization, higher throughput, and lower latency. Writing and tuning fork-join tasks is tricky. Parallel streams (Item 48) are written atop fork join pools and allow you to take advantage of their performance benefits with little effort, assuming they are appropriate for the task at hand.

A complete treatment of the Executor Framework is beyond the scope of this book, but the interested reader is directed to *Java Concurrency in Practice* [Goetz06].

Item 81: Prefer concurrency utilities to `wait` and `notify`

The first edition of this book devoted an item to the correct use of `wait` and `notify` [Bloch01, Item 50]. Its advice is still valid and is summarized at end of this item, but this advice is far less important than it once was. This is because there is far less reason to use `wait` and `notify`. Since Java 5, the platform has provided higher-level concurrency utilities that do the sorts of things you formerly had to hand-code atop `wait` and `notify`. **Given the difficulty of using `wait` and `notify` correctly, you should use the higher-level concurrency utilities instead.**

The higher-level utilities in `java.util.concurrent` fall into three categories: the Executor Framework, which was covered briefly in Item 80; concurrent collections; and synchronizers. Concurrent collections and synchronizers are covered briefly in this item.

The concurrent collections are high-performance concurrent implementations of standard collection interfaces such as `List`, `Queue`, and `Map`. To provide high concurrency, these implementations manage their own synchronization internally (Item 79). Therefore, **it is impossible to exclude concurrent activity from a concurrent collection; locking it will only slow the program.**

Because you can't exclude concurrent activity on concurrent collections, you can't atomically compose method invocations on them either. Therefore, concurrent collection interfaces were outfitted with *state-dependent modify operations*, which combine several primitives into a single atomic operation. These operations proved sufficiently useful on concurrent collections that they were added to the corresponding collection interfaces in Java 8, using default methods (Item 21).

For example, `Map`'s `putIfAbsent(key, value)` method inserts a mapping for a key if none was present and returns the previous value associated with the key, or `null` if there was none. This makes it easy to implement thread-safe canonicalizing maps. This method simulates the behavior of `String.intern`:

```
// Concurrent canonicalizing map atop ConcurrentMap - not optimal
private static final ConcurrentMap<String, String> map =
        new ConcurrentHashMap<>();

public static String intern(String s) {
    String previousValue = map.putIfAbsent(s, s);
    return previousValue == null ? s : previousValue;
}
```

In fact, you can do even better. `ConcurrentHashMap` is optimized for retrieval operations, such as `get`. Therefore, it is worth invoking `get` initially and calling `putIfAbsent` only if `get` indicates that it is necessary:

```java
// Concurrent canonicalizing map atop ConcurrentMap - faster!
public static String intern(String s) {
    String result = map.get(s);
    if (result == null) {
        result = map.putIfAbsent(s, s);
        if (result == null)
            result = s;
    }
    return result;
}
```

Besides offering excellent concurrency, ConcurrentHashMap is very fast. On my machine, the intern method above is over six times faster than String.intern (but keep in mind that String.intern must employ some strategy to keep from leaking memory in a long-lived application). Concurrent collections make synchronized collections largely obsolete. For example, **use ConcurrentHashMap in preference to Collections.synchronizedMap.** Simply replacing synchronized maps with concurrent maps can dramatically increase the performance of concurrent applications.

Some of the collection interfaces were extended with *blocking operations,* which wait (or *block*) until they can be successfully performed. For example, BlockingQueue extends Queue and adds several methods, including take, which removes and returns the head element from the queue, waiting if the queue is empty. This allows blocking queues to be used for *work queues* (also known as *producer-consumer queues*), to which one or more *producer threads* enqueue work items and from which one or more *consumer threads* dequeue and process items as they become available. As you'd expect, most ExecutorService implementations, including ThreadPoolExecutor, use a BlockingQueue (Item 80).

Synchronizers are objects that enable threads to wait for one another, allowing them to coordinate their activities. The most commonly used synchronizers are CountDownLatch and Semaphore. Less commonly used are CyclicBarrier and Exchanger. The most powerful synchronizer is Phaser.

Countdown latches are single-use barriers that allow one or more threads to wait for one or more other threads to do something. The sole constructor for CountDownLatch takes an int that is the number of times the countDown method must be invoked on the latch before all waiting threads are allowed to proceed.

It is surprisingly easy to build useful things atop this simple primitive. For example, suppose you want to build a simple framework for timing the concurrent execution of an action. This framework consists of a single method that takes an executor to execute the action, a concurrency level representing the number of actions to be executed concurrently, and a runnable representing the action. All of the worker threads ready themselves to run the action before the timer thread starts the clock. When the last worker thread is ready to run the action, the timer thread "fires the starting gun," allowing the worker threads to perform the action. As soon as the last worker thread finishes performing the action, the timer thread stops the clock. Implementing this logic directly on top of wait and notify would be messy to say the least, but it is surprisingly straightforward on top of CountDownLatch:

```java
// Simple framework for timing concurrent execution
public static long time(Executor executor, int concurrency,
            Runnable action) throws InterruptedException {
    CountDownLatch ready = new CountDownLatch(concurrency);
    CountDownLatch start = new CountDownLatch(1);
    CountDownLatch done  = new CountDownLatch(concurrency);

    for (int i = 0; i < concurrency; i++) {
        executor.execute(() -> {
            ready.countDown(); // Tell timer we're ready
            try {
                start.await(); // Wait till peers are ready
                action.run();
            } catch (InterruptedException e) {
                Thread.currentThread().interrupt();
            } finally {
                done.countDown();  // Tell timer we're done
            }
        });
    }

    ready.await();     // Wait for all workers to be ready
    long startNanos = System.nanoTime();
    start.countDown(); // And they're off!
    done.await();      // Wait for all workers to finish
    return System.nanoTime() - startNanos;
}
```

Note that the method uses three countdown latches. The first, ready, is used by worker threads to tell the timer thread when they're ready. The worker threads then wait on the second latch, which is start. When the last worker thread invokes ready.countDown, the timer thread records the start time and invokes start.countDown, allowing all of the worker threads to proceed. Then the timer thread waits on the third latch, done, until the last of the worker threads finishes running the action and calls done.countDown. As soon as this happens, the timer thread awakens and records the end time.

A few more details bear noting. The executor passed to the `time` method must allow for the creation of at least as many threads as the given concurrency level, or the test will never complete. This is known as a *thread starvation deadlock* [Goetz06, 8.1.1]. If a worker thread catches an `InterruptedException`, it reasserts the interrupt using the idiom `Thread.currentThread().interrupt()` and returns from its `run` method. This allows the executor to deal with the interrupt as it sees fit. Note that `System.nanoTime` is used to time the activity. **For interval timing, always use `System.nanoTime` rather than `System.currentTimeMillis`.** `System.nanoTime` is both more accurate and more precise and is unaffected by adjustments to the system's real-time clock. Finally, note that the code in this example won't yield accurate timings unless `action` does a fair amount of work, say a second or more. Accurate microbenchmarking is notoriously hard and is best done with the aid of a specialized framework such as jmh [JMH].

This item only scratches the surface of what you can do with the concurrency utilities. For example, the three countdown latches in the previous example could be replaced by a single `CyclicBarrier` or `Phaser` instance. The resulting code would be a bit more concise but perhaps more difficult to understand.

While you should always use the concurrency utilities in preference to `wait` and `notify`, you might have to maintain legacy code that uses `wait` and `notify`. The `wait` method is used to make a thread wait for some condition. It must be invoked inside a synchronized region that locks the object on which it is invoked. Here is the standard idiom for using the `wait` method:

```
// The standard idiom for using the wait method
synchronized (obj) {
    while (<condition does not hold>)
        obj.wait(); // (Releases lock, and reacquires on wakeup)
    ... // Perform action appropriate to condition
}
```

Always use the wait loop idiom to invoke the `wait` method; never invoke it outside of a loop. The loop serves to test the condition before and after waiting.

Testing the condition before waiting and skipping the wait if the condition already holds are necessary to ensure liveness. If the condition already holds and the `notify` (or `notifyAll`) method has already been invoked before a thread waits, there is no guarantee that the thread will *ever* wake from the wait.

Testing the condition after waiting and waiting again if the condition does not hold are necessary to ensure safety. If the thread proceeds with the action when the condition does not hold, it can destroy the invariant guarded by the lock. There are several reasons a thread might wake up when the condition does not hold:

- Another thread could have obtained the lock and changed the guarded state between the time a thread invoked `notify` and the waiting thread woke up.

- Another thread could have invoked `notify` accidentally or maliciously when the condition did not hold. Classes expose themselves to this sort of mischief by waiting on publicly accessible objects. Any `wait` in a synchronized method of a publicly accessible object is susceptible to this problem.

- The notifying thread could be overly "generous" in waking waiting threads. For example, the notifying thread might invoke `notifyAll` even if only some of the waiting threads have their condition satisfied.

- The waiting thread could (rarely) wake up in the absence of a notify. This is known as a *spurious wakeup* [POSIX, 11.4.3.6.1; Java9-api].

A related issue is whether to use `notify` or `notifyAll` to wake waiting threads. (Recall that `notify` wakes a single waiting thread, assuming such a thread exists, and `notifyAll` wakes all waiting threads.) It is sometimes said that you should *always* use `notifyAll`. This is reasonable, conservative advice. It will always yield correct results because it guarantees that you'll wake the threads that need to be awakened. You may wake some other threads, too, but this won't affect the correctness of your program. These threads will check the condition for which they're waiting and, finding it false, will continue waiting.

As an optimization, you may choose to invoke `notify` instead of `notifyAll` if all threads that could be in the wait-set are waiting for the same condition and only one thread at a time can benefit from the condition becoming true.

Even if these preconditions are satisfied, there may be cause to use `notifyAll` in place of `notify`. Just as placing the `wait` invocation in a loop protects against accidental or malicious notifications on a publicly accessible object, using `notifyAll` in place of `notify` protects against accidental or malicious waits by an unrelated thread. Such waits could otherwise "swallow" a critical notification, leaving its intended recipient waiting indefinitely.

In summary, using `wait` and `notify` directly is like programming in "concurrency assembly language," as compared to the higher-level language provided by `java.util.concurrent`. **There is seldom, if ever, a reason to use `wait` and `notify` in new code.** If you maintain code that uses `wait` and `notify`, make sure that it always invokes `wait` from within a `while` loop using the standard idiom. The `notifyAll` method should generally be used in preference to `notify`. If `notify` is used, great care must be taken to ensure liveness.

Item 82:   Document thread safety

How a class behaves when its methods are used concurrently is an important part of its contract with its clients. If you fail to document this aspect of a class's behavior, its users will be forced to make assumptions. If these assumptions are wrong, the resulting program may perform insufficient synchronization (Item 78) or excessive synchronization (Item 79). In either case, serious errors may result.

You may hear it said that you can tell if a method is thread-safe by looking for the synchronized modifier in its documentation. This is wrong on several counts. In normal operation, Javadoc does not include the synchronized modifier in its output, and with good reason. **The presence of the synchronized modifier in a method declaration is an implementation detail, not a part of its API.** It does not reliably indicate that a method is thread-safe.

Moreover, the claim that the presence of the synchronized modifier is sufficient to document thread safety embodies the misconception that thread safety is an all-or-nothing property. In fact, there are several levels of thread safety. **To enable safe concurrent use, a class must clearly document what level of thread safety it supports.** The following list summarizes levels of thread safety. It is not exhaustive but covers the common cases:

- **Immutable**—Instances of this class appear constant. No external synchronization is necessary. Examples include String, Long, and BigInteger (Item 17).

- **Unconditionally thread-safe**—Instances of this class are mutable, but the class has sufficient internal synchronization that its instances can be used concurrently without the need for any external synchronization. Examples include AtomicLong and ConcurrentHashMap.

- **Conditionally thread-safe**—Like unconditionally thread-safe, except that some methods require external synchronization for safe concurrent use. Examples include the collections returned by the Collections.synchronized wrappers, whose iterators require external synchronization.

- **Not thread-safe**—Instances of this class are mutable. To use them concurrently, clients must surround each method invocation (or invocation sequence) with external synchronization of the clients' choosing. Examples include the general-purpose collection implementations, such as ArrayList and HashMap.

- **Thread-hostile**—This class is unsafe for concurrent use even if every method invocation is surrounded by external synchronization. Thread hostility usually results from modifying static data without synchronization. No one writes a thread-hostile class on purpose; such classes typically result from the failure to consider concurrency. When a class or method is found to be thread-hostile, it is typically fixed or deprecated. The `generateSerialNumber` method in Item 78 would be thread-hostile in the absence of internal synchronization, as discussed on page 322.

These categories (apart from thread-hostile) correspond roughly to the *thread safety annotations* in *Java Concurrency in Practice*, which are `Immutable`, `ThreadSafe`, and `NotThreadSafe` [Goetz06, Appendix A]. The unconditionally and conditionally thread-safe categories in the above taxonomy are both covered under the `ThreadSafe` annotation.

Documenting a conditionally thread-safe class requires care. You must indicate which invocation sequences require external synchronization, and which lock (or in rare cases, locks) must be acquired to execute these sequences. Typically it is the lock on the instance itself, but there are exceptions. For example, the documentation for `Collections.synchronizedMap` says this:

It is imperative that the user manually synchronize on the returned map when iterating over any of its collection views:

```
Map<K, V> m = Collections.synchronizedMap(new HashMap<>());
Set<K> s = m.keySet();  // Needn't be in synchronized block
   ...
synchronized(m) {  // Synchronizing on m, not s!
    for (K key : s)
        key.f();
}
```

Failure to follow this advice may result in non-deterministic behavior.

The description of a class's thread safety generally belongs in the class's doc comment, but methods with special thread safety properties should describe these properties in their own documentation comments. It is not necessary to document the immutability of enum types. Unless it is obvious from the return type, static factories must document the thread safety of the returned object, as demonstrated by `Collections.synchronizedMap` (above).

When a class commits to using a publicly accessible lock, it enables clients to execute a sequence of method invocations atomically, but this flexibility comes at a price. It is incompatible with high-performance internal concurrency control, of the sort used by concurrent collections such as `ConcurrentHashMap`. Also, a client can mount a denial-of-service attack by holding the publicly accessible lock for a prolonged period. This can be done accidentally or intentionally.

To prevent this denial-of-service attack, you can use a *private lock object* instead of using synchronized methods (which imply a publicly accessible lock):

```
// Private lock object idiom - thwarts denial-of-service attack
private final Object lock = new Object();

public void foo() {
    synchronized(lock) {
        ...
    }
}
```

Because the private lock object is inaccessible outside the class, it is impossible for clients to interfere with the object's synchronization. In effect, we are applying the advice of Item 15 by encapsulating the lock object in the object it synchronizes.

Note that the lock field is declared final. This prevents you from inadvertently changing its contents, which could result in catastrophic unsynchronized access (Item 78). We are applying the advice of Item 17, by minimizing the mutability of the lock field. **Lock fields should always be declared final.** This is true whether you use an ordinary monitor lock (as shown above) or a lock from the java.util.concurrent.locks package.

The private lock object idiom can be used only on *unconditionally* thread-safe classes. Conditionally thread-safe classes can't use this idiom because they must document which lock their clients are to acquire when performing certain method invocation sequences.

The private lock object idiom is particularly well-suited to classes designed for inheritance (Item 19). If such a class were to use its instances for locking, a subclass could easily and unintentionally interfere with the operation of the base class, or vice versa. By using the same lock for different purposes, the subclass and the base class could end up "stepping on each other's toes." This is not just a theoretical problem; it happened with the Thread class [Bloch05, Puzzle 77].

To summarize, every class should clearly document its thread safety properties with a carefully worded prose description or a thread safety annotation. The synchronized modifier plays no part in this documentation. Conditionally thread-safe classes must document which method invocation sequences require external synchronization and which lock to acquire when executing these sequences. If you write an unconditionally thread-safe class, consider using a private lock object in place of synchronized methods. This protects against synchronization interference by clients and subclasses and gives you more flexibility to adopt a sophisticated approach to concurrency control in a later release.

Item 83: Use lazy initialization judiciously

Lazy initialization is the act of delaying the initialization of a field until its value is needed. If the value is never needed, the field is never initialized. This technique is applicable to both static and instance fields. While lazy initialization is primarily an optimization, it can also be used to break harmful circularities in class and instance initialization [Bloch05, Puzzle 51].

As is the case for most optimizations, the best advice for lazy initialization is "don't do it unless you need to" (Item 67). Lazy initialization is a double-edged sword. It decreases the cost of initializing a class or creating an instance, at the expense of increasing the cost of accessing the lazily initialized field. Depending on what fraction of these fields eventually require initialization, how expensive it is to initialize them, and how often each one is accessed once initialized, lazy initialization can (like many "optimizations") actually harm performance.

That said, lazy initialization has its uses. If a field is accessed only on a fraction of the instances of a class *and* it is costly to initialize the field, then lazy initialization may be worthwhile. The only way to know for sure is to measure the performance of the class with and without lazy initialization.

In the presence of multiple threads, lazy initialization is tricky. If two or more threads share a lazily initialized field, it is critical that some form of synchronization be employed, or severe bugs can result (Item 78). All of the initialization techniques discussed in this item are thread-safe.

Under most circumstances, normal initialization is preferable to lazy initialization. Here is a typical declaration for a normally initialized instance field. Note the use of the `final` modifier (Item 17):

```
// Normal initialization of an instance field
private final FieldType field = computeFieldValue();
```

If you use lazy initialization to break an initialization circularity, use a synchronized accessor because it is the simplest, clearest alternative:

```
// Lazy initialization of instance field - synchronized accessor
private FieldType field;

private synchronized FieldType getField() {
    if (field == null)
        field = computeFieldValue();
    return field;
}
```

Both of these idioms (*normal initialization* and *lazy initialization with a synchronized accessor*) are unchanged when applied to static fields, except that you add the static modifier to the field and accessor declarations.

If you need to use lazy initialization for performance on a static field, use the *lazy initialization holder class idiom*. This idiom exploits the guarantee that a class will not be initialized until it is used [JLS, 12.4.1]. Here's how it looks:

```
// Lazy initialization holder class idiom for static fields
private static class FieldHolder {
    static final FieldType field = computeFieldValue();
}

private static FieldType getField() { return FieldHolder.field; }
```

When getField is invoked for the first time, it reads FieldHolder.field for the first time, causing the initialization of the FieldHolder class. The beauty of this idiom is that the getField method is not synchronized and performs only a field access, so lazy initialization adds practically nothing to the cost of access. A typical VM will synchronize field access only to initialize the class. Once the class is initialized, the VM patches the code so that subsequent access to the field does not involve any testing or synchronization.

If you need to use lazy initialization for performance on an instance field, use the *double-check idiom*. This idiom avoids the cost of locking when accessing the field after initialization (Item 79). The idea behind the idiom is to check the value of the field twice (hence the name *double-check*): once without locking and then, if the field appears to be uninitialized, a second time with locking. Only if the second check indicates that the field is uninitialized does the call initialize the field. Because there is no locking once the field is initialized, it is *critical* that the field be declared volatile (Item 78). Here is the idiom:

```
// Double-check idiom for lazy initialization of instance fields
private volatile FieldType field;

private FieldType getField() {
    FieldType result = field;
    if (result == null) {  // First check (no locking)
        synchronized(this) {
            if (field == null)  // Second check (with locking)
                field = result = computeFieldValue();
        }
    }
    return result;
}
```

This code may appear a bit convoluted. In particular, the need for the local variable (result) may be unclear. What this variable does is to ensure that field is read only once in the common case where it's already initialized. While not strictly necessary, this may improve performance and is more elegant by the standards applied to low-level concurrent programming. On my machine, the method above is about 1.4 times as fast as the obvious version without a local variable.

While you can apply the double-check idiom to static fields as well, there is no reason to do so: the lazy initialization holder class idiom is a better choice.

Two variants of the double-check idiom bear noting. Occasionally, you may need to lazily initialize an instance field that can tolerate repeated initialization. If you find yourself in this situation, you can use a variant of the double-check idiom that dispenses with the second check. It is, not surprisingly, known as the *single-check idiom*. Here is how it looks. Note that field is still declared volatile:

```
// Single-check idiom - can cause repeated initialization!
private volatile FieldType field;

private FieldType getField() {
    FieldType result = field;
    if (result == null)
        field = result = computeFieldValue();
    return result;
}
```

All of the initialization techniques discussed in this item apply to primitive fields as well as object reference fields. When the double-check or single-check idiom is applied to a numerical primitive field, the field's value is checked against 0 (the default value for numerical primitive variables) rather than null.

If you don't care whether *every* thread recalculates the value of a field, and the type of the field is a primitive other than long or double, then you may choose to remove the volatile modifier from the field declaration in the single-check idiom. This variant is known as the *racy single-check idiom*. It speeds up field access on some architectures, at the expense of additional initializations (up to one per thread that accesses the field). This is definitely an exotic technique, not for everyday use.

In summary, you should initialize most fields normally, not lazily. If you must initialize a field lazily in order to achieve your performance goals or to break a harmful initialization circularity, then use the appropriate lazy initialization technique. For instance fields, it is the double-check idiom; for static fields, the lazy initialization holder class idiom. For instance fields that can tolerate repeated initialization, you may also consider the single-check idiom.

Item 84: Don't depend on the thread scheduler

When many threads are runnable, the thread scheduler determines which ones get to run and for how long. Any reasonable operating system will try to make this determination fairly, but the policy can vary. Therefore, well-written programs shouldn't depend on the details of this policy. **Any program that relies on the thread scheduler for correctness or performance is likely to be nonportable.**

The best way to write a robust, responsive, portable program is to ensure that the average number of *runnable* threads is not significantly greater than the number of processors. This leaves the thread scheduler with little choice: it simply runs the runnable threads till they're no longer runnable. The program's behavior doesn't vary too much, even under radically different thread-scheduling policies. Note that the number of runnable threads isn't the same as the total number of threads, which can be much higher. Threads that are waiting are not runnable.

The main technique for keeping the number of runnable threads low is to have each thread do some useful work, and then wait for more. **Threads should not run if they aren't doing useful work.** In terms of the Executor Framework (Item 80), this means sizing thread pools appropriately [Goetz06, 8.2] and keeping tasks short, but not *too* short, or dispatching overhead will harm performance.

Threads should not *busy-wait*, repeatedly checking a shared object waiting for its state to change. Besides making the program vulnerable to the vagaries of the thread scheduler, busy-waiting greatly increases the load on the processor, reducing the amount of useful work that others can accomplish. As an extreme example of what *not* to do, consider this perverse reimplementation of CountDownLatch:

```
// Awful CountDownLatch implementation - busy-waits incessantly!
public class SlowCountDownLatch {
    private int count;

    public SlowCountDownLatch(int count) {
        if (count < 0)
            throw new IllegalArgumentException(count + " < 0");
        this.count = count;
    }

    public void await() {
        while (true) {
            synchronized(this) {
                if (count == 0)
                    return;
            }
        }
    }
```

```
    public synchronized void countDown() {
        if (count != 0)
            count--;
    }
}
```

On my machine, SlowCountDownLatch is about ten times slower than Java's CountDownLatch when 1,000 threads wait on a latch. While this example may seem a bit far-fetched, it's not uncommon to see systems with one or more threads that are unnecessarily runnable. Performance and portability are likely to suffer.

When faced with a program that barely works because some threads aren't getting enough CPU time relative to others, **resist the temptation to "fix" the program by putting in calls to Thread.yield.** You may succeed in getting the program to work after a fashion, but it will not be portable. The same yield invocations that improve performance on one JVM implementation might make it worse on a second and have no effect on a third. **Thread.yield has no testable semantics.** A better course of action is to restructure the application to reduce the number of concurrently runnable threads.

A related technique, to which similar caveats apply, is adjusting thread priorities. **Thread priorities are among the least portable features of Java.** It is not unreasonable to tune the responsiveness of an application by tweaking a few thread priorities, but it is rarely necessary and is not portable. It is unreasonable to attempt to solve a serious liveness problem by adjusting thread priorities. The problem is likely to return until you find and fix the underlying cause.

In summary, do not depend on the thread scheduler for the correctness of your program. The resulting program will be neither robust nor portable. As a corollary, do not rely on Thread.yield or thread priorities. These facilities are merely hints to the scheduler. Thread priorities may be used sparingly to improve the quality of service of an already working program, but they should never be used to "fix" a program that barely works.

CHAPTER 12

Serialization

THIS chapter concerns *object serialization*, which is Java's framework for encoding objects as byte streams (*serializing*) and reconstructing objects from their encodings (*deserializing*). Once an object has been serialized, its encoding can be sent from one VM to another or stored on disk for later deserialization. This chapter focuses on the dangers of serialization and how to minimize them.

Item 85: Prefer alternatives to Java serialization

When serialization was added to Java in 1997, it was known to be somewhat risky. The approach had been tried in a research language (Modula-3) but never in a production language. While the promise of distributed objects with little effort on the part of the programmer was appealing, the price was invisible constructors and blurred lines between API and implementation, with the potential for problems with correctness, performance, security, and maintenance. Proponents believed the benefits outweighed the risks, but history has shown otherwise.

The security issues described in previous editions of this book turned out to be every bit as serious as some had feared. The vulnerabilities discussed in the early 2000s were transformed into serious exploits over the next decade, famously including a ransomware attack on the San Francisco Metropolitan Transit Agency Municipal Railway (SFMTA Muni) that shut down the entire fare collection system for two days in November 2016 [Gallagher16].

A fundamental problem with serialization is that its *attack surface* is too big to protect, and constantly growing: Object graphs are deserialized by invoking the readObject method on an ObjectInputStream. This method is essentially a magic constructor that can be made to instantiate objects of almost any type on the class path, so long as the type implements the Serializable interface. In the process of deserializing a byte stream, this method can execute code from any of these types, so the code for *all* of these types is part of the attack surface.

The attack surface includes classes in the Java platform libraries, in third-party libraries such as Apache Commons Collections, and in the application itself. Even if you adhere to all of the relevant best practices and succeed in writing serializable classes that are invulnerable to attack, your application may still be vulnerable. To quote Robert Seacord, technical manager of the CERT Coordination Center:

> Java deserialization is a clear and present danger as it is widely used both directly by applications and indirectly by Java subsystems such as RMI (Remote Method Invocation), JMX (Java Management Extension), and JMS (Java Messaging System). Deserialization of untrusted streams can result in remote code execution (RCE), denial-of-service (DoS), and a range of other exploits. Applications can be vulnerable to these attacks even if they did nothing wrong. [Seacord17]

Attackers and security researchers study the serializable types in the Java libraries and in commonly used third-party libraries, looking for methods invoked during deserialization that perform potentially dangerous activities. Such methods are known as *gadgets*. Multiple gadgets can be used in concert, to form a *gadget chain*. From time to time, a gadget chain is discovered that is sufficiently powerful to allow an attacker to execute arbitrary native code on the underlying hardware, given only the opportunity to submit a carefully crafted byte stream for deserialization. This is exactly what happened in the SFMTA Muni attack. This attack was not isolated. There have been others, and there will be more.

Without using any gadgets, you can easily mount a denial-of-service attack by causing the deserialization of a short stream that requires a long time to deserialize. Such streams are known as *deserialization bombs* [Svoboda16]. Here's an example by Wouter Coekaerts that uses only hash sets and a string [Coekaerts15]:

```
// Deserialization bomb - deserializing this stream takes forever
static byte[] bomb() {
    Set<Object> root = new HashSet<>();
    Set<Object> s1 = root;
    Set<Object> s2 = new HashSet<>();
    for (int i = 0; i < 100; i++) {
        Set<Object> t1 = new HashSet<>();
        Set<Object> t2 = new HashSet<>();
        t1.add("foo"); // Make t1 unequal to t2
        s1.add(t1);  s1.add(t2);
        s2.add(t1);  s2.add(t2);
        s1 = t1;
        s2 = t2;
    }
    return serialize(root); // Method omitted for brevity
}
```

The object graph consists of 201 HashSet instances, each of which contains 3 or fewer object references. The entire stream is 5,744 bytes long, yet the sun would burn out long before you could deserialize it. The problem is that deserializing a HashSet instance requires computing the hash codes of its elements. The 2 elements of the root hash set are themselves hash sets containing 2 hash-set elements, each of which contains 2 hash-set elements, and so on, 100 levels deep. Therefore, deserializing the set causes the hashCode method to be invoked over 2^{100} times. Other than the fact that the deserialization is taking forever, the deserializer has no indication that anything is amiss. Few objects are produced, and the stack depth is bounded.

So what can you do defend against these problems? You open yourself up to attack whenever you deserialize a byte stream that you don't trust. **The best way to avoid serialization exploits is never to deserialize anything.** In the words of the computer named Joshua in the 1983 movie *WarGames*, "the only winning move is not to play." **There is no reason to use Java serialization in any new system you write.** There are other mechanisms for translating between objects and byte sequences that avoid many of the dangers of Java serialization, while offering numerous advantages, such as cross-platform support, high performance, a large ecosystem of tools, and a broad community of expertise. In this book, we refer to these mechanisms as *cross-platform structured-data representations*. While others sometimes refer to them as serialization systems, this book avoids that usage to prevent confusion with Java serialization.

What these representations have in common is that they're *far* simpler than Java serialization. They don't support automatic serialization and deserialization of arbitrary object graphs. Instead, they support simple, structured data-objects consisting of a collection of attribute-value pairs. Only a few primitive and array data types are supported. This simple abstraction turns out to be sufficient for building extremely powerful distributed systems and simple enough to avoid the serious problems that have plagued Java serialization since its inception.

The leading cross-platform structured data representations are JSON [JSON] and Protocol Buffers, also known as protobuf [Protobuf]. JSON was designed by Douglas Crockford for browser-server communication, and protocol buffers were designed by Google for storing and interchanging structured data among its servers. Even though these representations are sometimes called *language-neutral*, JSON was originally developed for JavaScript and protobuf for C++; both representations retain vestiges of their origins.

The most significant differences between JSON and protobuf are that JSON is text-based and human-readable, whereas protobuf is binary and substantially more efficient; and that JSON is exclusively a data representation, whereas protobuf offers *schemas* (types) to document and enforce appropriate usage. Although protobuf is more efficient than JSON, JSON is extremely efficient for a text-based representation. And while protobuf is a binary representation, it does provide an alternative text representation for use where human-readability is desired (pbtxt).

If you can't avoid Java serialization entirely, perhaps because you're working in the context of a legacy system that requires it, your next best alternative is to **never deserialize untrusted data.** In particular, you should never accept RMI traffic from untrusted sources. The official secure coding guidelines for Java say "Deserialization of untrusted data is inherently dangerous and should be avoided." This sentence is set in large, bold, italic, red type, and it is the only text in the entire document that gets this treatment [Java-secure].

If you can't avoid serialization and you aren't absolutely certain of the safety of the data you're deserializing, use the object deserialization filtering added in Java 9 and backported to earlier releases (`java.io.ObjectInputFilter`). This facility lets you specify a filter that is applied to data streams before they're deserialized. It operates at the class granularity, letting you accept or reject certain classes. Accepting classes by default and rejecting a list of potentially dangerous ones is known as *blacklisting*; rejecting classes by default and accepting a list of those that are presumed safe is known as *whitelisting*. **Prefer whitelisting to blacklisting**, as blacklisting only protects you against known threats. A tool called Serial Whitelist Application Trainer (SWAT) can be used to automatically prepare a whitelist for your application [Schneider16]. The filtering facility will also protect you against excessive memory usage, and excessively deep object graphs, but it will not protect you against serialization bombs like the one shown above.

Unfortunately, serialization is still pervasive in the Java ecosystem. If you are maintaining a system that is based on Java serialization, seriously consider migrating to a cross-platform structured-data representation, even though this may be a time-consuming endeavor. Realistically, you may still find yourself having to write or maintain a serializable class. It requires great care to write a serializable class that is correct, safe, and efficient. The remainder of this chapter provides advice on when and how to do this.

In summary, serialization is dangerous and should be avoided. If you are designing a system from scratch, use a cross-platform structured-data representation such as JSON or protobuf instead. Do not deserialize untrusted data. If you must do so, use object deserialization filtering, but be aware that it is not guaranteed to thwart all attacks. Avoid writing serializable classes. If you must do so, exercise great caution.

Item 86: Implement `Serializable` with great caution

Allowing a class's instances to be serialized can be as simple as adding the words `implements Serializable` to its declaration. Because this is so easy to do, there was a common misconception that serialization requires little effort on the part of the programmer. The truth is far more complex. While the immediate cost to make a class serializable can be negligible, the long-term costs are often substantial.

A major cost of implementing `Serializable` is that it decreases the flexibility to change a class's implementation once it has been released. When a class implements `Serializable`, its byte-stream encoding (or *serialized form*) becomes part of its exported API. Once you distribute a class widely, you are generally required to support the serialized form forever, just as you are required to support all other parts of the exported API. If you do not make the effort to design a *custom serialized form* but merely accept the default, the serialized form will forever be tied to the class's original internal representation. In other words, if you accept the default serialized form, the class's private and package-private instance fields become part of its exported API, and the practice of minimizing access to fields (Item 15) loses its effectiveness as a tool for information hiding.

If you accept the default serialized form and later change a class's internal representation, an incompatible change in the serialized form will result. Clients attempting to serialize an instance using an old version of the class and deserialize it using the new one (or vice versa) will experience program failures. It is possible to change the internal representation while maintaining the original serialized form (using `ObjectOutputStream.putFields` and `ObjectInputStream.readFields`), but it can be difficult and leaves visible warts in the source code. If you opt to make a class serializable, you should carefully design a high-quality serialized form that you're willing to live with for the long haul (Items 87, 90). Doing so will add to the initial cost of development, but it's worth the effort. Even a well-designed serialized form places constraints on the evolution of a class; an ill-designed serialized form can be crippling.

A simple example of the constraints on evolution imposed by serializability concerns *stream unique identifiers*, more commonly known as *serial version UIDs*. Every serializable class has a unique identification number associated with it. If you do not specify this number by declaring a static final `long` field named `serialVersionUID`, the system automatically generates it at runtime by applying a cryptographic hash function (SHA-1) to the structure of the class. This value is affected by the names of the class, the interfaces it implements, and most of its members, including synthetic members generated by the compiler. If you change any of these things, for example, by adding a convenience method, the generated serial version UID changes. If you fail to declare a serial version UID, compatibility will be broken, resulting in an `InvalidClassException` at runtime.

A second cost of implementing `Serializable` is that it increases the likelihood of bugs and security holes (Item 85). Normally, objects are created with constructors; serialization is an *extralinguistic mechanism* for creating objects. Whether you accept the default behavior or override it, deserialization is a "hidden constructor" with all of the same issues as other constructors. Because there is no explicit constructor associated with deserialization, it is easy to forget that you must ensure that it guarantees all of the invariants established by the constructors and that it does not allow an attacker to gain access to the internals of the object under construction. Relying on the default deserialization mechanism can easily leave objects open to invariant corruption and illegal access (Item 88).

A third cost of implementing `Serializable` is that it increases the testing burden associated with releasing a new version of a class. When a serializable class is revised, it is important to check that it is possible to serialize an instance in the new release and deserialize it in old releases, and vice versa. The amount of testing required is thus proportional to the product of the number of serializable classes and the number of releases, which can be large. You must ensure both that the serialization-deserialization process succeeds and that it results in a faithful replica of the original object. The need for testing is reduced if a custom serialized form is carefully designed when the class is first written (Items 87, 90).

Implementing `Serializable` is not a decision to be undertaken lightly. It is essential if a class is to participate in a framework that relies on Java serialization for object transmission or persistence. Also, it greatly eases the use of a class as a component in another class that must implement `Serializable`. There are, however, many costs associated with implementing `Serializable`. Each time you design a class, weigh the costs against the benefits. Historically, value classes such as `BigInteger` and `Instant` implemented `Serializable`, and collection classes did too. Classes representing active entities, such as thread pools, should rarely implement `Serializable`.

Classes designed for inheritance (Item 19) should rarely implement `Serializable`, and interfaces should rarely extend it. Violating this rule places a substantial burden on anyone who extends the class or implements the interface. There are times when it is appropriate to violate the rule. For example, if a class or interface exists primarily to participate in a framework that requires all participants to implement `Serializable`, then it may make sense for the class or interface to implement or extend `Serializable`.

Classes designed for inheritance that do implement `Serializable` include `Throwable` and `Component`. `Throwable` implements `Serializable` so RMI can send exceptions from server to client. `Component` implements `Serializable` so GUIs can be sent, saved, and restored, but even in the heyday of Swing and AWT, this facility was little-used in practice.

If you implement a class with instance fields that is both serializable and extendable, there are several risks to be aware of. If there are any invariants on the instance field values, it is critical to prevent subclasses from overriding the `finalize` method, which the class can do by overriding `finalize` and declaring it final. Otherwise, the class will be susceptible to *finalizer attacks* (Item 8). Finally, if the class has invariants that would be violated if its instance fields were initialized to their default values (zero for integral types, `false` for `boolean`, and `null` for object reference types), you must add this `readObjectNoData` method:

```
// readObjectNoData for stateful extendable serializable classes
private void readObjectNoData() throws InvalidObjectException {
    throw new InvalidObjectException("Stream data required");
}
```

This method was added in Java 4 to cover a corner case involving the addition of a serializable superclass to an existing serializable class [Serialization, 3.5].

There is one caveat regarding the decision *not* to implement `Serializable`. If a class designed for inheritance is not serializable, it may require extra effort to write a serializable subclass. Normal deserialization of such a class requires the superclass to have an accessible parameterless constructor [Serialization, 1.10]. If you don't provide such a constructor, subclasses are forced to use the serialization proxy pattern (Item 90).

Inner classes (Item 24) should not implement `Serializable`. They use compiler-generated *synthetic fields* to store references to *enclosing instances* and to store values of local variables from enclosing scopes. How these fields correspond to the class definition is unspecified, as are the names of anonymous and local classes. Therefore, the default serialized form of an inner class is ill-defined. A *static member class* can, however, implement `Serializable`.

To summarize, the ease of implementing `Serializable` is specious. Unless a class is to be used only in a protected environment where versions will never have to interoperate and servers will never be exposed to untrusted data, implementing `Serializable` is a serious commitment that should be made with great care. Extra caution is warranted if a class permits inheritance.

Item 87: Consider using a custom serialized form

When you are writing a class under time pressure, it is generally appropriate to concentrate your efforts on designing the best API. Sometimes this means releasing a "throwaway" implementation that you know you'll replace in a future release. Normally this is not a problem, but if the class implements `Serializable` and uses the default serialized form, you'll never be able to escape completely from the throwaway implementation. It will dictate the serialized form forever. This is not just a theoretical problem. It happened to several classes in the Java libraries, including `BigInteger`.

Do not accept the default serialized form without first considering whether it is appropriate. Accepting the default serialized form should be a conscious decision that this encoding is reasonable from the standpoint of flexibility, performance, and correctness. Generally speaking, you should accept the default serialized form only if it is largely identical to the encoding that you would choose if you were designing a custom serialized form.

The default serialized form of an object is a reasonably efficient encoding of the *physical* representation of the object graph rooted at the object. In other words, it describes the data contained in the object and in every object that is reachable from this object. It also describes the topology by which all of these objects are interlinked. The ideal serialized form of an object contains only the *logical* data represented by the object. It is independent of the physical representation.

The default serialized form is likely to be appropriate if an object's physical representation is identical to its logical content. For example, the default serialized form would be reasonable for the following class, which simplistically represents a person's name:

```
// Good candidate for default serialized form
public class Name implements Serializable {
    /**
     * Last name. Must be non-null.
     * @serial
     */
    private final String lastName;

    /**
     * First name. Must be non-null.
     * @serial
     */
    private final String firstName;
```

```
/**
 * Middle name, or null if there is none.
 * @serial
 */
private final String middleName;

    ... // Remainder omitted
}
```

Logically speaking, a name consists of three strings that represent a last name, a first name, and a middle name. The instance fields in Name precisely mirror this logical content.

Even if you decide that the default serialized form is appropriate, you often must provide a readObject method to ensure invariants and security. In the case of Name, the readObject method must ensure that the fields lastName and firstName are non-null. This issue is discussed at length in Items 88 and 90.

Note that there are documentation comments on the lastName, firstName, and middleName fields, even though they are private. That is because these private fields define a public API, which is the serialized form of the class, and this public API must be documented. The presence of the @serial tag tells Javadoc to place this documentation on a special page that documents serialized forms.

Near the opposite end of the spectrum from Name, consider the following class, which represents a list of strings (ignoring for the moment that you would probably be better off using one of the standard List implementations):

```
// Awful candidate for default serialized form
public final class StringList implements Serializable {
    private int size = 0;
    private Entry head = null;

    private static class Entry implements Serializable {
        String data;
        Entry next;
        Entry previous;
    }

    ... // Remainder omitted
}
```

Logically speaking, this class represents a sequence of strings. Physically, it represents the sequence as a doubly linked list. If you accept the default serialized form, the serialized form will painstakingly mirror every entry in the linked list and all the links between the entries, in both directions.

Using the default serialized form when an object's physical representation differs substantially from its logical data content has four disadvantages:

- **It permanently ties the exported API to the current internal representation.** In the above example, the private `StringList.Entry` class becomes part of the public API. If the representation is changed in a future release, the `StringList` class will still need to accept the linked list representation on input and generate it on output. The class will never be rid of all the code dealing with linked list entries, even if it doesn't use them anymore.

- **It can consume excessive space.** In the above example, the serialized form unnecessarily represents each entry in the linked list and all the links. These entries and links are mere implementation details, not worthy of inclusion in the serialized form. Because the serialized form is excessively large, writing it to disk or sending it across the network will be excessively slow.

- **It can consume excessive time.** The serialization logic has no knowledge of the topology of the object graph, so it must go through an expensive graph traversal. In the example above, it would be sufficient simply to follow the `next` references.

- **It can cause stack overflows.** The default serialization procedure performs a recursive traversal of the object graph, which can cause stack overflows even for moderately sized object graphs. Serializing a `StringList` instance with 1,000–1,800 elements generates a `StackOverflowError` on my machine. Surprisingly, the minimum list size for which serialization causes a stack overflow varies from run to run (on my machine). The minimum list size that exhibits this problem may depend on the platform implementation and command-line flags; some implementations may not have this problem at all.

A reasonable serialized form for `StringList` is simply the number of strings in the list, followed by the strings themselves. This constitutes the logical data represented by a `StringList`, stripped of the details of its physical representation. Here is a revised version of `StringList` with `writeObject` and `readObject` methods that implement this serialized form. As a reminder, the `transient` modifier indicates that an instance field is to be omitted from a class's default serialized form:

```java
// StringList with a reasonable custom serialized form
public final class StringList implements Serializable {
    private transient int size   = 0;
    private transient Entry head = null;

    // No longer Serializable!
    private static class Entry {
        String data;
        Entry  next;
        Entry  previous;
    }

    // Appends the specified string to the list
    public final void add(String s) { ... }

    /**
     * Serialize this {@code StringList} instance.
     *
     * @serialData The size of the list (the number of strings
     * it contains) is emitted ({@code int}), followed by all of
     * its elements (each a {@code String}), in the proper
     * sequence.
     */
    private void writeObject(ObjectOutputStream s)
            throws IOException {
        s.defaultWriteObject();
        s.writeInt(size);

        // Write out all elements in the proper order.
        for (Entry e = head; e != null; e = e.next)
            s.writeObject(e.data);
    }

    private void readObject(ObjectInputStream s)
            throws IOException, ClassNotFoundException {
        s.defaultReadObject();
        int numElements = s.readInt();

        // Read in all elements and insert them in list
        for (int i = 0; i < numElements; i++)
            add((String) s.readObject());
    }

    ... // Remainder omitted
}
```

The first thing `writeObject` does is to invoke `defaultWriteObject`, and the first thing `readObject` does is to invoke `defaultReadObject`, even though all of `StringList`'s fields are transient. You may hear it said that if all of a class's instance fields are transient, you can dispense with invoking `defaultWriteObject` and `defaultReadObject`, but the serialization specification requires you to invoke them regardless. The presence of these calls makes it possible to add nontransient instance fields in a later release while preserving backward and forward compatibility. If an instance is serialized in a later version and deserialized in an earlier version, the added fields will be ignored. Had the earlier version's `readObject` method failed to invoke `defaultReadObject`, the deserialization would fail with a `StreamCorruptedException`.

Note that there is a documentation comment on the `writeObject` method, even though it is private. This is analogous to the documentation comment on the private fields in the `Name` class. This private method defines a public API, which is the serialized form, and that public API should be documented. Like the `@serial` tag for fields, the `@serialData` tag for methods tells the Javadoc utility to place this documentation on the serialized forms page.

To lend some sense of scale to the earlier performance discussion, if the average string length is ten characters, the serialized form of the revised version of `StringList` occupies about half as much space as the serialized form of the original. On my machine, serializing the revised version of `StringList` is over twice as fast as serializing the original version, with a list length of ten. Finally, there is no stack overflow problem in the revised form and hence no practical upper limit to the size of `StringList` that can be serialized.

While the default serialized form would be bad for `StringList`, there are classes for which it would be far worse. For `StringList`, the default serialized form is inflexible and performs badly, but it is *correct* in the sense that serializing and deserializing a `StringList` instance yields a faithful copy of the original object with all of its invariants intact. This is not the case for any object whose invariants are tied to implementation-specific details.

For example, consider the case of a hash table. The physical representation is a sequence of hash buckets containing key-value entries. The bucket that an entry resides in is a function of the hash code of its key, which is not, in general, guaranteed to be the same from implementation to implementation. In fact, it isn't even guaranteed to be the same from run to run. Therefore, accepting the default serialized form for a hash table would constitute a serious bug. Serializing and deserializing the hash table could yield an object whose invariants were seriously corrupt.

Whether or not you accept the default serialized form, every instance field that isn't labeled transient will be serialized when the defaultWriteObject method is invoked. Therefore, every instance field that can be declared transient should be. This includes derived fields, whose values can be computed from primary data fields, such as a cached hash value. It also includes fields whose values are tied to one particular run of the JVM, such as a long field representing a pointer to a native data structure. **Before deciding to make a field nontransient, convince yourself that its value is part of the logical state of the object.** If you use a custom serialized form, most or all of the instance fields should be labeled transient, as in the StringList example above.

If you are using the default serialized form and you have labeled one or more fields transient, remember that these fields will be initialized to .their *default values* when an instance is deserialized: null for object reference fields, zero for numeric primitive fields, and false for boolean fields [JLS, 4.12.5]. If these values are unacceptable for any transient fields, you must provide a readObject method that invokes the defaultReadObject method and then restores transient fields to acceptable values (Item 88). Alternatively, these fields can be lazily initialized the first time they are used (Item 83).

Whether or not you use the default serialized form, **you must impose any synchronization on object serialization that you would impose on any other method that reads the entire state of the object.** So, for example, if you have a thread-safe object (Item 82) that achieves its thread safety by synchronizing every method and you elect to use the default serialized form, use the following write-Object method:

```
// writeObject for synchronized class with default serialized form
private synchronized void writeObject(ObjectOutputStream s)
        throws IOException {
    s.defaultWriteObject();
}
```

If you put synchronization in the writeObject method, you must ensure that it adheres to the same lock-ordering constraints as other activities, or you risk a resource-ordering deadlock [Goetz06, 10.1.5].

Regardless of what serialized form you choose, declare an explicit serial version UID in every serializable class you write. This eliminates the serial version UID as a potential source of incompatibility (Item 86). There is also a small performance benefit. If no serial version UID is provided, an expensive computation is performed to generate one at runtime.

Declaring a serial version UID is simple. Just add this line to your class:

```
private static final long serialVersionUID = randomLongValue;
```

If you write a new class, it doesn't matter what value you choose for *randomLongValue*. You can generate the value by running the `serialver` utility on the class, but it's also fine to pick a number out of thin air. It is *not* required that serial version UIDs be unique. If you modify an existing class that lacks a serial version UID, and you want the new version to accept existing serialized instances, you must use the value that was automatically generated for the old version. You can get this number by running the `serialver` utility on the old version of the class—the one for which serialized instances exist.

If you ever want to make a new version of a class that is *incompatible* with existing versions, merely change the value in the serial version UID declaration. This will cause attempts to deserialize serialized instances of previous versions to throw an `InvalidClassException`. **Do not change the serial version UID unless you want to break compatibility with all existing serialized instances of a class.**

To summarize, if you have decided that a class should be serializable (Item 86), think hard about what the serialized form should be. Use the default serialized form *only* if it is a reasonable description of the logical state of the object; otherwise design a custom serialized form that aptly describes the object. You should allocate as much time to designing the serialized form of a class as you allocate to designing an exported method (Item 51). Just as you can't eliminate exported methods from future versions, you can't eliminate fields from the serialized form; they must be preserved forever to ensure serialization compatibility. Choosing the wrong serialized form can have a permanent, negative impact on the complexity and performance of a class.

Item 88: Write `readObject` methods defensively

Item 50 contains an immutable date-range class with mutable private `Date` fields. The class goes to great lengths to preserve its invariants and immutability by defensively copying `Date` objects in its constructor and accessors. Here is the class:

```
// Immutable class that uses defensive copying
public final class Period {
    private final Date start;
    private final Date end;

    /**
     * @param  start the beginning of the period
     * @param  end the end of the period; must not precede start
     * @throws IllegalArgumentException if start is after end
     * @throws NullPointerException if start or end is null
     */
    public Period(Date start, Date end) {
        this.start = new Date(start.getTime());
        this.end   = new Date(end.getTime());
        if (this.start.compareTo(this.end) > 0)
            throw new IllegalArgumentException(
                            start + " after " + end);
    }

    public Date start () { return new Date(start.getTime()); }

    public Date end () { return new Date(end.getTime()); }

    public String toString() { return start + " - " + end; }

    ... // Remainder omitted
}
```

Suppose you decide that you want this class to be serializable. Because the physical representation of a `Period` object exactly mirrors its logical data content, it is not unreasonable to use the default serialized form (Item 87). Therefore, it might seem that all you have to do to make the class serializable is to add the words `implements Serializable` to the class declaration. If you did so, however, the class would no longer guarantee its critical invariants.

The problem is that the `readObject` method is effectively another public constructor, and it demands all of the same care as any other constructor. Just as a constructor must check its arguments for validity (Item 49) and make defensive copies of parameters where appropriate (Item 50), so must a `readObject` method. If a `readObject` method fails to do either of these things, it is a relatively simple matter for an attacker to violate the class's invariants.

Loosely speaking, readObject is a constructor that takes a byte stream as its sole parameter. In normal use, the byte stream is generated by serializing a normally constructed instance. The problem arises when readObject is presented with a byte stream that is artificially constructed to generate an object that violates the invariants of its class. Such a byte stream can be used to create an *impossible object*, which could not have been created using a normal constructor.

Assume that we simply added implements Serializable to the class declaration for Period. This ugly program would then generate a Period instance whose end precedes its start. The casts on byte values whose high-order bit is set is a consequence of Java's lack of 'byte literals combined with the unfortunate decision to make the byte type signed:

```
public class BogusPeriod {
    // Byte stream couldn't have come from a real Period instance!
    private static final byte[] serializedForm = {
        (byte)0xac, (byte)0xed, 0x00, 0x05, 0x73, 0x72, 0x00, 0x06,
        0x50, 0x65, 0x72, 0x69, 0x6f, 0x64, 0x40, 0x7e, (byte)0xf8,
        0x2b, 0x4f, 0x46, (byte)0xc0, (byte)0xf4, 0x02, 0x00, 0x02,
        0x4c, 0x00, 0x03, 0x65, 0x6e, 0x64, 0x74, 0x00, 0x10, 0x4c,
        0x6a, 0x61, 0x76, 0x61, 0x2f, 0x75, 0x74, 0x69, 0x6c, 0x2f,
        0x44, 0x61, 0x74, 0x65, 0x3b, 0x4c, 0x00, 0x05, 0x73, 0x74,
        0x61, 0x72, 0x74, 0x71, 0x00, 0x7e, 0x00, 0x01, 0x78, 0x70,
        0x73, 0x72, 0x00, 0x0e, 0x6a, 0x61, 0x76, 0x61, 0x2e, 0x75,
        0x74, 0x69, 0x6c, 0x2e, 0x44, 0x61, 0x74, 0x65, 0x68, 0x6a,
        (byte)0x81, 0x01, 0x4b, 0x59, 0x74, 0x19, 0x03, 0x00, 0x00,
        0x78, 0x70, 0x77, 0x08, 0x00, 0x00, 0x00, 0x66, (byte)0xdf,
        0x6e, 0x1e, 0x00, 0x78, 0x73, 0x71, 0x00, 0x7e, 0x00, 0x03,
        0x77, 0x08, 0x00, 0x00, 0x00, (byte)0xd5, 0x17, 0x69, 0x22,
        0x00, 0x78
    };

    public static void main(String[] args) {
        Period p = (Period) deserialize(serializedForm);
        System.out.println(p);
    }

    // Returns the object with the specified serialized form
    static Object deserialize(byte[] sf) {
        try {
            return new ObjectInputStream(
                new ByteArrayInputStream(sf)).readObject();
        } catch (IOException | ClassNotFoundException e) {
            throw new IllegalArgumentException(e);
        }
    }
}
```

The byte array literal used to initialize serializedForm was generated by serializing a normal Period instance and hand-editing the resulting byte stream. The details of the stream are unimportant to the example, but if you're curious, the serialization byte-stream format is described in the *Java Object Serialization Specification* [Serialization, 6]. If you run this program, it prints Fri Jan 01 12:00:00 PST 1999 - Sun Jan 01 12:00:00 PST 1984. Simply declaring Period serializable enabled us to create an object that violates its class invariants.

To fix this problem, provide a readObject method for Period that calls defaultReadObject and then checks the validity of the deserialized object. If the validity check fails, the readObject method throws InvalidObjectException, preventing the deserialization from completing:

```
// readObject method with validity checking - insufficient!
private void readObject(ObjectInputStream s)
        throws IOException, ClassNotFoundException {
    s.defaultReadObject();

    // Check that our invariants are satisfied
    if (start.compareTo(end) > 0)
        throw new InvalidObjectException(start +" after "+ end);
}
```

While this prevents an attacker from creating an invalid Period instance, there is a more subtle problem still lurking. It is possible to create a mutable Period instance by fabricating a byte stream that begins with a valid Period instance and then appends extra references to the private Date fields internal to the Period instance. The attacker reads the Period instance from the ObjectInputStream and then reads the "rogue object references" that were appended to the stream. These references give the attacker access to the objects referenced by the private Date fields within the Period object. By mutating these Date instances, the attacker can mutate the Period instance. The following class demonstrates this attack:

```
public class MutablePeriod {
    // A period instance
    public final Period period;

    // period's start field, to which we shouldn't have access
    public final Date start;

    // period's end field, to which we shouldn't have access
    public final Date end;
```

```java
    public MutablePeriod() {
        try {
            ByteArrayOutputStream bos =
                new ByteArrayOutputStream();
            ObjectOutputStream out =
                new ObjectOutputStream(bos);

            // Serialize a valid Period instance
            out.writeObject(new Period(new Date(), new Date()));

            /*
             * Append rogue "previous object refs" for internal
             * Date fields in Period. For details, see "Java
             * Object Serialization Specification," Section 6.4.
             */
            byte[] ref = { 0x71, 0, 0x7e, 0, 5 }; // Ref #5
            bos.write(ref); // The start field
            ref[4] = 4;       // Ref # 4
            bos.write(ref); // The end field

            // Deserialize Period and "stolen" Date references
            ObjectInputStream in = new ObjectInputStream(
                new ByteArrayInputStream(bos.toByteArray()));
            period = (Period) in.readObject();
            start  = (Date)   in.readObject();
            end    = (Date)   in.readObject();
        } catch (IOException | ClassNotFoundException e) {
            throw new AssertionError(e);
        }
    }
}
```

To see the attack in action, run the following program:

```java
public static void main(String[] args) {
    MutablePeriod mp = new MutablePeriod();
    Period p = mp.period;
    Date pEnd = mp.end;

    // Let's turn back the clock
    pEnd.setYear(78);
    System.out.println(p);

    // Bring back the 60s!
    pEnd.setYear(69);
    System.out.println(p);
}
```

In my locale, running this program produces the following output:

```
Wed Nov 22 00:21:29 PST 2017 - Wed Nov 22 00:21:29 PST 1978
Wed Nov 22 00:21:29 PST 2017 - Sat Nov 22 00:21:29 PST 1969
```

While the `Period` instance is created with its invariants intact, it is possible to modify its internal components at will. Once in possession of a mutable `Period` instance, an attacker might cause great harm by passing the instance to a class that depends on `Period`'s immutability for its security. This is not so far-fetched: there are classes that depend on `String`'s immutability for their security.

The source of the problem is that `Period`'s `readObject` method is not doing enough defensive copying. **When an object is deserialized, it is critical to defensively copy any field containing an object reference that a client must not possess.** Therefore, every serializable immutable class containing private mutable components must defensively copy these components in its `readObject` method. The following `readObject` method suffices to ensure `Period`'s invariants and to maintain its immutability:

```
// readObject method with defensive copying and validity checking
private void readObject(ObjectInputStream s)
        throws IOException, ClassNotFoundException {
    s.defaultReadObject();

    // Defensively copy our mutable components
    start = new Date(start.getTime());
    end   = new Date(end.getTime());

    // Check that our invariants are satisfied
    if (start.compareTo(end) > 0)
        throw new InvalidObjectException(start +" after "+ end);
}
```

Note that the defensive copy is performed prior to the validity check and that we did not use `Date`'s `clone` method to perform the defensive copy. Both of these details are required to protect `Period` against attack (Item 50). Note also that defensive copying is not possible for final fields. To use the `readObject` method, we must make the `start` and `end` fields nonfinal. This is unfortunate, but it is the lesser of two evils. With the new `readObject` method in place and the `final` modifier removed from the `start` and `end` fields, the `MutablePeriod` class is rendered ineffective. The above attack program now generates this output:

```
Wed Nov 22 00:23:41 PST 2017 - Wed Nov 22 00:23:41 PST 2017
Wed Nov 22 00:23:41 PST 2017 - Wed Nov 22 00:23:41 PST 2017
```

Here is a simple litmus test for deciding whether the default `readObject` method is acceptable for a class: would you feel comfortable adding a public constructor that took as parameters the values for each nontransient field in the object and stored the values in the fields with no validation whatsoever? If not, you must provide a `readObject` method, and it must perform all the validity checking and defensive copying that would be required of a constructor. Alternatively, you can use the *serialization proxy pattern* (Item 90). This pattern is highly recommended because it takes much of the effort out of safe deserialization.

There is one other similarity between `readObject` methods and constructors that applies to nonfinal serializable classes. Like a constructor, a `readObject` method must not invoke an overridable method, either directly or indirectly (Item 19). If this rule is violated and the method in question is overridden, the overriding method will run before the subclass's state has been deserialized. A program failure is likely to result [Bloch05, Puzzle 91].

To summarize, anytime you write a `readObject` method, adopt the mind-set that you are writing a public constructor that must produce a valid instance regardless of what byte stream it is given. Do not assume that the byte stream represents an actual serialized instance. While the examples in this item concern a class that uses the default serialized form, all of the issues that were raised apply equally to classes with custom serialized forms. Here, in summary form, are the guidelines for writing a `readObject` method:

- For classes with object reference fields that must remain private, defensively copy each object in such a field. Mutable components of immutable classes fall into this category.

- Check any invariants and throw an `InvalidObjectException` if a check fails. The checks should follow any defensive copying.

- If an entire object graph must be validated after it is deserialized, use the `ObjectInputValidation` interface (not discussed in this book).

- Do not invoke any overridable methods in the class, directly or indirectly.

Item 89: For instance control, prefer enum types to `readResolve`

Item 3 describes the *Singleton* pattern and gives the following example of a single-ton class. This class restricts access to its constructor to ensure that only a single instance is ever created:

```
public class Elvis {
    public static final Elvis INSTANCE = new Elvis();
    private Elvis() { ... }

    public void leaveTheBuilding() { ... }
}
```

As noted in Item 3, this class would no longer be a singleton if the words `implements Serializable` were added to its declaration. It doesn't matter whether the class uses the default serialized form or a custom serialized form (Item 87), nor does it matter whether the class provides an explicit `readObject` method (Item 88). Any `readObject` method, whether explicit or default, returns a newly created instance, which will not be the same instance that was created at class initialization time.

The `readResolve` feature allows you to substitute another instance for the one created by `readObject` [Serialization, 3.7]. If the class of an object being deserial-ized defines a `readResolve` method with the proper declaration, this method is invoked on the newly created object after it is deserialized. The object reference returned by this method is then returned in place of the newly created object. In most uses of this feature, no reference to the newly created object is retained, so it immediately becomes eligible for garbage collection.

If the `Elvis` class is made to implement `Serializable`, the following read-`Resolve` method suffices to guarantee the singleton property:

```
// readResolve for instance control - you can do better!
private Object readResolve() {
    // Return the one true Elvis and let the garbage collector
    // take care of the Elvis impersonator.
    return INSTANCE;
}
```

This method ignores the deserialized object, returning the distinguished `Elvis` instance that was created when the class was initialized. Therefore, the serialized form of an `Elvis` instance need not contain any real data; all instance fields should be declared `transient`. In fact, **if you depend on `readResolve` for instance**

control, all instance fields with object reference types *must* **be declared transient.** Otherwise, it is possible for a determined attacker to secure a reference to the deserialized object before its readResolve method is run, using a technique that is somewhat similar to the MutablePeriod attack in Item 88.

The attack is a bit complicated, but the underlying idea is simple. If a singleton contains a nontransient object reference field, the contents of this field will be deserialized before the singleton's readResolve method is run. This allows a carefully crafted stream to "steal" a reference to the originally deserialized singleton at the time the contents of the object reference field are deserialized.

Here's how it works in more detail. First, write a "stealer" class that has both a readResolve method and an instance field that refers to the serialized singleton in which the stealer "hides." In the serialization stream, replace the singleton's nontransient field with an instance of the stealer. You now have a circularity: the singleton contains the stealer, and the stealer refers to the singleton.

Because the singleton contains the stealer, the stealer's readResolve method runs first when the singleton is deserialized. As a result, when the stealer's readResolve method runs, its instance field still refers to the partially deserialized (and as yet unresolved) singleton.

The stealer's readResolve method copies the reference from its instance field into a static field so that the reference can be accessed after the readResolve method runs. The method then returns a value of the correct type for the field in which it's hiding. If it didn't do this, the VM would throw a ClassCastException when the serialization system tried to store the stealer reference into this field.

To make this concrete, consider the following broken singleton:

```
// Broken singleton - has nontransient object reference field!
public class Elvis implements Serializable {
    public static final Elvis INSTANCE = new Elvis();
    private Elvis() { }

    private String[] favoriteSongs =
        { "Hound Dog", "Heartbreak Hotel" };
    public void printFavorites() {
        System.out.println(Arrays.toString(favoriteSongs));
    }

    private Object readResolve() {
        return INSTANCE;
    }
}
```

Here is a "stealer" class, constructed as per the description above:

```
public class ElvisStealer implements Serializable {
    static Elvis impersonator;
    private Elvis payload;

    private Object readResolve() {
        // Save a reference to the "unresolved" Elvis instance
        impersonator = payload;

        // Return object of correct type for favoriteSongs field
        return new String[] { "A Fool Such as I" };
    }
    private static final long serialVersionUID = 0;
}
```

Finally, here is an ugly program that deserializes a handcrafted stream to produce two distinct instances of the flawed singleton. The deserialize method is omitted from this program because it's identical to the one on page 354:

```
public class ElvisImpersonator {
    // Byte stream couldn't have come from a real Elvis instance!
    private static final byte[] serializedForm = {
        (byte)0xac, (byte)0xed, 0x00, 0x05, 0x73, 0x72, 0x00, 0x05,
        0x45, 0x6c, 0x76, 0x69, 0x73, (byte)0x84, (byte)0xe6,
        (byte)0x93, 0x33, (byte)0xc3, (byte)0xf4, (byte)0x8b,
        0x32, 0x02, 0x00, 0x01, 0x4c, 0x00, 0x0d, 0x66, 0x61, 0x76,
        0x6f, 0x72, 0x69, 0x74, 0x65, 0x53, 0x6f, 0x6e, 0x67, 0x73,
        0x74, 0x00, 0x12, 0x4c, 0x6a, 0x61, 0x76, 0x61, 0x2f, 0x6c,
        0x61, 0x6e, 0x67, 0x2f, 0x4f, 0x62, 0x6a, 0x65, 0x63, 0x74,
        0x3b, 0x78, 0x70, 0x73, 0x72, 0x00, 0x0c, 0x45, 0x6c, 0x76,
        0x69, 0x73, 0x53, 0x74, 0x65, 0x61, 0x6c, 0x65, 0x72, 0x00,
        0x00, 0x00, 0x00, 0x00, 0x00, 0x00, 0x00, 0x02, 0x00, 0x01,
        0x4c, 0x00, 0x07, 0x70, 0x61, 0x79, 0x6c, 0x6f, 0x61, 0x64,
        0x74, 0x00, 0x07, 0x4c, 0x45, 0x6c, 0x76, 0x69, 0x73, 0x3b,
        0x78, 0x70, 0x71, 0x00, 0x7e, 0x00, 0x02
    };

    public static void main(String[] args) {
        // Initializes ElvisStealer.impersonator and returns
        // the real Elvis (which is Elvis.INSTANCE)
        Elvis elvis = (Elvis) deserialize(serializedForm);
        Elvis impersonator = ElvisStealer.impersonator;

        elvis.printFavorites();
        impersonator.printFavorites();
    }
}
```

Running this program produces the following output, conclusively proving that it's possible to create two distinct Elvis instances (with different tastes in music):

```
[Hound Dog, Heartbreak Hotel]
[A Fool Such as I]
```

You could fix the problem by declaring the favoriteSongs field transient, but you're better off fixing it by making Elvis a single-element enum type (Item 3). As demonstrated by the ElvisStealer attack, using a readResolve method to prevent a "temporary" deserialized instance from being accessed by an attacker is fragile and demands great care.

If you write your serializable instance-controlled class as an enum, Java guarantees you that there can be no instances besides the declared constants, unless an attacker abuses a privileged method such as AccessibleObject.setAccessible. Any attacker who can do that already has sufficient privileges to execute arbitrary native code, and all bets are off. Here's how our Elvis example looks as an enum:

```java
// Enum singleton - the preferred approach
public enum Elvis {
    INSTANCE;
    private String[] favoriteSongs =
        { "Hound Dog", "Heartbreak Hotel" };
    public void printFavorites() {
        System.out.println(Arrays.toString(favoriteSongs));
    }
}
```

The use of readResolve for instance control is not obsolete. If you have to write a serializable instance-controlled class whose instances are not known at compile time, you will not be able to represent the class as an enum type.

The accessibility of readResolve is significant. If you place a readResolve method on a final class, it should be private. If you place a readResolve method on a nonfinal class, you must carefully consider its accessibility. If it is private, it will not apply to any subclasses. If it is package-private, it will apply only to subclasses in the same package. If it is protected or public, it will apply to all subclasses that do not override it. If a readResolve method is protected or public and a subclass does not override it, deserializing a subclass instance will produce a superclass instance, which is likely to cause a ClassCastException.

To summarize, use enum types to enforce instance control invariants wherever possible. If this is not possible and you need a class to be both serializable and instance-controlled, you must provide a readResolve method and ensure that all of the class's instance fields are either primitive or transient.

Item 90: Consider serialization proxies instead of serialized instances

As mentioned in Items 85 and 86 and discussed throughout this chapter, the decision to implement Serializable increases the likelihood of bugs and security problems as it allows instances to be created using an extralinguistic mechanism in place of ordinary constructors. There is, however, a technique that greatly reduces these risks. This technique is known as the *serialization proxy pattern*.

The serialization proxy pattern is reasonably straightforward. First, design a private static nested class that concisely represents the logical state of an instance of the enclosing class. This nested class is known as the *serialization proxy* of the enclosing class. It should have a single constructor, whose parameter type is the enclosing class. This constructor merely copies the data from its argument: it need not do any consistency checking or defensive copying. By design, the default serialized form of the serialization proxy is the perfect serialized form of the enclosing class. Both the enclosing class and its serialization proxy must be declared to implement Serializable.

For example, consider the immutable Period class written in Item 50 and made serializable in Item 88. Here is a serialization proxy for this class. Period is so simple that its serialization proxy has exactly the same fields as the class:

```
// Serialization proxy for Period class
private static class SerializationProxy implements Serializable {
    private final Date start;
    private final Date end;

    SerializationProxy(Period p) {
        this.start = p.start;
        this.end = p.end;
    }

    private static final long serialVersionUID =
        234098243823485285L; // Any number will do (Item 87)
}
```

Next, add the following writeReplace method to the enclosing class. This method can be copied verbatim into any class with a serialization proxy:

```
// writeReplace method for the serialization proxy pattern
private Object writeReplace() {
    return new SerializationProxy(this);
}
```

The presence of this method on the enclosing class causes the serialization system to emit a SerializationProxy instance instead of an instance of the enclosing class. In other words, the writeReplace method translates an instance of the enclosing class to its serialization proxy prior to serialization.

With this writeReplace method in place, the serialization system will never generate a serialized instance of the enclosing class, but an attacker might fabricate one in an attempt to violate the class's invariants. To guarantee that such an attack would fail, merely add this readObject method to the enclosing class:

```
// readObject method for the serialization proxy pattern
private void readObject(ObjectInputStream stream)
        throws InvalidObjectException {
    throw new InvalidObjectException("Proxy required");
}
```

Finally, provide a readResolve method on the SerializationProxy class that returns a logically equivalent instance of the enclosing class. The presence of this method causes the serialization system to translate the serialization proxy back into an instance of the enclosing class upon deserialization.

This readResolve method creates an instance of the enclosing class using only its public API and therein lies the beauty of the pattern. It largely eliminates the extralinguistic character of serialization, because the deserialized instance is created using the same constructors, static factories, and methods as any other instance. This frees you from having to separately ensure that deserialized instances obey the class's invariants. If the class's static factories or constructors establish these invariants and its instance methods maintain them, you've ensured that the invariants will be maintained by serialization as well.

Here is the readResolve method for Period.SerializationProxy above:

```
// readResolve method for Period.SerializationProxy
private Object readResolve() {
    return new Period(start, end);  // Uses public constructor
}
```

Like the defensive copying approach (page 357), the serialization proxy approach stops the bogus byte-stream attack (page 354) and the internal field theft attack (page 356) dead in their tracks. Unlike the two previous approaches, this one allows the fields of Period to be final, which is required in order for the Period class to be truly immutable (Item 17). And unlike the two previous approaches, this one doesn't involve a great deal of thought. You don't have to figure out which fields might be compromised by devious serialization attacks, nor do you have to explicitly perform validity checking as part of deserialization.

There is another way in which the serialization proxy pattern is more powerful than defensive copying in readObject. The serialization proxy pattern allows the deserialized instance to have a different class from the originally serialized instance. You might not think that this would be useful in practice, but it is.

Consider the case of EnumSet (Item 36). This class has no public constructors, only static factories. From the client's perspective, they return EnumSet instances, but in the current OpenJDK implementation, they return one of two subclasses, depending on the size of the underlying enum type. If the underlying enum type has sixty-four or fewer elements, the static factories return a RegularEnumSet; otherwise, they return a JumboEnumSet.

Now consider what happens if you serialize an enum set whose enum type has sixty elements, then add five more elements to the enum type, and then deserialize the enum set. It was a RegularEnumSet instance when it was serialized, but it had better be a JumboEnumSet instance once it is deserialized. In fact that's exactly what happens, because EnumSet uses the serialization proxy pattern. In case you're curious, here is EnumSet's serialization proxy. It really is this simple:

```
// EnumSet's serialization proxy
private static class SerializationProxy <E extends Enum<E>>
        implements Serializable {
    // The element type of this enum set.
    private final Class<E> elementType;

    // The elements contained in this enum set.
    private final Enum<?>[] elements;

    SerializationProxy(EnumSet<E> set) {
        elementType = set.elementType;
        elements = set.toArray(new Enum<?>[0]);
    }

    private Object readResolve() {
        EnumSet<E> result = EnumSet.noneOf(elementType);
        for (Enum<?> e : elements)
            result.add((E)e);
        return result;
    }

    private static final long serialVersionUID =
        362491234563181265L;
}
```

The serialization proxy pattern has two limitations. It is not compatible with classes that are extendable by their users (Item 19). Also, it is not compatible with some classes whose object graphs contain circularities: if you attempt to invoke a method on such an object from within its serialization proxy's `readResolve` method, you'll get a `ClassCastException` because you don't have the object yet, only its serialization proxy.

Finally, the added power and safety of the serialization proxy pattern are not free. On my machine, it is 14 percent more expensive to serialize and deserialize `Period` instances with serialization proxies than it is with defensive copying.

In summary, consider the serialization proxy pattern whenever you find yourself having to write a `readObject` or `writeObject` method on a class that is not extendable by its clients. This pattern is perhaps the easiest way to robustly serialize objects with nontrivial invariants.

Items Corresponding to Second Edition

Second Edition Item Number	Third Edition Item Number, Title
1	1, Consider static factory methods instead of constructors
2	2, Consider a builder when faced with many constructor parameters
3	3, Enforce the singleton property with a private constructor or an enum type
4	4, Enforce noninstantiability with a private constructor
5	6, Avoid creating unnecessary objects
6	7, Eliminate obsolete object references
7	8, Avoid finalizers and cleaners
8	10, Obey the general contract when overriding `equals`
9	11, Always override `hashCode` when you override `equals`
10	12, Always override `toString`
11	13, Override `clone` judiciously
12	14, Consider implementing `Comparable`
13	15, Minimize the accessibility of classes and members
14	16, In public classes, use accessor methods, not public fields
15	17, Minimize mutability
16	18, Favor composition over inheritance
17	19, Design and document for inheritance or else prohibit it

Second Edition Item Number	Third Edition Item Number, Title
18	20, Prefer interfaces to abstract classes
19	22, Use interfaces only to define types
20	23, Prefer class hierarchies to tagged classes
21	42, Prefer lambdas to anonymous classes
22	24, Favor static member classes over nonstatic
23	26, Don't use raw types
24	27, Eliminate unchecked warnings
25	28, Prefer lists to arrays
26	29, Favor generic types
27	30, Favor generic methods
28	31, Use bounded wildcards to increase API flexibility
29	33, Consider typesafe heterogeneous containers
30	34, Use enums instead of `int` constants
31	35, Use instance fields instead of ordinals
32	36, Use `EnumSet` instead of bit fields
33	37, Use `EnumMap` instead of ordinal indexing
34	38, Emulate extensible enums with interfaces
35	39, Prefer annotations to naming patterns
36	40, Consistently use the `Override` annotation
37	41, Use marker interfaces to define types
38	49, Check parameters for validity
39	50, Make defensive copies when needed
40	51, Design method signatures carefully
41	52, Use overloading judiciously

Second Edition Item Number	Third Edition Item Number, Title
42	53, Use varargs judiciously
43	54, Return empty collections or arrays, not nulls
44	56, Write doc comments for all exposed API elements
45	57, Minimize the scope of local variables
46	58, Prefer for-each loops to traditional `for` loops
47	59, Know and use the libraries
48	60, Avoid `float` and `double` if exact answers are required
49	61, Prefer primitive types to boxed primitives
50	62, Avoid strings where other types are more appropriate
51	63, Beware the performance of string concatenation
52	64, Refer to objects by their interfaces
53	65, Prefer interfaces to reflection
54	66, Use native methods judiciously
55	67, Optimize judiciously
56	68, Adhere to generally accepted naming conventions
57	69, Use exceptions only for exceptional conditions
58	70, Use checked exceptions for recoverable conditions and runtime exceptions for programming errors
59	71, Avoid unnecessary use of checked exceptions
60	72, Favor the use of standard exceptions
61	73, Throw exceptions appropriate to the abstraction
62	74, Document all exceptions thrown by each method
63	75, Include failure-capture information in detail messages
64	76, Strive for failure atomicity
65	77, Don't ignore exceptions

Second Edition Item Number	Third Edition Item Number, Title
66	78, Synchronize access to shared mutable data
67	79, Avoid excessive synchronization
68	80, Prefer executors, tasks, and streams to threads
69	81, 81, Prefer concurrency utilities to `wait` and `notify`
70	82, Document thread safety
71	83, Use lazy initialization judiciously
72	84, Don't depend on the thread scheduler
73	(Retired)
74	85, Prefer alternatives to Java serialization 86, 86, Implement `Serializable` with great caution
75	85, Prefer alternatives to Java serialization 87, Consider using a custom serialized form
76	85, Prefer alternatives to Java serialization 88, Write `readObject` methods defensively
77	85, Prefer alternatives to Java serialization 89, For instance control, prefer enum types to `readResolve`
78	85, Prefer alternatives to Java serialization 90, Consider serialization proxies instead of serialized instances

References

[Asserts]   *Programming with Assertions.* 2002. Sun Microsystems.
              http://docs.oracle.com/javase/8/docs/technotes/guides/language
              /assert.html

[Beck04]   Beck, Kent. 2004. *JUnit Pocket Guide.* Sebastopol, CA: O'Reilly
              Media, Inc. ISBN: 0596007434.

[Bloch01]   Bloch, Joshua. 2001. *Effective Java Programming Language
              Guide.* Boston: Addison-Wesley. ISBN: 0201310058.

[Bloch05]   Bloch, Joshua, and Neal Gafter. 2005. *Java Puzzlers: Traps,
              Pitfalls, and Corner Cases.* Boston: Addison-Wesley.
              ISBN: 032133678X.

[Blum14]   Blum, Scott. 2014. "Faster RSA in Java with GMP." *The Square
              Corner* (blog). Feb. 14, 2014. https://medium.com/square-corner
              -blog/faster-rsa-in-java-with-gmp-8b13c51c6ec4

[Bracha04]   Bracha, Gilad. 2004. "Lesson: Generics" online supplement to *The
              Java Tutorial: A Short Course on the Basics,* 6th ed. Upper Saddle
              River, NJ: Addison-Wesley, 2014. https://docs.oracle.com/javase
              /tutorial/extra/generics/

[Burn01]   Burn, Oliver. 2001–2017. *Checkstyle.*
              http://checkstyle.sourceforge.net

[Coekaerts15]   Coekaerts, Wouter (@WouterCoekaerts). 2015. "Billion-laughs-style DoS for Java serialization https://gist.github.com/coekie/a27cc406fc9f3dc7a70d … WONTFIX," Twitter, November 9, 2015, 9:46 a.m. https://twitter.com/woutercoekaerts/status/663774695381078016

[CompSci17]   Brief of Computer Scientists as Amici Curiae for the United States Court of Appeals for the Federal Circuit, Case No. 17-1118, Oracle America, Inc. v. Google, Inc. in Support of Defendant-Appellee. (2017)

[Dagger]   *Dagger.* 2013. Square, Inc. http://square.github.io/dagger/

[Gallagher16]   Gallagher, Sean. 2016. "Muni system hacker hit others by scanning for year-old Java vulnerability." *Ars Technica,* November 29, 2016. https://arstechnica.com/information-technology/2016/11/san-francisco-transit-ransomware-attacker-likely-used-year-old-java-exploit/

[Gamma95]   Gamma, Erich, Richard Helm, Ralph Johnson, and John Vlissides. 1995. *Design Patterns: Elements of Reusable Object-Oriented Software.* Reading, MA: Addison-Wesley. ISBN: 0201633612.

[Goetz06]   Goetz, Brian. 2006. *Java Concurrency in Practice.* With Tim Peierls, Joshua Bloch, Joseph Bowbeer, David Holmes, and Doug Lea. Boston: Addison-Wesley. ISBN: 0321349601.

[Gosling97]   Gosling, James. 1997. "The Feel of Java." *Computer* 30 no. 6 (June 1997): 53-57. http://dx.doi.org/10.1109/2.587548

[Guava]   *Guava.* 2017. Google Inc. https://github.com/google/guava

[Guice]   *Guice.* 2006. Google Inc. https://github.com/google/guice

[Herlihy12]   Herlihy, Maurice, and Nir Shavit. 2012. *The Art of Multiprocessor Programming, Revised Reprint.* Waltham, MA: Morgan Kaufmann Publishers. ISBN: 0123973376.

[Jackson75]   Jackson, M. A. 1975. *Principles of Program Design.* London: Academic Press. ISBN: 0123790506.

[Java-secure]   *Secure Coding Guidelines for Java SE.* 2017. Oracle. http://www.oracle.com/technetwork/java/seccodeguide-139067.html

[Java8-feat]   *What's New in JDK 8.* 2014. Oracle. http://www.oracle.com/technetwork/java/javase/8-whats-new-2157071.html

[Java9-feat]   *Java Platform, Standard Edition What's New in Oracle JDK 9.* 2017. Oracle. https://docs.oracle.com/javase/9/whatsnew/toc.htm

[Java9-api]   *Java Platform, Standard Edition & Java Development Kit Version 9 API Specification.* 2017. Oracle. https://docs.oracle.com/javase/9/docs/api/overview-summary.html

[Javadoc-guide] *How to Write Doc Comments for the Javadoc Tool.* 2000–2004. Sun Microsystems. http://www.oracle.com/technetwork/java/javase/documentation/index-137868.html

[Javadoc-ref]   *Javadoc Reference Guide.* 2014-2017. Oracle. https://docs.oracle.com/javase/9/javadoc/javadoc.htm

[JLS]   Gosling, James, Bill Joy, Guy Steele, and Gilad Bracha. 2014. *The Java Language Specification, Java SE 8 Edition.* Boston: Addison-Wesley. ISBN: 013390069X.

[JMH]   *Code Tools: jmh.* 2014. Oracle. http://openjdk.java.net/projects/code-tools/jmh/

[JSON]   *Introducing JSON.* 2013. Ecma International. https://www.json.org

[Kahan91]   Kahan, William, and J. W. Thomas. 1991. *Augmenting a Programming Language with Complex Arithmetic.* UCB/CSD-91-667, University of California, Berkeley.

[Knuth74]   Knuth, Donald. 1974. Structured Programming with go to Statements. In *Computing Surveys* 6: 261–301.

[Lea14]   Lea, Doug. 2014. *When to use parallel streams.* http://gee.cs.oswego.edu/dl/html/StreamParallelGuidance.html

[Lieberman86] Lieberman, Henry. 1986. Using Prototypical Objects to Implement Shared Behavior in Object-Oriented Systems. In *Proceedings of the First ACM Conference on Object-Oriented Programming Systems, Languages, and Applications*, pages 214–223, Portland, September 1986. ACM Press.

[Liskov87]   Liskov, B. 1988. Data Abstraction and Hierarchy. In *Addendum to the Proceedings of OOPSLA '87* and *SIGPLAN Notices,* Vol. 23, No. 5: 17–34, May 1988.

[Naftalin07]   Naftalin, Maurice, and Philip Wadler. 2007. *Java Generics and Collections.* Sebastopol, CA: O'Reilly Media, Inc. ISBN: 0596527756.

[Parnas72]   Parnas, D. L. 1972. On the Criteria to Be Used in Decomposing Systems into Modules. In *Communications of the ACM* 15: 1053–1058.

[POSIX]   9945-1:1996 (ISO/IEC) [IEEE/ANSI Std. 1003.1 1995 Edition] Information Technology—Portable Operating System Interface (POSIX)—Part 1: System Application: Program Interface (API) C Language] (ANSI), IEEE Standards Press, ISBN: 1559375736.

[Protobuf]   *Protocol Buffers.* 2017. Google Inc. https://developers.google.com/protocol-buffers

[Schneider16] Schneider, Christian. 2016. SWAT (Serial Whitelist Application Trainer). https://github.com/cschneider4711/SWAT/

[Seacord17]   Seacord, Robert. 2017. *Combating Java Deserialization Vulnerabilities with Look-Ahead Object Input Streams (LAOIS).* San Francisco: NCC Group Whitepaper. https://www.nccgroup.trust/globalassets/our-research/us/ whitepapers/2017/june/ncc_group_combating_java_deserialization _vulnerabilities_with_look-ahead_object_input_streams1.pdf

[Serialization] *Java Object Serialization Specification.* March 2005. Sun Microsystems. http://docs.oracle.com/javase/9/docs/specs /serialization/index.html

[Sestoft16]   Sestoft, Peter. 2016. *Java Precisely*, 3rd ed. Cambridge, MA: The MIT Press. ISBN: 0262529076.

[Shipilëv16]   Aleksey Shipilëv. 2016. *Arrays of Wisdom of the Ancients.* https://shipilev.net/blog/2016/arrays-wisdom-ancients/

[Smith62]   Smith, Robert. 1962. Algorithm 116 Complex Division. In *Communications of the ACM* 5, no. 8 (August 1962): 435.

[Snyder86]   Snyder, Alan. 1986. "Encapsulation and Inheritance in Object-Oriented Programming Languages." In *Object-Oriented Programming Systems, Languages, and Applications Conference Proceedings*, 38–45. New York, NY: ACM Press.

[Spring]   *Spring Framework.* Pivotal Software, Inc. 2017. https://projects.spring.io/spring-framework/

[Stroustrup]   Stroustrup, Bjarne. [ca. 2000]. "Is Java the language you would have designed if you didn't have to be compatible with C?" *Bjarne Stroustrup's FAQ.* Updated Ocober 1, 2017. http://www.stroustrup.com/bs_faq.html#Java

[Stroustrup95] Stroustrup, Bjarne. 1995. "Why C++ is not just an object-oriented programming language." In *Addendum to the proceedings of the 10th annual conference on Object-oriented programming systems, languages, and applications*, edited by Steven Craig Bilow and Patricia S. Bilow New York, NY: ACM. http://dx.doi.org/10.1145/260094.260207

[Svoboda16] Svoboda, David. 2016. *Exploiting Java Serialization for Fun and Profit*. Software Engineering Institute, Carnegie Mellon University. https://resources.sei.cmu.edu/library/asset-view.cfm?assetid=484347

[Thomas94] Thomas, Jim, and Jerome T. Coonen. 1994. "Issues Regarding Imaginary Types for C and C++." In *The Journal of C Language Translation* 5, no. 3 (March 1994): 134–138.

[ThreadStop] *Why Are Thread.stop, Thread.suspend, Thread.resume and Runtime.runFinalizersOnExit Deprecated?* 1999. Sun Microsystems. https://docs.oracle.com/javase/8/docs/technotes /guides/concurrency/threadPrimitiveDeprecation.html

[Viega01] Viega, John, and Gary McGraw. 2001. *Building Secure Software: How to Avoid Security Problems the Right Way.* Boston: Addison-Wesley. ISBN: 020172152X.

[W3C-validator] *W3C Markup Validation Service.* 2007. World Wide Web Consortium. http://validator.w3.org/

[Wulf72] Wulf, W. A Case Against the GOTO. 1972. In *Proceedings of the 25th ACM National Conference* 2: 791–797. New York, NY: ACM Press.

Index

compiler-generated casts, 117, 119, 127

components, 2

composition, 8, 89
  `equals` and, 44
  vs. inheritance, 87–92

conceptual weight, 7

concurrency, 311
  documenting method behavior for, 330–332
  improving via internal synchronization, 322

concurrency utilities, 323–329
  vs. `wait` and `notify`, 325–329

concurrent collections, 321, 325–326

conditionally thread-safe classes,
  documenting, 331

consistency requirements
  `equals`, 38, 45
  `hashCode`, 50

consistent with `equals`, 68
  unreliable resources and, 45

constant fields, naming conventions for, 290

constant interfaces, 107

constant utility classes, 108

constants, 76
  in anonymous classes, 114
  naming conventions for, 290

constant-specific behaviors, 162–166
  lambdas for, 195

constant-specific class bodies, 162

constant-specific method implementations
  See constant-specific behaviors

constructors, 4
  calling overridable methods in, 95
  checking parameters of, 353
  `clone` as a, 61
  copy and conversion, 65
  default, 19
  defensive copying of parameters, 232
  deserialization as, 344
  establishing invariants, 82, 86
  noninstantiability and, 19
  private (*see* private constructors)
  `readObject` as a, 353
  reflection and, 282
  replacing with static factories, 5–9
  safely overloading, 240–241

for singletons, 17–18
  summary descriptions of, 257
  `SuppressWarnings` annotation and, 124
  validity checking parameters of, 229

contention, synchronization and, 321

contracts
  `clone`, 58
  `compareTo`, 66
  documentation as, 304
  `equals`, 38–46
  `hashCode`, 50
  `toString`, 55

corrupted objects, 12, 30, 227, 309

countdown latches, 326

covariant arrays, 126

covariant return typing, 16, 60

creating objects, 5–33

cross-platform structured-data representations,
  341

custom serialized forms, 346–352

D

data consistency
  maintaining in face of failure, 308–309
  synchronization for, 311–316

data corruption, 285, 312

`Date`, replacements for, 232

deadlocks
  resource ordering, 320, 351
  thread starvation, 328

Decorator pattern, 91

default access
  See package-private access level

default constructors, 19

default implementations, 104

default methods on interfaces, 99, 104–105

default serialized forms, 346–352
  disadvantages of, 348

defensive copies, 231–235
  of arrays, 234
  builders and, 14
  `clone` and, 233
  deserialization and, 353, 357
  documenting, 234
  immutable objects and, 83